THE KING'S DAUGHTERS

Compiled by
B.A.Ramsbottom

2003

Gospel Standard Trust Publications
12(b) Roundwood Lane
Harpenden
Herts
AL5 3DD
England

ISBN 1 897837 24 0

This edition first printed 2000.
Reprinted 2003.

Printed by
The Cromwell Press
Trowbridge

INDEX

PREFACE

The publication of *Six Remarkable Ministers* a few years ago was exceedingly well received and requests have since been made that something similar might be produced. The result is *The King's Daughters*, the lives of sixteen godly women, the title of the book being taken from Psalm 45, verse 13. Some of "the King's daughters" were rich, some poor, some with remarkable lives, others living in obscurity; but all were witnesses of the power of God in salvation.

As some of the accounts are autobiographical while others are written by a minister or friend, there is obviously a difference in style and length.

We hope the publication of *The King's Daughters* will prove of interest and spiritual profit to young and old.

B.A.Ramsbottom
October 2000

BUT I OBTAINED MERCY

Cecilia Sloane

By Christopher Woollacott, minister at Little Wild Street Chapel, London, from 1834.

It has been said that "truth is stranger than fiction". The following narrative confirms the saying, while it also illustrates the distinguishing grace of God.

The subject of this memoir was related to a noble family. To give publicity to their name might gratify a morbid curiosity, but could not yield any advantage to the reader. She will, therefore, be known only by her husband's name.

Cecilia Sloane, from early infancy, was surrounded with every gratification which high station and great wealth could command. One of the first impressions she received was in harmony with the satire of the wise man: "There is nothing better for a man than that he should eat and drink, and that he should make his soul enjoy good!" She lived in a splendid mansion, around which the park, with its green covering, extended several miles. The deer silently cropped the rich herbage, or playfully sported among the trees. Her dress was elegant, the table was covered with every luxury, and numerous servants were ever ready to gratify her desires. Her life was like a beautiful summer day, in which no envious cloud obscured the brightness of the sun. Who that saw her then would have hesitated to say, "The lines are fallen unto her in pleasant places; she has a goodly heritage"?

The education of young ladies at this period rarely included more than external accomplishments, which enabled them to shine amidst the gay circle of fashion. Such, at least, was the extent of Cecilia's attainments. She knew very little of the God who made her, or His design in her existence. She was taught the Church catechism, yet even this was never explained, and she remembered it only as a burdensome task. A little girl in our Sunday schools knows more than Cecilia knew, for almost the first sentence the child is taught to lisp contains the germ of all divine truth: "Man's chief end is to glorify God, and to enjoy Him for ever." It is lamentable that even now there are many parents utterly indifferent to the inspired precept: "Train up a child in the way he should go." Their neglect is productive of the most fearful consequences: "They sow the wind and they reap the whirlwind." Such was the result, as the sequel will show, of Cecilia's defective education.

There were no incidents in her early life sufficiently interesting to require notice. She was without care. The river at the extremity of the park, whose waters flowed so tranquilly that they could scarcely be seen to move, may be regarded as an emblem of her existence. The words of the prophet precisely point out the character of her life: "Tomorrow shall be as this day, and much more abundant."

When she had nearly reached her seventeenth year an event occurred which gave a new and painful character to her future history. The gardens belonging to the house were large, and contained almost every variety of plants and flowers, delighting the eye with their beauty, and perfuming the air with their fragrance. Among the persons employed there, one, a young man of showy exterior, attracted Cecilia's attention, and she frequently conversed with him respecting the names and properties of certain flowers. The distance between them* was as so great that no suspicion was entertained by her friends of any improper intimacy. It seems, however, that a mutual attachment was formed, and for many months they carried on a clandestine correspondence without discovery. An accident disclosed their secret, and Cecilia's family was exceedingly distressed that she had so far forgotten her station in life, and the duty she owed to her parents and friends. The young man was immediately dismissed from his situation, and Cecilia was threatened with the lasting displeasure of her parents. She seemed to be overwhelmed with shame at her folly, and engaged in the most solemn manner that she would never see him or hold any further communication with him. After some time, her apparent contrition and humility were believed to be sincere; she was again restored to favour, and her life began to move on almost as tranquilly as it did prior to the discovery of this unhappy circumstance.

How painful it is to witness duplicity, especially in the young, from whom we had expected ingenuousness and sincerity! Cecilia was deceiving her friends. The correspondence was continued notwithstanding her solemn pledge to the contrary, and in an unhappy hour she left her home and married the man she had engaged to see no more. Her folly and guilt must be apparent to every reader. Perhaps, however, the evil

---

* While we can in no way excuse Cecilia's deceiving her parents, yet we cannot see that it is scriptural to regard "marrying beneath one's station" as such a terrible crime, however unwise.

consequences of this false step are so evident in the following pages that Cecilia's sufferings will form the strongest appeal to young persons, inducing obedience to parental counsels, in reference especially to that connection which death only can terminate.

From the uniform kindness of her indulgent parents Cecilia expected to be forgiven, and also that some lucrative situation would be obtained for her husband. In this she was painfully disappointed. From the moment her marriage was known, they discarded her for ever. She never saw them again, nor received any intimation that she was forgiven. Solomon says, "The way of transgressors is hard," and Cecilia proved the truth of that saying. She mourned in secret her disobedience and deceit, but it was too late then!

Cecilia's husband brought her to London and engaged an apartment in the neighbourhood of the Seven Dials. The contrast between her former and present abode must have been exceedingly distressing to her feelings. At a very late period of her life the impression continued, though its bitterness was then gone. The magnificent and airy mansion was exchanged for one confined room, and the extensive prospect for the chimneys of the adjacent houses; the superb furniture for a few articles of the plainest kind; the luxurious table for the coarsest fare; and instead of servants anticipating her wants, she now had to perform the most menial services for herself. But in the humiliating comparison there was one thing more difficult to endure than all the others. Instead of companions whose elegant manners gave a charm to all they did, she had the society of her husband only, while every day rendered her more sensible of her imprudence in the choice she had so foolishly made. She was as unsuited to him as he was to her, and now, when she wanted sympathy, there was no one to whom she could impart her cares, no one from whom she could receive consolation. Her neighbours were all poor, and many were depraved. She was as poor as any, but she never sank to their level or practised their vices.

It is due to her husband to state that, although he was bitterly disappointed by the continued silence of Cecilia's friends, he treated her kindly, and laboured hard to supply her wants.

The birth of a son, when she had been married rather more than a year, though it increased her difficulties, lessened their pressure; she had something to love now. For her child's sake she cheerfully endured privation and toil. There were moments when her thoughts would revert sadly to her former condition when she dwelt with her family and knew no want, yet even then the sight of her child would banish the feeling of regret and fill her heart with gladness. How tender and self-sacrificing is a mother's love! The God of all grace refers to it to illustrate His affection to His chosen people: "As one whom his mother comforteth, so will I comfort you; and ye shall be comforted in Jerusalem."

Thus the first ten years of her married life were spent. She had at intervals endeavoured to obtain some notice from her family, but her efforts were entirely unsuccessful; her letters were returned unopened, and not one indication of remembrance ever reached her. Between her parents and herself there was a great gulf. She could not pass it, and they adhered to their resolution; they would not pass to her.

Her mind was now more reconciled to her painful lot, and she clung with increased fondness to her child. There was nothing withheld from him that Cecilia could possibly procure, and she sought continually to promote his happiness. But she never taught him to look to heaven and pray. Alas! she knew not God, and was as unable as unwilling to speak to her boy concerning Him. All this time she had no Bible. Unsanctified afflictions harden, and poor Cecilia's heart was as hard as a rock. She had never said with the prodigal, "I will arise and go to my Father," nor with the publican, "God be merciful to me a sinner." In those days there was no Bible Society to seek out the destitute poor and give the best of books. Even now, ignorance and vice abound, but the company is great who publish "glad tidings", and the Lord has said, "My Word...shall not return unto Me void, but it shall accomplish that which I please, and it shall prosper in the thing whereto I sent it."

About this time an event occurred which plunged Cecilia into the depths of affliction and despair, far exceeding anything she had previously experienced. It is probable that her early habits prevented that union of feeling between her and her husband which is so essential to happiness in the married life. They were "unequally yoked". Perhaps, also, the consciousness of his inferiority was mortifying to himself and induced him to regret the step he had taken, by which her position in life was so painfully changed. It is only in this way that she could account for the mysterious and distressing event which must now be related.

Her son was just entering his tenth year; he was an interesting lad and was greatly attached to his mother. One Sabbath morning, when the sun was brightly shining and the church bells were sending forth their cheerful peal, he went out with his father, not to attend the house of God but to take a walk, intending to return in time for dinner. Cecilia made the usual preparation, and after waiting some considerable period after all was ready, she began to feel angry at their stay; but hour after hour passed, and her anger was exchanged for alarm. *From that day she never saw her husband or her child, nor heard anything concerning them.* They had not quarrelled, nor had he ever by a single word led her to suspect that he entertained an intention of leaving her. Everything connected with his absence continues to be involved in the deepest obscurity.

It would be vain to attempt a description of the anguish that was felt by the bereaved mother. As the day closed, and the dreary night succeeded, she listened with intense eagerness to every footstep that seemed to approach her dwelling, but as the steps receded she sank down in mute despair. The longest night will end; so did that long night of suffering; yet the day brought no relief, for the sad truth began to force itself on Cecilia's breaking heart: she was forsaken! Her poor neighbours, from whom she had usually stood aloof, now came around her, and with affectionate earnestness sought to encourage her still to hope. The poor are not destitute of sympathy, and they often help those who are poorer than themselves. But their efforts were in vain; Cecilia had ceased to hope, and like Rachel "she refused to be comforted".

When she began to think upon her past life, she remembered with bitter grief her ungrateful conduct to her friends. Her duplicity and disobedience had wrought upon her a heavy punishment, yet she did not confess her sin against God or offer up one prayer to Him for pardon or for succour. He was "an unknown God". "Like a bullock unaccustomed to the yoke", she was stubborn and rebellious; and she said as Cain, "My punishment is greater than I can bear." Her condition and prospects were indeed most dreary and distressing. There was no ray of light to relieve the gloom, no cheering remembrance to lessen her woe. All was *hopeless, helpless misery!* The language may seem too strong, and yet it simply expresses the state of her mind.

In after life, when she knew the grace of God and had become familiar with the sacred oracles, she used to say that David's "horrible pit and miry clay" must have been very similar to her experience at this period of her existence. In the sunshine of her days she never sought the Lord; in her poverty and toil she had always neglected the means of grace; and now, in her utter bereavement, she had no God to go to!

Reduced by the loss of her husband's earnings to absolute poverty, she was obliged to part with her furniture and clothes to buy bread. She was too proud to solicit charity and she knew no way by which she could obtain the meanest provision, when the remainder of her little property was gone. She had clung to life while there was any hope that her child would return; but now, when every inquiry had been made, and all had proved fruitless, she only wished to lie down and die.

Affliction is a dark lane, where the enemy of souls is always watching that he may gain advantage over those who have to travel in that path. He was busy with Cecilia now, and she readily listened to his artful suggestions. The temptation was in unison with her feelings: it was self-murder! Poor thing – she had no dread of a future state, for she thought of death only as the end of her existence and of her misery. Her plan was soon formed, and she waited only for the approach of night as the fittest season for her deed of darkness. Scarcely had the shades of evening spread their gloom over her poor abode than she wrapped her cloak around her and went forth, firm in her purpose to end her life and her sufferings for ever.

How awful is the spectacle! An immortal being is about to rush into the presence of her Maker: a sinner, to the tribunal of her Judge. See the destroyer, as with malicious triumph he urges his victim onwards to eternal ruin. Is there no friendly arm to snatch the brand from the burning? There are but a few steps between Cecilia and the pit. Man's aid is vain. Lord, save, or she will perish!

She was walking swiftly up Tottenham Court Road, a solitary path then, when she saw a number of persons entering Whitefield's Chapel. She stood still, scarcely knowing what to do. She thought that if she attempted to execute her purpose then, she would be observed and hindered. While she was hesitating, a young man very kindly invited her to accompany him into the chapel. He was quite a stranger, but his manner evinced so much affection and sympathy that she felt herself unable to refuse, and for the first time for many years she found herself in the house of God. She had not, at that time, relinquished her fatal purpose, but was as firm as ever in her determination not to live. She had only for an hour or two postponed the execution of her design. The service, and especially the singing, had soothed her troubled mind, but beyond this the service had made no impression. When the congregation began to disperse, the young man gave her a shilling, and entreated her to come again the next evening. She promised to do so, and they separated. The supply, small as it was, which had been sent just as providentially as the bread and flesh which the ravens brought to the prophet, enabled her to provide a little nourishment, which she greatly needed. Her feelings were also tranquillized, and for the time she put away from her the horrid thought of self-destruction.

At the appointed time she again went to the chapel and saw the young man to whose kindness she was so much indebted. Nothing particular occurred during the service, but when it ended he gave her a shilling, as he did on the previous evening, and very earnestly pressed her to come on the following day, which was the Lord's day. Such was her destitute condition that it was with great difficulty she could make herself sufficiently decent to be seen in the daytime at such a place. But she went. And now she obtained a blessing for which she had infinite cause for gratitude to that young man and to Almighty God for ever. The preacher seemed to have singled her out from all the congregation, as if his message were only for her. He set before her the ingratitude and rebellion of her whole life. While hearing him she felt that the Lord might, with strict justice, have cut her off in her sins. And now, the thought of the future, as it is set forth in the Scriptures, filled her with dreadful anguish: "the worm that never dies – the fire that is never quenched". Cecilia felt that if her purpose had not been prevented, this would have been her portion. But the minister was not a Boanerges only; he was also a son of consolation; and as the cry burst from her broken heart, "What must I do to be saved?" he pointed to the cross, and to the risen and ascended Saviour. The Holy Spirit applied the Word with power, and Cecilia felt that there is a charm in the name of Jesus. An old writer, commenting on the first chapter of Matthew and the twenty-first verse, thus writes: "O sweet name of Jesus! It is honey in the mouth, music in the ear and a jubilee in the heart." It was all this to Cecilia. She had now entered on a new existence. Satan was defeated and shrank away ashamed, but there was joy in heaven.

When this service, so interesting and important to Cecilia, had terminated, the young man pressed her very earnestly to continue her attendance. She wept, but her tears were those of joy, for she had now found a "great treasure", of the existence of which she was previously in utter ignorance. He gave her a shilling, and they separated, to meet no more in this life. It is very remarkable that she never knew anything concerning him. Perhaps he was detained by illness or perhaps he was removed, in the providence of God, to some other part of the great city. But it is idle to inquire. Our safest course is suggested by the prophet when he says. "This also cometh forth from the LORD of hosts, who is wonderful in counsel and excellent in working." He never knew the consequences resulting from his kindness, but the act shall be had in everlasting remembrance.* This young man was an instrument in the hand of the Holy Spirit of "saving a soul from death", a holier and happier deed than the conquest of a kingdom. "Suffer the word of exhortation," and

---

* What a lesson there is in the simple, humble witness of this young man!

"Go, thou and do thou likewise."

Cecilia had been unable to thank her benefactor, but she went home with a lightened heart. She was willing to live now, that she might praise Jesus. She had found a Friend, one who "loves at all times" and is "a Brother born for adversity"; others had cast her off, but He would "never leave her nor forsake her". Happy Cecilia! She served the Lord with gladness, and often longed to have her husband and child with her again, that she might tell them "how great things the Lord had done for her"; but this privilege she never enjoyed.

Perhaps some persons, who are inclined to "limit the Holy One of Israel", as if He were bound in every instance of conversion to certain rules, will conclude that there is not sufficient evidence that the "work was of God". They think it essential to a sinner's salvation that he should endure for a certain period all the horror and distress of soul which they have endured; but Cecilia was no sooner wounded than she was healed. Such objectors are reminded that there are "diversities of operations, but the same Spirit". The interval was very short between the hour when the multitude on the Day of Pentecost were "pricked in their heart" and that in which they "gladly received the Word". Those who knew Cecilia Sloane never doubted the reality of her conversion.

With some difficulty she obtained employment, and cheerfully toiled for her daily bread. She cared not how hard she laboured, if at the close of the day she could reach the chapel in time for the worship of God. Sometimes she suffered pain in her limbs, from having overtaxed her strength, and at other times she endured great privation, when she had but little employment: yet in every trial, she felt as the poet, when he said:

"And though my cup is mixed with gall,
There's something secret sweetens all."

"We glory," said the apostle, "in tribulations also: knowing that tribulation worketh patience; and patience, experience; and experience, hope: and hope maketh not ashamed; because the love of God is shed abroad in our hearts by the Holy Ghost which is given unto us."

She now lived in the liberty of the gospel for several years, during which there was no change in her outward circumstances. She laboured hard, but she had great enjoyments. The poor frequently possess a larger share of spirituality and comfort than the rich, and thus their covenant God compensates for the privations and toils they endure. "God hath chosen the poor...rich in faith."

One evening, after her day's work was done, Cecilia was returning home. Her path led her through Little Wild Street, and when she had reached the chapel which is situated there, the sound of voices singing the praises of the Saviour attracted her attention. The tune was familiar, and this encouraged her to enter. Doctor Stennett* was preaching, and though his manner was less energetic than that of her favourite ministers, yet his soft persuasive tones interested her greatly, and she left the place with a gladdened heart. From that time she frequently attended there, as it was much nearer her residence than Tottenham Court Road, though she still preferred the chapel where the Lord had so graciously changed her heart.

After some time, she was kindly noticed by several of the Doctor's members, and as she had not up to this period formed any spiritual acquaintance, their attentions were much prized. Familiar intercourse with the children of God tended also to enlarge her views of divine truth, and promoted greatly her establishment in the things of God. Solomon says that as "iron sharpeneth iron, so a man sharpeneth the countenance of his friend". It is much to be lamented that the example of primitive saints is so little imitated. Christians too much resemble a flock of sheep on a summer day, scattered over the common, and mindful only of their individual ease. Were the clouds to indicate a storm, or the dog to bark, they would soon congregate together, as if they knew that "union is strength". May the Church consider this, and even now "speak often one to another". Days of persecution may be nearer than many think; but under any circumstances, the "communion of saints" will greatly advantage the people of God, by the strength and courage it will impart to endure and perform all the will of their divine Master.

While occasionally hearing the good Doctor, she heard with surprise of believers' baptism. The subject was quite new. Like many others, she had always believed that infant sprinkling was the good old way, and that any change from that must be an unauthorized innovation. She attempted to convince her new friends of their error, yet she could not help wondering that all the evidence of the New Testament was in their favour, and there was not one single text to support her views. One argument only remained, and that for some time seemed to her quite conclusive: "The good men whom she had heard with so much profit at Whitefield's Chapel baptized infants: and surely they ought to know what was right." Yet this did not satisfy her friends, nor even herself entirely: for she soon saw that the question is not, "What do others say?" but, "What saith the Scripture?" She now examined the subject with seriousness and prayer, and the result of her convictions became apparent in her conduct: she was

---

* This would be Samuel Stennett (1729-1795), whose hymns appear in Gadsby's selection.

13

baptized, and united herself in Christian fellowship with the church in Little Wild Street.

Dr. Stennett, whose name is still fragrant in the church, having heard from Cecilia the history of her eventful life, endeavoured to effect a reconciliation with her relatives. In this he failed, and they still adhered to their determination never to see her again. His intercession, however, induced them to settle on her a small annuity, to be paid quarterly. By this arrangement, she was mercifully relieved from the necessity of labouring for the bread that perisheth, just at the time when her strength began to fail. When the writer of these pages became the pastor of the church, he several times had the pleasure of paying her the quarterly allowance, which was handed to him for that purpose by the agent of the family. At her death, also, when he submitted an account of charges for her funeral, and for previous medical attendance, the amount was immediately paid, without any comment.

In making a public profession and uniting with the church Cecilia found, like many others, that "in keeping the Saviour's commandments there is great reward", and, as the eunuch, she "went on her way rejoicing". Her days were now free from anxiety respecting temporal things, and she was permitted constantly to attend the means of grace. Her cheerful godliness, also, rendered her society valuable to her fellow Christians. Indeed, there was always a sweet savour of Christ in her conversation, and the apposite manner in which she would introduce a text of Scripture, part of a hymn, or a sentence from the sermons of Whitefield, Berridge and others, whose names were embalmed in her memory, was exceedingly pleasant and profitable. The writer of this memoir remembers the solemn manner in which, a short time after he became acquainted with her, she addressed him in the following lines:

> "O servant of God, your Master proclaim,
> And publish abroad His wonderful name;
> The name all-victorious of Jesus extol;
> His kingdom is glorious, and rules over all."

The death of Dr. Stennett was a great loss to the church, and was painfully felt by Cecilia. His worth is too well known to require a tribute now. He was succeeded by other pastors, among whom the names of Coxhead, Waters and Hargreaves are still held in affectionate remembrance. All of these, after labouring for a few years, were removed to other places, and have now entered into their eternal rest. In the month of January 1834, when the present pastor entered on his ministerial labours in Little Wild Street, his acquaintance with Cecilia commenced. At that time, she had just entered on her ninetieth year. She was still in the possession of her faculties; indeed her memory was remarkably retentive, but her bodily strength was nearly gone, and she was unable without assistance to come to the house of God.

Her enjoyments were very great. Every sermon was to her a "feast of fat things, a feast of wines on the lees, of fat things full of marrow, of wines on the lees well refined". She found, as she often said. "a full Christ for empty sinners; a rich Christ for poor saints". Her pastor heard her express her strong confidence in God, saying, *"No! how can I doubt after all the Lord has done for me?"* and then added with singular emphasis:

"He by Himself hath sworn,
I on His oath depend;
I shall, on eagles' wings upborne,
To heaven ascend.
I shall behold His face,
I shall His power adore,
And sing the wonders of His grace
For evermore."

Thus she seemed as "a shock of corn, fully ripe in its season"; she was willing to wait the Lord's time, yet she had "a desire to depart and be with Christ, which is far better".

When on any occasion her husband and son were mentioned, she always referred to them with the confident expectation of meeting them in heaven. She had prayed for them, and she believed that a faithful God would not permit any of his children to pray in vain. Of her other connections she ever spoke with gratitude. Her parents were dead, and scarcely any who had formerly known her were now alive. She felt that if they still existed, the change in her religious views and habits would have unfitted her for their society. She sighed not for her former splendour, for she had "learned to be content with the things that she possessed". Indeed "Christ and a crust" were sufficient to make her happy. Of death she had no fear. He was a chained enemy, and she knew that her best Friend held the chain. She would frequently say:

"And when I'm to die, 'Receive me,' I'll cry,
For Jesus hath loved me, I cannot tell why;
But this I do find, we two are so joined,
He'll not stay in glory, and leave me behind."

Her last Sabbath was spent in the house of God. She was on the mount. In answer to an inquiry respecting the state of her mind, she said, "Thy words were found, and I did eat them; and Thy word was unto me the joy and rejoicing of mine heart: for I am called by Thy name, O LORD God of hosts." That night she went to bed as usual, but she never left it. Before the morning an attack of paralysis deprived her of the use of her limbs, and of the power of speech. Yet even then she indicated by signs that she was happy. In this state she remained two or three days and then, without a struggle or a groan, she fell asleep in Jesus.

In the original account the author here makes various comments on Cecilia's life, and then concludes:

In concluding the memoir of Cecilia Sloane, the reader is assured that it is a truthful narrative. The facts have been obtained by the author from several sources, all of which may be relied on with entire confidence. He gratefully acknowledges the kindness of an aged gentleman, who acted as agent for the family in the payment of her annuity; to whom he is indebted for much interesting information in reference to Cecilia and her parents. Other parts were communicated to him by his much esteemed friend and deacon, the late William Paxon, to whom she was personally known during many of the latter years of her life. But the principal part of the narrative was from Cecilia herself. She seemed to derive both pleasure and profit while she related the interesting and affecting events by which her life had been so remarkably distinguished. It may be further remarked that she ever sought to magnify the sovereign grace of her heavenly Father, "who remembered her in her low estate: because His mercy endureth for ever." Such also has been the sincere desire of the author. May the Holy Spirit deign to make this little account a blessing to many.

Gospel Standard 1990. First published as a pamphlet c. 1835.

SEARCH FOR REALITY

Henrietta Gilpin

Early Memories

My mother having died when I was an infant, and my father being much engrossed in human learning, and not till many years afterwards impressed with the importance of religion, I do not recollect receiving any early religious instruction beyond hearing a chapter in the Bible and one of Spinkes's prayers read daily, morning and night, in the family. I was also required to take my stand among my brothers and sisters while we repeated the Church catechism with perfect correctness to my father every Sunday evening, and this was followed by the reading of a sermon. I used to pay little attention to these forms, which constituted at that time the extent of our family religion. On the contrary, I often found them most irksome, my spirit being wholly set upon this world.

Still I felt sometimes convictions of sin when very young, but they were transient. The first I remember occurred when I was about five or six years old. I was unaccountably urged, out of mere curiosity, to try a foolish experiment, which though really harmless, I childishly supposed might prove dangerous. I pursued my purpose, however, in a reckless spirit till suddenly a cutting conviction of sin struck into me. I thought I was hardened, daring and presumptuous above other children, and I felt a measure of terror, with a vague expectation of judgment to come, that I long remembered with fear.

When I was about seven or eight years old, I used to hear more about the importance of the soul from my elder sisters, and then I would frequently make resolutions of being very religious, and set about the business most earnestly; but my natural disposition being very inconstant, I never could persevere long together. This was a great distress to me, but I would try again and again, and sometimes kept up for a good while, very constant in private prayer and laboriously striving against sin. I was often warned by my friends of the necessity of continuance in well-doing, and was taught to believe that converted people might turn back to the ways of sin again, and be eventually lost, which I always pondered with distress, believing it would be my own case. I thought it a most grievous pity that those who had at any time been in a state of salvation should outlive that and become heirs of hell again. This used to make me consider death, even in its most violent form, as the greatest blessing that could possibly befall a person as soon as ever he was once religious. Accordingly, as soon as I had kept on (as I supposed) long enough in private prayer, etc., I began to long to die, as my best chance of ever getting to heaven. Once on a walk, I found I had got into a field with a bull, and though exceedingly afraid of those animals, I really felt glad in the hope that it would kill me, for I thought my pain would soon be over and I should be out of the danger of becoming wicked again. So again, when I awoke with a noise in the night, I really hoped there were thieves and that they would kill me. (We lived in a lonely house and were more than once robbed.) But death would not come, and after some time I got wearied out with my laborious religion, which was as hard to me as Egyptian bondage, and I began by degrees to relax a little and at last to let all go and return to the world again, but not without grievous smitings of conscience and bitter regrets. These efforts were thus repeated with little variation, and with shorter or longer success, at intervals during the remaining years of my childhood.

The Unpardonable Sin

One circumstance occurred, however, when I was about nine years old, which I will relate because my sin on that occasion was sorely visited on me many years afterwards. One day my eldest sister was reading some of the Scripture to us, and coming to that chapter where "the sin unto death" is spoken of, she stopped to comment on it, saying that it was a great mystery and that no one can tell what that sin is, adding that it was a great warning to us to resist sin in every form, lest we should commit it unawares. I felt while she was speaking an amazing curiosity to know what this secret mysterious sin could be, and indulging this curiosity I thought of little else. At last, something seemed to whisper, "Commit that sin." I was in the greatest horror, but still the temptation haunted me. I tried in vain to drive it away. "How can I commit it?" I said. "I don't even know what it is." And now I was glad I did not, lest I should be hurried into the commission of it, which I felt would be deplorable indeed. In spite of this, I was tormented by this fearful and unaccountable temptation to that degree that at last I desperately shut myself up in a dark cupboard and tremblingly said, "I commit it."

Thus I sought to obtain quiet, but the moment the words were out of my lips, I was terrified. I would have borne anything to have recalled them; surely I thought myself sealed for destruction. I feared and trembled greatly, but still a hope glimmered within that perhaps it would not be imputed to me, that perhaps that sin was kept secret on purpose to keep people from committing it. With this little hope, I knelt down and begged the Lord very earnestly to tell me if I had committed it, for I knew that if I had, it was useless to ask for forgiveness contrary to His positive determination expressed so strongly in Scripture. I therefore confined myself to entreating Him to let me know if I had absolutely committed it past hope. I had never in my life heard a word that could lead me to think that God ever sensibly speaks to the souls of His people nowadays, and therefore I have often been surprised to think what could put me upon asking such a thing. I kept begging and watching for an answer, and when none came in the day, I implored Him to speak to me in a dream and reveal the truth of my case to me. I so feared the answer that I hardly dared close my eyes at night, yet I longed to be at some certainty, for nothing, I thought, could be worse than suspense. However, days and nights passed, and nothing occurred from which anything could be gathered, and by degrees the follies and pleasures of childhood wore away my terrors. My impression is, though I have forgotten particulars, that the remembrance would frighten me for about a year, but after that I completely lost sight of the whole transaction, insomuch that I am not aware of its recurring to my memory till many years afterwards.

Legal Bondage

When I was about fourteen, I was confirmed, on which occasion I again set hard to work at my religion, which I continued as long as my natural inconstancy of disposition would permit, and then gave up as before. Many efforts of this kind all leading to the same issue recurred during my early youth. On my coming home from school at the age of sixteen, my father required me to attend the sacrament. This excited many anxious fears in my mind, for at that time I was quite worldly and dared not attend in that state. Yet I was kept by shame and fear from refusing to attend, which I thought would be deliberate avowal of irreligion. So after many debates in my mind, and some distress, I came to this conclusion—that as I must be religious some day or else perish, I had best set about it at once. Indeed I thought it an excellent opportunity, for I hoped that receiving the sacrament would be a strong tie to bind me to perseverance, vainly presuming that I should never be so wicked as to live in deliberate sin again after joining in that sacred ordinance.

I therefore prepared myself with great earnestness and many long prayers, together with diligent self-examination according to the routine prescribed by Spinkes and Doddridge and such authors, and approached the table pretty confident of the goodness of my state. Often did I pity and wonder at those poor creatures who could dare to receive the sacrament unworthily, as I called it, though the most ungodly among them could not possibly be more ignorant of all that is signified by that ordinance, even Jesus Christ and Him crucified, than I was. My mouth indeed was full of the mention of His name, but I spoke what I did not understand.

After my return to school, I found it hard work to maintain my strict religion among my thoughtless companions. However, I succeeded pretty well on the whole, and as I patiently endured some ridicule and stood through one or two strong temptations, I began to think myself established. In about three quarters of a year more, I finally left school and returned to live with my family at Petersham, near Richmond. Here my religion seemed to flourish well. I became more and more earnest and constant in private prayer and more self-denied in my daily walk.

I have often looked back with surprise at the strict scrutiny I used to keep over my thoughts and actions; though I was perfectly my own mistress and had my time at my own disposal, yet I seldom ventured to undertake the smallest employment without seriously asking myself, not whether it was most agreeable to *me,* but whether I had reason to believe it was more pleasing in the sight of God than anything else I could be engaged in. This, of course, obliged me often to sacrifice even my strongest inclinations, which I found frequently very painful, but was supported by the thought that surely now I must be a converted character. Sometimes I would set apart a day for secret self-examination and humiliation before God. On these occasions I would take great pains to call to mind all the sins of my early youth and infancy, of which indeed I had a black catalogue to reflect on, for between my fits of religion I had been much given to deceit and lies and in many other ways was worse than other children. All these I would reflect on, dwelling upon all their aggravated circumstances till I have often lain prostrate on the ground with shame and remorse, and wept over, confessed, and begged forgiveness for them; and I have more than once felt at such times that there was no indignity the meanest servant could insult me with, that I should feel *able* to resent. All this I used to suppose must be godly sorrow and genuine repentance, though I now see nothing in it but what was *self*-wrought. In this way I went on, supposing I had found all that was to be found in religion and that nothing now remained but to persevere to the end and so be saved. Thus I made great account of prayer and searching the Scriptures, but of the answer to prayer or finding the God of the Scripture I knew nothing.

The Unpardonable Sin: Fresh Concern

In this state I was when one morning I rose and began to repeat hymns or psalms as usual, while dressing myself. All of a sudden it was darted into my mind, "What is the use of all your prayers, etc? You had better leave them alone, for it is utterly impossible you should ever be saved; you have deliberately and of free choice committed the unpardonable sin." And immediately the transaction I have already related was brought quite fresh to my memory. My spirit was thrown into great hurry and alarm, and I tried hard to fortify myself against it and withstand the fearful conclusion which was pressed on me as hard. I thought how pious I had become and endeavoured to consider that a proof to the contrary. After a while, I calmed myself a little and as an infant was going to be buried close against my window, which looked into the churchyard, I thought I would sit at the open sash and follow the funeral service, a thing I was particularly fond of doing.

Just at this moment, I heard the bell ring for family morning prayer below, and I felt much tempted to absent myself, so strong was my desire to witness this funeral. After some struggles, my conscience seemed to drive me to give up my inclination and go down, which I did. It happened that the chapter in course was not read that morning, but instead of it that one that contains our Saviour's mention of the sin against the Holy Ghost, saying, "It hath never forgiveness, neither in this world nor in that which is to come." I cannot describe the terror that seized me while these words were being read. It seemed to me that the remarkable circumstance of this chapter being selected, just after the conviction I had had upstairs, was ordained to prove my guilt and stop my mouth. My whole soul was in an agony. I shut myself up in my room and spent the day in the bitterest anguish.

I dared not open the Bible nor pray, for I thought that I was utterly forbidden to do either. I can never forget the value and blessedness I then saw in the Scriptures and the envy I felt for those that might read them. I shut the book and laid it at the further end of the table and sat looking at it in deep distress. I thought I must give up all profession of religion and never presume to go to a place of worship, and how I was to drag on the rest of my existence, I knew not.

At last I ventured to go and tell my distress to one of my sisters in the faint hope that she might help me to a glimmer of encouragement. She answered that the exact nature of that sin was not revealed and therefore it was not our part to enquire into it. I replied that I feared the way in which I had committed it cut off all hope that I was mistaken in the sin, for that I had actually been so mad as to say, "*Whatever* it is, I commit it." I then confessed all the circumstances to her, which quite staggered her, and after some silence she only said, "Well! It's astonishing how wicked children can be." Thus I got small comfort from her and went again to my room worse than ever.

Encouragement

At last as I was wandering about the house, I found a heap of books that had lain undisturbed for a length of time, and carelessly picking up one of them, I was somewhat struck with its title, which was *The Redeemer's Tears*. I therefore carried it to my room, for though I dared not read the Bible, I thought as this was only a man's writing, I would venture. Still I expected to be greatly cut up by reading precious things of a Saviour in whom I had no interest. I sat down on the floor in one corner and, opening the book, found a little treatise quite distinct from the book of Howe's, whose title had struck me, but bound up under the same cover, whether by the same author or not, I do not know. This little tract was entitled, *On the sin against the Holy Ghost, addressed to tempted souls*. I was agitated and astonished. I had never before in my life met with anything on that subject, and thought it could not be chance that it should have come into my hands at such a crisis. I therefore had a sort of expectation that it would pronounce my sentence one way or the other, and therefore began to read it through with much attention and anxiety. From what I recollect, I think the author must have treated the subject according to truth and with wisdom. He did not attempt to enter much into the nature of the sin, but shewed clearly that such as are under the guilt of it are utterly destitute of the strivings of the Spirit in their hearts; consequently they are hardened, insensible and dead, or else given over to desperation, with rebellion and hatred to God, His ways and His people. "And therefore," the author continued, "how black soever the circumstances of your sin may have been; how exactly soever (to human judgment) it may seem to resemble the sin against the Holy Ghost, yet, if you feel compunction and grief for your folly and madness − if the love and favour of God seem more desirable in your eyes than all the world − if you long for the influences of the blessed Spirit, whom you fear you have everlastingly offended − I may venture to assert that you have not been suffered to sin the sin unto death. On the contrary, you have ground to hope that there is already a seed of grace springing up in your heart, which has provoked the malice of the accuser of the brethren against you. He seldom molests any in this way but those whom he is in danger of losing. Possibly you can remember that he never haunted you with this suggestion while you were worldly and careless, but now it may be you have begun to seek the salvation of your soul. There's nothing the devil fears like prayer, and he will surely be put to shame." The treatise was as nearly as I can recollect to this effect, and I found it very encouraging. Indeed, I could not but hope it would in the end prove true for *me,* and though still in doubt and fear, I thought I would venture to the church as the bells were ringing for service.

Deliverance

The first lesson was Isaiah 43, and contained the words, "Fear not, for I have redeemed thee, I have called thee by thy name; thou art Mine. When thou passest through the waters, I will be with thee; and through the rivers, they shall not overflow thee: when thou walkest through the fire, thou shalt not be burned; neither shall the flame kindle upon thee...For I am the LORD *your* Holy One, the creator of Israel, your King." These words fell so sweetly upon my spirit and infused such calm, peace and joyfulness that all my fears vanished at once, and if I had tried to recall them, I could not have done it; and from that hour to this, they have never been suffered to return, even weakly – I mean on that one particular subject.

A week or two after, I was pondering the whole circumstance and thinking I should like to read again the tract which had been such a comfort to me in my trouble. I went to seek the book from its place, to which I had restored it after reading, but when I sat down to read the tract, I sought for it in vain. I turned leaf by leaf through the whole book and it was not there – nor any allusion to it in the index. I could not tell what to make of this, but so certain was I that I had been made to read it there, and so certain that it was not there now, that I was ready to think it miraculous, but I never told a creature what had happened.

The Mystery Solved

Several years after, this mystery was cleared up thus. My elder sister (not the same whom I had consulted in my distress) was employed with me in sorting my father's books after a family removal, and we fell into conversation about some of the authors and their writings. She observed that even good men were often very injudicious, and brought up as an example their publishing treatises on the blasphemy against the Holy Ghost, which, she said, was the very way that such things were put into people's heads, adding that for her part, she never allowed such things to be in the house. Of course, this called to my mind all that I had gone through, and I said, "What then, have you destroyed any?" "Yes," she said, "there was one in one of our books and I got it out without hurting the book at all – you can't think how cleverly it could be done, and the place, too, where it was noticed in the table of its contents. I would defy anyone to find out that anything had been removed from the book." "I know what the book was," said I. "It was Howe's *Redeemer's Tears*." She answered, "What then, have you seen it?" I only said, "Yes," but I felt a good deal, and thought what a mercy it was that, although it had been for years in the house, she had not been suffered to lay hands on it till just after it had done what it had for me! I think that doubtless there must have been some working of the Spirit in what I have related, though it was soon smothered and obscured again in the clouds of self-righteousness and legality.

A Deficient Religion

After I was thus delivered from that fearful temptation, I went on very smoothly and made, as I thought, great progress; and think I may say that after the strictest sect of our religion, I lived a Pharisee. I prayed, read, strove, denied myself in every way. In *word* I renounced all my own righteousness, and I truly thought I trusted wholly in Christ. But I now see, as clear as the sun, that all this while I was wholly ignorant of Christ and was under the law, though couched in gospel terms, and being under the law whose demands are infinite, the more I did, the more it required. Nevertheless, I kept on the whole pretty comfortable, because my gospel notions, such as they were, came in to patch up the deficiencies. It is awful to think how I, like others in this state, could teach and talk of Christ and fill my long prayers with the continual mention of His name and righteousness and yet know nothing in the world of Him experimentally, not having been brought through that tedious and killing work of pulling down off the natural foundation of self-righteousness, without more or less of which none can be built upon the Rock. How did I neglect full one half of the Word of God, and thus never discerned that the promises are made to the *lost,* the *blind* and the *prisoners,* to which states I had *never* been *really* reduced.

As for *sensible* answers to prayer, I may say I never truly looked for any, and the forgiveness of sins I thought to be what would of course take place without our knowing it, if we were very religious; and that we must take it for granted without any inward experience of it. As for such texts as these: "I will *manifest Myself* unto him as I do not unto the world," I either explained them away or neglected them altogether, and I made no doubt whatever that I was a *doer* of the Word and not a hearer only, because of the strict watch I used to keep over my thoughts, words and actions, striving after usefulness to others, as well as inward holiness. I was on the whole very successful. My temper seemed quite subdued and every passion brought into subjection.

In this state I had a short illness, of which I thought I might die, but was so confident of the goodness of my state that I longed for death, and was quite disappointed when the complaint began to yield to the remedies. I am persuaded that, had I died in such a state, I should have said many triumphant speeches about my entrance into glory and being with Christ, etc. This has shown me since that a false hope may support a soul through natural death and therefore that an exulting death does not *prove* a profession of religion to be genuine, as Bunyan implies when he makes "Ignorance" to be carried over the river high and dry by "Vain-hope"; and the Scriptures say the same. For I firmly believe that it was of professors of this kind that our Saviour spoke when He declared: "*Many* shall say unto Me in that day, Lord, Lord, have we not prophesied in Thy Name" (taught Thy Name to others) "and in Thy Name cast out devils" (as the Church catechism says – renounced the devil and all his works) "and in Thy Name done many wonderful works. And then will I profess unto them, I never knew you; depart from Me, ye that work iniquity" – for workers of iniquity all will be accounted who have not known Christ and been known of Him, whatever apparent excellence they may have attained to.

Thus I was alive without the law, and sin was dead; and as I made so sure of my being in a state of grace, it is no wonder that I had often seasons of much happiness. This natural joy and satisfaction I took for the peace of God and thought it one of my tokens for good because the word says, "Rejoice evermore," etc. Therefore I nursed it and knowing nothing (in reality) of the plague of my own heart and the temptations of the enemy, I could pretty easily maintain it, insomuch that I have often taken such delight in prayer and meditation as to pass the *whole* day two or three times in a week in those employments and have thought "If the world did but know this pleasure, they would leave all their vanities to enjoy it."

All this while I knew nothing of Christ, nor of that state of spiritual destitution set forth throughout the Scriptures by numberless figures, as the state to which He brings His people, and wherein He reveals Himself to them as a Saviour in *time of need*.

The heart is deceitful above all things, and therefore I did not suspect at the time what I have clearly discovered since, and that is that my comfort was *secretly* based on my perseverance and success in religion. I used to go to bed very happy, and after I had lain down commonly repeated aloud two favourite hymns, one of which contained these words, "Jesus, Thou my guardian be, Sweet it is to trust in Thee," and in the other were these words:

> "Mean as we are, by sins and griefs beset,
> We glory that in Him we are complete."

These last lines especially I used greatly to enjoy on my best days, but I recollect I could not say them if I had given way to spiritual sloth, worldliness or any other sin during the day. I would then feel very uncomfortable and used to pray for forgiveness, but knew nothing of finding the blood of sprinkling to purge my conscience, whereby I should have experimentally entered into those lines, and without which they are but empty sound. I would secretly take comfort from resolving to be more watchful next day and generally lost the pressure of the sense of sin during the night; so that I began pretty clear afresh next morning, and if I succeeded better, which I usually did, all was right again.

"Are you sure you are born again?"

In this state I continued till some time after my removal with my family to Hampstead, and then I remember two occasions on which my confidence received a sudden shake inwardly, the effect of which was very terrible to me.

The first was this. I had been praying very earnestly in private as usual and came out of my room more than ordinarily happy and well satisfied with my state. As I went downstairs I was suddenly arrested by this question inwardly suggested: "Are you sure you are born again?" "Yes," I answered, "surely I must be." The question was repeated. I stood still and wondered what could put such a thing into my head, and answered it as before, only more at length, bringing up, as I thought, Scripture proofs. Again, the same question was repeated more solemnly and, as it were, preceded by a "nevertheless". I was chilled throughout in a way I cannot describe, but held fast my integrity and tried to have the last word. Still it presented itself and I was obliged to go away with it sounding unanswered in my heart. This caused a dreadful feeling. I believe it was a conviction of the Spirit, but I thought it came from the enemy, and wore it off by constantly resisting it.

The second occasion was just before a sacrament. I had been earnestly preparing myself all the week and was at the time engaged in fervent prayer after long self-examination. If I remember right, I had been blessing God for enabling me to devote myself to His service, and begging Him to enable me to increase. Just at this moment I was conscious of an inward conviction that all this my religion was to come to nothing, to be utterly destroyed. I thought this came from my own imagination and was afraid of giving it force by opposing it; I therefore coolly tried to turn my eyes another way, as it were, and to pursue my former train of thoughts. However, I could not put it aside, for it increased to a most positive intimation of the dreadful truth, for such it was to me at that time. I was horror-struck and in great agony of mind, for I had no idea that the destruction foretold could be in mercy, as it is written: "Thou turnest man to destruction; and sayest, Return ye children of men." Little did I think that in the loss of that specious religion I should but be losing *the shadow, the letter, the form,* to find *the substance, the spirit and the power.* I thought rather it implied final apostasy from grace (a doctrine which I held at that period).

The terrifying effect abode long; indeed, it never went off, for I believe the hopeless feeling it wrought went far towards making me reckless and desperate in the spiritual declension which commenced soon after this. In a few weeks more I found I had lost all relish for religion and private duties; gradually I left off prayer and watchfulness, and at last got quite thoughtless and worldly. I used to have intervals of bitter misery and anguish of soul, in which I would strive in the very fire to regain what I had lost. This was the very utmost bound of my desire, for I really believe I would have ventured my life for it, that that religion was the religion of the Bible.

Marriage (and Deeper Concern)
We had now removed to Buntingford and I was just twenty years of age. I was looking forward to my approaching marriage with a sort of hope that in becoming the wife of a clergyman, a sense of responsibility would urge me to greater exertion to regain and retain my religion, for I had never been brought to discover in any measure the depth of powerful truth which lies hid in those easily quoted words, "By *grace* are ye saved through *faith;* and that *not of yourselves:* it is the *gift* of God."

It was at this time that I first had the doctrine of election brought to my particular notice. I found that some of my husband's family, whom I looked up to in religion, strongly held this doctrine and those allied to it, such as the believer's perseverance and the impossibility of *finally* falling from grace. I rather argued against them for the sake of making them bring forth their proofs, for these things came quite new to me, and I secretly longed that they might be true as they opened a door of hope unknown before, my belief that I had once been a believer being still unshaken.

It was somewhat more than a year after my marriage, on the 5th May, 1830, that I began to feel a return of more abiding concern for my soul. I received a shock on that day by hearing of the sudden death of a worldly relation in the prime of youth and health. This caused much working of fear on my heart. Throughout that summer, I was in a very peculiar state. A little glimmer of light gradually began to "shine in the darkness", but truly, "the darkness comprehended it not", for I thought I was getting into a worse state than ever. The enmity of my heart was roused in a way I had not felt before. At times I felt irritated, as I may say, against the Lord for not giving me better success in my religion. Besides this, some of those books which in my former state had been my greatest favourites now excited in me bitter indignation; I allude to Baxter and Doddridge. I did not yet understand their legal bias, so unlike Owen, Bunyan, Romaine, etc. but supposed them to be every way faultless, so that I really thought my dislike was only against what was good, and yet could not restrain it. Doddridge's *Rise and Progress* especially I had formerly delighted in, and governed every day of my life by its rules, to the very uttermost of which I had been able to conform. But now that I was beginning to be brought into a state of spiritual poverty like the Israelites, I was without straw and therefore could not deliver the tale of bricks. Wherefore I hated the task-masters. This arose to such a height that one day I took that book and angrily flung it across the room resolving never to pick it up wherever it might fall. It lighted on the top of an old wardrobe and I don't recollect that I ever saw it again, though I felt for a long time exceedingly guilty whenever I thought of the top of that piece of furniture.

At this time secret doubts and suspicions used to arise as to the nature and reality of my former profession, but I could find no fault in it whenever I examined it, for there is not a grace of the Spirit mentioned in Scripture but what I had had the counterfeit of in times past. Then I would set apart a day for prayer and fasting before God, in which I would beseech Him most earnestly to shew me the truth of the matter. I would spend hours in examining my religion by Scripture and always came to the same conclusion that it certainly was genuine, that I would harbour no more of these evil questionings; but I was never suffered to rest long so. Soon all my doubts returned, and I very often wondered what would be the end of all this and what it could mean. During that year and the next, my state grew worse and worse to my own feelings. I gradually lost all power to offer one connected prayer, though I had formerly been very fluent. I could no longer pray for others or even ask for faith or any other grace for myself. I would kneel down with my heart very full, but so dark and confused that I could not possibly put two words together. I would remain perfectly dumb for a length of time and rise without having uttered a word.

Prayer for Reality

At one time for weeks and months together the only prayer I could put up was: "Lord, I know not what conversion means. Thou knowest. O give it me!" I must have repeated this hundreds of times, I think. I was also brought to such a sense of blindness, that really some of the rooms in the Rectory used, for a long while after we had left the house, to convey to my mind the impression of dark rooms without windows, from the exercises of mind I had gone through in them.

After I had gone on thus for a long while without finding any answer or light on my path, or hearing anything from others that could explain my case, I began to give up all for lost. I was in despair of ever succeeding and resolved I would try no more, and even pray no more, except just to repeat over and over as I went about: "Lord, I am weak, be Thou my might; Lord, I am *blind,* be Thou my sight." Here I seemed at the worst, for having given up all hope of finding religion, I was dreadfully afraid of death and feared I should not get through my approaching confinement (my second), and to make my fear greater, the cholera came to our shores, and at last to our town and very door. This dreadfully alarmed me, but I did not betray my fears to others and seldom spoke of religion to anyone.

"They shall be all taught of God"

One evening when things were in this sad condition, I went to drink tea with a sister who lived at Hertingfordbury. There I met my brother Charles, who was staying with her. He was then in the Established Church and had been brought to some experience of the *power* of religion, which was gradually breaking him off in spirit from the prevailing empty profession around. He shared my husband's duty at that time for a while, and I had been a good deal in his company, but never said a word about religion to him. However, that evening after tea, he said these words in an accidental way, as it seemed: "It is very easy for a person to have an amazing deal of outward religion, and of *closet* religion too – prayer, reading, self-mortification, and everything else that seems good, with their mouths, heads, and (as they think) their hearts full of the Name of Christ, while they are all the while turning their backs upon Him and the salvation He wrought." This fell with an unspeakable weight of conviction on my spirit and the words, "Thou art the man," seemed to sound through my heart. My sister thought the statement unguarded and somewhat over-wrought, and said a good deal to soften it down a little. He heard her through, and then quietly repeated all, even more strongly than at first.

I believe I betrayed my emotion, for I remember he addressed me afterwards, but I was so utterly amazed and lost that I neither heard nor heeded a word more that either of them spoke. How I went home I know not; I only came to sufficient consciousness to perceive where I was when I arrived at my own door. Then I remembered with great regret that I had not required Charles to explain to me what the fault of such a religion was, for I had as yet no suspicion in what direction the error lay, and thought myself as far from finding out the matter as ever, when these words came unsought into my mind: "And they shall be all taught of *God.*" For a moment I was comforted, but as I did not understand the voice then, I concluded it was merely a suggestion of my own mind, and therefore put it almost quite from me, saying in my ignorance: "O, that is only in the Old Testament spoken to the Jews. I don't know that it means to allude to the cases of individuals like me now, in such a literal manner as I should need." Soon after, I opened the Testament on the place where Jesus renews that promise, saying: "As it is written in the prophets, And they shall be all taught of God." It came to my heart then very sweetly for a while.

"Freely"–The Power of the Word

After I was in my room at night, I felt a spirit of prayer come upon me, and a resolution to cry till I obtained this effectual teaching from God. I knelt by my bedside and thought I *could* not rise from prayer all night, but all in a minute, almost before I could lift up a thought to the Lord, a wonderful inward light flowed into my soul accompanied by a verse in the Revelation which contains the word "*Freely*". "Whosoever will, let him take of the water of life *freely*"; but it was only the word "*freely*" that was spoken to my soul, and that with an indescribable power. I saw in it what I had never conceived before. It spoke thus: "Let go all your prayers, all your earnest spiritual desires, all your victories over sin and self; turn away your eyes from beholding such vanities and take my salvation *freely*." The feeling conveyed to my mind was that that one word "*freely*" filled heaven and earth. The light that came with it, and the discovery made by it astonished me so that I was quite overcome with amazement. "Oh," I said to myself, "does every Scripture doctrine contain such a depth within it when revealed by the Spirit? I wonder whether anyone else understands the word *"freely"*; if they do, I wonder they can help speaking more of it to each other!" Many other such things I said in my ignorance, thinking I should have such wonders to tell of it, whereas when I tried to explain the word to others, I found I was only saying the oldest and most commonplace things such as I myself had over and again taught the school children.

Then I found that the difference lay not in the letter, but in the *experience* and *power*. I am very sure that by our natural powers we can get hold of nothing but the letter; and therefore, if a person be not sensible of the infinite difference between these two kinds of knowledge of every truth, and cannot understand and sympathise in the feelings of astonishment excited in the breast of one who is beginning to have these things discovered to him, it is because they have never themselves got beyond the letter, and probably are ignorant that any better knowledge is to be found, and truly I can say that I found none among my former religious acquaintance that could understand me when I laboured hard, as I sometimes did, to convey to their minds what I had found in the word *"freely"*. I was like one that talked strangely to them; not that they denied the truth of what I held, but rather spoke as in this sort of spirit: "Of course it is so; have you never known that before? Don't you remember the Scripture says so and so?" as if I could have learnt it from the letter alone! I felt that I could not make myself understood and quite gave up trying to speak of these things to others, not laying the fault to them, but rather to my own confusion of mind.

A Bright Light

A few days after this circumstance, my confinement took place and I remember that the power of what I had lately felt in some measure abode with me, and often returned afresh in a remarkable way thus. Almost as soon as ever I began to lift up my heart in prayer, I used to receive the impression of a bright light far, far away, and with it would come such a sense of utter nothingness in myself that I seemed to cease from everything – even from breathing – while the Lord Jesus carried on alone the work of my salvation. I don't mean to assert that I did actually cease from breathing, or that the light did shine before my natural eyes. It was rather the figure or similitude by which the Lord saw fit to convey to my mind the lesson He designed to teach me; and I desire simply to relate these things just as they were, conscientiously, fearing on the one hand to add anything for the sake of increasing the effect, or, on the other, to suppress any part for fear of giving offence. Indeed, I have one conclusive evidence that it was not to my bodily eyes, but to those of my mind, that this light appeared, which is this. I remember that it seemed shining through clouds, whereas the situation of my bed in that room was such that no part of the sky could have been visible to a person lying down in it. But for this proof to the contrary, I really should have believed I actually *saw* the light.

This happened in May 1832. It lasted a fortnight or three weeks, and after that, the effect in some measure abode with me, though it is surprising what darkness and legality still encompassed me. The Lord says: "I taught Ephraim also to go, taking them by their arms, but they knew not that I healed them." So I was utterly ignorant of the way in which the Lord was teaching me by little and little, and therefore, because the sensible feeling of the above experience did not abide, I gave it up to a great extent as if it had all come to nothing, and thus lost sight of it to such a degree that I should never have been able to give a consistent account of it had it not been sweetly revived to my heart many times since.

Meeting with a Sister

At this time, I was entirely unacquainted with the principles of such of my sisters as had separated from the Establishment. Circumstances had never brought us together, nor had we exchanged a line since they left the Church [of England]. When I therefore heard that my brother Charles, after leaving Hertford (with the intention of merely passing a day or two with them) had found such union with the members of their connection that he had determined to cast in his lot among them, I felt astonished and mortified, not doubting but that he was sadly beguiled. At this I was the more disappointed as I had held him in very high esteem ever since what had passed on the occasion I have related, always feeling convinced that he had found that *reality in religion* which I was but darkly seeking after, as it is written: "The *secret* of the Lord is with them that fear Him, and He will *shew* them His covenant." But I felt no desire to communicate with any of them, especially as I had heard and believed numbers of false reports of various extravagancy and errors which they were *said* to hold.

But at the end of August following, circumstances obliged me to pass through town, and I slept one night at my sister Harriet's house. I had no intention of speaking on the subject of religion to her. However, a very few words passed between us as we were about to part next morning which had an effect on me I did not expect. She began to say something on those subjects. I interrupted her by saying: "I really am not able to judge of anything you advance, for I am very ignorant." She answered: "Dear sister, pray don't be too sure you know what being ignorant and blind means." I rejoined: "O, but I am ignorant and blind, and that to such a deplorable degree that for months together I have not been able to make out the simplest prayer, but just to repeat over and over, 'Lord, I know not what conversion means.' "

Her emotion betrayed the pleasure and surprise with which she heard me, and for my part, I was fully as much surprised at the lively interest and tender sympathy excited in her by a confession of what seemed to me so bad. After covering her face with her hands quite silently for some time, she at last said rather abruptly: "Then how can you keep friends with such authors as Doddridge? What can you find in them to suit a case like what you describe? I soon parted company with Doddridge, etc., when I began to understand anything of true inward work; and while I was burning those books I thought, What would my Hertford sisters think of me if they could see what I am about?" "Well," I said, "I can't say but that I think Baxter and Doddridge must have been very good men, yet what you have said makes me confess that my *Rise and Progress* lies covered with dust at the top of an old wardrobe where I flung it in my despair, but I have always thought I did very wrong." She smiled significantly, as much as to say that I should see more on that subject by and by, and she put into my hands Hart's Hymns and a manuscript book wherein was a copy of a few letters of Mr. Bourne's and Mr. Burrell's, and we parted with more than usual affection.

Prejudice

Short as this conversation was, it kindled a feeling of union with her which I had never felt in any religious intercourse with former acquaintances. Indeed, I believe I felt then for the first time in my life a little spark of the true unity of the Spirit. This, however, was soon obscured, for shortly after, circumstances occurred which excited very strong prejudices in my mind against my relations and their friends, whose conduct and sentiments were indeed represented to me under a fresh load of evil report.

However, another sister wrote me a few lines in consequence of what Harriet had told her of my state of mind, wherein she spoke affectionately and said she was sorry she had not come to see me when I had been in town, but had supposed me to be in such a different state as would have made our meeting only a painful one. The prejudices of my mind were so strong that I did not feel any impression made by her letter. However, one expression abode by me. She said she had been stripped of *all* her former religion, and, truly, thought I, so have I.

This by degrees wrought with me to write and enquire of her whether she had found a better, for I was sure I had not. But no one can tell the jealousy, fear and mistrust with which I wrote that letter, in consequence of which it was not in the least a true index of the state of my mind. I was inwardly much broken and brought down by what I had gone through, but yet the terror I had lest I should be led into error made me express myself in many parts in what must have appeared haughty and positive language, implying that I was predetermined thoroughly to canvass, if not to reject, whatever was said in answer. This letter did not, I suppose, much invite a reply. Certainly, I received none, and this made me the more determined to have nothing to do with them, for I thought theirs was a very bad spirit.

"What, now? in 1832?"

Throughout the rest of that year I went on by myself, groping for the wall of salvation like the blind, and in spite of my resolutions to the contrary, I was conscious of my eyes being often turned inwardly towards Charles and his friends as being possessed of something I had not found. This was exceedingly strengthened by the persual of those letters of Mr. Bourne's which Harriet had lent me. Had I read them before I understood them *at all*, I should probably have seen little more than common in them; but now, if I may so express it, I understood them sufficiently to see how little I understood of them. They made an impression on me I can never forget. I would read them till I was lost, and would keep turning back and back in the most absurd way to look at the date almost every half page I read. I kept saying: "What, now? in 1832? Is there any religion like this really existing? Is there anybody living just at such a simple place as Somerset Street, Portman Square, Titchfield Street or Oxford Street to whom the Lord really and sensibly speaks in these present days, and to whom He manifests Himself in this beautiful manner? I thought all such things had ceased since the Bible days. I do not think it can be true, yet I feel that this letter is no lie and written by no liar."

The inward drawing I now had to go and hear what they had to say came, I believe, from the same source as Cornelius's direction to send for Peter to hear words of him, which words his heart had been previously prepared to receive; and so had mine. And I had no more will or power to disobey the inward voice than he had.

Visit to the London Friends

Accordingly I made an excuse for my going to town in January 1833, having heard nothing from them in the interval. I was kindly received and introduced to some of their friends, especially to Mr. Abbott,* and in the evening, we met for the purpose of their entering into conversation with me. I felt much embarrassed at first, expecting from past experience that I should have very great difficulty in making myself understood sufficiently to convey to their minds any just idea of the state I was in, and had been in so long. But no sooner had I begun to stammer out a few words all in confusion than, to my utter surprise, I found them received with entire sympathy and such a perfect understanding of my meaning that whenever I was at a loss to express myself, my sentence was taken up and finished for me by others exactly to my heart's content. Mr. Abbott, who especially spoke on that occasion, would take up the thread of what I was trying to say and add: "And then I dare say you often felt so and so, etc., and then such suggestions as these would come continually through your mind, and the enemy would suggest such and such things, and it would seem to you that you were only getting further and further from what you desired to find?" In this manner he would go on describing the secret workings and windings of my experience so minutely and so faithfully that it was to my feelings little short of a miracle. I found I had not come to inform others of what I had felt and where I now stood, but to be informed myself.

This was indeed new to me and convinced me that the truth of God was among them in the same way that the woman of Samaria was convinced that Jesus was the Lord when she said: "He told me all things that ever I did; is not this the Christ?" which words of hers came strongly through my mind at the time. I found my heart to join in unreserved union with theirs, and though I heard many things in their experience far above what I had yet reached, yet even such things did sweetly accord with, and explain to me, what little I had been brought to the knowledge of.

The instruction I received here, combined with the various exercises I had gone through, enabled me now to form a decisive judgment, and one which I know will be found according to truth, of the zealous profession I had formerly walked in. It was, as I may say, *crumbled to dust before my eyes,* "so that there was not found in the bursting of it a sherd to take fire from

---

* Deacon at the chapel in London where Joseph Burrell preached.

the hearth, or to draw water withal out of the pit". I saw it to be a tissue of refined self-righteousness, and the sum of all that could be said of my then state is that I had "a zeal for God, but not according to knowledge". All my attainments in that kind of religion I did now heartily renounce and have never since desired to regain them.

Return to Hertford

I returned to Hertford very happy, sweetly assured that I was in the footsteps of Christ's flock. Being still very ignorant of the Lord's way of dealing with His people, I took it for granted that the light and comfort I now enjoyed would abide and increase and that I should never get into such darkness again, and that the rest of my way would be comparatively smooth. Especially I thought that as my great enemy, self-righteousness, was now unmasked and detected, it would no longer be able to deceive me to my great loss as formerly. I had been seriously warned by my friends to beware of being built up by others before I had been well pulled down; and above all, to let no one persuade me to *rest* short of finding some sensible manifestation of Jesus Christ to my own soul, and of His blood to my conscience, giving me the knowledge of salvation by the remission of my sins. I had heard some of the friends to whom I had been introduced give an account of the way in which they had been brought again and again to this soul-satisfying experience, and the continual necessity they found of obtaining a fresh application of the blood of sprinkling, whereby alone the believer can be cleansed from his daily sins and infirmities and walk with God in peace and equity.

The exceeding sober-mindedness and godly fear evident in those from whom I heard these things gave a just weight to what they said. Besides this, I had an inward testimony of the truth of them in the experience I had had, small as it was, of the experience and power with which the Lord could make His voice to be heard and understood in my soul, and that too in a time when I did not in the least expect any such communication, never having heard that such a thing was to be looked for. I had sometimes been told, I believe, that some deluded people trusted to frames and feelings and pretended to visions and revelations, but I had never met with such people. I have now no doubt that there are many under awful delusions of this kind as well as every other, but still I am very sure that those who are brought to experience the power of vital religion must take up the cross of having to bear the character of deluded persons and bigots among the great mass of high professors who know nothing but the letter.

I was at this time set upon obtaining the testimony of God by the witness of His Spirit in my heart, but little did I know the difficulties that lay between me and the accomplishment of my soul's desire. Little did I think I had almost everything yet to learn, and, if possible, more to *un*learn; that I had yet an amazing deal further to come down. I feared opposition from without, but knew next to nothing of the opposition from within – the opposition that my own heart would keep up in every form against the new principle implanted, as it were a grain of mustard seed, and which would be amply sufficient utterly to destroy it, if it were upheld by any power short of the power of God. I had to discover that the discernment of self-righteousness is one thing, and the power to subdue and expel it quite another. O, what a monster have I since found self-righteousness (or legality, which is but another name for the same thing) to be to my cost! The different shapes it assumes are past man's finding out. Though it seem slain at times, it always revives, and repulsed in one direction, comes on in another. Truly it may be compared to "the beast which had the deadly wound and did *live*". Nothing has ever wrought such self-despair in me as the continual fresh discovery of this sin has brought me to on many occasions. Indeed I have found the path to be most painful to the flesh up to the present time, and have never gained any real token for good but through much tribulation.

From this time I was quite at a point about my own past state, but had very little discernment of the professors by whom I was surrounded, or the nature of their profession. I dared not judge of the religion of those I had always looked upon as great lights, though I uniformly found their society bring on fresh darkness and misery to me, while they evidently considered the change that had taken place in me to be sadly for the worse. I found no refuge but in leaving them and their religion quite alone (as far as my judgment of them was concerned), and endeavouring to mind only myself and to give heed to the things which I had heard, lest by any means I should let them slip.

No Fellowship

Still I used to be present at the Jewish and Missionary Meetings which were held monthly in our drawing room. Though I found nothing to edify or encourage me to attend, yet I feared I might be doing wrong if I absented myself, for I had no light on the subject. These meetings consisted of most of the seriously disposed ladies within some miles of Hertford, and used to be conducted by one or other of those among them who were considered the most experienced Christians. My only wish was to conduct myself there so as to escape all notice. Nevertheless, I soon made myself very conspicuous by my utter inability to put in a word of assent when the promises contained in Scripture used to be handed about as a matter of course from one to another and appropriated in the most easy, confident manner. I always held my tongue unless the customary words: "Is not this promise sweet?" or, "Is it not very encouraging?" happened to be personally addressed to me, and then I would say, "*Sweet* indeed if we can but obtain the Holy Spirit's application of it," or something to that purpose. These answers were received with a marked silence of dissatisfaction, as if they were judged to proceed from a morose or morbid spirit. And I am sure on the other hand, I was chilled to the heart by this sensible want of sympathy and union from those with whom I was still trying to keep up Christian fellowship. I felt my spirit withdraw further and further from theirs, but still I was in such bondage about the matter that I feared to absent myself.

The principal reason for which I have introduced the subject of these meetings at all is because I wish to give a short account of the breaking of this bondage, since it was connected with the first sensible help and light I obtained from the Lord after my return from my visit to my friends in London, and which came at a time of great need, as follows.

Further Prejudice

The joy I had felt when I first returned from them shortly abated, and my impatient expectation of finding great things all at once was disappointed. Especially I found that the earnest spiritual violence, with which I made sure of taking the kingdom of heaven by force, was not always at my command, so that I too often felt as dead, hard and indifferent to all spiritual things as possible. All this in my ignorance I had not laid my account for and did not understand. Therefore it disheartened me, and filled me at times with doubts as to the truth of those things which I had lately heard and believed. Though I had found such sweet union with my friends when with them, yet after I had parted from them, and the savour of my visit was over, I found I could not recall to mind what I had felt with any power. Our Saviour said that when the Spirit should come, *He* should bring all things to their remembrance that had been said unto them, and it is only He that can do it to any purpose. I had felt very confident that I should henceforth be proof against all that I might continue to hear laid to their charge of the principles and character of those whom I now so highly valued, but in my dark and bewildered state I found this was by no means the case. The enemy did not fail to help forward my calamity, and often succeeded in filling my mind with suspicions and prejudices, especially by means of some painful and protracted circumstances.

One morning I was especially exercised in this way, and when the post came in, it brought me a letter in which I was assured, with great apparent justice (and that by one I much respected), that certain among my friends were actuated by a very bad spirit. The enemy took this advantage to come in like a flood indeed. He crowded in his proofs with such force that I was quite carried away. He made it seem as clear as possible to me that they were walking in a false light, insomuch that I resolved utterly to renounce all intercourse with them, and inwardly trembled at the narrow escape I had had of being entangled in a dreadful snare.

"I AM THE WAY"

All this seemed certain, but still the question proposed itself: "What then will you do?" I could not answer, for I could not bear the thought of betaking myself to my old empty religion again where, like Baal's priests, I found neither voice nor hearing nor anything that regarded. "What is true religion?" I cried. "Where is it?" "Who is right? There is a heaven, but as far as I can see, there is no way to it in all the world. As for *men,* they are all deceivers, *one* and *all.*" I do not think I ever felt such anguish as filled my soul while I uttered these words under the pressure of deep temptation. Never did I feel more hopeless or further from the possibility of help. At last I threw myself on the floor in misery and cried out: "There's *no* way, *all* men are liars. *All! All!*"

At this moment, these words were spoken to my soul with indescribable power: "I AM THE WAY, THE TRUTH." In an instant, I was set upon my feet again, delivered from all my trouble, and the discovery of *this way* was quite as new to me as if I had never heard of it before. Well may the Lord say: "Behold, I make all things new," even in this sense, for I am sure that the very oldest and most well-known truth, when revealed by the Spirit to the soul, is new indeed, and that again and again so often as it is revived. I was now full of joy and made to feel Christ alone to be perfectly enough, so that for some time I forgot to think about any *man* or set of people. But when I came by degrees to call them [the London friends] to mind, I found the present light shone upon and revived what I had found before among them, so that my union with them was sweetly confirmed. Thus, like Israel of old, I ate of the old corn because of the new.

Profession and Possession

Afterwards I was reading in the Bible and came to this verse: "Who of God is made unto us *wisdom,* and *righteousness,* and *sanctification,* and *redemption.*" I dwelt long on this and felt much awe on my spirit in considering what a depth lay under those words, and felt a longing desire that the Lord would some day open them to me as He had just done with respect to those, "The Way and the Truth," which I had found very blessed.

On the next day was one of the monthly meetings I have described, and I attended as usual. Though I had so lately been happy, yet my spirit sank to such a degree that I believe I looked more dejected than usual, for the lady who conducted the meeting addressed herself particularly to me. What she said and what I answered I forget, but I well recollect that she rejoined again in a tone of expostulation (though I had not referred to the text in any way): "Well, but surely we know that Christ is our wisdom, righteousness, sanctification, and redemption?" And then she looked round the room for confirmation of what she had said, and some motion of assent was immediately made by all the rest except one, whose case strongly resembled my own. I can hardly convey an idea of the way in which these words fell on my spirit, and in the light that I had obtained the day before I saw so clearly the hollowness of that showy profession that my soul sickened, and glad was I to flee from among them. I can truly say that this final separation was not made in a lofty spirit, for my heart felt as if it were bursting and I found it difficult to refrain myself from giving way to a flood of grief till I should have got into my room. My bondage about this matter was from this time effectually broken. I never was present again, and they soon after, of their own accord, withdrew from our house and found another room for their purpose, which I was very glad of.

Sympathy from her Husband

It was a great mercy to me that my dear husband gave me full permission to act according to my conscience in this and other cases. In truth, the very same work was being carried on in his heart about the same time, wholly independent of what was passing in mine, except that the account I gave him of my first visit to London tended exceedingly to convince him that those who had conversed with me were themselves taught of God. He had not been in the same sort of state with myself formerly; accordingly there was afterwards some variety in the way he was led into the full truth. Yet I think I may say that the teaching in his heart and mine did truly harmonize, and brought us each separately to receive or reject the very same things, so that we found sweet unity of spirit continually.

I remember well so long ago as the first or second year after our marriage, when I would bemoan myself to him in the thickest of my darkness, he would say to me: "I believe some day you'll find that self-righteousness has in some way come in, but I have not light enough to explain how." I *could* not believe this then, because in the letter I did so strongly hold Christ to be all in all, but I have since found he spoke very true. Another thing he used to say, which I could as little believe then, but which has been happily verified, and that was: "I believe firmly that God has begun to shew you some especial thing and I hope we shall both be enabled to watch what it is." He was thus made very tender of attempting to stifle any conviction either in himself or me.

I feel a desire to record two very sweet and remarkable dreams I had in the year 1833. The first I wrote an account of at the time of its occurrence, though I did not do so in the case of the second, yet I retain the most perfect recollection of it, and can faithfully declare that I here relate nothing but the simple truth without one addition or embellishment of the most trivial kind.

In my childhood, I never put the least faith in any dreams, and indeed grew up with the most sovereign contempt for those that paid any regard to them. Nevertheless, I can truly say that these have each of them afforded me great encouragement in the reflection, and though unbelief and the effect of early prejudice sometimes prevail to make me question whether they might not have been mere illusions like the generality of dreams, still, on the whole, I must express the fullest conviction that they came from the Lord to convey a hopeful expectation to my soul at a time when I stood much in need of it. Certainly the Scriptures fully declare that He has been pleased from the beginning often to hold communication with the souls of His people while their bodies have slept. Most, if not all, of the *Old* Testament saints had His will made known to them at times in this manner, and so had Joseph, Paul, etc. in the *New*. I have often thought the instance of Solomon a very remarkable one. Not only did God speak to him, but he was also made to reply in his dream, and his answer was favourably accepted of the Lord and the great blessing was pronounced upon him, the abundant fulfilment of which he found when he awoke. In the Chronicles, it merely says: "The LORD appeared to him by night," but in the account given in the Kings we are expressly told that it was in a *dream* by night, and the relation closes with these words: "So Solomon awoke, and behold it was a dream."

The First Remarkable Dream

In the summer of 1833, I was in much anxiety to come to a comfortable assurance of the genuineness of the work of religion in my soul, with some evidence of the Lord's favour towards me. Some of my friends kept urging me to appropriate the precious promises of the gospel, to lay hold on Christ, representing it as a *duty* to believe His love toward us individually. In my former profession of religion I had made no small attainments in this sort of *self-wrought* faith, but I had gradually yet powerfully been made to feel its insufficiency, and I was now desirous above all things to obtain faith that stands in the power of God, *not* in the wisdom of man. Still, my soul was in a very dark and bewildered state, with the feeling sense of blindness and ignorance; and when I cried to the Lord for some token of His favour and seemed to get no answer, I was sadly perplexed and often ready to conclude that I was wrong and presumptuous in looking for any such thing. Then I would think that perhaps my friends were right and that I ought to be contented with that self-application of the promises which seemed to satisfy them as it used to satisfy me. Yet I could not for a moment bear the idea of being driven back to betake myself to that empty religion again, and thus I was grievously tossed about and distressed. In this state I was when one night I slept and dreamed the following dream.

I found myself standing with one of my sisters in a sort of gallery enclosed by high, strong, iron rails, on the other side of which, and at a great depth below, stood a person whom it was infinitely our interest to prove to be our father. My sister said of course he was so, and looked very contemptuously at me for putting myself at such needless anxiety as to doubt it. "But," answered I, "I cannot see that he takes any notice of us, and that does not seem as if we were his children." I did everything I could to attract his attention in vain, and my fear and anxiety became intense. My sister then turned from me and went away, and I saw her no more.

As soon as she was gone, I cried out: "O dear, what shall I do? C. has so much more faith than I. I cannot possibly believe that he is my father because he does not look at me." I then seized hold of the railing and a great trembling came over me, for I thought the person began to withdraw. Just as he was within one step of being quite gone, he stood still and looked at my feet. I cannot describe the state of anxiety I was now in, of fear and of hope. After a while he gradually raised his eyes till at last he looked full in my face. The moment his eyes met mine, his whole countenance was enlightened with an inexpressible smile, full of the tenderest paternal love. "Now I know well enough that he is my father," cried I in an ecstasy. "Now I can love him indeed."

As I said this, a thrill of mingled love and joy ran through my frame. I sprang towards him, and neither the railing nor the great depth offered any impediment. He opened his arms and I was in his bosom in a moment. "Now," I said, "I am safe from all doubting; it is utterly impossible I should ever doubt again." He then, tenderly embracing me, took me by the hand and led me on. I had not gone far before I felt a misgiving in my mind. "What if I should be deceived? Perhaps after all he is going to destroy me." But when I looked at his face, he gave me the same sweet smile again, and I was as safe and happy as before. This happened several times over as we went along.

The road lay straight before us as far as I could see, but instead of continuing in it as I expected, he very soon led me out of it to a place where was a narrow, black-looking river. The path lay along the bank of this water and sloped so much that it was as much as I could do to keep from falling in. When first we entered this path, my fears and suspicions returned, and I thought he meant my harm, but on my asking him where it would lead me, he smiled again and gave me an answer that satisfied me, and I went on rejoicing.

After a little while, I looked behind and saw a man seated on a white horse coming at a somewhat swift walking pace down a path that led into mine. "O dear!" said I with some fear. "When he overtakes me, he certainly will throw me into the river." I looked again earnestly for satisfaction to my conductor who still kept near me, and he smiled still and all was right. I then felt assured that the horseman would indeed throw me into the river, but I was as happy as I could be and perfectly willing that he should. Soon he overtook me and threw me in. My father smiled still, and as I was sinking, I uttered some exclamation of joy, declaring that my father had not cast me off. So I awoke, and behold, it was a dream.

At first I thought I never should lose the powerful impression it made on me. I believed and wondered at the kindness of the Lord in sending me so sweet and suitable a dream to instruct and comfort me. And I rose from my bed with a determination to cry mightily to Him for the fulfilment of it. But the enemy came in, and I gave my fool's ear to him and suffered him to rob me almost entirely. Carnal reasoning and early prejudice went far to deprive me of that sweet consolation which simple-minded people would have drawn from it, as I am sure Elihu would. Many times since it has returned to my memory and been made (as I believe) the means of helping me with a little help at times when I have been so much in need of it that I have been glad to gather all that He gave.

The Second Remarkable Dream

A few months after the dream I have just related, I had a second, which was as follows. In the autumn of the year 1833, I was in much fear in the prospect of my confinement lest I should die without coming to a good supporting hope in my soul, the thought of which was a great terror to me. I had a trying time but was carried safely through on November 6th. About the second or third night after, I had no sooner dropped asleep than I was awakened with a cold perspiration all over me which I had never felt before in my life. I thought it had a very deathly feeling and I was much frightened. On being made dry and warmed, I fell asleep again and the same cold perspiration woke me again directly. This happened several times over; though I had hot flannels round me and a good fire in my room, I was ready to shiver with cold. I was now in great terror indeed. I could not endure the thought of death or even of dangerous illness in the dark and bewildered state my soul had long been in. I dared not go to sleep, and though I cried to the Lord, I seemed to get no relief. In this state I at last dropped asleep and had the following dream.

I found myself in a very dismal place. It seemed to be underneath some great building, for it was almost quite dark. The roof was low and vaulted and I could discern long rows of arches. I was exceedingly anxious to get out to the light, but every effort to extricate myself was in vain. Run which way I would, I was stopped by a dead wall at the end of the dismal, dark passage. At last I thought I could discern a glimmer of light through a very distant arch, but on rushing towards it I found I was disappointed of my hope of finding a door out. Instead of that I found myself in a square place, the walls of which were covered with tablets like tombstones, only these were black and frightful. There was light enough here to read, and I found that instead of epitaphs, they contained nothing but fearful accusations, which I felt to be directly pointed against myself. Some of them I have forgotten. One I remember was *A Lover of Mammon*. Another was *A Friend to Lies*. An unspeakable horror fell on me. I dared read no more but stood trembling with my eyes fixed on the ground, utterly afraid to raise them. As I trembled there, I heard someone approach and bid me follow him. Though I fully concluded he was going to destroy me, I could not help obeying, but still without raising my eyes from the ground.

He then led me some way and stopped, desiring me to look up and read the tablet before me. I told him I dared not, but he again desired me, I think once or twice. I obeyed with great trembling, when, behold, instead of these accusations, I read in large fair characters: *Food for the Hungry; Rest for the Weary.* My heart bounded and I ventured to look in the face of my guide and found He was Jesus Christ. He smiled most sweetly and asked me in the softest voice if that frightened me. I said, "No, Lord."

He then touched the tablet, which proved to be a door, for it flew open and displayed a vast variety of most beautiful things of very resplendent colours. With the choicest of these He immediately began to present me, and threw over my shoulders a long sort of cloak or robe of exquisitely beautiful feathers. Whilst He was thus enriching me, He smiled with such melting and softness and spoke so endearingly that I cannot describe it at all. And it seemed as if the same tender love kept flowing back from me to Him. He said I might present Him with some of the things He had given me and He would accept them. "O, may I?" exclaimed I, and the heart-thrilling endearments that kept passing between us by looks, smiles and words, as I offered and He accepted, I cannot by any words convey. Never have I on any other occasion, asleep or awake, been conscious of such sensations, except in my former dream, but this (to my feelings at the time) exceeded even that.

Then I awoke, and behold, it was a dream. My fears were quite gone, and I found myself looking to the Lord very earnestly with peace and a degree of joy on my spirit, telling Him I wanted no more than the fulfilment of the sweet dream He had condescended to send me, and which I felt did most strikingly set forth the desire of my soul.

After this time I was very earnest to obtain some clear manifestation of Jesus Christ to my soul, but was still like the man whose sight was but half restored, who saw men as trees walking. So I was yet very ignorant, and truly I knew not what manner of spirit I was of; for I have been made to discern so much sin, mixing itself with all the earnestness, that I have seen abundant cause to justify the Lord for keeping me so long in darkness. Especially I have been convicted of an inordinate desire of obtaining the testimony of men, that is, of those whom I now looked up to in religion. I longed to be able to commend myself to their favourable opinion by having something great to tell them of my prevalence in prayer, and I have often since seen the wisdom and mercy of God in frustrating these fleshly desires. Nevertheless, in great and undeserved compassion, He did not leave me long together even at that time without some little help to encourage me to keep on waiting upon Him.

Encouragement to Wait

One day when my anxiety was at the height, and I was constantly entreating the Lord Jesus to reveal Himself to my soul, I was all of a sudden perfectly conscious of His approach. I heard as it were the footsteps of His coming. To those who have *not* known by experience what this means, no explanation will convey it: to those who *have,* none is necessary, for they have felt how every faculty of the soul seems to wake at the sound in breathless expectation, while its inward language is, "Speak, Lord, for Thy servant heareth." This is what our Lord meant by saying: "My sheep *hear* my voice," and again: "They *know* my voice...they know not the voice of strangers." Also it is written: "They shall know in that day that I am He that doth speak; behold, it is I." This was indeed the case with me then, though I was thinking of other things when it came, for I was busily engaged in giving some orders to a servant. I had never felt this before, yet I wanted no one to explain it to me, and I hurried the servant away, big with expectation of what was coming, nothing doubting but that I was now going to receive the accomplishment of all my desires and prayers.

I went toward a chair, intending, as far as I remember, to kneel down by it, but before I had taken two steps, the Lord spoke to me. I heard nothing with my outward ears: indeed, I think He conveyed His meaning without any words at all, but certain I am that the exact purport of what was said to me was this: "Not *yet,* it would not suit you yet; but *wait on,* and the time will come that you long for, for you shall not be finally disappointed of your desire."

This was done in a moment, and all was past, but the power that accompanied it wrought such a transformation in me that I was as happy and contented as could be. Had any man told me a minute before that I was going to get nothing but the information that I must wait, without knowing how long, for that *sensible* pardon of my sins which I was expecting that minute, I should have been ready to die with disappointment. Nothing that any man could have said could have reconciled me to it, whereas when the Lord spoke, my will was brought in a moment to such sweet and cheerful submission to His will that I kept thanking and blessing Him for intending to answer me at the time that pleased *Him* best, and this in the simplest way without the least force or constraint on my feelings. My heart overflowed with thankfulness and I was quite happy.

But I was yet such an ignorant babe that I understood these things no longer than I actually felt them, so that after a few weeks, when the power of this was gone, I knew not what to make of it. I thought of it with disappointment, and even wondered at myself for having felt contented.

Indeed, so little did I comprehend the work of the Spirit, that I actually repented of and regretted the sweet submission He had wrought in me, and thought I had given up the point so easily and thereby lost the blessing. I only mention this to show how much folly and ignorance are bound up in the heart of a child.

A Bitter Trial

Friday, August 12th, 1836, I was taken very ill with an attack which ended in a premature confinement. I had had a similar trial the year before, but on that occasion was carried through with much less suffering. This time I felt very ill and had scarcely any hope of recovery. I really believed I had, at the most, but a very few hours to live and can scarcely describe what I felt. None but those who have had a near view of eternity can have any idea of what it seems at such a time. I had been very long in a state of dreadful spiritual death, engrossed in this world's cares, business and enjoyments, not without perpetual checks of conscience and temporary seasons of distress. I had also received many severe strokes, for I had been bereaved of both my boys in succession, to whom I was tenderly attached, besides being afflicted the previous year with a stillborn child. And now again, after having long looked forward to the possession of this babe, hoping it would prove a boy, I was sorrowfully conscious that it was also dead.

When first this bitter conviction came upon me, I was like one mad, full of desperate rebellion, and I could not even bring myself to ask for submission. In vain did my husband urge me to do so. I could do nothing but cry in an agony unconditionally for its life, that I might be mistaken in my fears and that animation might return. But I was soon made indeed to cease from my impetuous anxiety about my child's life, for at this time I was not materially ill myself, but dropping asleep from fatigue. I soon awoke with such sensations and other symptoms of serious illness that I, as well as the members of my family that were around me, really believed I was about to die.

"Through Much Tribulation"

Now I was willing enough to give up my child – its life did not seem to me worth thinking about. I was in such terror for myself. My worldliness and backsliding, after I had had some hope that the Lord had begun a work in my soul, stared me in the face. Bitterly did I lament my madness and folly in wasting away the precious hours of health in vanity; and now death was come, I had no token of the Lord's favour towards me.

I sought indeed now in my desperate case to cry to the Lord, if so be there might be one ray of hope; but my head was so weak that my understanding began to fail when I attempted. Flashes of fearful despair came across me, during which I seemed to see the countenance of poor Mr. B (a person who had been well known to me and who had destroyed himself a week or two before) just before my face. I thought he was hopelessly bewailing and cursing his madness and folly, and that in a minute or two I should join him in that dreadful employment *for ever.* Yet I was not *left* to utter despair, for many passages in Psalm 107 and other parts of Scripture seemed to say that the mercy of God *could* reach even *me.* Once I even believed that it not only *could,* but *would.* About twenty-four hours after, my child was born. It was a fine little boy, but quite dead – my rebellious tongue was silenced by what I had undergone, and I dared say nothing against it.

As I was gradually raised up again, I was filled with hope that better things were in store for me, and I believed it was for good that the Lord had spared me, and O, how exceedingly did I wish that I might have grace to employ my lengthened days in seeking till I should obtain that token for good, that clear, sure, evident work in my soul, the value of which I had lately had some idea of! Sometimes I seemed to faint so in my mind, and was conscious of such returning worldliness in my spirit, such hardness and deadness and indifference, being so easily kept off from spiritual things by the presence and foolish gossip of my nurse, that I feared all was going from me. Still a struggling cry was kept up through such violent and forcible opposition from the enemy as I do not remember ever to have experienced before, which has made me often to think I could enter into the word: "through much tribulation".

Divine Comfort

This continued about three weeks, and then I obtained a little help one day, which came as follows. I woke with my heart hard and dull on the morning of Saturday, September 3rd, but felt a desire to seek the Lord, and thought I would endeavour to do so when I should be quietly dressed and moved onto my couch for the day. But my heart felt so hard and dull and averse to prayer that I did not think I should be able. However, while the maid was dressing me, without any effort on my part, my heart seemed to kindle within me, and such a spirit of prayer was given me that I could not wait till I should be dressed, but began to cry to the Lord most earnestly in my heart. This continued after I was laid on my couch, with such a melting in my spirit that the tears kept running down my face, and I was obliged to cover my face (by pulling up the blanket that was thrown over me) to conceal my feelings from the servant who was still present, cleaning and arranging the room. I was not in the least disturbed by her moving about and pushing by and against me as she took up the carpet to shake it and again laid it down. My heart and all my thoughts were lifted entirely above everything here, and I felt indeed to abound in hope. For hours was this crying kept up within, and when it had gradually subsided, the comfortable savour still remained.

But the next day, Sunday, it was quite gone. In vain did I try to regain something of it. The whole day was spent in fruitless efforts, and all the beginning of the next week I was barren and dull within. It was a week of particular business, for I had decided upon going down to the seaside for the furtherance of my recovery the following week, being strongly urged to do so by my friends; and as I expected to be absent for some time, I had much to settle and arrange before I left. Thus my time, or at least my strength, was quite engrossed (for I was still very weak), and I could not fix my thoughts on anything but business, though I felt frequently a longing desire to find the Lord, and a very great dread of spiritual death, which made me look forward to my intended journey with the greatest fear lest the hurry of travelling, change of scene, and separation from such as fear God, with the loss of outward means, should quench the little spark of life which had lately been kindled within.

I continued to feel languid and lifeless in my soul until the afternoon of Friday, when, after having lain down to rest for an hour before tea time, I awoke with a sweet feeling upon me and found my spirit looking to the Lord. I said, "What is this, Lord? Is it from Thee?" And these words came in very sweetly: "I will not leave you comfortless" – very gently, as if they were whispered. My soul was still, and felt very peaceful. After I rose, and all the evening, I continued looking to the Lord, telling Him I really thought He had just given me a little sip of His kind tenderness and applied the above promise, and that I desired greatly to thank Him for His mercy.

The Promised Blessing

Next morning, Saturday, September 10th He did indeed fulfil this promise with much greater power than I had ever before experienced. I woke in the morning heavy and dull as usual, and some vexatious trifles occurred that disquieted me and entailed some trouble, some business upon me which fatigued me considerably, so that I went into my husband's study to lie down on the sofa till dinner time, as it yet wanted full two hours to dinner. The maid brought me some coffee and a little dry toast, by my dear husband's desire.

I sat up to partake of this, and before I had finished, a feeling came over me which I had never felt before, but once in a much lesser degree. I can only describe it in Hart's words, of which it forcibly reminded me at the time, and which exactly express it: "I felt myself melting away into a strange softness of affection which made me fling myself on my knees before God." I did not fall on my knees literally, yet my spirit fell down before the Lord and sweet comfort flowed from Him. I could not suppress my tears: and it was as much as ever I could do to refrain from crying out aloud. Had I been alone, I must have done so, but my husband was sitting in the room, and though I knew he would only have rejoiced in my joy, yet at that moment I wanted to be quite undisturbed, to enter into no explanations, but to lie quite still and listen to what the Lord would say concerning me.

So I restrained my feelings, though with much difficulty, and multitudes of passages of Scripture kept pouring into my mind with wonderful sweetness and power. Many accusations also from the enemy, who envied my happiness and tried to mar it, were all silenced and answered from the Word as fast as ever they came. I am sorry I did not write down any account of this sweet visitation while it was quite fresh and the power of it lasted, for now I only write from recollection and very much has escaped from my memory. Most of the texts I have forgotten, and the manner and words with which the accuser was answered, though some were very striking and all flowed in quite unsought and unstudied on my part.

Abounding in Hope

One I recollect. The enemy suggested strongly that what I felt was only fleshly excitement, self-wrought, that it did not come from the Holy Spirit, and that at the best it was but hope, though in a greater measure than I had ever felt before. Then this word came in: " That ye may abound in hope through the power of the Holy Ghost," and the temptation vanished, and I wondered with delight at the goodness of the Lord, and at His power and wisdom, who could make even the fiery darts of Satan to be the occasion of increasing my comfort rather than dispelling it, as he maliciously designed. This continued some time till the enemy seemed to retire for the time quite defeated in his attempts against me, and indeed, he could not venture any more for a long while to deny that the Lord had been with me of a truth.

My husband soon left me as he had to visit a friend in Hertford and would not return till late. He perceived that something unusual was passing in my mind, and therefore, to avoid disturbing me, he went out quietly without speaking, and also gave orders to the servants not to go up to me at all for any reason unless I should ring the bell.

The Blessing Abides

Soon after he left, the great power and sweetness I had enjoyed began to subside and leave me. I felt sorry for this, but I thought to myself. "I know we are not to expect such great indulgences to be lasting. To have any at all is a great favour." Thus I was going to be contented it should go, when these words were powerfully whispered to me: "He made as though He would have gone further, but they constrained Him saying, Abide with us... and He went in to tarry with them." Such a suggestion coming at such a moment seemed to me as a promise of the like happy success, and so indeed it surely was, for on my pleading it earnestly as such to the Lord, He owned it by an immediate fulfilment. All my comfort came again – if anything, increased – and tarried the whole of the rest of the day, so that I had no thoughts to spare for my meals, and dinner hour and tea hour came and went without my observing them, so that (as I did not ring the bell) I saw no one till my husband returned at night.

I cannot describe half of what I felt during that day, but I particularly remember that I did sensibly receive the answers to petitions long past and even quite forgotten by me until they were at that time strangely recalled to my recollection, and, I can truly declare, most sensibly answered. These very petitions, at the time of my making them, had, I well remember, seemed to myself put up, as it were, against a dead wall. I also remember that it seemed to me that the Lord had dealt more wonderfully and beautifully with *me* than with anybody else, for I could believe none so undeserving as myself, none so helpless, none so obstinately opposing. I saw and felt that He had led me from first to last in such a manner that heaven, earth and hell must be constrained to give Him all the glory of salvation. I could freely beg Him to take the sole management for ever of all that related both to my soul and body. I could unreservedly thank Him and bless Him for all that He had ever done to me, even in taking away my children. My whole soul seemed filled with gratitude and wonder, and I kept saying: "Lord, I never knew it was for this!"

Though the enjoyment gradually abated that night, yet a very sweet savour remained with me a long while, and a delightful remembrance of what I had felt that happy day, September 10th, 1836. I never could think

51

of it suddenly, after having been occupied with other things, without a thrill throughout my frame, and I used to say: "Lord, I know of a truth that Thy love is better than wine (the wine of all earthly enjoyments whatsoever)."

Upheld in Deep Tribulation

(January 1839). It is now about two to three years since I wrote the foregoing account and I have kept no notes of anything that has occurred since; but O, if a faithful record could be made of the way I have walked from that time to this, I should, I think, be utterly ashamed that anyone should see it. It would be nothing but a register of mercies abused, patience and longsuffering trifled with, warnings disregarded, instructions slighted and perverted, and deliverances forgotten. How many times I have found the Lord to be to me a God that restoreth the soul, while I have been so often a base backslider. All that I have ever done can only be included in this sentence: "I have sinned and perverted that which was right."

Twice again I have been visited with a stroke similar to the two I have before alluded to. On 30th June, 1837, I was again carried through a premature confinement, giving birth to a stillborn son under circumstances of imminent peril, in which the medical attendant every minute expected my death for about an hour or so. Throughout that night, when I was supposed to be insensible, I shall ever remember the wonderful clearness of my spiritual senses. It was as if the spirit were clearer and livelier in its actings when disencumbered of the body. I seemed to fall into the hands of the Lord with awe and deep seriousness, but was kept from that agitation which would have proved fatal to my body by these texts, which were a sufficient stay to me: "Remember the word unto Thy servant, upon which Thou hast caused me to hope"; and, "He will have mercy upon whom He will have mercy."

The following year again I was for the fourth time seized in a similar way, though I was not this time in the real peril I had been in the time before; yet, from a very singular circumstance which was not discovered till the next day, everyone – even the medical man as well as myself – apprehended a fatal issue. I was dreadfully alarmed because I was in a very backsliding state when it came on, but I was powerfully kept from despair, and Psalms 78 and 107 were made "more precious than gold, yea, than much fine gold", to the removing of all my fears. This happened on 2nd September, 1838.

"The Same Lump"

(Written 1840). The Lord was pleased to give me a very sweet and seasonable help which I did not put down at the time, but which I desire to keep in remembrance. My soul had been for some weeks in very peculiar exercise, sometimes relieved by a sense of support from the Lord. But these seasons were so short that it seemed as if I had not time to catch my breath before I was down again, grappling hard with such miserable sensations and such discovery of sin that I thought I had no more ground to think that the Lord had any favour towards me than the most abandoned wretches on earth, for I could see no difference between myself and them. Once, under this feeling, these words came very sweetly: "Hath not the potter power over the clay, *of the same lump* to make one vessel unto honour, and another unto dishonour?" This sweetly relieved me, and my soul kept saying: "Truth, Lord, for it is indeed of the *same lump,* the *very same lump.* I never knew that before."

This lasted but a little while, for in about a day I lost all handhold and foothold and was down again so low that I said: "If this is the only way, I can never, never endure. I may have years of life before me, and it is quite out of the question to think of going on in such a path. The thought of even another month like this is dreadful. Like Pliable, I must get out on which side I possibly can." For many days my case got darker and darker. It was impossible for me to think that the Lord had one thought or care for me, or that one of my groanings reached His ear. He seemed so utterly to disregard me.

Light Shining in Darkness

Things went on so, till one evening I was sitting with a friend who had dined with us, and my husband was reading to us. I began to feel so restless in spirit that I could no longer listen and felt inwardly urged to retire by myself into my husband's vacant study. When I could no longer resist this urging, I went. But on seating myself by the fire there, I thought: "What have I come here for? I have no thought either to read or pray; I'll go back again. I'm no better here than there."

Just then, to my sweet surprise, the Lord showed me His face, and such a light shone on my dark path as I cannot describe. I was astonished and quite overcome to see that He had all the while been close by, carefully ordering every step, and that He would never leave me, but in the end would bring me to Himself. This wrought a mighty change indeed. My headstrong will was quite subdued in a moment, and I felt the sweetest submission to drink of what cup He pleased. Then I knew what it means:

"My yoke is easy, and My burden is light," for all the perverse opposition that makes it otherwise was gone. My will flowed so freely out after His will that I kept telling Him in the simplest way that I then deliberately and freely chose beforehand every dispensation, be it what it might, that He might intend to allot to me during life. The blissful feelings this submission brought with it have made me know experimentally from that time that our happiness consists, not in what the Lord's will concerning us is, but in our will being swallowed up in His will. For some time there was a sweet interchange of smiles on His part and tears of joy and blessing on mine, praising Him not merely for now showing His kindness to me, but for all that He had ever appointed me; yea, for the very things that I abhorred and so lately would not consent to endure. What power but the Lord's could have made such a transformation in my soul?

At Christmas 1839, which was soon after this, I composed the following hymn which was wrought out of the last few months' experience. The 2nd, 3rd, 4th and 5th verses have peculiar reference to this particular exercise here relate:

Jesus, wilt Thou condescend
Still to be the sinner's Friend,
    Saviour, wilt Thou hear me?
Since for sin Thy blood was spilt,
Let it still remove my guilt,
    Let me find Thee near me.

When Thou leav'st me, Lord, alone,
All my evils to make known,
    Ease and sloth benumb me;
Sins of every shape and kind
In the flesh and in the mind,
    Rise and overcome me.

When for help I try to pray,
And that help Thou dost delay,
    Angry murmurs seize me.
Grov'lling in that dreadful case,
Atheistic thoughts find place
    And no friend can ease me.

When no sun nor stars appear,
And my soul is urged to fear,
    Lest Thou never own me;
When a beam of heavenly light
Lets me see that all is right,
    That e'en there Thou'st known me;

Then submissive to Thy will,
Patiently my soul lies still;
    Who like Thee can teach me?
From the miry clay and pit,
On the Rock to set my feet,
    Thy kind hand can reach me.

Grant me by Thy Spirit, Lord,
To retain each wholesome word,
    When Thou dost instruct me;
To Thy feet with nought to give,
Full remission to receive,
    Thus Thou dost conduct me.

When again from Thee I stray,
Nor can I regain Thy way,
    Unless Thou direct me;
When my fainting spirits droop,
And the tempter hides my hope,
    Saviour, then protect me!

When he spreads the hidden snare,
Some kind whisper to beware
    By Thy Spirit send me.
Or when taken in the net,
Struggling, I but faster get,
    Even then befriend me.

Fill me, Lord, with godly fear,
And my praises deign to hear,
    For what Thou hast taught me.
Still reveal Thy smiling face,
That with joy I may retrace
    All the way Thou'st brought me.

Out of the Horrible Pit

(26th February, 1840). I desire to set down in simplicity, if the Lord will enable me, a short note of the very precious help I have received tonight. I have been in the horrible pit and miry clay indeed for some time (that is, for about ten days), everything that I had experienced during the last four or five months contradicted, and as it appeared to me, disproved. I felt dreadful murmurings and rebellion and enmity; then checks of conscience and a conviction that I was kicking against the pricks; intervals of bitter misery; utter powerlessness to repent, believe or pray; yet many seasons of earnest desire to find the Lord and a struggling cry which did not feel like prayer. Truly I began to feel myself empty, void and waste –

"My heart a desert waste and wild". I have been getting worse and worse till today, when I seemed right gone for ever.

Tonight, after I had been complaining to Miss S. and she was gone to bed, my case seemed to have become desperate at last, and I felt I must prevail with the Lord or perish from the way altogether, for I could not possibly get myself out of the miseries, which I now saw and felt I had brought myself into, any other way. As I said, "Lord, are Thy strength and power great enough to reach me even here?" a little faith sprang up and I said strongly, "Yes, they are, but are Thy mercy and willingness great enough?" The spark of faith rose higher and added still stronger, "Yes, they also are." This surprised me, for I could not have said this for many days past. Then a mighty cry came into my soul in which I felt faith work. I had no plea but the desperateness of my condition, nor any hope but in the Lord as a "help in time of need", a Saviour in time of trouble.

Before I rose from the floor, onto which I had flung myself in my distress, I felt a great change. My heart was meekened and I could hear, as it were, the footsteps of His approach. I was very conscious of a power at work within, though but a still, small voice. When I opened the Bible, though I did it with sure belief and expectation that it would not be quite such a sealed Book and dead letter as it had been for some time, I was not at all prepared to find so great a change. I was quite astonished to find it talk with and instruct me everywhere. Every verse seemed alive and alight. O, the understanding and light that flows in when the Spirit shines upon the Word! It must be experienced in some degree to be in the least understood. Psalm 22 in connection with Hebrews 2 were unspeakably sweet to me. I feel at this time a great awe on my spirit at writing what I am going to put down, but I think the Lord knows that it is true.

Fellowship with Christ

He showed me that He had Himself been in my dreadful place and reminded me of petitions that I had often put up that He would conform me to His image. Every word of that 22nd Psalm was made most beautiful, especially the way in which He mixes up His people's case with His own. I did see and feel that I had brought my distress on by my own sins entirely, yet it was as if the Lord would tell me He had been in my case too. At first, I kept trying to put this from me, and I said, "No, Lord, for this is all my sin, and Thou never didst sin." I was quite ashamed to take it; I thought it too much. Still He would make me to feel Him very near as a Brother. And then I lighted on those words: "He is not ashamed to call them brethren," and it seemed quite to break my heart. O, these words kept sounding in my heart: "And we indeed justly, for we receive the due reward of our deeds, but this man hath done nothing amiss." All the Bible seemed to speak the same way. I kept finding unexpectedly such words as these: "Who was in all points tempted like as we are, yet without sin"; "Wherefore in all things it behoved Him to be made like unto His brethren, that He might be a merciful and faithful high priest."

He has by this commanded a great calm in my tempest-tossed soul. Though I do not feel great joy, yet I feel sweet peace and encouragement. The light is real and powerful, though not brilliant. It seems like the early morning which, though inferior to the blaze of noon, is yet quite clear enough to put one beyond all doubt of the reality of the objects discerned. Lord, grant that it may prove the dawn of day.

Another Bitter Stroke

During much of the remainder of the year 1840, I have to confess to my shame that I got back to my own sad place of backsliding and deadness to all spiritual things – not quite as entirely as I have too often done, but still very worldly in spirit and conversation, and consequently obtaining none of the Lord's sensible presence. Gradually, however, during the last month or two of the year, I began to anticipate with hope a return in *spirit,* because I used often to find my heart drawn out greatly in prayer to seek it and to plead with much wrestling at times, and many arguments drawn from former favours; and a secret cry seemed to go about with me when I walked or went anywhere, which I have never yet found vain in the issue.

Early in January 1841, after taking a little gentle walk for exercise (as I was desired to do), I returned so ill that it became too evident to me that the rod was again lifted up over me and would probably descend for the fifth time with the stroke I so much dreaded. I was sorely afflicted, but not suffered to rebel. On the contrary, I was enabled in a great measure to justify the Lord and to confess that my sin had called for this stroke. At first, I was much alarmed, for it was somehow very unexpected to me, and though I believed the Lord would restore my soul, yet it was very long since I had heard from Him, and I thought no doubt it would be by terrible things in righteousness His voice would first come. I thought I should find it very hard work to bear this in weakness and suffering of body. For some days, these lines of a hymn had kept running through my mind in a way of prayer:

"When Thy rod is lifted up,
Let me on Thy love repose.

Stay Thy rough wind,
When the chilling east wind blows."

Now I had not read these lines for years, as far as I know, and had neither considered nor sought to remember them at this time, insomuch that I did not perceive their meaning till my attention was attracted by finding myself continually uttering them to the Lord.

Encouragement

When I considered them, I thought them very suitable and found much encouragement to hope that the Lord's intention was to answer the cry He had (as I thought) put into my heart and that He would deal gently with me in my time of extremity; and truly He did, and that most wonderfully. This expression of Hart's came into my mind: "It is the glory of God to bring good out of evil," with such a realising belief as I cannot express. My soul became filled with a living hope which I have several times felt before, and which has never been disappointed of its object.

This continued for days and was so powerful that I was sure it would find a happy fulfilment, but I could not quite discern what its object was. I knew that its chief expectation was for spiritual mercy, but it did overflow so at times and seemed so large that I thought perhaps it included a temporal deliverance also from the threatened trial. But I always felt an inward misgiving upon that head so that, on the whole, though the medical opinion was favourable, I expected that the uplifted rod would descend. Still I was kept very cheerful during the whole period of suspense, for I was much supported within. I was surprised indeed that the Lord should begin to return in this very kind and gentle way without chiding and rebuking first, but I kept telling Him that He is a Sovereign and giveth not account of any of His matters, and needeth not to be instructed how to deal with His people. Scarcely a day passed but I had something to cheer me in the course of it, which made patience very easy work.

One day I had a clear sense of being included in the everlasting covenant. This was accompanied with a great sense of emptiness and sin in myself. I saw that I was in no wise better than those who are left, and indeed, worse than many of them. But yet I could come boldly to the throne of grace and tell the Lord that He had Himself been pleased to put an everlasting difference between me and them for His dealings with me were in Christ, and that I came to Him at that moment sheltered under cover of His death and righteousness, which was what they never could do. O what firm standing I found here! Another day, He gave me much light upon His dealings with me and cleared up many perplexities of such long standing that I had begun to think I should never have any understanding of their meaning.

Support in the Distressing Hour

Thus my mind was so well entertained that I had no time to brood over my outward trouble much, so that I did not look forward to that impending crisis with anything like the fear and dread I should otherwise have done, considering how very severe these times of trial have always been proved with me. Indeed, it is surprising how little I dreaded it. I thought it would be very easy. But herein I was much mistaken. During the night of January 14th, 1841, my trial came on, and death with it, as it seemed to all appearances. This was so unexpected that I was thrown into much confusion and alarm. I could not feel the presence of the Lord, and the enemy represented all I had felt as presumption. I cried in great fear and distress and had a reviving remembrance of His past mercies, so that hope sprang up high again. Then it was suggested that this hope was on a false foundation for it rested only on past experience. This alarmed me, but this word came in most seasonably: "Experience worketh hope, and hope maketh not ashamed."

For some time (that is, for about eleven hours) I was to my own feelings in the very article of death, often thinking that one sigh would release my spirit: but I was perfectly sensible inwardly, though not to outward things. For some time I was up and down with fears as to whether I had ever been really founded on the Rock, till the Lord gave me this text: "Christ Jesus came into the world to save sinners, of whom I am chief." I cannot describe the childlike simplicity with which I was made to rest on this. Everything else, within and without, was quite out of sight and the impression of my mind was that I had got hold of the hem of His garment. This was enough for me during the rest of my extremity. I was satisfied that I should not make shipwreck. Bunyan's allegory was on my mind and I kept saying: "I am going through with my head quite above water; the Lord does not suffer it to go under."

Divine Compassion

Afterwards I gradually recovered and the Lord still continued to deal most kindly with me. One day especially He gave me a most sweet view of all the way He had led me, of my own exceeding baseness, and of His own unwearied love and patience towards me. I was lying on my couch pondering on what I had been reading in Judges, especially these words: "His soul was grieved for the misery of Israel." Here the Lord showed me to my surprise that He had always shown the same sympathy with me in all my afflictions, outward or inward, and then numbers of instances, which sweetly proved this, kept coming before me without my troubling my natural memory to recall them, till I could truly say that through all my peculiarly perverse behaviour towards Him, and at the very worst of times with me, He had never once been able to refrain Himself when He heard my cry of distress. This was quite a new discovery to me and very beautiful. Very often from want of spiritual understanding, I had not perceived His hand, though I felt the support, and very often through unbelief I quickly lost sight of the help I had at the time been able to acknowledge. But I could now discern that His bowels of compassion had in every case yearned over me, and in proportion to the greatness of my trouble had been the clearness of the relief.

This sight seemed to endear the Lord Jesus greatly to my soul, and while it was quite fresh, my husband came up, and, without knowing what was in my mind, began to read some of the last three or four chapters of Isaiah to me. I heard with much comfort, and at last he came to this verse (I had forgotten there was such a verse in the Bible): "Where are the sounding of Thy bowels towards me? are they restrained?" This was indeed sweet to me. This sight of the way He had led me has in a measure either abode with me or else been revived again and again ever since that time.

Another thing He certainly showed me, which I had at times before had some intimation of, and that was that all the many severe afflictions I have been visited with have been, in the strictest sense, the answer to my own petitions in the following way.

About seven years ago, that is in the year 1833, I was under a peculiar influence in prayer for some months. I was groping in darkness and anxiety and in much confusion to find religion *in the power of it*. Here I was made continually to cry to the Lord to use *whatever* means He saw necessary to overcome the carnality and self-righteousness I was made so sorely conscious of. This cry followed me incessantly. I could pray nothing else. I think I must have said these words hundreds of times, and that without vain repetition: "God of the means as well as the end, be pleased to hear me. All the means in the universe are at Thy command; choose out any, ever so severe, but bring me to the knowledge of Thee. If Thou seest the rod necessary, spare it not. If one stroke fails in its effect through my stubbornness, inflict another and another, neither leave off till Thou dost bring forth judgment unto victory. Lord, I know I shall kick hard against Thee in this: I acknowledge that I shall rebel, murmur, complain:

moreover, I shall pray to Thee to hold Thy hand, but Lord, I do here earnestly beseech Thee, let not Thy soul spare for my crying."

These were the very words (only the sentences were more broken than they look on paper) that I kept crying from my soul to the Lord. I did not plan them, nor did I intend from one hour to another to continue using them, so that I feel sure the Lord set me to pray them for those months together. Often as I walked up and down the room with my eldest boy in my arms, I would look at his face with dread as to what the issue of my prayer would be, for I doted on him, but I found I could do nothing but begin the very same cry again. Soon after this cry had subsided, I laid that boy in the grave. The next year, his fine, healthy little brother followed him, and since then, I have sent child after child to the grave and been many times brought down to death's door myself with much suffering.

But at this time, these things were shown me in so different a light that the very same circumstance, which before seemed to add a keener edge to my afflictions, now worked in the very opposite way. It made my heart to sing for joy and to welcome all my trials, and quite disarmed them of their sting, for the Lord showed me He had foreseen all these strokes to be really necessary because I was so peculiarly obstinate and a greater spiritual fool than any living; that He could have inflicted them without asking or consulting me, but that He had wonderfully condescended to obtain my consent first and even to convert them into tokens of His favour by giving me the power to number them among the sensible answers to prayer I have received. In this sweet light I can truly say I rejoice in them and would not part with one.

Revelation of the Trinity

Some days after this, I got into great darkness and sorrow, being harassed by much temptation. This continued for several days, and rebellion began to work against the Lord for leaving me, as I thought, to be tempted above that I was able, when on Saturday, January 30th, I received a letter from Mr. Abbott, in the reading of which a little light seemed to glimmer (faintly at first). He spoke of Mr. Burrell's having mentioned the darkness he had felt on Sunday and of his having obtained a full deliverance while addressing the three persons of the Trinity distinctly in prayer. I felt while reading this a spiritual resolution to try the same way, but all that day I was resisted and hindered by the enemy, who declared it would not succeed with me, for I had been always very confused in my ideas on the subject of that great mystery.

However, next morning while they were at chapel, I felt that I must try, let the issue be what it might, and to my surprise, I found the Lord very near indeed. He gave me great access with much power to lean on the merits of Christ and come to the Father through the Son. The power of the temptation was quite gone, and I could feel the Lord so kind that I was filled with shame and sorrow at my sinful ingratitude. I knew what Hart meant: "A sinner may repent and sing, rejoice and be ashamed." All that week I had daily, more or less, communion with Father, Son and Spirit. I wrote to Mr. Abbott, but on Sunday was thrown into much affliction and confusion by hearing of his sudden death, so that he had never got my letter. I had much searching of heart and much sin worked up, and through the week was dark mostly.

Last Sunday, February 14th I had a *good* day. I was sweetly sensible of the presence of the blessed Spirit. This increased gradually till evening when the Lord condescended again to give me the clearest light on all His dealings with me from first to last, with a sweet and unspeakable sense of peace with God, through the blood of Christ, applied by the Spirit to my conscience. I felt this to be a sweet and powerful entrance into the doctrine of the Trinity beyond anything I had felt in this way before, and far exceeding any mere light in the understanding. It did sensibly deliver me from guilt, and made me to feel assured that I should never come into condemnation; so that I could say (and still can in some measure), "Bless the Lord, O my soul, and all that is within me, bless His holy Name."

All the Way

(May 28th, 1841). I have many times found a great sweetness in the review of all the way the Lord has led me. How peculiarly perverse and unteachable have I been! Like Israel of old, how soon have I forgotten His deliverances out of trouble and returned to the very evils that brought me into those troubles! I have done nothing but return evil for the great goodness which He has shown me, and to this hour I have to confess to my grief that I am bent to backslide continually, being tormented by an evil heart of unbelief, causing me to depart from the living God, so that I can feelingly say with Hart:

> "If ever it could come to pass,
> That sheep of Christ might fall away,
> My fickle, feeble soul, alas!
> Would fall a thousand times a day."

On the other hand, with what infinite patience and forbearance has He borne with my manners in the wilderness! How has He instructed me line upon line, precept upon precept, here a little and there a little, gradually bringing me to a clearer knowledge of Himself, when by my sins I have brought myself again into darkness and trouble! How often has He had compassion on me and surprised me with His mercy, delivering my soul from death, my eyes from tears, and my feet from falling, so that I can at times joyfully sing:

> "His love in time past forbids me to think
> He'll leave me at last in trouble to sink;
> Each sweet Ebenezer I have in review
> Confirms His good pleasure to help me quite through."

This concludes Mrs. Henrietta Gilpin's gracious account of the Lord's dealings with her.

The following is an account of the last days of Henrietta (wife of Bernard Gilpin), written by her husband. She died on October 12th, 1841, aged 34.

September 28th, 1841

She was in darkness and labour of spirit which now reached its height. She said to me, "My darkness is exceedingly great. I do not see how it can possibly be turned into light again. I remember the words: 'Darkness which may be felt'; that is like the darkness of my soul now." I encouraged her to hope in the Lord, and found she was very tender and had a hope, but it seemed this way: "Hope that is seen is not hope."

About three o'clock I heard her groaning in prayer and she added very gently, "Will this dark, *dark* night never end?" I replied with an energy which surprised myself, "You are near Christ's deliverance." We both of us continued praying secretly for about two hours, but she soon told me that she felt herself better. After a while she added, "There is a light in my heart," and bid me look at the dawning of the natural light. "That", said I "is the light of the morning." "Yes," she answered, "and I think there is the light of a better morning in my soul. Don't you remember how you told me at three o'clock that I was near His deliverance? Just as you spoke, I was tempted to reply in bitterness that you were wrong; instead of which, a check passed through my heart and made me say inwardly, 'Perhaps I am near His deliverance.' This gave me a little turn and immediately I began to pray in hope." After a further while she added, "O, this light, this glorious light! The hope has visited my soul. It has laid hold upon everything that the Lord has wrought in my heart *from the very first,* and it points forward into heaven itself."

In answer to further enquiries, she spoke to this effect: "The Lord

Jesus has most clearly and in the tenderest manner revealed His love in my heart, and while I was entirely taken up with admiring and adoring His kindness, He made me to understand His peculiar attention to the circumstances of my outward condition. I felt ashamed, as thinking His kindness was too great, but the more I shrank from it, the more He pressed it upon me, till at last I was made entirely willing to resign myself, my family and every other concern, together with the newborn hope which had visited my soul, into His safe keeping, so that I could not feel a shadow of mistrust nor fear of any kind. At the same time He plainly intimated to me that this peculiar support was intended to strengthen me in some approaching trial, which now therefore I expect."

September 29th

Later in the morning it began to appear that her labour was coming on at the period of seven months, though the symptoms were not at that hour very urgent.

I went to Hertford at her request to desire the surgeon to be in readiness, and to bring back our kind friend Mrs. F. While I was there, she was suddenly taken worse and wrote me a line by messenger: "I am worse, return quickly with Mr. Evans, Mrs. F. and the nurse; but be not alarmed, for I am not." On my return I found her very quiet; she seemed for a time in a happy state of surprise, and her spirit full of communion with God. She said, "I have not the shadow of a fear. He is with me and enables me to resign myself entirely into His hands. I am quite happy. Soon after you left, I rose and went to lie down on the couch thinking I had in prospect a long, tedious day of suspense. Beginning to ponder on what might follow, I opened the book of Proverbs and read. These words arrested my attention: 'In all labour there is profit, but the talk of the lips tendeth only to penury.' I soon passed them and found a gentle and very peaceful impression from another passage: 'He that spareth the rod hateth his son, but he that loveth him, chasteneth him betimes.' I felt satisfied of the love of God as my Father and that all my trials would work together for my good, and while I was sucking honey out of these things, the former words returned with a weight of the Lord's reproof. It was as if He said, '*Attend to it – In all labour there is profit, but the talk of the lips tendeth only to penury.*' Immediately these words were clinched by the following: 'All Scripture is given by inspiration of God, and is profitable for doctrine, for reproof, for correction, for instruction in righteousness.' I was frightened and brought very low and entreated the gracious help of the Spirit to keep me from offending Him. I also prayed: 'Lord, deliver me from this vain talking.'

Afterwards this further word was added and He restored my peace and hope: 'The ear that heareth the reproof of life abideth among the wise.' O, how I did cry with all my heart that I might always abide among the wise! When this was over, I suddenly became worse in body. I was alarmed for a moment, not having the requisite helps at hand, but the Lord's tenderness took my fears clean away. He kept assuring me that I should find Him at hand to supply all my need. So now I say again: 'Be not any of you alarmed, for I am not.' "

Throughout the morning she continued very ill but happy. In the afternoon, both body and spirit seemed spent and she had a time of dark temptation. She said, "The enemy presses hard upon me. He would have me mistrust the Lord, and maintains that my hope is only a delusion. At times I have yielded to him, which has made me very miserable." Later in the evening she spoke to this effect: "I have found a return of help from the Lord and my doubts are again scattered."

September 30th

Early in the morning, her state became very critical for a time. She had one severe and distressing fainting fit, and when it began to pass away, she fully considered herself to be dying. She said afterwards, "I was at that time in a state of unclouded peace; no shadow of a doubt perplexed me. I was also both ready and willing to die and indeed sorry to find that I was to return back again. Yet I can now submit to the Lord's will in everything." Afterwards all went on favourably till about seven in the morning when she was delivered of a stillborn son. Her first words to me were: "All is right. I have not one word of complaint to make." However, before that day was spent she began to be very unhappy at times through the intrusion of murmuring thoughts.

October 1st and 2nd

She complained, sometimes very bitterly, of these inward sins. Her rest in the Lord's lovingkindness was broken and she said, "I am afraid that sometimes in conversation I have betrayed the sinful want of submission I have felt within." All bodily symptoms were favourable and she quite expected her recovery.

October 3rd

She passed a day of conflict, though not without some victories, but towards the evening became alarmed with symptoms of oppression on the brain. There was a favourable intermission, however, though she afterwards passed a wild and restless night.

October 4ᵗʰ

She continued slowly getting worse, though the symptoms were yet by no means clear. In the evening she was in great pain and anxiety. At the same time her soul became oppressed with sore darkness and it was as though "sin revived and she died", though not without vehement cries to the Lord Jesus. From eight o'clock till eleven, I continued by her bedside entreating for mercy and endeavouring to direct her oppressed spirit to the Saviour. She said, "O, what sin and rebellion I have found within, and how I have dared to entertain murmuring thoughts and at times strengthened them by giving them utterance, as I fear! Will He ever return and pardon me and blot out my transgressions as a cloud? I am now labouring in the dark. What fears I feel! What mountains of fears! Lord Jesus, Thou knowest my heart. It is neither life nor death, ease nor pain that I now care about, but my whole cry is for mercy, Thy rich *mercy,* Thy full *mercy,* Thy *free mercy.* That is all I seek, Thou knowest it." I repeated the hymn, "Rock of Ages, cleft for me!" She said, "That hymn seems to me good a *little;* it expresses the thing that I want, but the thing I cannot now feel. O, how I long to feel it!" Afterwards I repeated to her the whole account of Hezekiah's great conflict: "I reckoned till morning, that, as a lion, so will he break all my bones: from day even to night wilt thou make an end of me. Like a crane or a swallow, so did I chatter: I did mourn as a dove: mine eyes fail with looking upward. O Lord, I am oppressed; undertake for me." She followed me till I arrived at the last passage and then outran my words very seriously: "O Lord, *I am oppressed,* undertake for me." She sank down oppressed with a heavy kind of sleep from which she awoke twice without apparent refreshment. The second time was about three in the morning when I perceived she was alarmingly ill. She said, "I fear lest I shall become distracted and die with the pain in my head" – and indeed, there was too much reason to apprehend this to allow of our speaking a word to her on spiritual subjects. Every medical means was most promptly attended to, but all was scarcely enough to avert the violence of the disorder.

October 5ᵗʰ

Throughout the whole day she could neither speak nor be spoken to. At night she was still worse.

October 6th

The symptoms were decidedly favourable, and as the power of speech returned, she began to utter expressions of adoration and joy. I am not aware that she described to any the manner in which the consolation was restored to her soul (her great weakness rendering it inexpedient to converse much with her), but her state during that and the three following days was a very blessed one, her faith full of resolution, and "for a helmet the hope of salvation".

October 7th

In the evening, her sister, Mrs. Latter, came down. As soon as she saw her, she said, "Is that my sister? God bless you; I love you; I believe I love you in the Lord and am glad to see you. I do not now expect to recover, but the Lord has been very gracious to me, very gracious indeed, full of tenderness. I cannot tell you how tenderly kind He has been." She then gave her an account of many of the particulars that have been related.

October 8th

She seemed to have a strong presentiment of her approaching end and a powerful revival in her heart of some very instructive spiritual teaching, which she had first had some time before.

Calling her sister and me to her bedside that she might describe this to us, she first asked me to read John 5. 24: "Verily, verily, I say unto you, He that heareth My word, and believeth on Him that sent me, hath everlasting life, and shall not come into condemnation; but is passed from death unto life." She then proceeded thus: "I had those words opened in a wonderful manner to me; it began with a glorious perception of the presence of the three Persons in the Godhead. My heart was filled with reconciliation through the blood of Christ, which brought in the Father's love, all through the application of the Holy Ghost. Had I never heard of the doctrine of the Trinity before, I should have believed it from that day forwards. My joy was for a time suspended by the appearance of an awful shadow. Nothing was unfolded in it, but I was made to understand that this was the shadow of eternal death; but it was said to me: 'This shall never be your portion.' I was then made to pass on and behold a very bright and glorious light, wherein, as before, nothing was unfolded, but I was made to understand that it was the representation of heaven, and these words followed: 'You are passed from *death* unto *life;* this glory – come it soon or come it late – shall be yours for ever.' Now all this I saw and felt. I was so convinced of the divine reality of it that I could have staked the life of my dearest husband or children *entirely* upon it. Yet, for all that, I cannot say the reality is so clear to me now. Nevertheless, Lord, I appeal to Thee; I believe that teaching was from Thee and I perceive that now while I speak to Thee, Thou dost not contradict what I say."

About the same time she requested me to read several passages to her, especially Psalm 42: "As the hart panteth after the water brooks, so panteth my soul after Thee, O God." She said, "That's like me; so do I pant and long after the mercy of the Lord, and it is not far from me. I feel Him near and He encourages me to go on praying and using all the pleas I can think of, and I don't think He will reject me any more than He rejected the Samaritan woman we read of in John 4."

In the afternoon, she was restless and anxious. She called me and said, "Unless *you* will stay and remain with me all the evening and through the night, I fear I shall get no rest." When I told her I must go presently to Hertford and preach, it being Friday, she said, "I am quite willing you should go, and be very cautious that you do nothing in compliance with my wishes which would bring a cloud over your own soul. Do be cautious of that; and when you return after service, come and stay with me if you feel it right, or I fear I shall get no rest." This conversation troubled me because I knew that I could not remove her restlessness. I left the room inwardly praying. In a few minutes she said to our kind friend Mrs. F., "Go to my husband and ask him to return. I wish to see him." When I came, she said, "The Lord has whispered a word *very softly*. It is that verse that begins: 'I will both lay me down in peace and sleep; for Thou, Lord, only makest me dwell in safety.' Now read that Psalm to me and perhaps the Lord will put me to sleep upon it." I read it and she begged to hear the last verse repeatedly, following it up herself very slowly: " 'I will both lay me down in peace and *sleep,* for Thou, Lord, *only* makest me to dwell in safety.' That's it; now, that's enough for me. I don't want anything better; now I think I can go to sleep." After this, though she got but little refreshing bodily sleep, yet she continued quiet and her fears of being left without me (she said – I think) never once returned.

October 9th

She was stronger in body and the hope of her spirit was more triumphant. After Mr. Evans had seen her, he told her he hoped she would now continue getting better. On this she said to him, "You consider me better; well, the Lord is able to restore me for a short time. But I can say now, that's not my concern but *His,* and I wish to abide in that mind, to leave it all with Him and to take no thought about it myself.

But I must say, my own belief is that I shall not recover, but *die* very soon; yet I have a hope in my heart. and I believe it is a good hope too, and I tell you it is worth ten thousand worlds to have such a hope when we come where I am now." Very soon after he had left the room, her countenance beamed with joy and she was so evidently in heavenly communion that her sister dared not speak lest it should disturb her, when presently she said herself, "The Lord Jesus is present and sweetly comforts me. I begged Him to open my mouth Himself, if it were His will I should speak to Mr. E. respecting my hope, yet no sooner had I done so than I heard a *taunting voice* within saying, 'You have been making a vain boast and will have hard work for this by and by.' I said, 'Lord, I don't think that's Thy voice, for it is *taunting* and Thy voice is not *taunting*,' when immediately the Lord smiled sweetly and told me that He loved me. Now. sister, did I say anything wrong to Mr. E.?" "No, indeed," (replied Mrs. L.) "for the Lord has shone upon it and approved it."

About seven in the evening of the day, her sister M. came to see her. As soon as she came into the room she said, "This was very kind of you. I have wished to see you, but you are come to see me do the hardest thing I ever did in my life, and that is to die. I have done many hard things, but this is the hardest of all." After this, she appeared in conflict for some time and then said, "I have been greatly exercised and I have waded through many deep waters and had many fears since your last visit in the spring, but now I have a hope, a good hope, a living hope, which the Lord has given me and I can put my trust in Him. He has delivered and He *will yet deliver*. God only knows the strength of the hope He has given me."

October 10th Sunday

She seemed still better in the morning and seemed to have a near view of the presence of the Lord. She spoke much of the continued conflict she was in because of the accusations of the enemy, which, she said, were very desperate; on this she added, "But the Lord comes in with the mighty torrent of His love and assuages all my grief. I feel I am in His hand whether for life or for death, and He has now given me that resignation to His will that I have no choice of my own; I only want to be assured of His love and I *am* assured of it, for I feel Christ's blood sprinkled upon my conscience, and He tells me that He has died for me, a vile sinner."

Here her language entirely changed and she cried out, "But is there a hope for me? Tell me, is there a shadow of a hope for me? I cannot tell you the fears with which I am sometimes overwhelmed; my heart fails me and I fear lest after all, I have been deceiving myself. O, to hear those words *'Depart from me'!* I have a great terror lest these words should be said to me." Here she changed again and proceeded, "Still, I have a hope, a living hope which hath its foundation in Christ. Every hope fails, but this hope fails me not. It does not fail me now and it is worth thousands of worlds. It is kept alive in Christ. Does it not say somewhere, 'We are saved by *hope*'? Now that is the hope that saves me, and I believe I am saved. Is it not wonderful that it should be so when I am such a vile sinner? I do not know how to express my gratitude, for sometimes all fear is taken away except a fear lest I should be raised up again and forget all His mercies and backslide again from Him. O, I fear that more than death, for I have done nothing all my life but grieve Him and pierce Him through and through with my untoward ways. I cannot tell you how I loathe myself, and yet I know I should be as bad again, if He suffered it, for all manner of abominations are in my heart, and more than all. But the Lord Jesus steps in and holds me fast; I am in His hands and He suffers me to touch Him – He suffers me, a sinner, to touch the hem of His garment."

A short time after this she said, "Now read to me; be all the day long reading to me and feeding me with the crumbs of the bread of life, for I am very hungry for the bread of life and I am very thirsty for the water of life; and while you read, the Lord keeps sending little sentences into my heart and they support me greatly; keep feeding me that way with little crumbs and drops all day." After this, she expressed great delight in hearing different passages, especially Psalm 27. 4: "One thing have I desired of the Lord, that will I seek after; that I may dwell in the house of the Lord all the days of my life." She said, "That is what I desire now, to dwell in the house of the Lord for ever. His house is in Christ, nowhere else but in Christ, and this the Lord teaches me now and He makes me to know what it is to dwell in Him, even in the Father, in the Son and in the Holy Ghost. Where is that passage: 'Praise waiteth for Thee, O God, in Zion'? Read it, for that is just what I feel now – praise waiteth in my heart. I cannot tell you how I feel that praise in my heart is stretching out its neck; yes, it is all on the stretch, ready to burst forth because of His mercy. Could you have thought it possible that He should have mercy upon me and pass by all my transgressions and put His love upon me and fasten it upon my heart and never let it go? Therefore, though I cannot praise Him now, yet praise waiteth in my heart and I am sure if I am saved, my praise must sound the loudest of all for no one has been a greater sinner. Could you have thought it possible that He should have mercy upon me, a vile, corrupt worm, a reptile? I cannot tell you how vile I am in my own sight – a scorpion! O, that is it! I feel myself so very venomous that I can compare myself to nothing but a scorpion."

I came myself into her room and heard the greater part of the above. Then, turning more especially to me, she repeated what she had said about *praise stretching its neck.* I said, "Do you know that is just the manner the apostle Paul describes the new creature in Romans 8, saying, 'The earnest expectation of the creature waiteth for the manifestation of the sons of God.' That word 'earnest expectation' describes in the Greek the *stretching forth of the neck.*" "Now does it?" she said. "How very sweet that is! Do turn to my sisters and tell them that. Now M., do you hear that? Is it not very encouraging?"

Knowing that I should be on that day (it being Sunday) a good deal engaged from her, she appeared at times anxious to take leave of me and to prepare my mind as tenderly as she could for the change she was convinced was approaching. Once she said, "It is almost over. We have lived together in the happiest union for nearly thirteen years, and now the Lord is about to dissolve that union. I thank you much for your unvaried kindness to me, and as He has blessed our union, so now may He bless our separation. And I tell you, I have prayed for this and I have found a promise that it shall be so, and I know it!" Also respecting our kind friend, Mrs. Furnival, she said repeatedly, "I have prayed, and I have found an answer, that the Lord will surely bless her and reward her sevenfold for her kindness to me, and I know the promise shall not fail; and if the Lord saw it needful to confirm it, I know that my faith could throw a mountain into the sea."

Her sister, Mrs. L., read to her part of Revelation 21, particularly this verse "It is done. I am Alpha and Omega, the beginning and the end. I will give unto him that is athirst of the fountain of the water of life *freely.*" She was much moved and said, "Lord, Thou didst give me that verse and it was that word which once appeared so wonderful to me; yes, it was large enough to fill heaven and earth."

After hearing part of Luke 15 read, she said, "I have been like that prodigal son indeed. Were it not for Thy free grace, O Lord, I should have run into all manner of evil and brought myself to shame and destruction, but Thy Holy Spirit has kept me and guided me. I did not formerly feel, as I do now, power to pray to the Holy Spirit, nor had I formerly that sweet and powerful sense of His divinity which I enjoy now. I can now address Him in my prayers, for O, Thou blessed Spirit, Thou knowest, after all that Jesus has done for poor sinners, notwithstanding His wondrous and great salvation, yet such is the hardness and deadness of my soul that it would all have been in vain for me hadst Thou not condescended to reveal these things to me."

On hearing the word: "When thou passest through the waters, I will be with thee; and through the rivers, they shall not overflow thee: when thou walkest through the fire, thou shalt not be burned; neither shall the flame kindle upon thee," she said, "The Lord is with me now in these deep waters I am now passing through. I have many fears at times, but my hope rises higher than my fears and I believe I shall not suffer shipwreck." At another time she said, "The Lord has dried Jordan to the bottom before He has required me to step one foot in."

Shortly after this she gave an account of the state of her mind when she was taken ill, saying, "Now I will tell you how merciful the Lord was to me when I was first taken ill. My husband was gone to H. and I was quite unexpectedly taken worse. I knew I was in great danger and my life might be gone before any assistance could be procured, yet the Lord came so fully into my heart that I had not the least dread of any kind, either temporally or spiritually, for He graciously condescended to talk with me and to hold up my soul in communion with Him, and He said that He was my physician both for body and soul. It was some time before the help I was expecting could arrive, but the Lord kept pouring in His comfort into my soul. I cannot tell you how near He was to me, and He told me He would do everything for me. I could touch Him and He touched me and allayed my fears so that not one rose up all the time. I do not know how long it was, but it was more than an hour, though I thought it was scarcely a minute, for I shut my eyes and threw myself into the hands of the Lord as my physician, which He said He would be, and when I opened them – which I thought was the next minute – I was surprised to find myself surrounded with husband, doctor, nurse, friends, and all possible assistance was rendered while I had nothing to do but to lie still in the hands of the Lord and let Him do what He pleased. Surely then I have cause to praise Him and to commit all things into His hands."

After lying quiet for some time, she asked for 1 Timothy 2. 15 to be read. She then repeated the words: " 'Saved in child bearing, if they continue in *faith* and *charity* and *holiness* with *sobriety*.' Lord, how is it that I am saved, for Thou knowest Thou canst not lay these things to my charge; I have them not. Tell me, Lord, how is this? It must be that Thou hast given me these good graces though I have none of them, and so Thou dost save me in Thyself with an everlasting salvation. Yes, Lord, it must be so."

Then she began to speak at intervals of the unchangeable love of God in Christ, saying, "Were it not for that unchangeable love of God, how often must He have cut me off who have been a continual backslider from

Him! I think if I am saved, my voice must sound the loudest, yes, the very loudest of all in His praise for having saved me. No one knows the treachery of my heart. Now all fear is taken from me but the fear of returning again to the world and of turning my back on such a Friend; *that* I fear greatly, for the Lord has given me such love to Himself that I would not for all the world grieve Him; yet such is the treachery of my heart that if left to myself, I should turn away in one moment."

In the afternoon she was rather worse and had also a return of conflict in hearing James, chapter 1. She said to her sister, "I want to ask you one thing. It says, 'For he that wavereth is like a wave of the sea driven with the wind and tossed. For let not that man think that he shall receive any thing of the Lord.' Now I cannot help wavering. Will He then reject me?" Mrs. L. replied, "Our minister often speaks of that and tells us that wavering is in the *old man* to whom the Lord pays no regard and he need not expect to receive anything; but He hears the voice of the new man of grace that is in all that are born again." She seemed satisfied and glad to hear this and reflected on herself as having been slow of heart, saying, "I am more brutish than any man." Afterwards she gave me an account of what had passed, adding that she was delivered from her fears then.

After this she had an hour's sleep, but woke much disturbed and harassed, as she had been once before, with the bitter accusations of the enemy; also bitter blasphemous suggestions against the Saviour. She was not a moment at a loss here but referred them at once to the tempter, saying with great vehemence, "'Do not I hate them, O Lord, which hate Thee? Yea, I hate them with perfect hatred.' O, what hatred the Lord has given me to Satan, for he keeps hurling in a host of fiery darts to tempt me to think hardly of the Lord's dealings with me; but the Lord is my stay!"

Many times during the day she referred to her death, saying, "They say I am better, but I know I am not. I know I shall not recover, but die." And once added, "I have been told so; the Lord has told me so, and I am in His hand." Several times she desired to see our friend Mr. Bourne, wishing us to send for him. "I do not want to speak to him, but to hear him speak, seeing the Lord has many times blessed his words to me and perhaps He may again."

After this, being fluttered and in pain, she was reminded of her need of patience, when she became calm and said, "Speak to me one word about Jesus." Her sister quoted the words: "Look unto Me and be ye saved, all ye ends of the earth, for I am God and there is none else." Then she said, "The Lord sees the heart. He knows that I cry to Him without ceasing." At last, turning to Mrs. Furnival, she said, "*Now tell my sister the Lord Jesus has looked upon me and smiled sweetly.*"

After this, she fell asleep but was roused for a short time by the arrival of her brother Julius whom she recognised and addressed tenderly, and at last said to him, "My tabernacle is being taken down, but I hope it will please the Lord to take it down." Previous to his coming, she had asked for the words to be repeated: "I will both lay me down in peace and sleep, for Thou, Lord, only makest me to dwell in safety." "The Lord has often put me to sleep with those words, and perhaps He will again."

Her brother having left, she sank gradually into a sound sleep which increased in depth and intensity till at last we became aware she would wake no more in this world. After continuing thus for thirty-six hours, she gradually expired at seven o'clock in the morning of Tuesday, the 12th October, 1841, in the 35th year of her age.

Thus it appeared how signally the Lord's first promise given her in her childhood had been fulfilled to the end: "When thou passest through the waters, I will be with thee; and through the rivers, they shall not overflow thee."

Gospel Standard 1973, published from an old manuscript, much of which appears in *Life and Ministry of Bernard Gilpin.*

AMAZING GRACE

Alice Shettlewood

By Bernard Gilpin (1803-1867), minister at Port Vale Chapel, Hertford.

Early Years of Wickedness

This poor woman was a younger member of a large family named Knight, living at Charlbury in Oxfordshire. She was far from being one of those who could say, "If any man have whereof he might trust in the flesh, I more"; for not only was her natural disposition extremely trying to others through fretfulness and violence of temper, but her early habits also were such as she had need to remember, and did remember, with shame and confusion of face.

I have reason to hope that she was not the only member of her family called by grace. She had a distinct recollection in her last years of the death of her brother Thomas many years before, though she did not understand what the scene meant when she was eyewitness to it. She remembered that he had been a very careless man till his last illness, which lasted fifteen weeks, during which period he expressed much distress, and was praying night and day. On the morning of his death he caused all his family to be assembled round him, but being at the time unable to speak, he begged them to retire, and return to him in half an hour. They did so, when he declared he had never known till laid on that sick bed the awful danger of his condition, but that now at last the Lord Jesus had heard his prayer, shown him the narrow way of life and the pardon of his sins, and that he was saved. Then lifting up one hand, he said in a way which deeply impressed the by-standers, "The way is but as a finger's breadth," and shortly afterwards he expired.

No good impression lasted on poor Alice. She went out early to service, both in London and the country, and from her last place was sent home ill, and had a long and most severe fever; after which she partly maintained herself by glove-making. It is probable that she was but indifferently treated, her friends being poor, and her conduct and temper disobliging. On one occasion, one of her relations in a passion threw upon her a quantity of boiling pitch. She wandered about, and became the

75

victim of temptation, and with some intermissions lived in an abandoned manner for nearly twelve years. Her friends at first endeavoured to reclaim her, and that it is to be feared in a harsh spirit, which she as harshly resented. Long before the end they had quite abandoned her, and her destitution was most deplorable.

A Strange Dream

In the middle of this dreadful period she resided for about six months with a married brother, who as well as his wife were Primitive Methodists (who are at once flighty in their spirit, and erroneous in their creed). Most of such as made a profession of religion in the neighbourhood were also of the like persuasion. Alice had no religion of her own, and no respect for theirs. She had a most remarkable dream, in which (as I now believe) the Lord intimated His purpose of mercy to her, but it was long before she found it verified.

She dreamed that after labouring with a heavy burden till she brought on a dreadful pain in her side, she lay down, gradually declined, and died. Her body was put into a coffin, and her soul was carried to a place which appeared as a great forge. Here, being in the utmost agony of fear, she saw two persons, one of whom she supposed to be Satan, and the other a servant of Christ's. The latter said, "Why do you tremble?" She replied, "Because I do not know whether I shall be saved or lost." He said, "You'll soon know that," and then opening a door beyond which was a flight of steps, bade her ascend, which she did. She found herself in a most splendid judgment hall, and right before her "a great white throne", and Jesus was sitting on it. As she entered, His eye met hers, and He said, " 'All manner of sin and blasphemy shall be forgiven unto *thee.*' Go and read the 12th chapter of Matthew."

She awoke overpowered with astonishment, and was not able to leave her bed. Her sister enquiring the cause, she begged her to read the 12th chapter of St. Matthew, and at the words "All manner of sin", her astonishment increased, and she related all that had happened. This, in the outward circumstance falling in with her sister's views, highly delighted her, and she called a number of her friends round her and told them. Some said, "Alice Knight has had a fine dream. She's surely converted now." "We wish we had had such a fine dream." "Will you see our minister?" But Alice replied, "I neither want to see you nor your ministers; for I am sure you must be wrong yourselves, because you say my dream has converted me, and I know better than that."

Powerful as the effect of this dream was, it soon wore off. For several succeeding years she continued a wretched outcast from her relations, in the utmost misery and destitution, loathing her wicked course, yet not knowing how to escape from it. She afterwards described to me in a feeling manner her anguish during this concluding period. "I thought I could be content to lie down all night under a shed, aye, to starve rather than to go on as I had done but, O, Mr. Gilpin, look which way I would, I had nowhere to go! The thing was I had nowhere to go! Now and then my dream flashed on my mind, and I would think to myself, 'What a wicked woman I am to forget that dream!' Then I would drive away the thought."

A Door of Escape

In the month of June 1839, it pleased God in His mercy to begin to open a door for her escape. A woman who kept a public house, deeply pitying her most forlorn condition, induced several persons who were lodging there to speak favourably of her to a young man named James Shettlewood (her future husband), who had come to the same place on his work. He had been for some time earning his bread honestly by mending china up and down the country, but he had not at that period more of the fear of God in his heart than poor Alice had. He made her an offer of marriage, which she most gladly accepted, but neither of them having any ready money, they agreed to defer the marriage till they had, and in the meantime, without feeling any compunction of heart at the first, they went from place to place together. She was exceedingly delighted with the change, but acknowledged afterwards that her thoughts were entirely on the worldly advantage of having found at last one who would support and protect her. But God in His sovereign mercy overruled the event for the spiritual advantage of both of them; and who could have supposed this?

Trials and Separations

Her temper became bitterly trying to him at times, and they often threatened to separate. Once, in a fit of anger, she told him she was resolved to leave him, and taking possession of some of his principal tools, she began to earn something for herself by mending china at neighbouring houses. But in three days she returned and begged to continue with him, being afraid (she said) of drowning herself in despair should she be left solitary.

On another occasion she had displeased him, and he left her abruptly, starting on before her, and she feared he would return no more. She followed him slowly in much distress, but as he turned aside for work to the houses on the right and left, she soon got before him. In this extremity, she remembered hearing her mother say, "If you pray God for anything, He can give it you." So she went over the hedge into a turnip field, and there cried aloud that she might find James again. A hope sprang into her heart, which seemed to say (as she described it to me), "Make haste – go forward – be in the town before he gets there." (It was Deddington in Oxfordshire.) She ran forward as fast as she could, and knocking at the door of a public house, enquired if one James Shettlewood were there. She was answered, "No, but come and sit down." She did so, and in an hour or two in came James. He had been very successful at his work, and was loaded with six shillings worth of copper. As soon as he saw her, her eyes swollen with tears, he went forward, and threw his weighty gain into her lap. She was perfectly overjoyed; but (as she afterwards said to me), "As soon as I had found James, sir, I forgot my prayer, and forgot the Lord too. I had found all I cared for."

The hand of God began to touch his heart, and perhaps hers also at times. One day, when they were in great distress, nearly penniless, wandering through the rocky valley of Todmorden, between Yorkshire and Lancashire, the fear of the wrath to come fell upon James. Something seemed to sound in his ears, "Hell, hell! The end of these things is death." As soon as he reached their lodging-house, he said to Alice for the first time, "Let us pray." She remembered the words of the Lord's prayer, and repeating them over to him, they prayed them together. He says, "Though we knew not the Lord, I believe we prayed indeed that day."

The Power of Grace

In April 1841, they went to Chelmsford to visit his relations. Here he was asked to attend at the baptizing of a nephew named after him. To this he consented, and on that occasion these words entered his heart with a divine impression which he could never afterwards forget, "Except a man be born again, he cannot see the kingdom of God." It seems that from that day forward, the power of the grace of God laid effectual hold upon him.

They went down to Reading and continued in that neighbourhood for some months, the work of spiritual conviction getting deeper and deeper in his heart. He regularly attended public worship in St. Giles's Church, and found the whole of the services very awakening; indeed everything he heard made him tremble more and more. This fear preserved him from the entrance of all errors, however otherwise they might have entangled him. The feeling of his sins became deep; and amongst other sins, the one he was living in, not being lawfully married, pressed his conscience intolerably. To continue thus he felt would prove destruction, yet how to order his course he knew not, for her temper gave him so much trouble, and proved so irritating to his own, that he sometimes thought a separation was absolutely needful to prevent the increasing of this evil. It was very remarkable that, ignorant though he was, he felt fully persuaded that none but God alone could resolve this difficulty. When he thought of asking counsel of men, a fear sprang up and stopped him. He prayed day and night, "Lord, what shall I do? Shall I leave her? Shall I marry her? If I leave her, perhaps she will kill herself; and her blood will be required at my hand. If I am joined with her, how can I lead a good life?"

She was glad on the whole to find him so turned to religion, because she perceived she could now trust him, and he left off all his bad ways. He also always induced her to attend with him service in St. Giles's Church, but further than this she showed no sign of a change.

Sometimes temptation prevailed against him. Once in an interval of his painful convictions, some young men persuaded him to spend a few hours at a diversion he was very fond of, and he did not return to his lodging till past midnight. She was exceedingly angry, and the effect of this, joined with a returning conviction of his own sinful backsliding, made him so thoroughly wretched that he thought, "I can endure this life no longer; I must separate from her at once." He told her so, and to his great surprise she answered mildly, "I think that plan will be best." He thought at first that perhaps God caused this change in her because it was His will that they should part; so giving her all the money he had about him, and wishing her goodbye, he left her early in the morning, and walked hard all day, intending to do so for several days till she should not be able to trace him. Just as he was entering Henley-on-Thames, he remembered having left a ball of wire worth one shilling and sixpence in his lodgings unknown to her, and reproached himself for having forgotten to inform her of what might prove to her advantage. While deliberating what to do, a woman met him whom he knew. He said, "Do you remember me and Alice?" "Yes," she said, "I remember you well; and I'm going to that same house in Reading where you used to be." "Then tell Alice," he replied, "that in such a corner of my lodging she will find some wire, which she may sell." "Very well," answered the woman, and going straight to Reading, said to Alice, "I met your husband just going into Henley. He bids you take his wire with you, and be with him as early as you can tomorrow morning." Poor Alice, overjoyed, set off running through rain and darkness, and reached Henley by breakfast time; and when James came downstairs, behold, she was the first to meet him.

At first he was troubled, but soon began to reflect that it was intended to show that he could not get rid of her, and must not attempt it any more, that he must cleave to her for better or for worse, and that this was certainly God's will. So returning back to Reading, as soon as ever they could raise sufficient money to meet the expense, they were married in St. Giles's Church on the 7th February, 1842.

A Good Prayer

During all this period, and afterwards, the good work was slowly going on in his heart. Going about this period to Oxford to work there, he found against the wall of his lodging-house a printed prayer, which so riveted his attention that the owner gave it to him. He kept it as a great treasure, and he and his wife got it by heart. It was the first thing that directed his attention to Christ. The beginning of it always made him tremble, "Let me know that I am a sinner before Thee, and exposed to Thy just wrath." Then it followed, "Grant me the saving knowledge of Christ; wash me in His blood, clothe me in His righteousness." He saw these were great things which he must himself find, whereas before this, whenever he heard about Christ and these favours, he had supposed they were blessings too good for him to seek at present. Further on the prayer said, "Let me know my interest in Christ." That word *interest* sank into his heart, and day and night, abroad and at home, for months together, he kept praying in these words, "Let me know my interest in Christ."

There was also another prayer which they found in a small book, which seems to have made a deeper impression upon Alice than the former one, though she did not acknowledge this till afterwards, when she repeated the words as nearly as she could recollect them as follows. "O Eternal God! I have lived in a careless, prayerless state, and have been altogether taken up with the things of this present evil world. I have never thought of my soul, and what I must do to be saved. And though I now kneel before Thee; and though I know that except I am born of the Spirit I cannot see the kingdom; that except I repent I must perish; that except I believe on Jesus I am condemned already – yet my heart is hard; I cannot repent. Yet hardened and careless as I am, Thou canst rouse me and convert me, and make me feel the evil of sin, that I have sinned against Thee, and that it is a fearful thing to fall into the hands of the living God."

At last, in the beginning of the autumn of 1842, they left Reading, intending after a short sojourn at some intermediate towns, to go to Chelmsford and other places. They passed the first Sunday at Henley, where they heard a sermon on these words: "Thou art the man." It cut James to the heart, so as to make him say that though he had often had his heart broken for sorrow, and felt much for his sins, yet he never had a truly broken heart for sin till that day. It brought all his sins to remembrance, worse, said he, than ever David's were. "Against Thee, Thee only have I sinned, and done this evil in Thy sight." Thus, truly mourning for sin, he reached Hertford, and his wife with him, in September 1842; and there, in consequence of what followed, they fixed their permanent abode.

James's Deliverance

They attended St. Andrew's Church, and were soon taken notice of by some of the congregation. One lady, who had been much struck with the account he gave of himself and his deep mourning for sin, said, "You should not only attend the service, but the Lord's Supper also, for it does good to such as you are." To confirm her words, she put a tract into his hands, which (though no good one) had a sentence in it to the above effect, that great sinners, being humbled, were welcome to the Lord's table, which sentence took full possession of his mind. It suggested to him a perfectly new idea of the purpose of the Lord's Supper, and after considering it over, praying and reading for several days, he came to the conclusion that he *must* attend, and could not help it. This he accordingly did. He did not think of it with self-complacency as a good thing which he was doing, but he remembered the words, "Let me know my *interest* in Christ," and if ever, prayed them with all his heart and soul. "What (thought he) does that *interest* in Christ mean?" The words of the confession in the communion service entered his heart with great power, "We acknowledge and bewail our manifold sins and wickedness, which we from time to time most grievously have committed, by thought, word, and deed against Thy divine Majesty; provoking most justly Thy wrath and indignation against us. We do earnestly repent, and are heartily sorry for these our misdoings. The remembrance of them is grievous unto us, the burden of them is intolerable," etc. Here he was enabled to fall down to the uttermost before Jesus, who at the same moment was pleased to break in upon his soul with unutterable love and mercy. In a moment he said to himself, "This is what *interest* in Christ means!" and he was filled with joy unspeakable and full of glory. The sensible pardon of sin, peace with God, and a conscience washed in the blood of Jesus, were things such as his eye had never before seen, nor his ear heard, neither had entered into his heart to believe.

His wife, though in a state of mind so different from his own, had been also recommended to go to the Lord's Supper, and had accordingly gone, but more to please man than in the fear of God. The same evening, when they met at their lodging, her husband related to her the glorious change he had found. She was struck with great awe, and cried out, "Yes, you were fit for it, and therefore were made happy: but I was unfit, and now I'm a lost woman! For the Book says, 'Whoso eateth and drinketh unworthily, eateth and drinketh damnation,' and that's what I've been doing!" The reality of her grief and fear was so apparent that for the first time a hope entered James's heart that she was quickened by the Spirit of God to feel her sins indeed.

After this, there followed in both much deep chequer work. He fell into deep trials, and after some months was restored to his former joy and to clearer establishment in the truth. She went on, showing remorse and contrition at times; then all seemed buried together through the tumults of sin in her heart. Her violent tempers, her opprobrious language when angry, her low (I do not mean immoral) habits of life contracted by her long intimacy with the very lowest dregs of society, were as so many mountains which seemed too high to be subdued. How many, who are not aware that they are themselves but as whited sepulchres, in contemplating a case like hers will join in the words,

"Shock'd at the sight we straight cry out,
Can ever God dwell here?"

For a time or two, under the same influence of pleasing men and not God, she continued to attend the Lord's Supper, but at last was thoroughly shaken out of it, and obliged by the vehemence of her convictions to quit the church in the middle of service.

I have sometimes thought that the despite she had till then shown to the convictions of the Spirit in her heart was one reason why the Lord at a later period covered her with a cloud upon this same point of the communion of His Supper, as shall be mentioned hereafter. Though He pardoned her sin, He took vengeance of her inventions.

First Meeting with Bernard Gilpin

It was about March, in the year 1843, that I unexpectedly met her myself in a poor woman's cottage, knowing neither her nor her husband. The course of conversation led me to make some allusion to the Lord's Supper, on which she broke out, and in a most feeling manner deplored her misery and danger, because she had profaned it. "O," she said, "that I were but as good as my husband! He can go to the ordinance! He can be very happy! He meets the Lord, go where he will! But I'm a lost woman." "As to your husband," I said, "I do not know him; but if he thinks he finds such wonderful things, go where he will, and in his own time and way, I fear he's a deceived man, and you are better off than he is after all." "No, sir – I'm not. He's right and I'm wrong; and you would say the same if you knew him." Her steadfastness and trembling united quite surprised me, and I began to think, "This is surely a living conviction for sin that shakes her soul." After conversation, I directed her to go to a good woman for counsel, who had formerly been exercised with temptations like hers, but had been graciously delivered from them.

I mention two favourable tokens for her at this time. The first was the reverence she thus showed for the work of God in her husband's heart, instead of being swallowed up with enmity because she had not the same in her own. The other was this: that long before the period I am now treating of, as well as afterwards to the very end of her life, her besetting sins, which had led to so detestable a course in her youth, were entirely chastened out of her, so that she loathed the very thought of them, and neither in word, demeanour, or deed, manifested the least tendency towards them. Those impure fires had, through God's mercy, entirely burnt out, and their ashes were left cold.

In a week or two, being told I was about to read (in a private house) the account of a young man, Isaac Clark, who had lately died in the Lord, she gladly went up to hear it. It pleased God powerfully to speak to her through it, and the words which had entered *his* heart entered *hers* with the same divine impression, so that ever afterwards, even to the time of her death, in every fresh conflict and every fresh deliverance, they seemed to be her watchword. "Jesus spake again unto them, saying, I am the Light of the world. He that followeth Me shall not walk in darkness, but shall have the Light of life" (John 8. 12). Immediately afterwards she began to attend my ministry, and the first sermon she heard was from Ecclesiastes 11. 9: "Know thou that for all these things God will bring thee into judgment." It made her tremble exceedingly, and shortly afterwards, relating to her husband the things she heard, he was brought to come and hear also.

I will not here say more about him, except only that after we became acquainted, I did indeed fully acknowledge that the Lord had been gracious to him, though without adding, as his poor wife had supposed I should, that she was wrong herself. It was also made clearly manifest that he found his direction from the Lord, and was humbled in heart to follow it.

The Unpardonable Sin

I urged them immediately to take a house for themselves, for up to this time they had been in a common lodging-house, which was very injurious, especially to her, inasmuch as evil communications had (already in her case) deeply corrupted good manners. They had hardly any furniture, and entered it without expectation of anything better than a lock of straw for their bed but they found that the Lord graciously prospered them, and gradually increased their substance. At first poor Alice was much delighted, and began to think that now she could control her evil tempers, and be (as the world would say) very good; but she was not suffered long to be deceived with such vanity as to suppose that she could find effectual religion, except in the path of tribulation.

I often felt convinced of her real sincerity. She fell deeply under the Word, and trembled from her very heart; yet her returns of violence, especially against her husband, who was now made increasingly tender, often brought me to fear lest my hope for her should prove vain.

Once, under this sad impression, I very seriously warned her, and said, "There are many who have deep convictions, and raise much hope for a time that they will prove to be right in the end; yet giving loose to their evil passions, they are suddenly suffered to make themselves manifest as professors without a root, so that God's people are obliged to give them up." Those words, *obliged to give them up*", sank into her very soul, and left a deep impression, from which she was not relieved till, after much earnest praying, she was surprised by some encouraging word of promise, which she mentioned to her husband, and afterwards to me, in a manner which fully restored our hope for her.

This comfort soon left her, and she sank deeper and deeper into spiritual convictions, till at last she feared exceedingly that she had sinned the unpardonable sin against the Holy Ghost. One morning, at the request of her husband, who was going out for a day or two, I called to converse with her on this subject. She expressed such tender remorse that I said, "No one who has really sinned as you fear finds such godly contrition as this"; but she could hardly receive any comfort. Soon after I had left her, as she kept on praying, the word fell, "Were you not told to read the 12th chapter of Matthew?" and suddenly the whole impression of her dream, more than ten years before, flashed upon her mind. She ran to a near neighbour and said, "Read the 12th of Matthew," who, opening the Testament, began at this verse, "All manner of sin and blasphemy shall be forgiven unto men." "O," she exclaimed, "those were the very words," and she nearly fainted away. It was the more remarkable because the end of that same verse speaks of the unpardonable sin, but this made no impression now, for all that fastened on her was the promise given to her in her dream. It entirely removed her despair, and never to the very end of her life did the fear of having sinned irremissibly ever enter into her heart again.

An Interesting Letter

Her husband did not return home till the next evening, immediately after which, as I happened to pass, I went in to see them both. She related all that had occurred, together with her dream and its effect in detaching her from light-minded professors, and all with such simplicity and deep spiritual awe, that I said to her husband, "James, there is a work in her heart which will stand." "I think so, too, sir," he replied. "She never told me this before; only now and then I have heard her mutter something indistinctly about a dream." Her state shortly after this time will be best shown by an extract from a letter she sent to her husband, then in London, November 23rd, 1843:

"I was in great distress when I went to the chapel last night. The sermon was on the 14th of Isaiah, 'The Lord will have mercy on Jacob, and will yet choose Israel.' That last part gave me comfort. But when I heard about Babylon in the same chapter, my sins came rolling over me like the great waves. It was as if I saw all my sins right before me; it has made me fear ever since. I prayed to know whether I was going to Zion or to Babylon, but the words came, 'O wretched man that I am!' Then I thought I was wretched indeed. When I got home I prayed, and thought I could never leave off, for the words came over and over and over which the Lord said to me in my dream. 'All manner of sin shall be forgiven unto *thee*.' Also those words in the account of Isaac Clark, 'Jesus spake again unto them, saying, I am the Light of the world: he that followeth Me shall not walk in darkness, but shall have the Light of life.' It made me hope I was going to Zion: not that I had got there, for the words came over several times, 'Ye must be born again,' and I cannot say that I am so now. But the promise about the sin being forgiven was very sweet, and something said, 'Why, you hardly believe God's words!' – this made me pray that I might believe them....I used to think at our old lodging-house that I could do a deal to make myself better, but now find that I can do nothing without the Lord. But last night, reading the 12th of Hebrews, the second verse, about *looking to Jesus,* came very powerfully. I felt that I had not been confessing my sins to Jesus, that He may wash them in His blood. I feel this now, I must do it. Lord, save, or I perish."

Words from the Lord

Soon after this she found much help in the application of several promises, and the manner in which these words entered, "Take up thy cross and follow Me," very sweetly confirmed in her a hope that Jesus loved her. She gave so simple an account of this that I entirely received her testimony; but being afraid lest some others in my congregation were deceived by a light spirit and satisfying themselves by words "coming" as it is called, without any effectual power, I preached a warning sermon on the subject. Alice was so terrified lest it was on account of what she had said, that on her return she dictated to her husband the following letter, which he brought to me:

" Dear Sir, I beg pardon, but I wish to ask you a few questions about what you said in your sermon, of persons who say they have clear words from the Bible, when they haven't. I thought you meant me. Now I never told you only what the Lord taught me. I never feared death till now. I am afraid the Lord will take me off in this dreadful state; then I am sure I shall perish: except the Lord will have mercy on me, and lets me seek like the poor woman (Luke 15) after the lost piece of silver. O, if I had been writing in the chapel, I could have filled a volume with my feelings. I thought you said I had a veil on my heart, which would never come off. Then I thought about the poor minister at Brighton (she had been reading a tract of Mr. Vinall's), how he was tempted, and that gave me a little hope. Then I thought, ' How can I compare my case to his? He was born again, but I'm not.' What a miserable wretch I am! O Lord, have mercy upon me! I am so uneasy I don't know what to do, or where to go. A. S."

Gospel Liberty

It was not surprising that this deep labour in the Lord was soon proved not to be in vain. It was on the 9th of January, 1844, that she could first say she was really brought clearly out. The manner of it was this. Her trouble brought her very low in body, and her feeble, unhealthy frame became almost exhausted. On Sunday, the 7th, she was unable to leave her bed, and indeed could hardly speak. I had been greatly impressed myself with these words at the administration of the Lord's Supper, "It came to pass, when Jesus was in a certain city, behold a man full of leprosy who, seeing Jesus, fell on his face, and besought Him, saying, Lord, if Thou wilt, Thou canst make me clean! And He put forth His hand and touched him, saying, I will, be thou clean!" So I went to my poor friend, and finding her, though sensible, yet unable to speak, I merely repeated those words and left her, commending her in my heart to the Lord. She afterwards acknowledged that the whole of the next day she fell right down before the Lord Jesus with these words, "Lord, if Thou wilt, Thou canst make me clean," and was so engaged till nine o'clock on the Tuesday morning, when her husband having left her, as he thought, too ill to stir, she suddenly sprang up, and going downstairs to him, said, "O, I could lie in bed no longer, for I've left all the burden of my sins there. The Lord answered me! He said, 'Though thy sins be as scarlet, they shall be white as snow.' 'I have clothed thee in the robe of My righteousness.' "

The next day, full of tenderness, awe, and love to Jesus in her spirit, she came up to me, and in stammering words made a confession of the dreadful sins of her early life. I said. "It is quite enough – now you have acknowledged this to your husband and to me, tell it to no one else. For what is the use of opening the mouths of hypocrites and Pharisees against you, and giving them fuel for their malice? It is enough that the Lord Jesus has covered you with the robe of His righteousness."

Soon after this, being greatly afflicted in body, she went into St. George's Hospital, London, for relief. While there she exceedingly prospered in spiritual things, being kept in a most earnest and humble frame, so as to find her way into the hearts and affections of all the kind friends who visited her. She would pray in the most simple manner that the Lord would direct her to such portions of His Word as should prove profitable; and in this way of proceeding found most seasonable helps. One of the most remarkable was from Job 5. 17–19, "Behold, happy is the man whom God correcteth, etc. . . . He shall deliver thee in six troubles and in seven there shall no evil touch thee." "From this last part (she said) I saw most clearly that the seventh trouble, which should not be evil to me, was the trouble of death." One day after her return, she gave a beautiful description of her enjoyment of the Lord's clear love, which she had found, after a painful intermission about an hour before I had called. The effect was so powerful that I said to her husband, "Neither you nor I have done this for her, have we? This is the Lord's work, marvellous in our eyes. We can only look on, while the Angel of the Lord does wondrously."

A Wonderful Testimony

This sweet and heavenly season, wherein the power of the enemy seemed wholly restrained, and her spirit kept entirely childlike, did not last long. Before the end of March, in consequence partly of some domestic trials, the old enemies began to lift up their heads. She had some hard but victorious fighting about this period, which proved the genuineness of the work, and in which I believe I may add, her dream was realised by faith. There had been some declension in her spirit, and fretfulness in her temper. Her husband left her for a few days on his usual business, during which time she became so much occupied with her little household matters that better things were much neglected; and one day she entirely omitted reading and praying with her husband's little niece, then newly come to live with them.

That same evening a horror of great darkness fell upon her. On which (to give her own very simple words to me) "I said, 'What's the matter with me? I'll take the Bible, and try and find out.' As I reached for the Book, the words, 'O thou hypocrite!' three times repeated, terrified me so, that I ran back, saying, 'What have I been doing? No harm, have I? The words are not for *me*.' But I soon found they *were* for me. It said, 'You live without prayer, you live without God - you do everything wrong.' I ran in to tell my neighbour of my trouble, who advised me to confess my sin; but I said, 'My heart is so hard that I cannot.' Everything seemed dry and dark. I passed the night in dreadful fear lest I should sleep, and wake in hell. Yet I had some faith at that time, and cried all night for mercy, though the words seemed to no purpose. In the morning my faith went away. My neighbour said, 'Are you better?' 'No (I said), I shall be better NO MORE' for the faith was gone away. I went back into my own house, and there cried, 'Lord, if Thou hast not pardoned me, whereas I thought before this trouble came that Thou didst pardon me, be pleased to show me my sins.' This He did. O how my sins came rolling over me! – more than ever I thought of! O how black! how many! I said, 'I am lost, and left to perish! – there can be no forgiveness for me!' So I went on crying, till I *breeded* a dreadful pain in my side, and I became very ill. My soul was worse so that from eleven to two I thought I was on the very brink of hell. I kept looking at a little loose twig on the creeper outside my window, which the wind shook as it hung by one thread: 'So (said I), am I shaken over the pit of hell, as if one puff of wind might send me there.' 'I'll send for Mr. Gilpin (thought I), and tell him that if I die he must not make a sermon to say I was the child of God, for I am the child of the devil.' Didn't it seem plain? For the devil kept putting my sins before me, and saying I should certainly perish, it was of no use my crying, I should never be heard. And I quite believed what he said.

"But about two o'clock, it was as if I saw the Lord Jesus a great way off, and the very first words He spoke were, 'Come, ye blessed of My Father,' etc. They seemed too good to take; yet they made me turn and pray and look to Him, and I found my hope grew stronger and stronger, till the words came three times, 'O woman, great is thy faith.' Now I prayed that the Lord Jesus would come closer and nearer. He did so, but the battle became very sore – it seemed to go between the Lord and the enemy; and it was as if the enemy said to the Lord, 'Touch her, and she will curse Thee to Thy face.' I cried still harder, and the Lord drew nigh and said, 'I am the Way, the Truth, and the Life. He that followeth Me shall not walk in darkness, but shall have the Light of life.' At these words the enemy gave way, he sank down and was gone. But O! what a battle it was; so that by this time my body was quite exhausted, and I had no strength left. Then it was Mr. Gilpin came in, and I could just say to him, 'I thought I was the child of hell this morning, but I find I am the child of God now – *so there's the difference!*' He said, 'Jesus says, "I am the Resurrection and the Life," ' etc. Then did the Lord draw nearer still at those blessed words, and the promises came rolling over me, the beautiful promises, more than ever my sins had done. This was the chief: 'Though your sins be as scarlet, they shall be white as snow'; also this, 'Yea, I have loved thee with an everlasting love.' I was musing that surely I could not believe; so when He came with these words, He said, 'Did not I tell thee before, "I have loved thee with an everlasting love?" ' For four days I could not speak, and for the first two the Lord kept so nigh that He would not suffer the enemy to put one bad thought into me. I lay quiet, and I looked at the twig; O, how I delighted to look at the twig then! The fever ran high, the inflammation and pain were great. I thought I should certainly die, but I was very happy. Jesus was waiting to receive me.

"O, I have seen Him on His milk-white throne! I have heard Him say, 'Come, ye blessed of My Father, inherit the kingdom prepared for you from the foundation of the world!' I shall not have one sin to answer for at the day of judgment, no, not one. Jesus has covered all!

"While yet I could not speak, Mr. Gilpin came to my bedside, and read me an account of what Mr. Dore, in London, found in his late illness. O, how it comforted me! I thought to myself, 'I don't know that dear gentleman, but my husband does, and I shall know him soon in heaven. Also I thought much of Mrs. Grimes, of this place, that she is dying in the Lord. Though I had never been able to see her, it seemed as if the likeness of her was brought to my bedside, and something said, 'Pray for her'; yes, and I did pray for her too, by the hour, and found great comfort. I find this trouble has done me good. It has made me humble and meek, to carry everything to the Lord, and not to neglect prayer. But the enemy is coming back, and tells me my prayers are no use; yet I have found help against him, and an answer from the Lord this morning, 'Be of good courage, thy sins are forgiven thee.' "

Received into Membership

Sometimes her heart sank; and this happened to be the case when the wind blew down her twig. "O! (she said to her husband) my twig is gone! my twig is gone! I fear I shall go too." Her returns were very clear and powerful. I called and read with her the 91st Psalm, and at that verse, "Thou shalt tread upon the lion and adder," etc., she replied, "That's what I'm doing now; but it's hard work though." Her illness continued some time, but on the 31st of March I found her decidedly better. On that day she repeated to me the lines of a hymn, the power of which she had that morning most clearly felt. O with what energy, as I then believed, and yet believe, truly from the Lord she spoke those words. Some of my readers will know what our feelings are when we believe that God bears witness in our hearts that the testimony of another is true. These were the words:

> "O my Jesus! Thou art mine,
> With all Thy love and power;
> I am now, and shall be Thine,
> When time shall be no more."

It was after this that I admitted her to join as a member in communion at the Lord's table. I had been afraid of doing this before; and though I most fully received her testimony, I was on one ground afraid still. For considering "the hole of the pit (as Isaiah terms it) whence she was digged", the tumultuous character of her passions, and that she was eminently one of those of whom the apostle Paul says (1 Timothy 5. 24), "Some men's sins are open beforehand, going before to judgment," I was aware that a season not only of trial, but of reproach, would probably come on. I knew not what might happen in those sifting days, when perhaps the enemy might be permitted to "come down upon her, having great wrath, knowing that he had but a short time". I warned others to expect this, but was scarcely prepared for it myself.

Blessing and Peace

I could give a long description of many trials with her, and many returns of the sweetest spiritual power of love in her heart. Yet before the summer was at an end, the plague of her fretful and violent temper began to gain ascendancy. I went one day to her house, burdened as I may say with a weight of reproof for her. It wrought kindly after a while, and not very long afterwards she was restored for a season to a clear and subdued spirit, and thanked me cordially for my reproving visit, saying. "O, how I needed it!" Soon afterwards, during one of her severe attacks of illness, she said to me, "O, Mr. Gilpin, ever since you preached three weeks ago, quoting these words, 'The children of the kingdom shall be cast into outer darkness,' I have sunk at the dreadful sound; not always without hope, but I've never come out clear. When I was taken ill this morning, I was greatly afraid. I cried, 'Let not the pit shut her mouth upon me.' I could pray for my husband at that time more than for myself. I thanked the Lord for showing him mercy, and for giving him a kind heart to nurse me tenderly. He waited on me like a child; but he could not comfort my soul, and left me in deep trouble. Since I have been alone by myself, the Lord has spoken peace. O His sweet, His beautiful voice! I knew it! He keeps telling me to come boldly; He assures me I shall not be lost; all my sweet words are coming back to me! I am waiting for the time when He will come Himself; for He is near, I know He is! Bless His name for ever!"

Another time she told me how she had persevered in prayer through much temptation, remembering her watchword, "Jesus spake *again*," etc. And while cleaning her house she had recollected how I had told her to improve such times by secret prayer, and said, "O Lord Jesus, be pleased to wash my soul as I wash these bricks: for Lord, if Thou *wilt* – if Thou wilt – Thou canst make me clean." At last the peace flowed in like a river, and this word had followed her for two days. "I have covered thee with the robe of righteousness."

Backsliding and Church Discipline

Though these seasons were multiplied, yet notwithstanding all, there came on by degrees a period of backsliding, wherein the keenness of her spiritual desires abating, she was left a more easy prey to the malice of the devil. Her falls were all of them occasioned by her violent temper; angry passions first upset her, and then, as she had formerly simply expressed it, her "faith went away". The little niece, of whom her husband had taken the charge, was continually the occasion, and often only the innocent occasion, of these falls. After some of her fits of anger, I have known her beg the child's pardon with tears, as if she had been a child herself, and entreat her to pray for her; yet all that the disciples could do was not strong enough to cast out this devil. Being very ill, about the end of August 1845, she went for several weeks into the Hertford Infirmary, and I perceived that her spiritual profiting did not appear there, as before in St. George's Hospital. The Lord in some measure fulfilled the awful threatening of His word, "My people would not hearken to My voice, and Israel would none of Me. So I gave them up to their own hearts' lusts, and they walked in their own counsels."

My grief for her was great at this time, because I saw that having thus departed from the Lord, she began gradually to lose her simplicity. Finding a lack of spiritual power, she would try and dissemble, and sometimes cloak her sin. This I often mentioned to her, and sometimes it made her tremble from her heart. I perceived, however, that after her return home, the evils continued to work, and even to gain ground. Through the encroachments of sin, her conscience was often deeply wounded, so that social prayer and spiritual conversation became painful, and sometimes she refused to join in family prayer, and instead of helping her husband, would interrupt him. Nay, sometimes her spirit seemed filled, as I may say, with curses, which she could with the greatest labour refrain from uttering; but if ever one passed her lips, she almost immediately fell down in trembling and self-reproach. Once, while things were in this sad condition, I called upon them and endeavoured to comfort her husband; and believing, as I did, that all the evil which was then working would not finally prevail, I repeated the words, "The floods have lifted up – the floods, O Lord, have lifted up their voice. The floods lift up their waves. The Lord on high is mightier–" "Ah! sir (he replied), but what shall we make of the last verse, 'Holiness becometh Thy house, O Lord, for ever'?" To which true remark I replied nothing, for I was as much confounded as he.

In the beginning of October, the evil wrought so tempestuously that she was forbidden to attend the Lord's Supper. It was a needful and a salutary measure, and she was brought to humble herself for the pride of her heart. Though she was never able after this to partake of the outward signs, yet there was a full spiritual clearing of the cloud, as will be seen. Perhaps, also, the Lord by this marked His remembrance of her former sin, when she attended the communion repeatedly, against the clearest convictions of her conscience.

A Precious Saviour

Yet, even at the worst times, it appeared now and then that the Lord had not *utterly* forsaken her. For instance, once, after being tossed by the fury of the enemy for several days, one night the Lord granted her a respite, and she lay quietly confessing her sin, expressing her self-abhorrence, and earnestly imploring mercy for a considerable time. She was not the least aware that her husband overheard the whole, and he said nothing about it. Next morning, when the storm arose afresh, he said, "How has it been with you?" "O (she replied) if I could but retain that sweet refreshment in repentance and prayer which I had last night, how blessed it would be!" Indeed several times when she refused, and that angrily, to hear him pray, she asked his leave to pray herself; and when he allowed this, he wondered at the power and pureness of the words which she uttered, her feeling confessions of sin, and fervent entreaties for mercy. She would often complain that this or that outward circumstance (for example, her husband's little niece) was the cause of the evil. "What then, (said her husband), shall I send her away?" "No (she replied), for how do I know the reason for which God appoints the trial?" She was one day lying apparently either asleep or insensible, while two persons in the room were conversing about a hymn. "I don't know it (said one); it's not in *our* book." Then poor Alice cried out, "But do you know the hymn that *is* in our book? This one, I mean, which says:

> 'Sinners can say, and none but they,
> How precious is the Saviour.' "

"Yes (replied her friend); and do you feel that now?" "Indeed I do," was her answer; while the deep power and unction with which she kept repeating the words for several days, showed that she felt them indeed. "The house was filled with the odour of the ointment."

She became increasingly ill. A complication of disorders, and, as it seems, a general derangement of all the principal vital organs, made her life a most distressing burden to her. After severe suffering for several days in November, from erisypelas and inflammation, as soon as she became a little better, I enquired how she had passed the week. She replied that she had been in exceeding great darkness for several days at first, but she had found power to abhor herself, and to repent in dust and ashes. Afterwards she had found a return of the Lord's first testimony given to her, and during five happy hours had not been able to see one sin, for the Lord's mercy covered all. Then she felt great love for the brethren, and earnestly prayed for a blessing on many.

Her dreadful enemies again made head against her, but again they were beaten back. She gave a very consistent account of the entrance and effect both of several words of encouragement and caution. The first surprised her by the love it brought with it, "Rise up, My love, My fair one, and come away." Then, when her heart fell down in deep self-abasement, it followed: "Is there no balm in Gilead? Is there no physician there? Why then is not the health of the daughter of My people recovered?" Then this followed: "Gird up the loins of your mind, be sober, and hope to the end." Lastly, this: "Watch and pray, lest ye enter into temptation." She appeared about this time almost ashamed and confounded, while mentioning the power she had felt in another word, seemingly very unbefitting her present woeful condition. "Arise, shine, for thy light is come, and the glory of the Lord is risen upon thee." I must leave my readers who can appreciate her whole case, and what soon followed, to judge whether this word was not verified.

A Letter from James Bourne

But above all, parts of the 14th chapter of Romans instructed and meekened her spirit during the intervals of her painful temptation, and were revived again and again, almost to the end of her life. This part especially: "None of us liveth to himself, and no man dieth to himself. For whether we live, we live unto the Lord; and whether we die, we die unto the Lord. Whether we live, therefore, or die, we are the Lord's." And all this, though it roused a hope which no deluge of temptation could overthrow, was yet accompanied with great awe too. I was witness how she trembled while she hoped, from these words following the above: "So then every one of us must give account of himself to God."

My friend, Mr. Bourne, after witnessing some of these changes, and observing how clearly the voice of the *new man* was heard in her, though the *old man* strove fearfully to prevail, wrote to her as follows:

"I often think of your afflictions, and trust you begin to understand that the Lord is refining you as silver, that you may be a vessel unto honour. Think it not strange concerning the fiery trial, but call to mind the condition in which the Lord first found you, as represented by the prophet Ezekiel: 'Thy father was an Amorite, and thy mother a Hittite. Thou wast cast out in the open field in the day that thou wast born. And when I passed by thee (says the Lord), and saw thee polluted in thine own blood, I said unto thee Live. I spread My skirt over thee; yea I sware unto thee and entered into a covenant with thee. I washed thee with the water of regeneration. I girded thee with the robe of My righteousness. I decked thee with the ornaments of a meek and quiet spirit and thou becamest Mine.' See, my dear friend, what the Lord had done for you, nor ever loses sight of you. Be tender towards Him; do not prove ungrateful. The adversity He calls you to pass through, He has passed through before you. This sweetly seasons the affliction. You know, as you told me, that if the earthly house of this tabernacle were dissolved, you have a building of God a house not made with hands eternal in the heavens; for in this you and I often groan through the misery and guilt we contract, and long to have this wretched mortality swallowed up of life. Remember how surely you have believed that whether living or dying you are the Lord's. Let this encourage you to have a jealous eye over your tempers, and whatever else damps this holy confidence. Pray that no evil may slip by unnoticed, but be contended against and slain. For thus shall we find watchfulness in the hour of temptation; we shall retain the blessed presence of the Lord; we shall give glory to God for His free grace richly bestowed upon such miserable offenders; and walk profitably to the church of God. Nothing grieves me more than to tarnish the character of the people of God, either as individuals or as a body; and this the Lord will sorely resent. May He bless you and your husband, that you may never forget that whether living or dying you are the Lord's.

"From your affectionate and faithful,

J.B."

Last Days

But no one, who had not witnessed it, would believe how truly it might be said of her, "Pharaoh would *hardly* let the people go." Whenever her temper had upset her, and she began to pray for pardon and grace, the temptation rose again in her heart, "How often you've prayed, and you see what it is all come to! Leave off at once." This used to perplex her beyond measure. I have seen her so beaten down with it, as if she could rise no more. So that perhaps we may say of these days of her tribulation, except they had been shortened, she could not have been saved; but because she was elect and precious, they were shortened (Matthew 24. 22).

In the beginning of January she was again admitted into the infirmary, where she declined and died. The comfort she derived from skilful and attentive nursing was very great, and tended considerably to allay the painful irritation of her feelings. She was thankful for these advantages in her extremity, and her spirit on the whole was much quieter than when she was in the infirmary before. I do not believe that she gave no occasion for reproach; for could we have expected this, during the subsiding tumult of that great storm of sin and temptation which she had been passing through for months? Nevertheless it very soon became evident, both to me and others who had long watched her, that a favourable change was going on. This, indeed, was obscured during the last week of her life, but only because of the delirium caused by the strength of her disease.

One of the first things which struck me was the quiet manner in which she told me that she had been made earnestly to pray the Lord to pardon and heal the breach which her sin had caused in the matter of the communion of the Lord's Supper. To all which prayers, she said, and they were very many, the Lord had returned one answer, and only one, "Let your light shine before men."

As for myself, I acknowledge that I felt great concern for her upon this point; and was led to expect that if, as I hoped, she was in the bond of the everlasting covenant, something marked might take place, which would clear that point spiritually, and bring her distinctly back into our hearts and affections as a sheep of Christ indeed. In this hope I was not disappointed; and will proceed to state in a few words how, notwith-standing her great weakness, I was still satisfied that "the Lord bound up this breach of His people, and healed the stroke of their wound".

Conflict and Confusion

Her strength rapidly declined during the first week in February. On the evening of the 6th, I (having been from home for several days) went to see her, together with her husband. I found her not without hope, though apparently labouring in spirit, but too ill to say much. The next morning I returned to her; she was then worse, appearing dark, confused, and unable to give any account of her hope. This, I think, was intended by the Lord to bring me down very low. I thought she was dying, and dying still under a dark cloud which her sinful outbreaks had gathered round her. I thought, surely the Lord would have dispersed this more fully, if she had been truly His; whereas it now seemed impossible that it could be so broken as to enable us to see the change.

I went to her husband, and told him that I feared she was dying, and that if he would go and sit with her for a few hours, I would return there in the afternoon. I then prayed for her with many desolate feelings. I said, "Lord, she is a poor outcast, whom it seemed to have pleased Thee to gather from the ends of the earth, and to have committed to my charge; and now, behold, her case is covered with confusion." I thought as I prayed that the Lord granted me access, and I was encouraged for myself, and encouraged also to go on praying for her.

On my return to the infirmary, her husband met me smiling, as I entered the ward. "Sir (he said), she continued in the same confusion for about half an hour after I came. I could do nothing but secretly pray, and confess her sin and my own; and while I did so, I began to get clearer and clearer. Suddenly she broke out and said, 'O! I've found Him! a precious Saviour!' and now she is clear and happy." I turned to the poor woman, and she confirmed her husband's account, very slowly getting a few words out, "Comfort ye, comfort ye My people – saith your God."

I think the exertion of speaking proved too much for her; and soon after I left her, she sank into a kind of torpor. Her husband continued for the most part sitting by her till eleven o'clock at night. Soon he found she was roused from her torpor by severe conflict. Her sins seemed set before her, and the terrors of God laid hold upon her. She could only groan and sigh. She seemed as if she was continually trying to pray and was baffled. He said, "What's the matter?" "O!" she answered, "it's too bad to tell you! I'm afraid to tell you! Destruction, destruction, this is what I was warned that I should find on my death-bed, because of my sins." She continually mentioned the name of her poor little niece, for her unkindness to whom she had been often reproved. Her husband says he was overwhelmed with trouble; the conviction of his own sins and of hers together pressed him down, till he felt himself as low as she was; and he concluded they were two wretches, too bad to be saved. He had a small and very distant hope from John 11. 22, "I know that even now, whatsoever Thou wilt ask of God, God will give it Thee." Yet this did not remove the heavy cloud, and he said, "This is the judgment of God for our sins, and nothing is able to turn it aside." He was obliged to leave her in this state.

Grace Reigning in the Prodigal

The next morning, which was Sunday, I went early to his house to ask him how he had left her. He gave me the above account with a countenance of the blackest sorrow, on which I said, "I will go down immediately to the infirmary, and see her." I found her asleep, and gently waking her, said, "Are you happy?" She said, "Yes." I said again, "You were not so yesterday evening, were you?" "No, sir (she answered), but it came in the middle of the night, 'I will arise, and go to my Father,' etc; and I did go to Him, and He met me. O, sir! it was so beautiful, I cannot tell you half."

I had scarcely left the house when the husband arrived, and continued with her till near service time. After which I went with him and another friend to see her again. Finding her very weak, I slowly repeated to her the words (from Luke 15), "I will arise," etc, till I got to the part, "Bring forth the fatted calf and kill it, and let us eat——." Here she interrupted me, adding the clause, *"And be merry."* "What (said I), are you merry?" "Yes, sir (she answered), I am." So I left her, as I may say, "eating the fatted calf."

At night she was greatly exhausted, but recovering a little strength before her husband left her, she said to him, "Jesus is the Way, the Truth, and the Life. I'm going to be with Him. I know it's not my work, not a bit! It's the Lord Jesus Christ's. *He spilt his blood for me."* Her husband read to her about the penitent thief, and she replied, "I believe that I also shall be with Him in Paradise." Feeling the utmost willingness to resign her into the Lord's hands, he said to her, "Goodbye, you have the Lord Jesus Christ with you now, and He's dearer to you than I am." She replied, "O yes, yes yes. Bless Him! bless Him!"

After this, her mind became very weak through the increasing force of the disease; and she appeared after Monday hardly sensible. At times she wandered and was violent, so as to cause the nurses much trouble, till the Friday evening, when her husband was sorely cast down, looking upon this as a fresh visitation for sin, perceiving how she tried the patience of all the kind attendants. But about nine o'clock that evening the mortal change came on, and she remained quiet, but rapidly sinking through the night. The attendants would call her insensible, but I believe she was not so; for in the morning James was able distinctly to observe the clearness and tranquillity of her spirit; all the restlessness and wildness were gone; she was just able to say that she maintained her hope, and remembered the words, "Thou shalt be with Me in Paradise." Then gradually sinking lower and lower, she expired about half an hour after midnight, February 15th, 1846, aged about 35 years.

Her husband felt very happy, to think how, where sin had abounded, grace had much more abounded. He had been cautioned not to tell his little niece suddenly, she being just in the crisis of the measles: "But (said he), sir, I could not help telling her, for I was overwhelmed with a flood of joy from these words, 'Death shall be swallowed up in victory.'"

As for myself, on the very day that she died, persuaded as I was of Christ's eternal mercy to her, I was so impressed with a sense of judgment, with which that mercy was blended, that I found what I hope to find still more abundantly, that fear which is a holy grace of the Spirit; which because it is wrought by Him, is not alone in the heart, for where He comes, there are faith, and hope, and love, as well as fear; but often the fear is made to prevail, which proves very salutary, as I then felt it to be. And I preached in consequence (it being the Lord's day) from Psalm 119. 120: "My flesh trembleth for fear of Thee, and I am afraid of Thy judgments."

Gospel Standard 1974. Originally published as one of many pamphlets that were eventually gathered together in several volumes of *Witnesses of the Truth*.

JESUS ALL – THE SINNER NOTHING

Margaret Speakman

This and the three following accounts are by Thomas Bradbury (1831-1905), for many years minister at Grove Chapel, Camberwell.

Haydock! The very mention of the name will send a thrill through many a heart. Within its bounds Jehovah's mercies and judgments have been solemnly displayed. Here, precious jewels of electing love have been found in the rough, and polished by the all-skilful Lapidary. Here, the gospel of the grace of God has been sounded forth for many a long year, and weary pilgrims on the way to glory have been refreshed and comforted. At certain times appointed by the Father, faithful ministers of Christ visited the scattered flock and dealt forth, from a Spirit-wrought experience, God's precious truth, which was blessed to the quickening, comforting and establishing of many living souls.

Here, M'Kenzie[1] keenly discerned between a fleshly and a spiritual religion, and sighed out the glory of his covenant God in suffering oneness with the Man of sorrows. Here, dear old John Kershaw traced out the evidence of regenerating grace, and spoke so well of his Master that anxious souls were encouraged and established in the faith of God's elect. Here, Collinge[2] and Sinkinson[3], from exercised hearts, dealt out in rough, unmeasured terms the painful, yet profitable experience of God's despised few. Here, the uncompromising William Parks[4] was heard at times contending earnestly for the faith once delivered to the saints. Here, the writer sojourned for seven years and nine months declaring the testimony of the Lord in weakness, in fear, and in much trembling. Here, the gospel of the grace of God is still loved by a remnant reserved according to the election of grace. Here, in the Particular Baptist Chapel, Zion's mourners find spiritual rest and sweet refreshment.

But there is a dark background to this picture. Here, Arminianism

---

[1] John M'Kenzie (c. 1800-1849) pastor at Preston, first editor of the *Gospel Standard*.
[2] Thomas Collinge (1810-1872), pastor at Bury.
[3] Thomas Sinkinson (1811-1875), pastor at Bedworth.
[4] Vicar of Openshaw, Manchester.

has oftentimes run riot, denouncing God's sovereign right to save whom He will. Here, ritualism of the grossest type, and after the most pagan fashion, has flourished under episcopal supervision. The doctrines of grace have been hated, a gracious experience despised, "the simplicity that is in Christ" ridiculed, and the necessity for the Spirit's work laughed to scorn. Here I must record the fact that with Satan's display of ritualistic idolatry in Haydock, there came God's solemn judgments in a succession of fearful mining explosions unparalleled in the history of the place.

The bringing from darkness to light of dear old Margaret Speakman is a striking illustration of the truth that God has His own way in the gathering together of His scattered people. During the summer of 1859, the writer was led to deliver a course of outdoor addresses to numerous gatherings, in which the glad tidings of great joy were declared. At first many persons, who had evidently a greater desire to exhibit themselves than to learn of Him who is meek and lowly in heart, came and escorted the preacher to his post, singing vociferously all the way. This was repeated twice or thrice, much to the annoyance of the messenger of peace until, by the sheer force of truth, they all withdrew. Man's inability and God's sovereignty were truths too humbling for these self-satisfied professors. The declaration that the Ethiopian cannot change his skin or the leopard his spots roused the offended dignity of these opposers of God's righteousness. They retired, but only to deride the doctrines of distinguishing grace. A few remained in whose hearts the fear of the Lord, which is the beginning of wisdom, was found. The great day will declare that many souls were wooed and won to a precious Christ by God the Holy Ghost, through the preached Word at these meetings near to the Old Fold, Haydock, St. Helens, Lancashire.

With the few who remained was a young man who took an active part in the Wesleyan Sunday School. He tried to teach a class of boys. Light having dawned upon his mind, he could not but speak the things which he had seen and heard. He soon discovered that Bible teaching was not wanted there. The place became at length too hot for him, and schemes were concocted to cast the erring one out of the synagogue. The time of separation arrived, and he took his leave. This step was the cause of much grief to his mother, old Margaret Speakman. Busy professors, who were interested in everybody's concerns but their own, took care to poison the old woman's mind with base insinuations and false accusations concerning her son, and *the dreadful perverter of his faith*. She was cautioned not to allow such a dangerous man into her house; but He who taketh the wise in their own craftiness ordered matters otherwise.

During the summer of 1860, I was asked to call and see old Margaret, who was very ill. On Saturday, July 28th, my feet were directed to the Old Smithies, a cluster of cottages bearing that name because the buildings had formerly been used as such, in connection with an adjoining coal pit. They were situated in a very secluded spot, surrounded with green fields and game preserves. It was a beautiful summer's day. Heaven seemed to smile upon this lower world, which is so marred with that fearful plague-spot, *sin.*

With conflicting thoughts I rambled on, wondering what the issue would be, and begging of the Lord to go before me in the way. When I arrived at the place, the poor old creature was engaged in a little household work as she sat by the fire. I informed her of the nature of my visit, which was to read God's blessed Word, and converse a little on the best of all subjects – the love of God in Christ Jesus seeking and saving sinners. She welcomed me heartily. The name which is above every name, not mine, had been announced to her. I sat down beside her, and after a few words of greeting, I read John 5. 24-29. The Lord enabled me to speak very plainly and affectionately to her on the preciousness of Jesus' Word, which is life and love to poor broken-hearted sinners. It speaks of a perfect, glorious righteousness wrought for the unworthy, and reveals to them a fountain of atoning blood to cleanse them from all guilt and uncleanness. It declares, in unmistakable terms, the everlasting and unchanging security of all the children of God.

As she listened to these blessed truths, she seemed riveted to her chair. I paused a moment. She asked:

"Are you Mr. Bradbury?"

"That is my name," I replied.

She seemed not a little confused for a moment or two, and then stammered out:

"Why, those Methodists have been here many a time warning me against you. They said you were leading our Will astray, and making him very unsettled and discontented. I was vexed when he came here and *seemed to say* that only him and a few more could be saved. They begged of me not to let you come here, for they said you would do me no good. Well, if it is with this sort of talk that you unsettle the people, I hope you will come here as oft as you can. I am sure they have belied you."

"Well, never mind them," I replied. "God will look after them. Verily they have their reward! My business this morning is not with, or concerning them, but with you as a poor sinner, and the Lord Jesus Christ as a perfect Saviour."

"Yes, I see how it is you vex people. You make it out that Jesus does everything, and that we have nothing to do to be saved."

"I simply state God's truth, that Jesus saves His people from their sins. Those who object to this must have very bad memories, for they sing with their lips, though their hearts cannot be very much engaged with the words:

' Not the labour of my hands
Can fulfil Thy law's demands;
Could my zeal no respite know,
Could my tears for ever flow,
All for sin could not atone –
Thou must save, and Thou alone.'

But why should we trouble ourselves about them? The truth we sometimes sing holds good,

' None but Jesus
Can do helpless sinners good.'

He is precious to them, and they are precious to Him."

"Well, I hope the Lord may forgive them," she said. "They have spoken ill of you without occasion. What they said so turned my mind against you that I was determined you should never come into my house; but you are here, and I am so glad the Lord has sent you."

"Why are you glad?" I enquired.

"Because you speak nothing but the Bible," she replied. "I am sure it is comforting – I wish I knew more of it. One that speaks so well of Jesus, and gives Him the first place, must be right."

After some further conversation we knelt before our Father's throne, and commended each other to His kind care and keeping.

It is delightful for me to ponder over her subsequent history. Jesus, in His love and faithfulness, was very precious to her. The good old generous wine of the covenant cheered and revived her soul. It was her privilege once after this to enjoy the worship of God in the assembly of His people. The faithful William Parks was preaching in the Baptist Chapel at the works, when she managed with the aid of a stick to creep so far. Her heart rejoiced as she heard that valiant champion of the truth of God's discriminating and distinguishing mercy vindicate the honour of his Lord and Master. Many times afterward she referred to that gathering, and always with pleasure and delight. The valiant William of Openshaw had a warm place in the old woman's affections.

She had a longing desire oftentimes to have done with the world, and to cast aside her frail mortality. Humble, waiting resignation to God's will was graciously vouchsafed to her. The first verse of Toplady's sweet hymn was laid upon her heart, and was very precious to her:

"A debtor to mercy alone,
Of covenant mercy I sing;
Nor fear, with Thy righteousness on,
My person and offerings to bring.
The terrors of law and of God
With me can have nothing to do;
My Saviour's obedience and blood
Hide all my transgressions from view."

The following visit paid to her in company with an old friend faintly illustrates the happy state of this poor, infirm, old woman. She was, as usual, sitting by the fire. I addressed her as follows:

"Good morning, Mrs. Speakman. I have come to see you once more, and brought a friend with me."

"Come in. You know I am always glad to see you. You cannot come too oft."

My friend conversed with her for some time, and then read the first three verses of 1 John 3, and said:

"Now, if some poor anxious sinner were to ask you what he must do to be saved, what would you tell him?"

"I would tell him to trust simply in the Lord Jesus Christ," she answered.

"So, then, you know something about salvation by Him?"

"Ay, bless Him! I'm but a poor, helpless sinner; but I find Him all-sufficient."

"Well, the Lord be thanked for that. Now, how long have you been in the enjoyment of this?"

"Why, it will be three or four months."

"And how might it come about?"

"Well, I used to say my prayers, and I tried my best to get right; but there was always something wanting. I was very uneasy, and did not know what to do. I was in this state when Mr. B. called and read and explained the Bible to me. I was eased of my burden then. It was the sweetest time of my life."

"Well, Mrs. Speakman, you *are* a happy woman."

"Yes. I feel happy in my God and Saviour, and this makes me content with whatever He may place upon me."

We knelt, where the living members of the mystical body of Christ hold sweet fellowship — where the confession of sin and failure is made to a merciful High Priest — where the tale of sorrow and temptation is poured into His ear — and, where a precious Jesus blesses "His own" with the sweet assurance of His tender regard for them, and His unchanging affection toward them. Thanksgiving was rendered to the God of all grace for His tender mercy revealed in dear old Margaret. Supplication was made for the continuance of that grace which preserves from Satan's wiles, and carries the soul safe through every conflict, trial and perplexity to the everlasting kingdom of our Lord and Saviour Jesus Christ. On taking our leave of her, she shook us warmly by the hand, saying: "Good-bye. God bless you. God be with you."

Dear old soul, toward the close of her mortal existence her sufferings were severe, but she found sweet composure in the tender sympathies of the Man of sorrows and acquainted with grief. The merciful and faithful High Priest was with her in all her afflictions and temptations, and the suffering members of Christ around her knew her as a companion in tribulation.

It was on Thursday, November 28th, 1861, she left this vale of tears for the distant hills of everlasting peace and glory. Late in the evening she sent for me. Burdened with a sense of my utter unworthiness to enjoy the company of a sister of my Lord, and nervous with the consciousness of my perfect inability to speak one word of comfort home to her heart without the gracious power of the Comforter, I at once set off to her house. She had evidently entered the dark river running between corruption and glory. Perfectly conscious, she was able to converse freely, but faintly. She expressed a feeling of awe at the prospect of a solemn eternity, but her confiding trust in death's Destroyer was unshaken. With a trembling spirit I read part of Isaiah 43 and inwardly begged of the Lord to comfort and encourage her with the precious promises contained therein.

As I thus read of the Lord's covenant faithfulness, she smiled, and thanks and adoration ascended from her glowing heart to the God and Father of all her mercies for the bestowal of His love to one who felt herself so undeserving. The Saviour's gracious presence was vouchsafed to her. She was greatly refreshed with the enjoyment of that covenant love and affection which none but Jesus by His blessed Spirit can make known to waiting, longing souls. In the hearing of all in the house, she said:

"I am dying; but, with good hope through grace — all through your words — which have always been — Jesus all — the sinner nothing."

The power of Jesus' precious name melted our hearts into felt oneness, while our knees were bent in reverential worship before the throne of the heavenly grace. With a heart swelling with emotion I commended her to the rich grace of a precious Christ – the sweet love of a tender Father – and the strong consolation of the never-failing Comforter. Before the night was past, her ransomed spirit was freed from its frail but burdensome tenement, and the glories of heaven's bright morning without clouds burst upon her enraptured view.

Of dear old Margaret Speakman I can say with confidence, Jesus bought her! Jesus sought her! Jesus taught her!

> "When gloomy death, in dread array,
> Appears to call the saint away,
>   Faith looks beyond the flood;
> And when the soul to march prepares,
> Good hope sends out her fervent prayers,
>   And dies in peace with God."

Gospel Standard 1993.

THE LOST SHEEP FOUND

Sarah Hatton

By Thomas Bradbury.

Edge Green is a little hamlet, situated a few miles to the south of Wigan, and belongs to the firm of Richard Evans and Co., the extensive coal proprietors, of Haydock, near St. Helen's, Lancashire. In the spring of 1859, I first visited Edge Green. To the cottages of the people the gospel of the ever-blessed God was taken. A cottage meeting, with exposition of God's Word, was held weekly, and the precious truths of a covenant salvation for a covenant people met with the cordial hatred of the majority of the inhabitants. Yet a goodly number were found who, through the teaching which is from above, bowed not to the idol of human merit.

I generally found time during my weekly visit to step into the cleanest cottage in the vicinity. Here lived old Sarah Hatton. I always felt interested in her company. There was something so guileless and simple about her which won my affection and esteem. She was never ashamed to own and acknowledge her ignorance. Invariably she paid marked respect to the reading of God's Word, but remained totally destitute of the knowledge of that saving grace which abounds by Jesus Christ. Yet, though she knew Him not, she was well known to her covenant God and Father, who, in pure electing love before all worlds, gave to her a place and a name in His house better than of sons and of daughters.

During the long period of eighty-six years, she lived and knew not Jesus but in name. To hear of her total depravity and utter helplessness was news indeed to her, but to be stripped of every rag of her own fancied righteousness was painful in the extreme. How could it be otherwise? Her character was highly moral and, though poor, she was greatly respected by all who knew her. She was not what the world or deluded Pharisees would call a sinner, and now to be told that her righteousnesses were as filthy rags perfectly overwhelmed her. Many times, when I left the house, she expressed a hope that I might never call to see her again. But God's all-wise pre-determination could not be frustrated. This jewel in the rough must be polished, however painful the process.

> "Far off, depraved, and prone to stray,
> But they shall surely come;
> For covenant love marks out the way,
> And brings the outcast home."

The time due for Jehovah the Spirit to reveal a precious Christ in her at length arrived. I well remember visiting her in the afternoon of Thursday, July 28th, 1859. More than ordinary interest was manifested by her. Half smilingly, but with an expression of bewilderment in her countenance, she received me. I had scarcely entered the house when she said, "You have come to see us once more. You will make a prayer for me?"

These words she repeated three or four times.

Having taken a seat, I drew my Bible from my pocket, when she made as though she would have knelt down. I asked her to sit still.

"Are you not going to pray for me?" she asked, apparently greatly surprised.

"No," I answered. "We will see first what God may say to us in His Word, and then perhaps we shall be in a better state of mind to pray to Him."

I opened my Bible, when my mind was directed to the 23rd Psalm, which I read for her. When I had finished reading, I said, "David was one of those who could say, 'We are His people, and the sheep of His pasture.' What a mercy it must be to know that we are His sheep, and He our Shepherd!"

"Eh, mester! I wish I was fit for that."

"Fit! What do you mean by being fit?" I asked.

"Why," she answered with some little hesitation, "I am not good enough yet."

"Good enough, you never will be. Bad enough, you may be."

"Mester, you fricken (frighten) me."

"If God's truth frightens you," I replied, "I can assure you I am not sorry."

"If I am not to make myself better, how is it then?" she inquired, trembling in every limb.

I answered, "Let us see what God's Word says. David expresses his experience in these things thus – 'I have gone astray like a lost sheep; seek Thy servant.' Isaiah says - 'All we like sheep have gone astray.' Peter says – 'Ye were as sheep going astray.' Now, when a sheep goes astray, can it find its way back?"

"No, that it cannot: for there's nothing so silly as a sheep," she answered.

"Well, then, do you not see that Christ's sheep have this mark upon them – they have gone astray? The Lord Himself says, 'My people have been lost sheep.' How often have we confessed with our lips, 'We have erred and strayed from Thy ways like lost sheep. We have followed too much the devices and desires of our own hearts. We have offended against Thy holy laws. We have left undone those things which we ought to have done; and we have done those things which we ought not to have done; and there is no health in us.' * Now, then, do you believe this is all true concerning you?"

"Mester, you make me tremble!"

"Trembling at God's Word is a blessed evidence of being one of Christ's sheep."

"Eh, mester, I am a great sinner"

"Jesus Christ came into the world to save such. He says, 'I am not come to call the righteous, but sinners to repentance.'"

The poor old woman was silent. Her soul was troubled within her. Tears burst from her eyes, and ran copiously down her furrowed cheeks. I continued: "I am glad to hear you own that you are a great sinner. To feel the burden of sin, and hate it, can only be produced by the Holy Spirit of God. It is His to convince of sin. 'Sin is the transgression of the law.' God has declared concerning those who break His law, that they are cursed. Listen to Galatians 3. 10: 'As many as are of the works of the law are under the curse; for it is written, Cursed is everyone that continueth not in all things which are written in the book of the law to do them.' You see from this, that being accursed creatures – having sinned against God in thought, word and deed – His law stands dead against us, and curses us to our face. This law in the hands of the good Spirit of God shows poor sinners the painful truth that they cannot make themselves better. It reveals the deadly state of our nature and works, and that iniquity, which is our nature, like the wind, takes us still farther and farther away from God. By nature we can do nothing but sin."

"If that's it, what must I do then?"

"Nothing," was my reply.

With earnest anxiety pictured in her face, she exclaimed, "Then my poor soul must be lost forever. Musn't I pray?"

"If you are truly anxious after your soul's welfare you cannot help

---

* Part of the prayer book service which was said each Lord's day morning in the Church of England.

praying, can you?"

"No. I do pray. But you know I am very ignorant."

"Well, my dear old friend, do not think me merely inquisitive when I ask you, What kind of prayers do you offer to God?"

For a moment or so she hesitated, and then exclaimed, "Why, 'Our Father', th' 'I belief', and th' Ten Commandments."

I could scarcely suppress a smile; but remembering that I might be dealing with one of the lambs of Christ's flock, I observed. "Why, you read your own death warrant and call that praying."

"My own death warrant!" she exclaimed: "I do not understand you. How do you make that out?"

"May the Lord enable me to make the matter plain to you."

"Amen," she responded fervently.

"The Ten Commandments form God's holy law, which is binding upon you and me. It says, 'Obey Me perfectly; love Me above everything, or you are lost if you fail in the least.'"

"Eh dear! But that's hard!"

"Ay, you may be sure of that. It is hard indeed when we find that we have broken and disobeyed it in every part; and look at it in whatever way we will, it does nothing but curse and condemn. The law, contained in the Ten Commandments, is like an angry creditor; its demands must be met and answered or to the prison-house of hell we must go."

"Then we're all lost!"

"If you and I know that, we are among the favoured number, 'For the Son of Man came to seek and to save that which is lost.' Jesus says, 'I am not sent but to the lost sheep of the house of Israel.' Lost ones the good Shepherd seeks. Lost ones He finds. He tells them by His Word and Spirit that He endured the hell which they deserved; that He put away all their sins when He suffered on Calvary's cross; that He obeyed God's righteous law for them, and that His obedience is 'unto all and upon all them that believe'. He invites all such to confide, or trust in Him. He encourages them with the sweet assurance that He will see them safe through every trial, trouble and perplexity, and bring them safe home to heaven, washed from all sin in His precious blood, and in His righteousness they stand unblameable and unreproveable. Saved and safe they are in Jesus."

She stared! Her poor frame quivered.

"Convinced, and pierced through and through,
She thought herself the sinner chief;
And conscious of her mighty woe,

> Perceived at length her unbelief;
> Good creeds had stocked her head around,
> But in her heart no faith was found."

At length she found vent in the following words: "Then I've been making a mistake all the days of my life! I always thought I should make myself better by praying, and doing good things, and then the Lord would save me!"

"Ay, ay, you are not alone there. But God's ways are not as our ways. We do good to those who are kindly disposed toward us; but God does good to those who have done nothing but sin against Him. Listen to what His Word says: 'God commendeth His love toward us, in that, while we were yet sinners, Christ died for us.' 'When we were enemies, we were reconciled to God by the death of His Son.' 'But God, who is rich in mercy, for His great love wherewith He loved us, even when we were dead in sins, hath quickened us together with Christ.' Jesus has done all. He has left nothing for us to do, but to enter into His rest. The Father is satisfied with what He has done for His sheep; ay, and bless your life, He is satisfied, and delighted, with every poor, lost, sinful sheep that He sees drawn to a precious Christ by His good Spirit. O! how sweet is the Shepherd's voice to such: 'Come unto Me, all ye that labour and are heavy laden, and I will give you rest.' And then He says, 'All that the Father giveth Me shall come to Me; and him that cometh unto Me I will in no wise cast out.'

"Eh dear, mester! how different it all seems now! I feel that I could trust such a good Shepherd for everything. I didn't see that I was altogether lost before. I feel He has found me, a poor, lost sheep. You will pray with me now, won't you?"

Poor dear old creature, how her tears of joy and gratitude fell on her lap as she ran over these last words, forcibly reminding me of the word of the Lord by Jeremiah: "They shall come with weeping, and with supplications will I lead them: I will cause them to walk by the rivers of waters in a straight way, wherein they shall not stumble; for I am a Father to Israel, and Ephraim is My firstborn."

At her request, we knelt before our Father's throne to ask His blessing on the reading of His Word and the conversation we had held together. I felt my very soul drawn out to God for her. Her subsequent history (short as it was) proved that our prayers were registered in heaven. I left, promising to call and see her whenever I visited the Green.

Many were the precious seasons I had the privilege of enjoying in her company. Jesus' Person, love, blood and righteousness became more endeared to me through the artless confidence manifested by this dear old saint. At each succeeding visit she would ask me to clear up some difficulty which had troubled her mind. One afternoon, as I sat with her, conversing on the goodness and grace of the Lord to our souls, a neighbour woman came in, who exhibited great surprise when she heard that God would not notice her because of her prayers. Old Sarah spied her opportunity and exclaimed, "Eh, wench, and I was puzzled too once; but I see through it all now. It's what Jesus has done for us that makes it how God listens to us when we pray to Him."

I never met with one of a more teachable disposition. She continued to the last as a little child desiring the sincere milk of the Word.

On Christmas Day 1860 I called to see her. An experienced teacher and visitor to the poor accompanied me, to whom I said, "This is the oldest woman you have seen today."

He responded to my remark in speaking to Sarah thus. "I knew an old man who, when inquiries were made concerning his age, invariably asked, 'What life?' Now, how long may you have known Jesus?"

"Not long," she replied. "Before I came here, I used to go to a retired place and fall down on my knees, and pray for God to take me to some place where I could see no sin, and where I could be quiet and prepare for a better world. God heard my prayer and brought me here. Soon after, He sent Mr. B., and eh, how he frickened (frightened) me. He told me that all my good works would never do anything toward getting me to heaven. My prayers, he said, were good for nothing for that."

"All your props were being knocked from under you," said my companion, smiling.

"Ay, they were," said she. "Well, after he had come several times, I began to understand him better – I could see that Jesus had done all for me. He put away all my sins. He shed His precious blood for me and He's promised to see me safe all through. Eh, what a mercy that He should so think of me!"

"Well, if I were to ask you the question Jesus asked the Jews, 'What think ye of Christ?' what would you say?"

"Say!" she exclaimed; "why, I should say, I think well of Him. There is nothing in this world I would wish for beside Him. Eh! I feel if I had Him here I could clasp Him to my breast, like a mother does her baby."

As she thus dealt out the fulness of her heart concerning her love to a dear Redeemer, big tears rolled down her wrinkled countenance, which was beaming with joy.

During the last few months of her mortal life, she ripened fast for the kingdom above. Often, when in great pain, she would cry out, "Precious Jesus! What is this to what Thou didst suffer for me? Blessed Jesus!"

One day, as I sat by her bedside reading the blessed Book, and speaking of the dying words of Jesus – "It is finished" – she burst out in a strain of rapturous joy which surprised me, as she exclaimed, "One word from the lips of Jesus to my poor soul is worth more than bags of gold."

As I read for her John 10. 27-29, she said, "These are abiding words, burnt in."

Sometimes Satan assailed her very fiercely. She would complain of darkness, but never of indifference. The sensible absence of that Blessed One whom her soul loved was grievous indeed. But Satan's assaults were never of long duration. Good news from the far country soon revived her drooping spirits, and the communications of the ever-blessed Spirit cheered her on her wilderness journey.

On one occasion, after a night of conflict, she raised her failing eyes towards heaven, and cried, "Blessed Saviour! I would not part with Thee for a thousand worlds! Thou hast provided for me all my life long, a poor. helpless, unworthy sinner. Jesus! I would never offend Thee! I shall see Him when I get to His kingdom, shan't I, Mr. B.?"

I could scarcely answer. Loving, hallowed sympathy was truly experienced. The real communion of saints was sweetly enjoyed. I was humbled to the very dust with the sense of the coldness of my love to Jesus, in comparison with hers. Here was love without any creature effort. The spontaneous outburst of the inward movings of the Comforter, the genuine production of God the Holy Ghost. "We love Him, because He first loved us."

The day the summons descended from heaven for her departure "from these lower scenes of night", she called her daughter Hannah to her bedside, and faintly whispered, "Precious Jesus! Blessed Jesus!"

Then, in a louder tone, she cried, "O death, where is thy sting? O grave, where is thy victory?"

And when she had said this, she fell asleep.

The following is the inscription on the gravestone of this dear child of God in the churchyard of St. Thomas-the-Apostle, Ashton-in-Makerfield:

IN MEMORY OF
SARAH HATTON
Who entered into the joy of her Lord, March 8th 1862,
Aged 89 years.

Gospel Standard 1993.

"A QUEER SORT OF AN OWD BODY"

Peggy Greenall

By Thomas Bradbury.

Blackbrook, Haydock, near St. Helens, Lancashire, will not soon be forgotten. Our outdoor meetings and cottage gatherings were owned and blessed of God, and many were the sweet sessions of spiritual refreshing vouchsafed to the gathered ones in the cottage of old Jemmy Atherton. Here sinners were born again, and weary pilgrims found rest and refreshment by the way. In the contemplation of these never-to-be-forgotten times, my spirit sings with dear old John Kent:

> "O! bless'd devotion! thus to meet,
> And spread our woes at His dear feet;
> Call Him our own, in ties of blood,
> And hold sweet fellowship with God."

One evening I noticed a strange woman among the little cluster who were gathered together to hear something more of Him whom their souls loved. She paid marked attention, and was often in tears. After the service was over, and the people had departed to their homes, I said to dear old Jemmy, "Who was that old woman sitting next to the door at the meeting tonight?"

"Why, don't yo' know? It's owd Peggy Greeno'. Hoo [she] lives down by th' slitting mill — hoo towd me hoo'd be coming — I was reet glad to see her. Hoo's *a queer sort of an owd body.*"

"In what way is she queer?"

"O, in mony a way. Why, if yo'll just look at her, yo'll see what a strong bony woman hoo is. Hoo'll work with onny man at loading coal carts, and labouring about th' boats."

"Is that all in which she is queer?"

"O no - hoo's been fond of drink, and hasn't ta'en care of hersel'; but hoo's been steadier lately. I was walking down by th' canal t'other neet, an' hoo was theere — we had a bit of talk about better things — I'm sure th' owd lass knows something o' th' plague of her own heart."

"Why do you think so?"

"Well, hoo complained reetly about her sinfulness, and said hoo thowt hoo should never mend while hoo was i' th' flesh. Hoo said th' only hope hoo'd got was that salvation is aw [all] of grace; and if it isn't, it'll be aw up wi' her."

"How did she learn that?"

"Why, yo' know, God teaches His people onny way He likes. A good many years ago hoo went up and down hearing gospel preachers. Hoo was reetly fond of hearing Nunn* when he came down from Manchester to preach at Billinge Church. Hoo cannot do with Arminian stuff. God has some queer uns in His family, an' I do believe hoo's one of His."

"I am glad to hear you say so - she listened very attentively tonight."

"Hoo did - yo' may be sure hoo'd miss nowt — her eyes were *weet* more than once."

"I must call and see her one of these days."

"Do - hoo'll be reet glad to see yo'."

In fulfilment of my promise I called to see her. She was at home, and, upon seeing me said, "Come in; we owt to spare a bit of time when the Lord sends us owt that's good."

"But His Word says, 'There is none good but one, that is, God.'"

"Well, well, you needn't be so sharp; if there is none good, the Lord sends His good news, an' th' good things of His kingdom, in earthen vessels - owd mugs — and thuse cracked sometimes. You know Samson's water was good if it did come out o' th' jawbone of a jackass."

This was said with a seriousness and gravity which commended the old woman and her saying to my heart. I thought of the description friend Atherton had given of her, for she appeared in deed and truth *"a queer sort of an owd body"*. She was a woman of deep feeling, while she expressed herself in quaint but not foolish language.

What a lesson is to be learned from old Peggy's comparisons — the treasures of eternal life and love sent in *"owd cracked mugs"*. Those who do business in deep waters for the good of the tried and afflicted children of God, know well the force of this quaint simile. "We have this treasure in earthen vessels, that the excellency of the power may be of God and not of us."

On another occasion, as we sat chatting on the truths of God's Word, the imputed righteousness of Christ became the subject of conversation. She was patching an old threadbare coat, at which she looked intently for a moment or two; then, referring to the robe of Christ's righteousness, she

---

* William Nunn, minister of St Clements's, Manchester, a friend of William Gadsby.

exclaimed, "I say, there's no takkin' th' nap off that coat."

I laughed, and yet my heart was in no laughing mood. The truth, which above all others had been made exceedingly precious to my soul, was brought out with a reality, clearness and fulness I did not anticipate. "*That coat!*" The robe of Jesus' righteousness, which excels in glory, beauty, purity and splendour the shining garments of the seraphic host – the spotless obedience of the church's Husband and Surety – the God-Man's unremitting, unvarying conformity to Jehovah's law, imputed to poor bankrupt sinners. What a glorious righteousness! The old woman's words, "*There's no takkin' th' nap off that coat,*" forcibly reminds one of that sweet verse by the Moravian Count Zinzendorf:

> "This spotless robe the same appears,
> When ruined nature sinks in years;
> No age can change its glorious hue;
> The robe of Christ is ever new."

A year or more elapsed, when one evening old Peggy was in her usual place at the week-night meeting in Jemmy Atherton's cottage. The word of the Lord was sent from Zech. 2. 5: "For I, saith the Lord, will be unto her a wall of fire round about, and will be the glory in the midst of her." Dear old soul, she seemed to dwell in the land of Beulah that night. On passing away to her home, she shook me warmly by the hand, and said with a joyous chuckle, "The God of love is a wall of fire round about His people, to warm, cheer and comfort them; and if the devil gets too near, he'll be sure to get his nose burnt."

A keen insight into divine mysteries appeared to be given to her. How well she understood that Satan, in all his schemes and contrivances, is wholly at God's control! Satan has wonderful power; but it is all kept in check by Zion's King and Lord.

Not many days after I called to see her, and during a short conversation on the Lord being the defence and protection of His people, she quaintly observed, "*No! Neither death nor devil can ever find a gap in that hedge.*" A few days before old Peggy left these lower scenes of night for the land which sin can never defile, I went to see her. She lay in bed, unable to rise, and upon my entering her room, said with surprise, "And have you come all this way to see *me?* Eh dear! Why, what am I? Nowt but a heap o' rubbish; and yet God is so good, He not only comes *His self,* but He sends you, with a word or two of comfort for a poor body."

"He has sent me, no doubt; but it is more than I can do to speak words of comfort to your poor sinking soul."

"Nay – you musn't say that – I don't think my soul is sinking; the body is, and if it wasn't for grace, *free grace,* both body and soul would sink into hell. These folk about me want to bring some of those shouting Arminians to pray for me, but I will not have 'em – they'd only torment me with their rant. You know, *salvation reet and square at both ends'll only do for me.* Eh, I cannot tell you how glad I am to see you!"

I read for her the latter part of Romans 8: "Who shall lay anything to the charge of God's elect?" to the end: "For I am persuaded, that neither death, nor life, nor angels, nor principalities, nor powers, nor things present, nor things to come, nor height, nor depth, nor any other creature, shall be able to separate us from the love of God, which is in Christ Jesus our Lord."

When I had finished, she said. "That'll do. Paul's salvation was like David's, in a 'covenant ordered in all things and sure'. You see we're all o' one mind. It begins, first by God the Father electing whom He will, then God the Son redeems 'em, then God the Holy Spirit quickens 'em and keeps 'em alive, till they're aw safe i' heaven. That's my hope. I've no other."

I prayed by her bedside, and felt my heart drawn within the veil as she fervently responded to the petitions poured out on her behalf. No more after this did I see this stranger and pilgrim upon earth. She was in deed and in truth *"a queer sort of an owd body"*; the world knew her not, and very few were privileged to know her *in the Lord.* My dear departed friend Atherton was often refreshed by her godly conversation, and spoke to me many times of the deep work of grace in her heart, which appeared from the confessions of her mouth.

God's people are *queer,* odd, strange, peculiar, in the world's estimation. Queer bodies Jehovah's elect and redeemed ones are. They cannot enjoy themselves as others do. Why should they? But they can sing,

"Saviour, if of Zion's city
    I, through grace, a member am,
Let the world deride or pity,
    I will glory in Thy name!
Fading is the worldling's pleasure,
    All his boasted pomp and show;
Solid joys and lasting treasure
    None but Zion's children know."

OUT OF THE HORRIBLE PIT

Ann Simm

By *Thomas Bradbury.*

The subject of this narrative was for over thirty years buried as a jewel in the rough, beneath the mire and clay and rubbish of a hollow, shallow profession of religion. Stuck up and self-conceited she was, because the clergyman of the parish noticed her, and her voice blended with others in the parish choir during the appointed services. But He, who had marked her as His own, wrought effectually in bringing down her high looks and staining the pride of her glory.

During the month of July 1859, the Lord visited her with a very severe mental and spiritual affliction, which can be best described from notes taken down at the time.

On Sunday, July 24th the writer's mind was directed to a cluster of houses called North Boston, in the township of Haydock, near St. Helens, Lancashire. Groups of men idled away their time during the whole of those precious days which God has given to His church for hallowed intercourse and communion with Himself. I was moved to visit that part and drop a word of warning; speak, as opportunity served, to those careless ones – those home heathen – "the unsearchable riches of Christ". During the forenoon, while I was thus occupied, two women called at my house and left a request with my wife that I would go and see a woman who was given up to despair. They observed at the time that she roamed about the house in a distracted state, crying, "I am lost! I am damned! The devil has me captive at his will!"

In the afternoon, according to an appointment I had made in the morning, an open-air meeting was held in the lane, when I was enabled to deliver my Master's message from Psalm 130. 1–4. After the meeting was over, acting upon the information I had received, I set off to see this strange woman. When I arrived at the house, I found the women had not exaggerated her case; the poor creature was upstairs, moaning piteously. Hearing me in the house, she descended. As she came near, her low, plaintive wail of, "I am lost," produced a very solemn impression upon my mind. When she appeared, what a sight met my gaze! A perfect picture of misery and wretchedness! Wildness darted from her eyes! Despair was stamped upon every lineament of her countenance! Her hair flowed loosely over her shoulders, and with scarcely clothing sufficient to cover her trembling limbs, she stood before me; she was alone. I at once retired, and at my request, two neighbour women – the same who had called at my house in the morning – went in and clothed her. Upon my re-entering the house, she almost cried out, "O! I am so glad you have come."

I took my seat beside her, and said, "Well, my dear woman, why have you sent for me?"

She wrung her hands in bitter anguish and exclaimed, with a pungency which made my very flesh creep, "O dear! O dear! I am a lost woman! I am damned! The devil has me now!"

Seeing the poor woman in such a condition, I felt bewildered – I was a fool indeed. From a sense of my perfect incompetency to deal with this poor creature's case, and knowing that

"None but Jesus
Can do helpless sinners good,"

I cried inwardly, "Lord, who is sufficient for these things? Speak to the heart of this poor sinner. Enable me to shew this transgressor Thy way, that she may be converted unto Thee." In the strength of that sufficiency which is of God, I stammered out, "Well, my dear woman, I am *very glad* to hear it."

Poor soul! She was quite shocked, and completely overcome with astonishment. At length she said, "Well, that's a settler. The parson was here this week; he told me to pray. I told him I couldn't, and he said I was a very wicked woman. I screamed out, and told him I knew that a great deal better than he could tell me. He could make nothing of me, and he left. Then some *'Methodys'* came, and they gave me more to do than I was able, and, I think, much more than *they* could do *gradely* (properly). They left me a great deal worse in my mind than they found me. But this *bangs* all. You are very glad to see me in this state, are you?"

"I *am* very glad whenever I hear a poor sinner, like myself, coming to a just sense of her true character before God," I answered.

"What do you mean?" she anxiously enquired.

"I mean that you and I, and every other sinner by nature, are lost, ruined and under the curse. The devil leads us all captive at his will; and until God the Holy Ghost opens our eyes and convinces us of our sinful state, we are the children of wrath; we are not only led captive, but we are the devil's willing captives.'"

"Well, well!" she exclaimed, "*that* is true. For I have been his willing captive long enough."

"Then you are not his captive willingly now?"

"No, I am not," she replied; "but there is no mercy for me!"

"Who told you that?"

With some little hesitancy, she answered, "Why, my conscience – my heart."

"But God says, 'The heart is deceitful above all things, and desperately wicked; who can know it?' So you have evidently been believing *that*, which can do nothing else but deceive you."

"O, but all my thoughts haunt me, and tell me that it is so!"

"But God tells us 'that every imagination of the thoughts of the heart are only evil continually.' "

"Well, well!" she cried, "I cannot get it out of my head that I am lost. There's no mercy for me!"

"For you to say you are lost is perfectly right. You can find something about that in God's Word, but you cannot find there is no mercy for you. On the contrary, we read, 'The Son of man is come to seek and to save that which was lost.' Would you allow me to ask, Is there anything particular which has caused you all this trouble?"

"It's because I feel I am a sinner – a great sinner – a lost sinner!" she replied.

"But is it some particular sin you have committed?" I inquired. Here her countenance indicated deep mental anxiety.

She replied, "Eh, mester! It's because I have sinned against God, and nobody else, and He knows all about it."

"David, the man after God's own heart, was like you, for he says, 'If Thou, Lord, shouldest mark iniquity, O Lord, who shall stand?' 'Against Thee, Thee only, have I sinned, and done this evil in Thy sight.' He felt, as you do, that left to himself, he could not stand before God. He smarted under the lash of a broken law, and was blessed with the experience of the forgiveness of all his sins, because Jesus was his Surety for good. He transgressed the law; but Jesus obeyed it. He deserved to suffer the pains of hell; but Jesus endured them. He had gone astray like a lost sheep; but God laid upon Jesus all his iniquities. If you could feel yourself anything else but a lost sinner, you would not know your need of Jesus the only Saviour, and you would be in greater danger of eternal ruin than you suppose you are now in."

At this part of our conversation, I endeavoured to point out to her the nature and design of the obedience and sacrifice of Christ. From the Psalms I set before her Jesus' righteousness as David's only hope and confidence. Did he experience the dangers and difficulties of the narrow way? He prays, "Lead me, O Lord, *in Thy righteousness.*" Does he groan beneath the galling yoke of bondage? The language of his heart is, "Deliver me in *Thy righteousness*"; "*For Thy righteousness' sake* bring my soul out of trouble." When doubts and fears perplex, and Satan fiercely accuses, he cries, "Judge me, O Lord my God, *according to Thy righteousness.*" Distressed with the burden of the flesh, and mourning over his barrenness and deadness, he prays, "Quicken me *in Thy righteousness.*" With nothing of his own to plead in prayer, he sighs out his soul thus, "Answer me *in Thy righteousness.*"

From the Epistle to the Romans I pointed out the fact that God receives and accepts the believing sinner as righteous in the righteousness of Christ.

She listened in breathless suspense and anxiety, and at length said, "Well, that's something better; but O! I wish I was all right!"

"Jesus says, ' Blessed are they that mourn; for they shall be comforted.' "

"Blessed – comforted! what with?" she asked.

"With the blessed assurance of His own Word which says, 'Come unto Me, all ye that labour and are heavy laden, and I will give you rest.' Blessed and comforted with all spiritual blessings in heavenly places in Christ."

"Ay, ay! But what are these blessings?" she asked rather impatiently.

I smilingly answered, "Forgiveness of all sin – justification, or freedom from all that the law has against us – adoption into God's family – the enjoyment of Jehovah's presence and company – and the blessed foretaste of eternal and unchanging happiness."

"And can a poor sinner like me enjoy such blessings as these?" was her prompt inquiry.

"Yes," I answered. "None but sinners do enjoy them –

' Raise thy downcast eyes and see,
Numbers do His throne surround;
These were sinners once like thee,
But have full salvation found.'

Salvation because Jesus, His own self, bore their sins in His own body on the tree, that they being dead to sins, should live unto righteousness: by whose stripes they were healed."

"But how is it that His stripes can heal us?"

"How is it that the husband can, and does, pay the wife's debts?" I asked her in reply.

"And is it in that way He does it?"

"It is, my poor woman. As the Husband, Friend and Surety of His Church, which is composed of a countless multitude of sinners, Jesus stood in their room and stead. He paid all their debts – that is to say, He endured all the wrath and suffering which they deserved; He obeyed all the commands and precepts of the law for them, thus arching over the great gulf sin had made between them and an all-holy God. It is here the believing sinner meets with God on friendly terms; nay, they are friends indeed. Man now stands before God as though he never had sinned."

"What man?" she eagerly enquired.

"That man or woman," I answered, "who, mourning over sins committed against God, hears in such truths as these which I have spoken to you the voice of Jesus calling in His love, 'I am the way, the truth, and the life; no man cometh unto the Father but by Me.' 'He that believeth in Me, though he were dead, yet shall he live.' "

"Well, now, that is comforting, I wish I could see and hear it gradely" (properly).

After a little further conversation I left, commending her to God and to the Word of His grace.

The Thursday following I called to see her again. She gave me a hearty welcome, and appeared more composed than she was when I left her on Sunday. I read for her Psalm 130. After conversing with her a short time, she said, "I cannot think that God will forgive *me*, I am too great a sinner."

"Why do you think so?" I asked.

"Well, mester, to tell you the truth, one day when something happened i' th' house that I didn't like, I cursed God for letting it be so; and I feel sure He will never have mercy on such a guilty wretch."

"Hold, hold, a little!" said I. "You are sadly mistaken, I think. Don't you remember the apostle Paul? He says here: 'Jesus Christ our Lord – putting *me* into the ministry; who was before a *blasphemer*, and a persecutor, and injurious, but I obtained mercy.' "

"Ay, for sure he says he was as bad as I am in that respect; but there never was as great a sinner lived in this world as me."

"Well, well," said I, smiling, "Paul and you might be brother and sister, see what he says in stating the blessed truths of pardoning mercy: 'This is a faithful saying, and worthy of all acceptation, that Christ Jesus came into the world to save sinners; *of whom I am chief.*' Paul felt himself to be the greatest of all sinners; but he found Jesus to be an all-sufficient Saviour, just suited to his case; and for the encouragement of such as you, God the Holy Ghost caused him to write thus: 'Howbeit for this cause I obtained mercy, that in me *first* [a first-rate sinner, second to none] Jesus Christ might shew forth all long-suffering, for a pattern to them which should hereafter believe on Him to life everlasting.' Now then, what poor sinners, with Paul's case before them, can question the love and power of Jesus to save?"

"No, my word," she replied, "there is no mistake about it I see. There is no occasion for me to doubt any longer. He says He is able and willing to save me; and, O how I feel myself drawn to such a Saviour!"

"May you ever feel drawn to Him. He is a complete and perfect Saviour. He loves sinners, saves them, keeps them, and does them eternal good."

"Eh dear!" she ejaculated, "I wish I could do nothing else but love and serve Him; for it has comforted me to hear of what He has done for poor sinners like me."

"And hearing of what He *has* done for poor sinners, you feel you can trust the well-being of your never-dying soul in His hands, and to none other?" I asked.

"Ay, He is able to save," was her reply, "that's His work; and as you have shown from His own Word, He finished His work, and God is satisfied with Him; and why shouldn't I be? God knows I'm satisfied."

We now knelt at the throne of grace to ask the blessing of our covenant God on this, which was evidently His own good work begun.

Previous to my first visit to her it was fully expected she must be removed to an asylum. The doctor gave her husband a strict charge in the following words: "Do not let any of those parsons go near her; if you do, they will drive her mad." Poor fellow! Little did he understand her case; yet I verily believe he spoke the truth. All the parsons for miles round would have acted in like manner to the one who visited her, and the "*Methodys.*"

In the self-same cottage in Edge Green Lane, Ashton-in-Makerfield, Lancashire, Ann Simm, the subject of the above incidents, still lives. With her husband, and a numerous family of children, she has struggled hard with poverty; but for every step of her pilgrim-journey she has been enabled to praise and adore her covenant God for ordering all things well.

She considers herself highly honoured of God in being blest with the acquaintance and friendship of that distinguished saint, whom Jehovah has taken home to Himself, William Parks, late Rector of Openshaw. Upon every visit which he paid to the neighbourhood he was sure to make the inquiry, "Where's Ann Simm?" Poor Ann! She lived in our dear departed friend's affection; and O how he lived in hers! Sometimes, not often, she was privileged to listen to the clear, joyful sound of the gospel from his lips, but never did she hear him without shedding tears of spiritual joy and godly sorrow.

The old-fashioned truths for which our forefathers bled, and which can be learned exclusively at the feet of Jesus, are still Ann's meat and drink. I know of no person who has a clearer apprehension of the truths of Jehovah's covenant, electing, saving, mercy, and no one who carries the gospel into daily practice more. A short time since she wrote to me as follows:

"August 20th, 1885.

"How often have I thought of writing to you, and how often I have longed to take counsel with you, or hear the word of consolation which you would have spoken to us during all the long time of trial which it has been God's will we should pass through. I refer to the sickness and death of our dear boy Joe. His most painful illness lasted one year and three months. He was hurt, and after a little while, abscesses formed in different parts of his body which drained his system unto death. He lay in bed from November until July 25th, and during all that while we were up with him night and day. O! I can never describe his patient suffering through all those months, but God gave us precious seasons rich in blessing to our souls (at times) and at others we passed through deep waters, but, bless the Lord, for my dear lad left a bright evidence behind to cheer us, and we know he is with his Saviour. God matured His purpose in him."

Her husband is partner of her joy, and though poor, they esteem the reproach of Christ greater riches than all the treasures of this world. The blessed Book – the Bible, God's own Word – is their daily companion. In the sunshine of spiritual prosperity it has refreshed and delighted their souls, and in the deep gloom of temporal adversity has quickened their spirits, and confirmed their hope.

Covenant-keeping God, this work is all Thine own.

Gospel Standard 1993. This and the three previous accounts first appeared in the book *Strangers and Pilgrims.*

SOMETHING KNOWN AND FELT

Henrietta Emily (Annette) Benson

By J.H.Alexander (died 1980), author of More Than Notion.

In 1882 a small book was published called *Life and Love,* the memoir of one of Bernard Gilpin's daughters, named Henrietta after her mother and known as Annette. Although grace cannot be inherited, the Lord often graciously shows His lovingkindness to the children of praying parents, and displays it again under a different set of circumstances. So while the reader may say that Annette's language reflects the school in which her mother was taught (the school of James Bourne and Bernard himself), he will soon have to admit that Annette's path was quite different from her mother's and that her principal teacher was the Lord Himself.

Annette's natural character, says her biographer, was one of simplicity. She was affectionate and sympathising, ready to communicate what she most prized to those she loved. This trait endeared her to experienced believers who watched her case with interest. Later in life, when the gracious work wrought in her was matured through trials and experience, it gave a value to her spiritual friendship and letters.

A Smile from Jesus

Annette lost her mother when she was ten years old, and she and her older sister went to live in London, where they were educated in the family of James Bourne by his gifted daughters. Two years later this entry is in Bernard's diary:

"I had a serious conversation with Annette. Several things she said surprised me, but I restrained my feelings; only I afterwards prayed with her. She said, 'Just before I came home for the holidays, while at my Uncle Charles's (this was Charles Jeffreys, her mother's brother), my aunt read the chapter which says, Who is a God like unto Thee? In the night that verse brought on great fear: I never felt the like. I was afraid of the Lord. It was His might, yet it was His mercy too, and I saw I could not get away from Him. That night I was quite sure there was a God.

" 'I must tell you of a dream I had when I was very little. I thought that my sister and I and Mary Moore (a servant of her father's who was some years later called by grace) were all three together and a dreadful noise came, and a light too light to be seen. It was the judgment day. We were all frightened, thinking the Lord would not save us. Mary Moore cried out, "O Lord, we are great sinners, have mercy upon us!" And do you know, through all the noise and all the light, the Lord turned and smiled. I saw Him smile through it all. I awaked and was very happy.' "

She was thirteen when Elizabeth, her sister, wrote to their father:

"Last Friday night I heard Annette crying. She told me she was so wicked. 'Is it any particular sin?' I said. 'No,' she said, 'it is worse than any particular sin: it is all sin. My heart is so hard I cannot pray. Say something out of the Bible to me.' I told her all the texts I could think of and said, ' You must look to Jesus, Annette. Uncle Francis found comfort in only the Name of Jesus.' She replied, ' But I cannot, I cannot look to Jesus. Repeat to me that hymn, "Gird thy loins up, Christian soldier." ' I did. At the fourth verse, 'When assaulted sore by Satan,' she said, 'It is the devil that assaults me now and tells me to lie down and go to sleep, but I can't. I can't! I can do nothing but cry. O I had forgotten Him, I had forgotten the Lord. What a dreadful place I am in! I have done nothing but sin for thirteen years. I cannot pray or look to Jesus. I must get up and kneel down.'

"She did so and continued for some time sobbing violently. At last she cried out, 'O, I have got a little light, a very little, O such a little!' I said, 'Shall I read to you?' and managed to strike a light. Taking my Testament I said. 'Where? Shall I read Mr. Burrell's text last Sunday? Was it not in the 14th of John?' I began to read, but at the third verse she cried out, 'O I have got it! *I go to prepare a place for you.* I am quite happy. Jesus said He was gone to prepare a place for *me.* I know it was for me. I shall go to heaven now, I'm quite sure. I will go to sleep now. Mr. Bourne says he has such sweet sleep after the Lord has made him happy. How wonderful that you should have read the 14th of John! Mr.Burrell's text was in the 15th chapter. The Lord made you make that mistake. All is mercy. I see Jesus smiling. It is the very same smile I saw in my dream. I want to praise Him! I can't! Jesus, Thou knowest I want to praise Thee. I wish no one was near. We would sing that hymn, "Gird thy loins up." O, I am happy! Can anyone be happier than the highest pitch of happiness? When I knelt down, I said, "Lord, make Papa pray for me." I believe he did, dear, dear Papa. If I could but see him now, I would talk to him. The Lord has made me triumph. I can defy and trample upon the devil.'

"She stopped, and when I looked she had fallen asleep. It was quite light and we had not till then had any sleep."

Her father himself witnessed another such sharp conflict and deliverance from it, and several letters within the next few years told the same sort of experience, showing how spiritual life was maintained. In London the two girls attended Mr. Burrell's ministry and often met their Benson cousins from Norton-sub-Hamden, William, Joseph, Samuel, Charles, who came to London to train for different professions and stayed with their aunt, Miss Matilda Gilpin. Annette was fond of them all and could converse freely with them on divine things, which they were each seeking after.

"The dark cloud has not been cleared up till last night," she writes in a letter to her sister, "but I had, as I told Charles, felt more power in prayer on Wednesday...I have had many sweet visits, but never one like this..." And another time: "...I went to chapel but feared I should find nothing. But it was not so. Mr. Burrell said a great deal about living on every word of God and the sweetness of that feeding. I found it so indeed. How full that food is! How rich! (She had felt in reading Jeremiah 32 the Lord was indeed pleading her cause). How far living on God's Word surpasses all worldly pleasure, drawing (her favourite pursuit) and everything else! I found more enjoyment in reading the Bible than I can describe. I walked home with Joseph and told him all. But I did not know the sweetest part was yet to come. I went upstairs and when getting into bed felt I must praise the Lord. I never was happier, and these words were very sweet, 'Blessing, I will bless thee.' I could scarcely help going in to tell Miss Edmunda Bourne. I have since told her all about it and liked speaking to her very much."

The artlessness of these communications Annette was able to have with others was an unusual grace granted to her; it did not cheapen, but rather heightened the value of her conversation.

A Church Member

Before she was seventeen Annette joined her father's church, Port Vale, Hertford. Bernard Gilpin had left the Established Church and was pastor to a small but loving congregation of believers. They did not practise baptism but followed rather the Huntingtonian line of things. An interview with the minister decided the invitation to the Lord's table.

"For some years after it pleased the Lord Jesus to make manifest His work in my heart," she writes, "which was clearly made known to me in my childhood. I went on in the way that those who have gone before have taken, frequently backsliding, but 'True faith's the life of God, Deep in the heart it lies. It lives and labours under load: Though damped it never dies.' Never having been exercised on the subject of the ordinance of the Lord's Supper, and feeling a dislike to put myself forward, the foolish pride of my heart presenting it to me in that light, I endeavoured to forget it. But one Ordinance Sunday (the first Sunday in January 1848), I took my seat apart from the members, and secretly said, 'O that it might be made plain to me: I cannot act in it myself.'

"My father selected Exodus 12 to read and I soon felt my attention quite fixed and a very clear and beautiful light and hope entered my heart. I felt a great awe as though I could spiritually discern the judgment of God as that destroying angel passing over me. 'I will pass over you, and the plague shall not be upon you.' During the whole service this was all my thought, that God had said He would pass over me because of the blood of sprinkling washing away all my sin. After many conflicting thoughts, I determined not to speak of what I had felt unless I was spoken to. This conclusion, which for twelve months I was suffered to abide by, brought on much darkness and misery, together with a guilty feeling that caused the Lord's Supper to become a mere form to me. My conduct occasioned me many keen convictions. I saw it was carnal (not spiritual) humility that gave rise to it.

"Towards the close of that year, the subject returned with great weight. I had felt the words, 'I will cause you to pass under the rod, and will bring you into the bond of the covenant,' and now these words looked as though He would give me a fresh seal to that covenant: 'When they saw the star, they rejoiced with exceeding great joy.' The wise men had seen the star in the east, but instead of simply following it, they went up to Jerusalem, consulted with carnal sense, and, as it seems, lost sight of the star, for it was after they left Jerusalem they saw it again.

"The anniversary came round of the day on which I felt the subject clear, but as none of the people had spoken to me, my mouth remained shut, and I cried bitterly to Him in my trouble....I took my seat apart again, and raised the book that lay there. It fell open on the same chapter, and it seemed to me as though all the verses spoke to me. 'Ye shall take a bunch of hyssop and dip it the blood and strike the lintel....For the Lord will pass through to smite the Egyptians and when He seeth the blood....the Lord will pass over the door and will not suffer the destroyer to come in.... And ye shall observe this thing for an ordinance to thee for ever.'

"I now saw the meaning of the sign, the substance of which I had so truly partaken of. It was as the passover a sign to be observed in all our generations, young and old, as the sign marked on the lintel, blood sprinkled on every post: within, the Lamb was eaten, the substance was enjoyed: without, the sign of that substance should be observed in all the generations of the true Israel of God.

"I was deeply impressed and trembled. That day, on leaving the dinner table, my father turned to me and said, 'I have been thinking what your feelings may be respecting outwardly uniting with us. I wish to press nothing. If you have anything to say, speak freely.' The matter proceeded from the Lord. I was made willing in the day of His power."

The members received her with much affection and the unity between them was never broken. It received its final expression when, years afterwards, she sent them as her dying message Exodus 12. 11.

Charles Benson

There had been a growing attachment for several years between Annette and her cousin, Charles Benson. Charles was the fourth son of Frances, one of Bernard Gilpin's older sisters. She was married to a Church of England minister, John Benson, and lived at the vicarage of Norton-sub-Hamden in Somerset. All had gone smoothly with her as she brought up her family of seven sons and one daughter, and she had been a perfect pattern of a vicar's wife. But she was of a thoughtful nature, and was greatly impressed with her brother Bernard's secession from the Church in 1834. His letters to her searched her heart, and from that time for twelve years, she says, she felt the Lord gradually teaching her and bringing her away from the orthodox but profitless ministry of her husband. This was a most painful path for one of such a gentle, timid and loving nature, but as the light of God's Word shone more clearly, she was enabled at last to withdraw from her husband's church, and actually had a little meeting in the vicarage itself with several whom she had found, while visiting, were like-minded with herself. It was a situation that carried with it a weekly burden of pain. Her husband could not see her difficulties, and although for years her urgent prayer to God was that he and she together might leave the church, as Bernard and his wife had left the church at Hertford, it was not to be. Her sons were in their twenties when this spiritual estrangement showed itself, and were witnesses for many years of their gentle mother's faith being tried in this fire.

Charles, who had studied as an architect, was there to lead the first meeting in his mother's drawing room, and before any opening in business came to him was able to conduct it each week and speak acceptable words to the tiny congregation. His mother records many instances of being blessed despite the painfulness of the position and thanked God that

Charles "was defended from rebuke and harm". A year later the meetings were transferred to a friend's house. Here they continued for ten years, after which a small building became available for a chapel.

The Lord's blessing was manifested on this little cause, and Mr. Bourne, who was a most kind counsellor to all these young men, wrote to Charles:

"Although I have appeared to take but little notice of your letters, I have been much engaged in mind concerning your conflicts in the exercise of your ministry. I am sincerely glad to hear that your meeting with the people is profitable, and I believe the foundation of the profit is in keeping you low. The Lord will teach us that necessary lesson and if we cannot learn it in any other way He will teach it in the furnace of affliction... Now, my dear friend, if the Lord should put it into the heart of any of His people to entreat your help, let there be no idle excuse, lest the Lord should bring a cloud over you: but keep this in mind, ' Him that honoureth Me I will honour.' We cannot honour the Lord more than in a readiness to spiritual obedience... So if our movements are in this way according to the mind of the Lord, He will be our safeguard from all dangers, but idle excuses when the Lord calls always end in bondage and confusion. In all my long life I have never found it otherwise, and He has sweetly added, 'SURELY I will not leave thee till I have done that which I have spoken to thee of.' "

Difficulties about Getting Engaged

As well as ministerial misgivings, Charles could get no work and therefore had no prospects to set before Annette. It was two years before they were even engaged that Annette wrote in her Memoranda: "I have looked to Jesus as to the only quarter from which good can arise... something says, Go again and again (referring to Elijah); in the end you will see that little cloud... I have gone alone into my room and when thus heavily burdened, a secret hope springs up as if something said, Still you can go to the Lord: He can hear and will pity. It has been like coming to the mercy seat, there to pour out all my griefs, even when unable to utter a word. Sensibly I have felt the Lord Jesus hath not despised the affliction of the afflicted, with a sweet hope that my cry is heard. I can leave the rest, and cheerfully say, I know that He is able to keep that which I have committed to Him, for hitherto hath the Lord helped me."

Another entry reads:

"This evening while sitting sewing with the rest, the whole circumstance came with weight upon me, and I could not resist putting away my work and going alone to pray for a real blessing, especially upon Charles and all the various dispensations he is at present under. I took my Bible and went alone into the spare room. I believe I found some power to cast my burden and his upon the Lord... Were it not for a real hope that arises again and again and can never be quite crushed, I do not know what I should do. At times when I feel almost overcome, which is very often the case, I can never describe what that hope is that enables me to cast all weight of fear and sorrow at the feet of the Lord Jesus. It needs no words to make Him understand my troubles or necessities...

"Once in much trouble I opened on this, 'Though He had done so many miracles among them, yet they believed not.' I feared this was my case, and called to mind the many ways in which He had caused me to see His hand, and the evident answers I had received to prayer. This quite melted my heart, and I said, 'Lord, surely Thou didst hear my prayer in those little circumstances.' Almost immediately these words came with a sweet gleam of hope, 'Because I said unto thee, I saw thee under the fig tree, believest thou? Thou shalt see greater things than these.' The immediate cause of the exercises through which I was passing was a temporal one, but it was as if the Lord took that way to teach me in my soul..."

Again seven weeks later she writes:

"At present I can only say I feel as if I were standing before a blank wall. There is still no opening in outward things before Charles. At times I feel greatly perplexed about this, but cannot forget the injunction, If the cloud continue, thou shalt not journey. I feel much grief naturally; this is very painful, but nothing brings me into condemnation except sin. Still the Lord does sometimes seem to smile, and then I cannot help smiling too. None can understand this unless brought to experience it, but it is no fancy. Nothing but reality could bring such sweet quietness: it is indeed rejoicing in hope. What does the trouble signify if I may find the undeserved mercy of Jesus Christ? 'Thou, Lord, hast not forsaken them that put their trust in Thee.' "

Engaged at last

In February 1854 the engagement was arranged, and after praising the Lord for all His mercies, temporal and spiritual, Annette writes: "I have been made to cry over and over that we may both serve the Lord in this world and be made meet to stand before His throne in another. We are not our own. If He should be graciously pleased to unite us, it is not only that we may walk together on earth, but we have surely a work there which

He alone can enable us to fulfil to His glory. I feel persuaded that unless the Lord grant me that wisdom which is from above, which is first pure, I shall not serve Him as I ought and become a help meet for one whom the Lord has chosen to minister before Him... The days which are coming are serious days. Can we stand? Not unless the Lord is with us. Does not the prospect call for a sober life and conversation?"

Mr. Bourne, who was within four months of his death, wrote to Annette on this occasion thus:

"I have heard of your engagement with Charles. I believe the Lord has made his heart sincerely tender and I can honestly pray for a blessing on you both. But neither of you must forget my Sunday's text, 'We must through much tribulation enter the kingdom.' There are no doubts mentioned in this text; the words appear absolute: MUST ENTER. Enter you shall, let the tribulation be what it may. Whether your lives be long or short, you will be subject to many changes, but if the root of the matter is found in you, that will stand the trial. It is for want of this root that there is so much confusion when a faithful minister is removed. I remember long ago when I spoke of my sweet token of the Lord's love to me, I could perceive the hidden power was wanting in some and that they did not know the secret of the Lord... I sincerely hope you and your sister will be always looking at the certificate of your union with Christ. Prove that, and you will be a crown of glory in the hand of the Lord, and shall no more be termed desolate for the Lord will delight in thee.

Love, love, love, Yours etc.   J.B."

Setting up Home at Sherborne

Charles eventually found work in Sherborne, Dorset, and their marriage was arranged. Unable to get a house for his bride, Charles had to take lodgings for them. Annette writes about this (later) as follows:

"A few days before we went to Sherborne, I had one especially sweet promise ' They shall build houses, and inhabit them. They shall not build and another inhabit; they shall not plant, and another eat: for as the days of a tree are the days of My people, and Mine elect shall long enjoy the work of their hands.' Afterwards, when our prospects that had seemed to open were again clouded over, this sweet word was quite forgotten, and one day I cried to the Lord in bitter sorrow and unconsciously used David's words, 'Remember the word unto Thy servant, upon which Thou hast caused me to hope.' That same evening, going into a dressing room in the house of one who told me nothing but ruin was before me, I opened the Bible at this passage, 'They shall build houses and inhabit them,' etc. and instantly I said, 'Lord, this is the very word upon which Thou hast caused me to hope. Thou hast surely remembered it'...And the Lord brought us through all that trial."

Another thing that burdened Annette was the prospect of being so far removed from the preaching of the Word. She says: "To the little number at Norton-sub-Hamden and to the ministry of my future husband under which they were gathered, I felt the truest union. (She had, of course, stayed with her aunt and met with them all.) But a distance of nearly fourteen miles from Sherborne would render it very difficult for me to go with him. And when a friend remarked that some provision in the way of hearing might be in store for me, I could not believe it would be.

"A few days after this an old letter was put into my hands by someone who knew nothing about my going into Dorsetshire. The letter had been written twenty-seven years ago and came from a village near Sherborne, Long Burton. The letter found an immediate echo in my heart, and thinking it came from a neighbourhood that appeared so barren in prospect stirred a spring of faith and hope I had not had before. On making enquiries through Charles, I was deeply affected to hear that the writer still lived there, and even preached each Sunday in a small chapel in Sherborne, though Charles had no means of hearing him, being engaged himself at a distance."

Thomas Small

Seeking out this little chapel after their marriage, Annette was full of questionings and fears. The enemy, she says, had the upper hand.

"He bid me look at the outward appearance, the few in number, the mean station of the hearers; at the chapel itself, too, hidden away at the back of the stable yard of an old inn. How conspicuous I would make myself if seen associating with them! Thus by the fowls of carnal reasoning was the good seed carried away directly it fell from the sower's hand. Even my natural ears scarce heard the sound through the hurry of temptation; yet I was much struck at the time by the deep earnestness and sobriety of the preacher. I tried to carry home the sound, that Charles on his return from Norton might pronounce for me, but beyond telling him I thought it must have been the truth, I found no power to convey it.

"A fortnight passed before I went again, and this time even more distressed and harassed than before. I went like a criminal and was taunted from within that I was sure to get ensnared. I was no sooner seated, however, than my attention was fixed ere I had begun to call it up. I knew from that moment Mr. Small was commissioned to speak God's Word to me, and in the clearness of that light I felt myself to be made naked and open before God. No other thought turned my attention up to the conclusion of the service. What of consequences or appearances if we find ourselves standing in *this* light?

"I never heard the Scripture read with such authority and awe. The text was, 'I will seek that which was lost, and bring again that which was driven away.' It seemed to me the preacher was describing the lost, the really lost, and to each sentence I inwardly answered, That is my case, for I trembled at the Word and judgment of God. The things spoken brought the question to a point: In what relation do you stand to God this day? It had nothing to do with any past experience. The word came nigh to me, Are *you* among these lost, driven away, broken, sick? At last Mr. Small paused and fixed his eyes on me. (He told me since that he was struck by my evident attention to his past discourse.) And he said, 'Is anyone here before me now thus lost and driven away? To you I say you shall assuredly be brought again.' He then went through the returning promises in the text in language well known to me. I had not come to a people of strange speech, nor did he speak parables or things too high. To everything he said I set my seal, even to the last beautiful words called the blessing at the end of his short but very expressive concluding prayer. I looked up at him for one moment to say in my heart, 'Thy people shall be my people, and thy God my God,' and then left the chapel unashamed before God and man.

"Mr. Small's words to me subsequently were, 'I believe we are bound in one bundle of life,' referring to the particular sympathy in our experiences. From that day I regarded him as a spiritual father. He has prayed for me in times of need, and I in return have prayed for him... Speaking of his having become so late in life connected with us, ("us" includes her father, Bernard Gilpin, who came and preached for Mr. Small at this little chapel once when visiting Annette), Mr. Small even with tears repeated the text, 'Who hath begotten me these, seeing I have lost my children and am desolate?' alluding to the painful separation of some whom he had esteemed. He came to his grave some years afterwards, 'like as a shock of corn cometh in in his season.' His last days on earth were blessedly spent in the enjoyment of hope, which as his afflictions abounded, abounded still above them, and his end was peace."

Faith Honoured in Providence
Annette records that once Mr. Small was in much need.

"I had a sovereign by me which I had reserved to buy something our little one needed (for the Lord had now given us a precious little one). I was exercised to know whether I should be justified in using this for a present to Mr. Small, seeing we in some sense needed it ourselves. I felt a sure confirmation that I might trust our need with the Lord, and sent away the money.

"In the course of the week I received a letter, in the postscript of which was written, 'Mrs._____ drove here on Tuesday afternoon (that same Tuesday) and left a parcel containing (here were mentioned the exact things I had saved the pound to purchase) which she thought might be useful to you!' "

Another case was this. Annette writes:

"In the earlier years of our married life we often felt much perplexed as to means. Once during very cold weather, the case of a poor family pressed me, and I purchased a small pair of blankets to send to them. Afterwards I remembered we too needed more blankets and I did not see how to procure for both. This deterred me from my purpose till the words, 'He that hath pity on the poor lendeth unto the Lord, and that which he hath given will He pay him again,' so fully freed me from hesitation that I sent them without further anxiety. Soon after this a friend from a distance, who knew nothing of the circumstance, visited us and playfully threw down at my feet a large parcel containing a pair of beautiful blankets, worth fourfold my gift!"

The Cup of Christ's Sufferings

"From very early in the time that the Lord was pleased to quicken my soul and make me live to Him, He gave me also a serious fear concerning His work. I felt it was no light thing He would do. I knew there were deep things in His law and teaching on the heart. I used to think if the Lord were to say to me as he said to the sons of Zebedee, 'Can ye drink of My cup?' I must say, 'No, Lord, I cannot.'

"Under the ministry I now attended (Mr. Small's) I became more deeply exercised on this subject: not that it was often referred to, but it was evident the minister had indeed partaken above most of that cup. I have trembled under the Word many times, yet loved its searching power. I had an impression I should not die until in a degree I never yet had known, I should drink of Christ's cup and be baptized with His baptism. And truly through inward and outward trials, while I yet looked towards a future work, I was brought down lower and lower in that very path, until shortly after the birth of my first child, it pleased the Lord to withdraw His sensible presence altogether, and I sank in deep mire where there is no standing. But I did not then think I was partaking of Christ's sufferings. O no! I feared I was being manifested a deceiver, that I was as the man who built his house on the sand.

"At this time I was very ill and in much suffering and we were also in very trying circumstances: but I did not connect these things with my inward trouble, because that was so much greater. I constantly cried in the bitterness of my soul under a sense of desertion, 'My God, my God, why hast Thou forsaken me?' Yet I did not call to mind that those were Christ's words. In fact I could not have conceived that He who was God as well as man could possibly have sunk as I did. Yet Hart's lines,

'Are ye tempted? So was He:
Deserted? He was too,'

I would repeat for days and nights, and say, 'Ah, if I knew that was what I feel!' Through everything, such words did help me, and very many more. Now too the tempter set upon me in all kinds of ways: the most distressing was that I should pray for healing as a proof of Christ's love; but in answer to these commands I only seemed to cry in vain. In this temptation I believe he acted as he once did to the Lord Jesus when he bid Him turn stones into bread in proof of His Godhead. But I was bewildered and believed him. Yet the Lord did not wholly leave me in his hand and I am now quite sure He did not condemn me.

"At this time (my sister having taken the baby away with her), my suffering was great, and to this was added an intense thirst that I was not allowed to satisfy. Thirst is a cause of great suffering and it touched me much some years later when, thinking of this season, I was led to remember that the Lord Jesus uttered the words, 'I thirst,' the only allusion He made to the pains of His body.

"One day I was as usual mourning alone, when I thought I saw the Lord Jesus coming towards me as a Man of sorrows. There was no glory but, I thought, the tenderest compassion. My soul was filled with awe, love and desire after Him, but He passed by, and I seemed left. Truly there was none in earth or heaven that I desired as I did Jesus then, and there is none now. But after this the sense of desertion increased, and the words 'Without God in the world' sounded through my heart, and through the power of temptation I was made to believe that it was revealed to others whom I loved and respected that this was my dreadful case, and that I should have to separate from them. I speak of what was being continually sounded in my ears. There was still a struggling cry. I cannot forget the effects of the words, 'Like a crane or a swallow, so did I chatter: I did mourn as a dove: mine eyes fail with looking upward: O Lord, I am oppressed; undertake for me.'

"I remember the deep feeling of sorrow, and of being left in it, when my husband was called away from home for some weeks. It was very early, hardly dawn when he started. I had several hours to wait before anyone came to me. I believe the deepest touch in lifting up my eyes to the Lord was at that moment. Charles had been my one earthly stay, and his removal was part of the work intended. I turned now from man. I lifted up my soul in prayer and then resigned myself wholly into the hand of God. Though no comfort was given, a peculiar filial hope sprang up. I could not help feeling some love and help had been granted, and could say, 'They trusted, and Thou didst deliver them.'

"A week after this my sister's husband (Richard Benson) came down and took me home with him. There I was surrounded by kind friends, had my baby again, and was greatly relieved from suffering. But though I felt very thankful, I found my state spiritually unaltered. By day and night I found my fear abode and I thought I was about to realise a living death 'without God in the world'. As to speaking on the subject of religion, I thought my mouth had been closed for ever. But the Lord's thoughts are indeed not our thoughts, and in this case they were 'thoughts of peace and not of evil'.

Captivity Turned

"One morning my aunt Matilda Gilpin came to sit with me. At first she too was silent, but after a while she began to press me to speak. I determined not to utter a word; indeed I had nothing to communicate but my dreadful fear. However, after she had tried many times, I thought I will tell her the worst and then she can say no more. With this I began in great fear and told her that as to my religion, it had utterly failed me in the time of need, and all I could say was, having been no support then, I feared it never would be. Saying this I turned on the pillow and thought what would my aunt feel at hearing that. For a time she did not reply, and then very gently repeated the words, 'Ye are they that have continued with Me in My temptations.' After this, though alone for some time, neither of us spoke. But these words fell on my heart as a dew from the Lord. It was but little at first, but very wonderful to me. The sound of them I shall never forget: 'Ye are they that have continued with Me in My temptations.' Continued with Jesus! I said to myself, 'I have continued with Him!' Jesus, Jesus, Jesus! That one word seemed to fill heaven and earth.

"From this moment I found my captivity was turned, though such was the awe abiding on my spirit for months that my harp hung on the willows.

One morning as I was looking and longing in soul and still in some outward suffering, these words passed before me, 'Unto you it is given on the behalf of Christ, not only to believe, but also to suffer for His sake'... And it has been given me from that hour to this to prove, as I passed through seasons of much inward and outward affliction since, that as the sufferings of Christ have abounded in me, so also have the consolations the more abounded by Christ.

"From the time when some years afterwards the Lord fully removed the cloud and unveiled the clear light behind it, this promise has been my plea, for I know it was once made mine: 'Fear not, I will help thee.' It is prefaced thus: 'I the Lord thy God will hold thy right hand, saying unto thee, Fear not.' It was a promise given for my whole life, a word graven on that white stone which who receives shall read."

Bernard Gilpin's Visit

While they were still in their modest lodgings at Sherborne, Annette's father visited them, and thus describes it in his diary:

"Yesterday morning (Sunday) I was dark and tried, and could not believe there was anything right in my case. We went to Mr. Small's chapel. His text was Proverbs 10. 24: 'The fear of the wicked, it shall come upon him, but the desire of the righteous shall be granted.' In the state I was in my heart sank at the words, but he handled them in a truly able manner. He was exceedingly clear, both in doctrine and experience, and bent himself to encourage the lambs. He so fed these as to quieten them, not to lull them. One subject he touched upon was the faith of a truly convinced sinner who apprehends only the judgments of God and the threatenings of His holy law – this faith is one with that of the happy man who, through the aboundings of the Holy Ghost, is filled with joy and peace in believing. The faith is the same, though the objects on which it is fixed are different.

"I loved the Word and trembled at it. It awakened in me still deeper fear, so that I could scarcely bear the thought of preaching in the evening. I felt I knew so little of the Lord's divine work that I felt afraid of presumption, but I was enabled to say, I must confess all and look only to Jesus, and behold! a gentle spring relieved me from Psalm 37. 20: 'The enemies of the Lord shall be as the fat of lambs.' My guilt consumed away out of sight under these words, and left me resolved to preach from the Psalm, which I did. It was beautiful to me as I preached, and on the two words. 'The Lord loveth judgment,' and again, 'The mouth of the righteous talketh of judgment,' I told the people how I had entered into their pastor's spirit in the morning, and enforced the same things. He afterwards came to us to supper, and showed true liberty and love. It was very uniting. This I felt as a signal mercy. It is long since I found the Word clothed in such power."

A New House at Yeovil

The next spring they had moved into a house at Yeovil, six miles to the west, and six miles nearer to Norton-sub-Hamden for Charles's ministerial work. It was a home of their own now, but Annette writes concerning it:

"When we moved to Yeovil, I found a new trouble, which has been of use to me as a warning ever since. This was that we entered into our arrangements there without, I think, sufficient watchfulness and prayer. I hoped all would grow clear, but it grew darker and darker. I cannot describe my trouble. I felt sensibly that my folly had brought down a rod. I saw nothing but temporal confusion before me; our expenses were increased so much beyond our means. I one day shut myself up, and like Hezekiah turned my face to the wall and wept sore. I did fully and sincerely confess my sin and abase myself. From that time to this the Lord has seemed to put away my sin. At that very time I fell down before Him in confession, at that very time He proved Himself a God hearing and answering prayer. He filled me with praise and faith. Before the day was passed He sent the earnest of provision for the present time, and the very day that was gone He sent more, and again proved to us that 'the cruse of oil' should not fail. This was wonderful; I knew He had undertaken our cause. But may I never forget the bitter lesson I then learned. And may I never forget, 'In all thy ways acknowledge Him and He shall direct thy paths.' "

Three years later (1862) she writes thus to Mr. Small:

"On Friday evening it pleased the Lord Jesus to draw near to my spiritual sense and renew His covenant with me as at the first. It was as a Bethel to my soul for I could truly say, Now I know that God is my God and will be with me till He brings me to my end in peace. I could not tell you, and could but faintly tell Him, the fears that instantly arose in my mind, Satan strongly urging me to believe that in thus giving myself up entirely into the Lord's hands, I should now have nothing but trial and affliction to the end of my days, and representing before me in the strongest light my weakness, and reminding me that I always did sink and despond at the very sight of trouble. I still was helped to struggle against him, and finally said with great awe and tenderness, You know *nothing* of the way in which it will please the Lord to lead me. It seemed as if he then fled, and I felt satisfied, be my future path what it might, I should lose nothing by falling entirely into the hands of the Lord, while something secretly whispered, 'For very great are His mercies.' Indeed, great they have been to me. Never in my life before have I felt so sweet a blessing in watching for and receiving His providential mercies as lately... I have often felt as if I must pray for everything and could only meet the smallest trial by prayer. My fears have been equally high, almost overwhelming all... I often read Mr. Bourne's letters (these had been published the previous year) with tears, for I find in them all my own exercises most clearly set forth, and much advice which it will be my mercy to follow."

Thoughts Recorded after a Severe Illness, 1864

"Entering this illness (probably childbirth, which was often a long illness) I felt submission, looking on the hours of solitude I should have as specially given for the contemplation of death. My only thought was, Am I prepared? Can I stand? For a quarter of an hour last Tuesday week I was very ill, more so than ever before. It was then that I answered myself, I am not prepared, I cannot stand, and the sin of my thoughts rolled out before me like a scroll. It left a distant, awful feeling. I said to myself, What then must death be? The next morning while thinking about it a verse of Hart's respecting the sufferings of Christ came into my mind, followed by this question, Did you ever consider that Jesus died? The impression conveyed was that He had infinite compassion on those that must die, and it left a softness on my spirit throughout the day.

"Next day while again thinking of what I had felt when my thoughts rolled out before me like a scroll, this passage came, 'Come now, and let us reason together, saith the Lord; though your sins be as scarlet, they shall be as white as snow.' There was a sweetness in them all day. In the evening as Charles read Isaiah 1 I felt every word of it. The sin of Judah and Jerusalem – exactly such was mine: the true principle – left 'as a lodge', 'as a besieged city', beset on every side – our base backsliding – His judgment – His power as God to redeem and deliver such lost, undone, sinful creatures – the glory He would get by it and our great humiliation. Again and again I was reminded of that quarter of an hour and bid to look at the 'hole of the pit' whence I was digged, not with despair but with the breaking forth of sweet hope. That night was also one of great weakness but I was helped to feel patience. In the morning as I had my breakfast I was comparing my case with Isaiah 1 when a sweet feeling of inward praise sprang up and I said, O what praise must and shall resound even from that 'besieged city'.

A Glimpse of Immanuel's Land

"...To take up the language of the *Pilgrim's Progress*, I did by faith behold the river of the water of life: I did by faith smell the sweetest perfume in the valley of humiliation, and rejoiced with joy and singing. I did by faith see the gates of the celestial city. I was brought down to a mere cypher and could only shed tears in abundance while the mercy of the Lord compassed me on every side filling me with joy and gladness.

"Having suffered much from the weakness of my head the evening before, it was suggested to me that this was all excitement, that it was too much for me, and I must not suffer it. But over and over again, whenever through fear of the effects I seemed to shun the sight, these words were most calmly repeated as if still showing me more of those unknown glories: 'I am the Lord that healeth thee'; and it must have been true, for I grew better and calmer and most peaceful. I saw then how I felt on Tuesday night that I could not stand. I had not seen that which I needed – the robe of Christ's righteousness to cover me. At that moment, very gently as if in answer, these words came into my mind: 'When I passed by thee, and saw thee polluted in thy blood, I said unto thee, Live...and I spread My skirt over thee, and covered thy nakedness; yea, I sware unto thee and entered into a covenant with thee and thou becamest Mine.' There was what I felt and it was beautiful – that He had covered me with the robe of His righteousness, or I must have been consumed, yet at the time I knew it not.

"This was on Friday. On Saturday I saw the doctor was not satisfied with my state. This roused me afresh to know the ground of my hope. I first prayed in the words: 'Remember me, O Lord, with the favour that Thou bearest unto Thy people,' and kept telling Him that it was not great things for which I sought, but for true; for pure gold that would stand in every time of trial. I had no desire left to escape the cross, be it what it might. All my desires were summed up in one-that the Lord would really be with me. I do know that He made me seek His kingdom before any other thing. The world itself seemed to me at that time like a straw already broken in my hands. I can now understand what David meant when he said, Thou hast rewarded me 'according to the cleanness of my hands', referring to the heaven-born principle which can find no rest here...

Abundance of Peace

I was able to read but very little yet every word spake of the peace I now felt. Yet it seemed to say: Remember this is yours as long as you are empty enough to receive it. As soon as ever your vessel is filled with self or other trash, this peace will not be able to flow in. But I, the Lord, grudge not; I change not. I take delight in filling you with the finest of the wheat and making your heart rejoice with food and gladness.

"Since then I have found changes, but cannot forget what I have seen. I never knew such peace before. His strength was everlasting, His love the same; that as I had given myself into His hands so I also should prove that He would give me all I needed while life should last. He seemed to bid me eat without scarceness, for it should not fail, and the more I asked the more He would give. The way in which I felt it was – that not in Him are we straitened, but in ourselves. O how it has made me long after and prize it, and seek over and over so to walk as not to bring a cloud on my ways!. I have often been half afraid of taking peace lest I should pervert it; but I have seen and been assured that the Lord takes more delight in giving than we earth-bound creatures do in receiving His most precious gifts. Satan and my unbelieving heart say, You must not expect such seasons in every trouble; but I have searched again and again in the Bible and can find no such thing, but 'abundance of peace so long as the moon endureth'. Is it gone? Have you slighted it away? Well, but how did you find it? Was it not freely, while mourning and confessing your sins? Thus seek and you shall find. Time would fail to refer to all the passages that confirm this promise. 'O taste and see that the Lord is good...there is no want to them that fear Him.' A tender walk in the fear of God will end in peace. And does it not make the lame man leap as a hart and the tongue of the dumb to sing? Do I not desire this peace above all else? May the Lord keep my mouth with a bridle and set a watch at the door of my lips that I sin not against Him. Another mercy is to be 'warned of God of things not seen as yet,' especially of death, and 'moved with fear' diligently to seek for His help in a dying hour. Seek also for a blessing He has promised, even 'an expected end.'

Gold Tried by Fire

"May the Lord perfect that which concerneth me. He knows I have many fears now that the abundance of that peace has passed, yet it calls for my highest praise. It was not a light given to be put under a bushel. I do desire to set it in the candlestick of my heart, that the light may shine to His glory. 'Arise, shine, for thy light is come, and the glory of the Lord is risen upon thee.' 'Awake and sing, ye that dwell in the dust: for thy dew is as the dew of herbs.' 'From the uttermost part of the earth have we heard songs, even glory to the righteous.' 'This people have I formed for Myself. They shall show forth My praise.'

"I knew that for several years the Lord had been graciously sustaining and teaching me, although my mouth seemed closed in very great measure. How many times I had prayed, 'O Lord, open Thou my lips and my mouth shall show forth Thy praise.' At this season He truly did so."

At the foot of this memorandum is a pencil note, written three years later (1867): "Another season of trial. Abundantly satisfied with 'the memory of His great goodness'. 'Satisfied with favour and full with the blessing of the Lord.' Again I say, Amen."

The Death of Annette's Mother-in-Law

On the death of her husband, Rev. John Benson of Norten-sub-Hamden, Mrs. Frances Benson, Charles's mother, left that rectory and came to live with the family at Yeovil. She was with them five years and Annette writes:

"Truly she had been made a blessing to many and her light had shone, though as a natural character she was reserved and retiring. She watched and cared for my children as for her own, and many times come back to my memory in which she shared my little burdens, and in which I sensibly felt her prayers (as of one made righteous in God's sight) availed much. To lose such an one was in prospect bitter indeed to me. She was taken ill with severe bronchitis in January 1865, and almost from the first we saw the end. I was followed by these words which were spoken to Elisha: 'Knowest thou that the Lord will take away thy master from thy head today?' During the night after our last hope of her recovery began to fail, I found my heart much softened and with earnestness was led to cry that the Lord would not take her hence until He had promised that a double portion of her spirit should rest upon us. It seemed gently whispered, If you have faith. I said, O Lord, I have faith: for I felt that I had. And it followed, 'Open thy mouth wide, and I will fill it.' I said, I do open it wide, I ask a double portion.

"From this time outward things diverted me, and I sank again under the burden, but on hearing the words our mother had uttered during the night, I felt a springing of hope, perceiving the Lord had not left her comfortless. 'Jesus, Jesus, Jesus, do come!' and soon afterwards when in suffering, 'Ah, why should I complain seeing death has lost its sting?' This hope in my heart increased until it abounded, filling my soul with peace, and uniting me closely to our dear mother. Throughout the day she herself found peace, and the Lord's words, 'Peace be to this house: and if the son of peace be there, your peace shall rest upon it,' followed me, and surely I did know the son of peace had visited us.

"Although it thus appeared she had sure hope and strong confidence, yet she was kept waiting for a fuller manifestation of the Lord's favour and mercy, and had much conflict with the rebellion of her heart under the severe sufferings that attended her illness. But gradually special help was granted her in these words: 'Therefore wait ye upon Me, saith the Lord, until the day that I rise up to the prey: for My determination is to gather the nations, that I may assemble the kingdoms to pour upon them Mine indignation, even all My fierce anger: for all the earth shall he devoured with the fire of My jealousy.' She spoke of it in the following manner: 'Affliction brings much evil to light − murmuring, impatience, rebellion: but the word, "Therefore wait ye," has been a help to me. The Lord will contend against all these evils. He will have no compassion on the flesh but all to do us good. It is no idle thing to wait.'

"On one of the servants sobbing bitterly, I remarked to our mother, '*You* have no cause to weep.' She smiled sweetly. I added, 'More than conqueror at last.' Her expression of joy was beautiful. Later on she said, 'Peace, peace.' When asked if Jesus was with her, she quickly replied, 'Surely, surely, He is with me, or where should I be? Certainly not in peace.'

"During her illness, the spiritual love I felt towards her hourly increased. I did indeed cleave to her as Ruth to Naomi, and over and again with tender assurance was the promise sealed on my heart, 'A full reward be given thee of the Lord God of Israel, under whose wings thou art come to trust.'

"On Charles repeating, 'When thou passest through the waters, I will be with thee,' she said, 'Is it *I will be?* No, *I am with thee.*' The chapter being read, and coming to the 5th verse, 'Fear not: for I am with thee,' she said. 'That's it, that's it.' At intervals we heard her saying, 'The Word I have heard preached is the truth... Give my love to them at Norton.' Afterwards she appeared to be in deep conflict, her lips moving and her hands clasped."

Her sons had been sent for, those children she had wrestled and prayed for and several of whom were now, like Charles, preachers of the Word in small gatherings of believers. They read to her as she wished from time to time, and very sweet was that chamber of death to them all. Annette continues:

"I hardly know how to touch on what I myself felt during this time; but I believe it pleased God to make me a partaker of her joy, and He gave me power to look straight, as it were, into heaven, dwelling on her joy, not on my sorrow. And I believe that as truly as Elisha took up the mantle of Elijah and divided the water of Jordan, so did I by faith. Through an entrance into her joy, death lost its sting in my heart. I could sweetly triumph. Yes! those waters were divided. The Lord had heard my prayer.

"The account of this beautiful scene in the last hour of it appears in the writing to fall far short of the reality. But we know that the peace of God *passeth* all understanding. It is said. 'Except ye be converted and become as little children, ye shall not enter into the kingdom of heaven,' and to such an image after a long fight of affliction was our dear mother now conformed indeed. It is nevertheless true that the Lord does not light a candle to be covered with a bushel, and these few facts have been recorded with the hope that they may be the means of encouraging many who 'wrestle hard as we do now with sins and doubts and fears'. On the evening of January 20th, 1865, her happy spirit was released for ever from sorrow and from sin."

(Mrs. Frances Benson* is buried in Yeovil cemetery, and the large flat tombstone at the edge of the right-hand pathway can be seen today with a long and beautiful inscription on it.)

Bringing up Children

Annette made several jottings during the years at Yeovil, and this is what she says about bringing up her children:

"As my children grow older, I need wisdom truly to act towards them in the fear of God. I fear subjecting them to restraint that shall weary them or that shall expose them, while as yet they may not have grace, to remark by outsiders.

"I was looking at one of my little ones, and with a mother's feeling thought she was a bright little thing, and said to myself, Do I right in forbidding all mixing in general society? Might it not in the providence of God prove for their temporal good, and more I cannot confer though I keep them ever so far from the world? A vision of worldly good sprang up before me. They might find a blessing, both 'upper' and 'nether springs'; it looked exceedingly fair. But almost instantly something quelled it and I felt, No, let me rather go on as I have found light, and seek in the fear of God for Him to bless them and provide for them without harassing my mind by letting them pursue a path *I cannot follow them in myself.* A secret

---

* There is a short account of Mrs. Benson in *Life and Ministry of Bernard Gilpin,* considerable mention in *More Than Notion,* and a lengthy account in *The Six Sisters.*

feeling arose that the Lord would acknowledge and bless me in thus walking.

"A few minutes afterwards my dear husband read in Genesis about Lot and, without knowing what had been passing in my mind, remarked that it was a useful lesson to consider what became of Lot, with all his great substance, choosing the plain of Jordan. He selected the best of this world and Abraham accepted the rest. The Lord not long after destroyed not the Sodomites alone but all Lot's substance, and he only escaped with his life without bringing out any of the wealth he had before; also he lost his wife. and his daughters became a snare to him. To Abraham, on the other hand, it was said that to him and to his seed God would give the whole land of Canaan, and he grew exceedingly great. A really sweet hope flowed into my heart that the Lord had accepted my desire and would grant me a blessing in following this path.

"I believe we cannot too tenderly seek to be enabled to honour the Lord. We do not honour Him while bowing the knee to Baal, and doing things with an eye to the world and its opinion is nothing better. No one knows how tenderly I desire to speak here."

Intercourse in the World

"How shall I speak? In the first place, by the world I would not imply that all who do not walk just in our line are devoid of true heart-felt religion. I am sure there are many upon whom the Lord's mercy is likewise poured, though by reason of clouds and differences sometimes we are not permitted to see it. Many I esteem naturally, and I can truly say there is nothing I see in them but I see far worse in myself, while many things there are in them that cause me to be ashamed. It is one of the most painful crooks in my lot that I am unable to show all the natural love and esteem I feel. I return my neighbours' calls, and believe there is nothing I would not do for them if I could, yet how is it? Two cannot walk together except they are agreed. I know there is a line of separation laid, not by man, and I cannot pass it. It is not that I alone cannot; it is mutual; and in many cases the distance widens till the form of friendship alone remains, and not that without much that grieves me.

"I may set up a model, and do, over and over again, of some in whom I believe the grace of God shines and who walk in a different path; but I am no more able to regulate my path by theirs than the foot is able to make itself the hand. Every part of the Lord's work is beautiful after its kind, but 'the body is not one member but many'.

"These trials cost me many sad hours and lead to many prayers, even as the thorn in the flesh. I have sought over and again that they might be removed, but the only answer I find is, 'My grace is sufficient for thee...'

"The Lord Jesus spoke much of being in secret, of worshipping in spirit and of digging deep foundations, as well as of putting the candle in the candlestick that they that come in may see the light. Small as that light in my heart may seem (a candle is not seen from far), yet I have reason to believe, and have had proof that it is not altogether hidden from such as have come in contact with it, especially such as make no profession themselves. If ever I had a desire to bear a testimony in word, it would be before such. It is a subject I have much felt, and have often prayed for wisdom in it. To speak of secret personal religion before those who do not believe in it is accounted enthusiasm and pride, while we only speak of what we ourselves have known and tasted. This is a bitter grief. None but those who feel it know the pain of that path. 'Lo, the people shall dwell alone, and shall not be reckoned among the nations.' It is doubtless profitable in driving us to seek afresh the testimony of the Lord rather than the approval of men."

Great Help in Little Things

In a letter to her brother-in-law, William Benson, around this time she writes: "My chief help at times lately has been in pleading, Lord, Thou hast said, 'I knew that thou art obstinate' (Isaiah 48. 4). You cannot think how that stays me, when the sight and heart-felt experience of my inborn, never-ceasing sin would almost make me believe the Lord never could have mercy or never had; else, why such evil? I think it has been the secret support to submit patiently to the cloud within and the cloud without that has been made so real a blessing to me, even through weeks of darkness. I dare not pray importunately for any blessing except mercy; seeking over and over to be brought down to the will of God even in spiritual blessings, secretly cleaving to the hope that the work He was still carrying on was as precious in His sight as ever it was when most precious in my soul. Truly I have entered into the experience of that hymn:

> ' He'll cause thee to bring thy griefs to His throne,
> But answers of peace to thee shall send none;
> Then sorrow and sadness thy heart shall divide.
> Because He's determined His grace shall be tried.'

"How often I remark this: We feel our burdens so pressing and so immoveable that it seems as if the Lord Himself must do some great thing, as Naaman thought; instead of which He works by little and little, by simple means, and often puts those means into our own hands and lets us prove our weakness while working them out in such a way as to hide from us for a time that they are His means. And so we go on crying for the very help which He is secretly giving while we think it is no help at all, and yet presently the trouble has dissolved away. This has taught me to regard little things very tenderly and I have reason to be thankful, for under a very pressing trial I have found lately great help in little things."

Letter on Family Trials

To another brother-in-law, Joseph, she writes:

"I dare not say much but I believe you will come out of the trial when you least expect it. ' When the Lord hides His face, who then can behold Him?'...Satan fills your mind with your perplexities, but perhaps to baffle him the Lord will let you feel your entanglements so great as at last to make you willing to go down into the sea itself, and there a pathway may await you. You may be sure it was a dreadful venture to the Israelites.

"Perhaps the doctors' wish to take away all thought of religion (this was in a case of mental affliction – perhaps of his wife?) is not so much to be feared as it appears to you. First of all, mercifully, they cannot do it. The more that is crushed, the stronger it grows. Secondly, our minds are marvellous combinations of spiritual and natural. I am sure it does not always please God to carry on a continued uniform exercise. I really do believe He makes His people sometimes, after great spiritual exercise, lie down and sleep, and that almost literally because He knows how weak the flesh is. He will safely preserve His own ark. So I hope you will try and not be overburdened on that subject.

"As to your dear boy, you must feel that nothing but the mercy of God can preserve him. It is a question whether in any other line he would not be equally exposed to temptation. What would not Jacob have feared had he known his son, a youth, was living in the court of the heathen Egyptians? Yet he was preserved."

The Move to Martock, 1867

After eight years at Yeovil, the Benson family removed to Martock in Somerset. Annette writes:

"Many things conspired to make us wish to live nearer Norton, my husband retaining an office in Yeovil. But my past lesson (as related before, when she felt they moved there without sufficient guidance) was so fresh in my remembrance, I feared taking the least step in my own hasty spirit and in regard to our removal here I prayed over every step of the way, and found the sweetest earnest of the blessing I sought. Now the

Lord seemed to promise He would open the two-leaved gates, the gates of His spiritual and of his providential mercies, and He has fulfilled His promise to this day. I have never had one instant's cause to regret our removal. I believe the Lord has as surely directed our way here as He directed Abraham's servant to the house of his master's brethren..."

They were now within much easier walking distance to the meeting house at Norton. (Annette was now thirty-five and had a family of five or six.) Annette's sister and brother-in-law, Richard, who compiled the book *Life and Love,* from which the majority of these extracts are taken, make this loving note about her in these her maturer spiritual years:

"She tenderly watched over her own children, earnestly sought for them a blessing, and not in vain; while to all who manifested the fear of God, she walked in much love, supporting them with her prayers and ministering to them as she had opportunity. Her heart was also in no small measure open to the real need of her fellow-creatures who seemed to be without, so as to be exercised on their behalf, not knowing, as she used often to say, where the mercy of the Lord might fall; and feeling an especial sympathy with those entangled and fettered and those in darkness and ignorance, which led her in secret to watch for them, rather than urged her into any path of outward zeal for the conversion of others. Knowing the work was the Lord's and being regardful of His sovereign grace and mercy, she sought to bear their misery and need with her own before Him.

"Remarkably, it is believed, was that love put into her heart and exercised in this way on the behalf of some to whom the Lord was afterwards pleased to make known His eternal mercy and grace.

"In one instance she was thus drawn out in behalf of one member of a family between whom and herself there existed only a courteous kindness, when on their coming into trouble a spirit of prayer was poured out upon her, and, to use her own words with regard to the testimony given by the subject of her prayers before his death. 'The Lord had already prepared His blessing. Even while I was sowing in tears I was bid to reap in joy, and it will be everlasting joy.' "

Praying for the Uncared for

"In the year 1864," Annette writes, "one text followed me very frequently, and I always enjoyed pleading it – Laban's promise to give Jacob the ring-straked cattle. I asked the Lord to give me the ring-straked, that is, as I felt it, those who were uncared for. But I did not know that in this prayer I prayed for a poor little stranger lad of whom at the time I knew nothing; yet I now assuredly believe it was intended by the Lord that he should be given me, and that by a chain of circumstances I should myself prepare the way by which I should witness this sheaf gathered. I can never express what my feeling was when for the first time, not long before his death, I saw in this poor lad, whose waywardness had caused me so much anxiety, one whom the Lord had already given me for my hire. I knew it was so, and this caused me to look on with adoration when I beheld that young life given back to God who gave it.

She refers here to a nephew, Alfred Benson, who came under her care fifteen years later. An account of this will appear in its chronological order.

Sore Trouble

"In November 1870 when on the eve of my confinement, the scarlet fever took down first one and then another of our family. We had at the time six children in the house who had not had it, and my own health was precarious. A real resignation was given me, because of the fear of God which caused me to acknowledge He was justified in speaking and clear in judgment. The words, 'I will hold thy right hand,' were given me and I was helped to believe them and prove them true. At this time was given to us that precious little boy, of whom we were so soon to be deprived. The resignation I felt made all the Lord's work beautiful to me. I cannot describe the love I felt for His sake to this new gift. We named him Bernard Gilpin after my dear father who was drawing near to his end. (Her father died on January 10th, 1871.)

"After this our troubles increased on every hand. It appeared to me also as if the Lord covered the face of His throne, though He never once during those long weeks covered the heavens with blackness. Nor was I, as at a time before mentioned, bound in affliction and iron, for I knew His everlasting arms were underneath. My soul clave to the Lord Jesus although it seemed as if His face was hid...

"The outward trouble was very heavy. The weather was very cold and with so many ill, including one of the servants, it was impossible to procure efficient nursing, so that we had much to endure. I learned lessons I never knew before. When ill myself with the fever, I was at times too weak to think aright...Once in the midst of this the Lord drew sensibly near as I was reading about Abram and the smoking furnace and afterwards came to the words, 'By Myself have I sworn...that in blessing I will bless thee.' It was exceedingly blessed to me to believe this. At the same time the prophecy against Seir for rejoicing over Israel in the day of his calamity (as I had felt Satan accusing me) was very serious and encouraging (Ezek. 35.). The words are, 'Whereas the Lord was there.' This whole passage had reference to the blasts of temptation against me during those months of inward and outward sorrow. I felt satisfied to leave my judgment with the Lord. The effect of this abode with me through the trial and afterwards when I was called upon to part with that little one towards whom my love had been so much drawn out.

The Death of her Baby

"When, at two months, our precious baby was taken for death (I knew it was for death at seven o'clock in the morning), his suffering increased and was inexpressibly touching to witness. I was alone with him as I desired, and my wish was not to give him up to anyone, nor loose him from my arms, until that moment came when his soul should be yielded back to God who gave it, and then cheerfully with my own hands had it been possible to lay his body in the dust. Till then he was mine, a gift, a precious gift from the Lord Himself. I cannot convey the sweet feeling that gave me. I little thought at such a time I should be made to give thanks to God for His mercy and love in having given to my charge a child whose life was so soon to be taken away, but I did so. And I felt the Lord Himself did acknowledge the tender care I had shown towards that infant, not merely as a mother's love, but even as a cup of cold water given to one of His little ones. I remembered at the time of his birth I had been made to receive him as such. I felt I had none to deal with but the Lord Himself. 'The Lord gave, and the Lord hath taken away: blessed be the Name of the Lord.'

"Over and over again my prayer was that I might commit him to the everlasting arms that I knew were underneath. I knew his suffering was bitter but must soon cease. Taking his little convulsed hands in mind, I held them for nearly two hours until stiff in death. Hart's hymn,

> 'Jesus is the chiefest good;
> He hath saved us by His blood,'

was very sweet to me, both in reference to myself and to the child. As I witnessed what proved the last attack of suffering, the words, 'Who His own self bore our sins in His own body on the tree,' helped me. Could I or the child complain? Gradually his features settled into a perfect calm. He lay thus for nearly an hour, when I perceived he had breathed his last.

"Afterwards infidel thoughts began to rush in, and I feared my hope was unwarranted by the Word: when in a moment these words were spoken and sealed on my heart. 'Suffer the little children to come unto

Me, and forbid them not, for of such is the kingdom of heaven.'

(This baby's tombstone is clearly to be seen off the edge of the right-hand side of the main path striking through the churchyard from the west door of Martock Parish Church.)

Sanctified Affliction

Annette's health was greatly shattered by all she had gone through during those months and she went up to Pulverbach in Shropshire, the home of her aunts, the Misses Gilpin, to recuperate, and although very weak she was able to write to William two weeks later:

"With regard to our dear little child's death, I cannot tell you how I felt to have not one word to say either against his sufferings or his death. I can only use the word, which some might hardly understand, *unutterable* willingness to give him up: being persuaded, for it did amount to that, that all the Lord demanded of me was to trust my child with Him. He had bestowed that gift for a very short and sorrowful season. He now came to receive him for ever to Himself, to behold His glory. This is no temporary feeling: I felt the trial much but I now believe I shall grieve no more for ever over the death of that little one. The night before last that hope was given to me, and with all my heart I blessed the Lord for taking to Himself one I loved so very sincerely that like John Bunyan with his blind child, 'I could not bear the wind to blow upon him': and now, ere I could have believed, he was where no wind or trouble or care should ever afflict. This enables me to say, 'O grave, where is thy victory?' The truth is, 'Where your treasure is, there will your heart be also.' So it falls out, as the Apostle says, none of these things move us, so that we may finish our course with joy. The same mercy I look for to the end, and may both you, and all under such heavy afflictions, truly prove it likewise."

Annette's weakness and pain increased, so that little hope of her recovery was held out. Poor Charles, supporting the family at Martock, wrote of this season:

"It was a time I shall never forget. The thought of her removal was anguish to me. For three or four months (all the time Annette was away) I passed through deep teaching. I was led to pray earnestly for her recovery and the Lord graciously answered my prayer and granted an abundant temporal as well as spiritual blessing thereby. In a remarkable manner her health was in a great measure restored and her life lengthened for more than nine years — years in which her influence was of great value to our young and growing-up family and many others..."

For herself, Annette was brought to a clear and almost loving acceptance of death, and when she recovered, it was almost like a "coming back". She says she felt again, like the Israelites, shut in the wilderness. But she had the words, "Be strong and of a good courage", and knew that as the Lord was with Joshua, so He would be with her. One day, she writes:

"I prayed, 'Search me, O God, and know my heart...' and I especially had in mind past sins, secret sins, even sins I knew not were sins. I thought of the wonderful words, 'Father, forgive them, for they know not what they do.' I confessed all; I loved, yet trembled. The words distilled like dew as I read chapter after chapter in Isaiah, many verses speaking eternal, perfect forgiveness on my soul. Yet still I kept confessing my sins with tears and cries before the Lord; and in answer to all this there was a tender silence, not like anger, while the peace still abode, as if to say, Be at rest: it is enough.

"What afterwards gave a beam-like light on my prayer was this: as I was reading a sentence of Sukey Harley, that her 'blessedest tears were so blessed she could not understand why they were to be wiped away'. I saw the promise in such a beautiful light that it seemed to answer my prayer thus: God will hereafter wipe away all tears. He puts into His bottle now these tears of sorrow and repentance for sin. You were looking for God to wipe away your tears. He bids you know that He pardons now and will wipe away the tears one day. It was an answer of peace."

The Kingdom of God with Power

Back at home in the autumn, Annette writes:

"Although my strength is somewhat restored, I can hardly believe I shall fully recover. The truth is, Have I not borne something of the burden and heat of the day? What have been those years of seeking that I might be found watching, ready to open when He should knock? Was it not years ago, even in my childhood, I began to provide for this day? I remember the fear and the cry for mercy in my end when these words very much encouraged me, 'Verily, I say unto you, that there be some of them that stand here which shall not taste of death till they have seen the kingdom of God come with power.' My hope in them was that I was one to whom the Lord Jesus would truly reveal Himself, even to my full satisfaction, before He took me hence. This I believe He has done. Not that the sense of it abides to my full satisfaction. But I know He has sealed my heart for ever. He is mine and I am His...I believe in those months of affliction last winter the Lord tried me to prove my love, and to seal His."

Alfred Benson

It was a few years after this that Annette was given one of the uncared for, or Jacob's "ring-straked" as she affectionately called such. This was Alfred Benson, a boy of eighteen, son of Charles's half-brother. Mrs. Frances Benson was the second wife of the Rev. John, who, at the death of his first wife, apparently passed the care of the son of that marriage, John, to his mother's relatives, for there is no trace of him in the Gilpin-Benson archives. He died in 1868 leaving this boy aged eight. Alfred was placed at school and as he grew older, his father's half-brothers took an interest in him. He was a wayward lad and caused them much anxiety. Several attempts were made to get him into business. William, at Hertford, took great pains with him, and his Uncle Joseph was another who truly cared for the boy's soul. Annette wrote to him after Alfred's death:

"I truly believe as you sowed for him in tears, you have now reason to rejoice and to take courage that other sowings, less quickly followed by harvest, are as surely lying in the ground in hope. You say that I, with yourself, 'asked him of the Lord', and this I am satisfied was so. As I looked at his lifeless frame I felt he was one sheaf garnered and I rejoiced before the Lord. The promise says *sheaves*. May there be *sheaves!*"

At the age of seventeen symptoms of consumption appeared in Alfred. Annette writes the account:

"It was in the spring of 1878 that he came into this neighbourhood. He was a stranger to us, but having been asked to find, if possible, a home for him where he could receive the rest and care his declining state of health required, we succeeded in interesting on his behalf a truly God-fearing person who, having long experience in nursing the sick, was in every way fitted to undertake the charge. At this time I thought chiefly of giving help to my husband's brothers, on whom an anxious care on Alfred's behalf had already fallen, and was not at all aware of the gracious hand that was ordering the whole. I felt nothing beyond a general hope that a blessing might attend the step we had taken.

"There was a natural frankness in Alfred, but he was given to argue and was very determined and self-willed. He truthfully described his state at this time in these words, 'I see no fun in obeying other people.' Indeed this temperament marked his character to the very end. I therefore feel persuaded that wherein he was subsequently brought to submit his personal feelings by yielding to us or even to the Lord Himself, it was through the power of the Holy Ghost, not from any influence obtained over him by others. This he has feelingly declared himself.

"At the time of his coming here Alfred appeared to be wholly set on the world. Behind my back his conversation was frivolous in the extreme. He used to say he must 'keep his spirits up', and this he certainly tried to do by laughing at and making fun of other people, especially of those who feared God.

"I avoided all reference to religion for the first few weeks; but sitting with him one Sunday during evening service, I made it the excuse for beginning upon a subject he evidently wished to avoid. I found that in word Alfred was much set against real religion, and those who professed it, using many contemptuous expressions and unkind personal remarks. He told me that he hated dissenters (as we were), and intended going to church; and spoke freely of his own religious opinions. I told him he was perfectly at liberty to go to church, but as to his opinions they would have nothing to do with his salvation. I said that his day, most likely, was far spent, and unless he found a better religion, he would come short at last. He took up a religious romance saying he 'would rather read it than the Bible, and if there were more such books, and fewer Bibles, the world would be a better place.' (But this, I think, was said more to shock me than as the expression of his own conviction.) He added that he had had preaching enough before now, and would have no more....We parted kindly, but I think on both sides unhappily. I felt the all-important distinction between true religion and false is no mere question between Church and Dissent, and I shrank from discussing it in that light.

True Religion

"One Sunday evening, finding my father's *Memorials* open on his table, I asked had he been reading a part? 'I've tried, Aunt,' he said lightly, 'but it's horribly dry stuff.' On Whit Sunday he spent the day with us. He had been to church in the morning, but I could say nothing to him, deeply feeling that the kingdom of God is not in word but in power...During the week he spent a few days at Norton, and saw some of his friends there. On my calling after his return I found him leaning his head upon the table and very quiet. After a few words on other subjects, he said very seriously, 'I'll tell you, Aunt, I've seen true religion now. I've not a word to say against that.' I did not, however, know how deep his feeling was.

"The following Sunday evening as I sat alone, Alfred entered. He looked depressed, and at once began to speak of increasing illness, asking if I had noticed it. The subject was a painful one, and as I hesitated to reply, Alfred carelessly drew himself up and said cheerfully, 'Well, I didn't come up to tell you my troubles.' 'It is your troubles, Alfred, I wish to hear, if you have any.' 'Yes, I have,' he replied. 'One trouble is my temper; it has been dreadful.' And he then related how he had suffered and caused others to suffer by it during the week. He confessed with much sorrow the pride of his heart and other sins, saying, 'I find hatred, spite, rage, and yet I do pray and cry to the Lord to keep them back. I have spent hours this week at my bedside begging thus, but only to find the next night they have been worse than ever. I have been wretched, and could not think of one passage in the whole Bible – not one! Though at times there have been two passages following me – "In the midst of life we are in death;" this has alarmed me, and it happened to be repeated in church this morning. It darted into my mind, "Were I to die this instant, where should I go?" The other passage encouraged me: "God is faithful and just to forgive us our sins.'"

"There was the simplicity of a child, and such deep feeling in what he said, that my soul was knit to him. I read Isaiah 1 with him, to which he listened with a new and intense interest.

"He confessed later that he only went to church to hear the music (for which he had a decided ear and taste), to look at the dresses and fashions which always attracted him, and to be thought well of ! But when alarmed with the fear that destruction was close upon him, and realising the lack of true heart-searching in the preaching, he had to 'come out,' though he continued to feel great opposition against being a dissenter. He told of a visit he paid to Mary Pitman (one of the Norton friends), having one afternoon walked over with Miss W. At the sight of her cottage he came to the conclusion that he should soon wish himself out of it, but he added, 'Do you think I *did* soon wish myself out? O no! After an hour and a half I could hardly be persuaded to leave. I felt a love that formerly I disbelieved in, and I knew what she spoke was the truth.'

Hate Changed to Love

"To read to him now what a few weeks before he would have ridiculed, the experience of others gone before, produced manifest sympathy, and spiritual joy and union. To Mr. Dore's conversations or Mr. Bourne's letters he would listen with unwearied attention. 'O it is beautiful! I feel every word! How strange, exactly my own feelings written down!'

"One day he said, 'I want to know my sins are all forgiven. You cannot tell how ignorant I am, yet there is a *feeling,* and I see it set forth in the things you have read to me.' I said, ' Where heart joins with heart there is a sympathy, and you will one day understand that our separation from general professors of religion, for which you have ridiculed us, and said it was hypocrisy, has been due to the same thing, and not from any desire to be peculiar or to dissent from others, through mere pride or notion.' He answered, 'I see it to be so now, yet only a little time back I hated you, yes, *hated*.'

"He said again once, there was a verse he felt, 'I will restore health unto thee and will heal thee of thy wounds, saith the Lord, because they called thee an outcast, saying, This is Zion, whom no man seeketh after...' and felt that the Lord would restore his soul and take him to Himself, his body mattered nothing in comparison with his soul . He had been all day calling himself an outcast, and then saw that verse, ' Because they called thee an outcast,' etc., and felt that now the Lord had promised him that He did not call him so, and that he would not be cast out. He kept repeating this, saying, ' Beautiful! beautiful! I am ignorant and most sinful, but the Lord will not cast me out!' This abounding hope was no doubt graciously given to sustain him through the deep trial and temptations that were before him. His love also abounded. On one occasion he went with his Uncle Charles to see one greatly afflicted, but seeking after the Lord. He said afterwards, 'It was a blessed conversation. You can't think how sweet. Yet only a few weeks ago I should have seen nothing but what I should have made fun of !'

Alfred Benson's Last Days

"He went through a fortnight of much distress and pain, but he also had a beautiful night. He was very ill, but a beautiful hope came in, and he felt sure of heaven. His heart kept going up in praise. His kind nurse came in to him (she heard him singing), but he only wished to be left alone to praise the Lord. He had been in a temper with her that evening, and referred to it some time later very tenderly, even weeping, saying, 'When I saw that the book I had flung in my rage (I was in truth mad; there was nothing I would not have done had not grace prevented), but when I saw that the book was the Bible, that precious book, I can never describe the anguish that filled my soul. But it has been forgiven me. What passed between the Lord and my own soul is known to Him and me only, but my sin has been repented of, confessed, and forgiven.'

"The bodily and mental irritation his illness produced increased painfully. One night of severe pain, he said, had also had a blessing in it. He thought of Jacob's ladder, and really believed he too saw a ladder set up between earth and heaven, and he could cry and pray and pour out prayer.

"In the meantime I had left home," writes Annette, "and wrote to him thus:

"When Boaz bade Ruth abide fast by his maidens in that portion of the field where it had been her hap to come, he directed her to his reapers saying, 'Let thine eyes be upon the field that they do reap,' and Naomi bade her, 'See that they meet thee not in any other field.' And how manifest it became that in obedience to this Ruth found the blessing, for in due season Boaz spread his skirt over her and took her to himself! In this Boaz was the type of the Lord Jesus, and Ruth of those whom He redeems and clothes in the robe of His righteousness and in due time takes to Himself."

Alfred wrote back a very feeling letter:

"Dear Aunt, I feel the Lord has made you my friend in His things," and often said with emotion, "O, I trust it has been my hap to fall on that portion of the field belonging to the Lord Jesus."

Divine Teaching

Such was the searching effect of the work of the Lord in his soul that Alfred began to see more and more that he was indeed brought into a narrow way. He did not at once perceive it was the secret teaching of the Holy Spirit that made the way thus narrow, and would endeavour to shake himself from these impressions, and call them "my views", though the candle of the Lord so shone in his heart that on subjects on which his aunt had never spoken the discernment he showed was great....But he was very baffled about Christ dying for all the world, or not. Annette pointed out to him many passages from John 17. etc. He had thought that Christ knocks at the heart of every man and waits to see if they will open to Him.... She ended the argument by saying that he must look, not to man, but simply to the Lord Jesus to teach him if these things were so.

"I fell asleep at night" (writes Annette) "exceedingly anxious on Alfred's account, and the prayer for him continued as I slept...

He told me on my next visit that the whole had occasioned new thoughts, that he knew it was a scriptural truth, and that he prayed to be kept from contention and to abide fast where it had been his lot to come. He could never describe the opposition of his mind against believing what I said, which had led to earnest prayer, when light shone more and more clearly. Other things too. 'O death, where is thy sting?' 'I always thought they were in a poem,' he said. 'I have heard of a resurrection but never believed it.' The forgiveness of sins too. 'Things are brought back to my remembrance that happened years ago – one time in particular when one of my schoolfellows spoke to me (about religion) and I tauntingly told him to keep it to himself: it was all a pack of lies and humbug!' A look of anguish came across his face when he told me this, and with tears he said. 'I cannot feel *that* has been forgiven!'

"It was evident there had been times of conviction long since, yet for years they bore no fruit. He mentioned having once at school uttered an oath, knowing he did wrong. 'I felt,' he said, 'a dreadful terror seize me at the instant the words were out of my mouth. I was in the act of running to touch the wicket. It seemed as if a strong hand took hold of me and held me still on the spot, so that the ball hit my head with a blow I still remember. I knew it was a punishment for my sin.'

"To employ his listless hours he did woodwork; friends sent him orders and he hoped to buy a watch with the proceeds. The weeks dragged gently on. He said once, ' Don't think because I say little I am feeling nothing. I am weak, and go through many temptations, but the Lord teaches me blessed things in secret.'

" He left a short diary written during his illness, with little prayers and ejaculations throughout. One entry was that he had been reading the account of Lieut. Jeffreys [see *More Than Notion,* chapter 13], and was much struck how like to himself he was. What he felt was, 'Against hope *believe* in hope.' And again, ' How beautiful are those hymns of Hart's, "My soul is a riddle," etc. Yes, how true! " Yet ease cannot content, or pleasure please." How true!'

Sorrows and Trials

Many were the mercies, but great the sorrows that attended the last three months of his life, and varied the conflicts. At times he seemed to be lifted above the trial, and at others it nearly overwhelmed him.

Annette wrote to her sister at this time:

"Poor Alfred has spent five days here this week. What a reality we behold in that religion which is of God – His unspeakable gift, the knowledge of Jesus Christ through the forgiveness of sins! Who that knew Alfred six months ago, and know him now, but must perceive there is life given, which is endless life, newness of days, not of the flesh nor of the will of man, but of God? When his natural life ebbs lowest, then this springs highest. You cannot hear his simple, heartfelt expressions without seeing this, 'O that delicious night when I had that dreadful pain, that delectable night! Just like a little bit of heaven on earth. The pain was dreadful but it reminded me that I had asked the Lord to give me the bitter here if I might but have the sweet hereafter, and now I knew He answered prayer. So it made the bitter sweet.' He was up the entire night; he cried with pain like a child, and was like a child in gentleness. All the week before he had been a sore trial through his temper. His conversation comes out of heartfelt experience, good and bad alike.

"Through what steps in providence has Alfred been both temporally and spiritually given to my charge! Yet when I proposed his coming down here, I marvelled at my hardness of heart and could not, as I thought, lift up one prayer for him. I did not then know that, in a sense, I was not in his case to sow in tears, but rather to reap the fruit of former sowings. At that time, eleven years ago (how I remember the words, 'Except a corn of wheat fall into the ground and die'!), I thought the hope I had should die and live again. I also felt the words, 'They that are dead shall hear the voice of the Son of God, and they that hear shall live.' The Lord can give us a hope, let it die and even be buried, yet live again on His reviving.

"I did not in my last letter answer your question about the other case here in Martock in which I am so interested. As I received it the case was most endeared to me. The word given to me does not return void. I think most of these things pass through a kind of consuming fire, and then if established they prove as gold."

To return to the narrative:

"One day being more than usually tried because of the silence he had long maintained, I was made to cry continually that it might be removed. Just as I was about to go down to his cottage, I opened the Bible, and my eye fell on this verse, 'Take ye away the stone.' It had an instantaneous effect. The stress was laid on the little word *ye*, and I felt encouraged to seek help to do according to it by very kindly and very freely speaking to him myself. This evening was one of my sweetest visits. We were three in number and I believe the Lord Jesus fulfilled His promise of being in our midst. Alfred especially seemed to revive, and to return to the days of his youth, but I kept no notes of this conversation."

Alfred's Death

"Towards the end he said one day, 'Do you think I am dying? Well, I leave it with the Lord Jesus. With His blessing I shall sleep.' He turned gently round and slept quietly. Extreme illness hindered him from speaking for long intervals. On the morning of his death he showed much affection to me, but his sufferings being very great, we neither of us spoke. There was no look of terror, yet of deep sorrow and distress, even spiritually. As Bunyan says of Christian, so I believe Alfred 'felt the bottom and it was good'. His feet were not removed from the Rock, though the waters flowed over his head. At one time I had repeated the line, 'Once more reveal Thy face, O once more shine!' and asked, 'Does

He shine?' A very sweet but exceedingly sorrowful expression as he shook his head was all his answer. Soon after he whispered, 'I want Jesus.' We kept silence for about two hours. He was most patient, but could find no earthly resting place. Miss W. leaned over him and said, 'Is Jesus precious now?' 'He answered, ' Yes,' and having said this he fell asleep. It seemed as if almost at the same instant the vision for which he so long waited was opening to his view. It was a most beautiful, peaceful sleep. We knew that it was death, and that his spirit had already gone to be for ever with the Lord. He was just nineteen years of age."

The Christian's Path

Annette only lived herself a year after Alfred. She was now forty-seven years old, and although she had no organic disease, she suffered from a general failure of vital power. She kept a book of memoranda from which extracts are here given, some from a few years previously, and some nearer the end.

"I know," she writes, "there are so many opinions as to what a Christian may do, or not do, that no subject is more difficult to define. It is really a question not of words but of power. When one wanted to follow Christ but first bid farewell to his friends, he was reminded that looking back proved him (as by nature all are) unfit for the kingdom of God. So close may it please the Lord Jesus to hedge round the way of His people. The outward forsaking of all is nothing: that alone, which is from the spiritually constraining power of the love of Christ, is of value. Hence it is that a life-long conflict awaits all His true disciples. If Christ and His love in the heart is uppermost, other things must move down – human learning, arts, sciences, and things that may be lawfully followed in moderation.

"Watch one of the true children of God. It may be in early life he throws aside much in zeal before he has tried his armour. This is half-fleshly zeal. He goes into the conflict, passes through the battle with the world, sin and the devil, and learns what the Lord Jesus said, 'In the world ye shall have tribulation.' He flees from the world, and his legal heart enfolds him with as dangerous a grasp. He seeks a middle path and finds it not, but is ready, as Bunyan says, in escaping the ditch on the one hand to fall into the quag on the other. Hence the need of divers temptations, and he must betake himself to all-prayer. All-prayer, however, has a very chastening effect on the spirit. Let any really use it, and how little will he be able to follow mammon. How often lawful pleasures have seemed like enchanted paths before me, whilst to give them up has seemed like opening the door to a worse enemy! What then? Why, no way but to enter praying into the battle. Seek earnestly that the Lord may sanctify your heart and all your occupations. How soon you will find that sanctification is not putting to sleep! What thorns will be found in these lawful, needful occupations! Sufficient, yes, quite sufficient to teach you with travail and sorrow how to use the world without abusing it."

Fear of Hypocrisy

Another time she wrote (in a letter to Mr. Small):

"I had called on a God-fearing woman, and very deeply entered into her conversation. She spoke of submission to the will of God in a way truly striking to me. My own prayer for months had been that I might for ever be kept from opening my lips against any of God's dispensations. I spoke from my heart, and together we took sweet counsel, and could alike praise the Lord. On leaving, my own emptiness rose up before my face. It seemed nothing short of hypocrisy that I had spoken thus; it could not be consistent with my heart sins, my carelessness and pride. Then these words came into my mind, 'We preach not ourselves, but Christ Jesus the Lord.' I believe the Holy Spirit did at that moment bear witness that thus alone I had spoken. I know He had made me exalt Him, not in word but in deed and in truth. This kept me tender through the evening (with her aunts, for she was then staying at Pulverbach), and later, on being spoken to, I again opened my lips to speak good of His Name and of that faith in the fulfilment of His Word which I believed the Lord had wrought in me. Satan instantly tempted me that I was speaking mere notions and that my faith would give way. At this moment the Lord truly owned His own work and reassured my soul of His never changing mercy in the words, 'This God is our God for ever and ever: He will be our guide, even unto death.'"

Speaking too Strongly

"...I wish a more quickened earnestness might be shown in her. There is tenderness manifested at times, yet a deadness and unbelief also. She is evidently unhappy, yet the enemy seems to deaden her fear. She speaks too strongly: if she knew more, she would speak differently. Do not the people of God get into this place sometimes when they know but little and think that they feel the full extent of sorrow and fear? They speak of being without hope, without considering what it is to be really without hope. I was in something of that state for years, and I have at times, in looking back upon my past profession, thrown all down at the Lord's feet, and asked Him to restore what was right and let the rest be burnt. I have not in this rooted up the wheat, for that has been committed to Him who gave it, that He might teach me again and again the same truth. But O, the sin! ' Thou thoughtest that I was altogether such an one as thyself.'

The Fight of Faith

"Sanctified affliction can sometimes even be rejoiced in, but the deadening influence of the cares of this life is true misery to the child of God, whether arising from prosperity or adversity. It is sometimes very hard to me to believe that in this may lie the good fight of faith. There is no difficulty in believing that those who 'wandered in sheepskins and goatskins' were blessed, but to believe the blessing will be found in and under the frivolous snares cares and deadening affairs of this life is very hard. It is these things that seem like millstones to me: yet it is most graciously said, 'We have not an High Priest which cannot be touched with the feeling of our infirmities.' May you, as well as myself and all others who have tasted these things, be made to come boldly to the throne of grace..."

Seeking the Right Way

About this time Annette and Charles were very troubled about the settlement of one of their boys.

"You must not forget," writes Annette in a letter to a brother-in-law, "what long exercise we have had over this, and how very nearly what appears to us the most desirable opening for our boy has been put in our way, only to be closed again. I have thought of my father's expression about sitting down content in a lowly lot, praying the Lord's prayer all our life through. But how many days of darkness attend a true abiding in that low place!

...The fear of the Lord is always accompanied by a keen sense of our insufficiency and hence it is that though as a principle we believe there is this liberty set before us, to exercise our judgment or follow our inclinations in the things of this life, yet in the practice of it we are often brought to a stand. Either, as Moses found, a sea impassable before us, and an enemy behind, and a wilderness that shuts in on either side; or the fear lest we blind our eyes to a kind providence which stops our way for our ultimate good.

"Either of these exercises (and both are common) will bring us at times to real straits, and constrain us, like David concerning Ziklag, to beg for special assistance in choosing which way to go. These words in that passage about David really helped me once, concerning the many anxieties a growing-up family bring upon us: 'For the soul of the people was sore distressed for their sons and their daughters.' We are made to understand whatever knowledge we through grace attain, that with cares without and fears within the way to the kingdom is now, as it ever was, 'through much tribulation'. It is very remarkable what very small steps at times clear a difficulty we have felt unable to touch, and which, if these little helps in our way were overlooked, would still perplex our path. I have proved this again and again of late, as all my way through: 'Even the very hairs of your head are all numbered.' But do we believe this? I never do until it is brought sweetly to me in experience. I then feel how deep my unbelief is, and am ashamed..."

Spiritual Diligence for Others

"There is a need still in much want of supply, that is, of more spiritual diligence. Do any fall so short in this as I? When the Lord lifts me up out of my many lost places, it is by grace alone that quickens the dead worldly heart, or rather quickens the new nature to rise and overcome the old, 'not by might nor by power, but by My Spirit, saith the Lord.' That we go through such painful and dark paths ourselves ought to quicken our love for others, especially for those whom no man cares for, and who through their folly and the power of temptation get into such very desolate places as to become like 'dead men'. I have at times so little life and faith in exercise as to raise many fears whether I myself have not wandered as far out of the way in spirit, and have not even power to lift up a prayer for myself. Sometimes I find more power at such a time for another, sometimes for *all* that are 'lost' in the true sense, known to us or not. I am sure it is well for us thus to open our mouth for the dumb, yet feeling among that number too! Lately I have had some secret encouragement that way, and there are many texts that have much in them on that subject. Above all, think of the great love expressed by the Lord Jesus towards such. These are words I never read without a measure of the light once felt in them shining out again: 'For as the Father raiseth up the dead, and quickeneth them, even so the Son quickeneth whom He will...The dead shall hear the voice of the Son of God, and they that hear shall live.' "

True Unity

"This indeed has been the feeling I have often had while thinking of the case of N.P. from the time I heard of him again. There has been a secret cry very often in my heart. Unity, if we ever felt it, is not meant to be consumed by such trials any more than faith, yet the one is as hard to hold as the other. It was Vain-Confidence who was dashed to pieces, though unconsciously, by the fall in the By-Path, not the poor wretched pilgrims, who with him were likewise out of the way, but who would fain reach the highway once more, though first the flood, and then Giant Despair, hindered them for a while. One who walks crookedly and in the spirit of the world, all the while professing religion, is in great probability only a Vain-Confidence; but such have seldom kindled real love in the hearts of the Lord's people, whereas those wretched ones, ever seeking like Jonah to flee from the presence of the Lord, and crying like him once more out of the midst of their trouble, are often among those who have at various times drawn others to them with a love as strong as death. As I write this, what taunting I feel! But this is the chief mercy: 'The Lord knoweth them that are His'."

Lack of Unity

A letter to another friend.

"...I have carefully read D's reply to your last and feel in it exactly what we used to feel when for a time connected with some in the very same state. Of all such, the very memory of what I felt causes a secret sorrow; not because it was proved that they were wrong, but because something (what was it?) hindered that unity I longed after. They did not feel it so, but seemed to think it was union, while my heart was sad...In all these men the truth was clear enough in the letter; up to a certain point the clearest experience was spoken of; but the tender fruits of godly fear and spiritual love either were lacking, or through some cloud I failed to see them. I can only describe the effect both of the preaching and the intercourse as 'when a thirsty man dreameth and behold he drinketh, but he awaketh and behold he is faint.' I felt as if such professors might be saying to me, as the children in the market place, We have talked both of joy and sorrow and yet you do not unite. This is a complete mystery to me, and one of those crooked things we cannot make straight...

"The longer our experience, the more we must bow before the Lord instead of pronouncing on any case, at least where there is no open wickedness or denial of essential truth. Most undoubtedly it is a part of Satan's work to hide brother from brother if he can. I can hardly tell you the grief I have gone through on account of this veiling, through which, though I have prayed again and again, the Lord has never yet permitted me fully to look. I am certain of one thing: all these exercises reveal so much weakness and sin in ourselves that they may be sent for that end...That which has healed the wound most is prayer for others as well as myself."

Parting from All

"I now think the Lord is about to take down my earthly tabernacle, and truly it can never be said that that day will overtake me as a thief, for I have been made to look full at it and know that He will do what He pleases with His own. My treasure is not here though I have much to induce a desire for life – all that I love around me, and anxieties which my foolish heart imagines none can smooth a way through so well as myself, especially respecting my growing-up sons.

"Thinking of the exceeding closeness of the tie which binds me here for the sake of others – a tie which alone grieves me – I felt this morning almost ready to envy those on whose life little seems to depend. However, a rather sweet thought struck me. It was, how the man at the helm on board ship has to feel that the well-being of all depends on his abiding there, and so it does: but when he comes near the harbour and the pilot comes on board and takes the helm, the steersman cheerfully gives place and loses all responsibility. So may I. I feel assured the Lord will not bid me leave the wheel, as it were, in my own household, until He takes it into His own hand. The ship I leave shall not be given over to the waves because I leave it; but in all probability will never in one sense miss my care, because in taking me from it, the Lord Himself will undertake the charge of all...

"Yesterday reading the life of a good man, I felt convicted and tried to amend. This never answers. I thought I must try and follow the steps of this good man where I felt I came more short than he, but I could not do this either. Then I began to feel the Lord looked upon me as I was, and encouraged me to come to Him as my Father and Teacher and ask Him to do everything His way, not mine..."

Last Days

For the last three months of her life, Annette suffered seasons of intense pain and increasing weakness which was hard to bear. In her last letters, written in June 1880, she wrote:

"Some time ago I asked for the perfect love that should cast out fear. I have not, in this suffering, had to go and ask again, but to receive love without one fear. Not one wish but His. Many I love come before me. O that they might be made spiritually wise! I have laboured for some; the Lord has made me do it. But I cannot give it to them; I don't mean grace, of course, in this instance, but that they may be wise and not wrap up the Lord's talent without increase. Last night I felt I had received tenfold increase. I never believed this before. But read this only to yourself at present for I am not out of bow-shot. Do not think I rejoice as if not aware that the armour must not be put off. I cannot so much ask as tell the Lord I believe all He has promised. I feel like the virgins going forth to meet the Bridegroom...I truly can say I find my lamp has oil. I believe it will burn, with His blessing, till I reach that land where there is no need of it."

Two of her brothers-in-law were able to visit her, Richard from Pulverbach (who later compiled the book *Life and Love* about her), and William, then minister at Hertford in place of her father, Bernard Gilpin. She was able to speak to both, and by William sent her dying love to the congregation at Hertford, telling them to have their loins girded, their shoes on their feet and their staff in their hand, alluding to the manner in which the children of Israel were to eat the Lord's passover in the land of Egypt. She also sent for and affectionately spoke to several friends from Norton and Martock. One of them writes, "In these interviews the weakness and confusion of failing nature was not more apparent than the steadfast abiding of faith and hope and love in her spirit..."

A Written Testimony

One day she spoke as follows, and wished her daughter to write what she said:

"This has followed me for long, 'Let your loins be girded about and your lights burning, and ye yourselves like unto men that wait for their lord.' I knew this was my state and have felt it for years. I knew my foundation was on the Rock and for long have not sought for joy or anything else because I had Christ. I desire to make nothing else my hope. I have looked neither to the right nor to the left, and have only begged that He would undertake to purge and clear everything needful. O how I have felt that 'through much tribulation we must enter the kingdom' !"

Another time she said, referring to a visit of love from the Lord to her soul, "O if anyone had seen what I saw of the truth of God's Word! But I cannot say what I wish here. Remember, it is as a man lives he dies. If he lives in the tender fear of God, he dies in peace."

Referring to this visit again later she said, "I have felt something of pain in the spirit, if you can understand me, as to how I shall endure the sight of Jesus. I could not ask to see His face because I could not bear it. We cannot as we are see Him as He is; when we do we shall be like Him. His glory was so great I had a dread of entering heaven! The apostles and the prophets, when they saw His glory, felt all their comeliness turned into corruption."

The well-known lines on Rutherford's last words seemed always to soothe and comfort her. Every word, as she said or softly sang it, was her very own:

> "The sands of time are sinking;
> The dawn of heaven breaks;
> The summer morn I've sighed for,
> The fair sweet morn awakes.
> Dark, dark has been the midnight.
> But dayspring is at hand;
> And glory, glory dwelleth
> In Immanuel's land." etc.

Perfect Peace

From the time that she became fully aware that her mind had wandered she watched and prayed earnestly against it, often asking Charles to pray that she might sleep undisturbed by delirium; and she was never afterwards carried away by it. One morning after a pain she said, "I have had a beautiful night. The first part I got lower and lower but the glorious peace I have felt can never be described. Everything in nature is beautiful, but O the beauty of the words, 'God so loved the world, that He gave His only begotten Son, that whosoever believeth in Him should not perish, but have everlasting life'!"

That day was one of great suffering. In the afternoon she turned away from all who were with her and prayed aloud in broken words, saying afterwards, "God bid me ask to be relieved from my suffering; He showed me it was lawful. Then He said to me, 'Come up higher.' My Lord says, 'Welcome home!' I am overjoyed; my sufferings are nothing. I do not care what I suffer. O the surprising loveliness, truthfulness and faithfulness of dying in the Lord. I am in haste to be gone."

She gradually sank, with little revivals now and then during two slow weeks. Once she said, with an almost agonised look, "It seems so long. I have lost my faith." The Testament was handed to her and she eagerly tried to read, but could not see. One said to her, "I will see you again, and your heart shall rejoice." She said, "Yes, that is the promise He gave me," and remained silent for some hours. When Charles came into the room, she pointed suddenly upwards over and over again, and with the brightest smile said to him, "I am going there! It won't be long now. You have a place there, and I'm sure I have."

Throughout her last week on earth there was manifest the same fervent love and desire for the increase of the work of God on the earth, especially in her immediate neighbourhood, repeatedly saying she believed her prayers for many were heard. The last two days she lay quiet, perfect peace evidently filling her spirit. Charles said to her, "Are you happy'?" She said gently, "Happy! O yes!" and smiled sweetly. Before sunrise on September 24th 1880 her breathing became softer and softer and then her spirit fled, where

> "Glory, shadeless, shineth
> In Immanuel's land."

She was in the 49th year of her age.

Written specially for the *Gospel Standard* 1975 by J.H.Alexander.
A biography *Life and Love* was published in 1882.

CHOOSING RATHER

Elizabeth Howarth

By William Schofield (1838-1923), Mrs. Howarth's son-in-law, who was at one time pastor at Trowbridge.

Elizabeth Howarth was born in Rope Street, Rochdale, on July 22nd, 1813, and was placed very early in life under the care of her aunt and uncle, Abraham and Hannah Lord. She, with her aunt, attended Mr. Kershaw's ministry from childhood and was kept thoroughly under restraint, and although like the rest of mankind she was born in sin and shapen in iniquity, which she from her spiritual birth was ever ready to admit, yet in consequence of this restraint she was in great mercy preserved from those open sins into which so many young people run. Even when attending the Sunday school at Hope Chapel, Rochdale, at eight years of age, she was impressed with the solemnity of eternal realities, and being in the possession of a soul that must live for ever and ever, which solemn impression occurred in this way. She was reading in the class with others the 27th and 28th chapters of Matthew, when the fifth verse of the last mentioned chapter was fastened on her mind, especially the last clause, "Ye seek Jesus which was crucified." The writer has heard her say several times that she saw herself to be an exceedingly great sinner, and she felt she had sinned against a good and gracious God, and she evidently from that tune became a spiritual mourner, although so young in years. There was a special cleaving to her aunt and others of the Lord's people at that time for the truth's sake, and they were the company she sought when at the chapel and elsewhere.

The Lord by His Spirit began now to work more deeply in her heart, and showed her that although she had been kept strictly moral thus far through life, yet the plague of sin was deeply rooted within her heart, so much so that she sometimes feared she never could be saved, and this made her the more diligent and the more earnest, in reading the Word of God and attending the means of grace, to see if there was any hope of salvation for such a sinner as she felt herself to be; and it is clear that she did not seek the Lord's face in vain. For although she was often exercised about the beginning of her religion, not being so conspicuously called by grace or so deeply led as others, yet it is certain the Lord visited her soul manifestly by His grace, and by giving her a sense of His pardoning love, when only about fourteen years of age.

From this time she was much exercised about uniting with the people of God in church fellowship, under the pastoral care of dear Mr. Kershaw, having a very ardent love to the Lord Jesus Christ, as was evident from the fact that during that year she worked with her needle on canvas, the whole of the 106th [should be 186th] hymn (Gadsby's) written by Dr. Watts, the title being, "God my only happiness"; and she often spoke of the hymn to others as containing the feelings of her heart. This hymn framed in two sections, was given to my wife, her only daughter, before our dear mother's death and we valued it very much.

She made known to her aunt her wish to join the church, and Mrs. Kershaw soon made the matter known to Mr. Kershaw, who says in his autobiography:

"When this was made known to me by my wife, who had had frequent conversations with her, I was afraid of the storm of persecution that I knew would ensue, being well aware of what Mrs. Lord had to pass through when she joined the church. The girl declared to me what the Lord had wrought in her soul. I saw the grace of God in her and was glad. I enquired if the thing had been made known to her uncle; her aunt replied, 'No; we think you had better break it to him.'

"I sought an opportunity in the kindest manner I could. I told him the great things the Lord had done for his niece, also that it was her desire to be baptized and join the church. As I was narrating the facts of the case I perceived by his very breathing that evil was working in his mind against it. His reply was, 'Do you know what age our Betsy is?' I saw from the manner in which he asked the question that he meant to raise an objection against her baptism and communion with our church on the ground of her youth. In reply I said, 'Supposing your niece had gone as regularly to your chapel as she has come with her aunt to ours, and paid the same attention to her Bible, closet and prayer, and to every other religious duty which was in her power, would you raise an argument against her joining your society upon the ground of her youth? Would you not rather say, what a mercy it is that our Betsy "remembers her Creator in the days of her youth"? Would not you and your friends gladly receive her?' He replied, 'Perhaps we should,' and in an abrupt manner left the room.

"From that very day her uncle set himself to frustrate her intention to be baptized, questioned her, threatened her time after time, and sometimes he threatened to turn her out of doors, sometimes saying that he would not leave a penny in his will for her; but nothing deterred her, and it is astonishing at this early age how firm and reasonable she was in her statements to her uncle. One of these was, 'I am quite willing and anxious to do all that is my duty to do to you as my uncle and guardian, but when it becomes a matter of conscience as to how I ought to serve God, then I feel that I must obey God rather than man.' Upon this her uncle turned her out of doors, with no clothing but her nightdress, but as she was going out she seized hold of a cloak that was hanging on the back of a door and threw it around her, and thus she went along the street until she reached her father's house."

On another occasion she was the washing clothes belonging to the family, when her uncle attempted to get hold of them, wet as they were, and put them on top of her, saying, "I'll baptize thee," but she stepped back and in a good measure escaped the wetting. However she came before the church, and Mr. Kershaw says again:

"The Lord was with her, and enabled her to give a good reason of the hope that was in her with meekness and fear. Many of the friends sat in tears. I felt very thankful when she declared what benefit she had received from some sermons she had heard me preach. She stated to the church that while she was enduring persecution from her uncle, he threatening to put her away and disinherit her, she had received great comfort from that well-known hymn of Dr. Watts, 'My God, My Portion, and My Love,' especially from the sixth verse to the end, which she evidently repeated with much feeling:

' How vain a toy is glittering wealth,
  If once compared to Thee!
Or what's my safety or my health,
  Or all my friends to me?

' Were I possessor of the earth,
  And called the stars my own,
Without Thy graces and Thyself,
  I were a wretch undone!

' Let others stretch their arms like seas,
  And grasp in all the shore;
Grant me the visits of Thy face,
  And I desire no more.'

She was baptized and added to the church on March 1st, 1829."

Some time after this her uncle began to be very uneasy about the course he had taken in persecuting her, and especially in turning her out of his home. He therefore sent for her to come back, which she was willing to do upon condition that she was never again to be interfered with in the performance of her religious duties, which was granted to her. And besides this, in his own mind, he began to feel that he himself would like to attend Mr. Kershaw's ministry, which shortly after this circumstance took place he did, and continued to do so; and in many matters he acted a very friendly part towards Mr. Kershaw; but so far as is known he gave no signs of the fear of God being in his heart.

The subject of this memoir continued to go in and out amongst the people, often having special hearing and soul-humbling times under the preached Word, and was sometimes favoured to sit under the shadow of her heavenly Friend with great delight, and found His fruit to be sweet to her taste: yea, sweeter than honey or the honeycomb. She remained with her uncle until she was married to Mr. Kershaw's eldest son, William, which took place at the end of the year 1833. This was a very happy union, although a very short one (only being married ten months), as her husband, William was removed by a sudden attack of cholera, when doing business at Manchester. And although his wife and father, as soon as they heard of the seizure, drove off at once, they were only just in time to see him alive. This great loss she felt to her dying day, of which we have abundant proof in many ways.

Mr. Kershaw's autobiography says: "Her husband being a grocer and baker, she continued the business in the same premises, and some time after was married again to Mr. John Chadwick somewhere about the year 1836, but he only lived until the year 1841, leaving her with two children and a business to look after under very trying circumstances." [She would only have been 27 or 28.]

During this period of her life she became acquainted with Mr.Gadsby, of Manchester, Mr. Warburton of Trowbridge, and Mr.McKenzie of Preston, and with many other leading ministers of the Strict Baptist denomination, whom she dearly loved, and very highly esteemed in the Lord for their work's sake.

At this stage of her life, and for some years after, she was greatly afflicted with rheumatism, which sometimes laid her aside; yet notwithstanding this, she struggled hard to keep on her business, though often she had to go up and down stairs on her hands and knees, and yet she was nearly always in her place in the house of God; and to show how tenderly she felt about disturbing the worship of God by going late, I need only mention one circumstance, *viz.*, that when she was hindered, and could not get in time, she would stand all the time at the door, rather than go in to cause a noise; and would often say that she had a soul-comforting time in listening to the dear people pouring out their hearts in supplication unto God; and she always made it a standing rule that when she had been laid aside through affliction, which prevented her from attending the means of grace on a Lord's day or week-evening services, she would not, upon recovery, go to see the best friend she had on earth until she had been to the chapel, as she considered the Lord had a just right to the first fruits of her services; and no minister, no matter how little in the eyes of others he might appear, would cause her to be absent from the house of God; nor would any person ever hear her complain of the want of gifts in the preacher, so long as he preached the truth, and power attended it to the souls of the godly hearers.

She seldom took a step in her business, or in any other important matter, without consulting her dear minister, Mr. Kershaw, who was a skilful and wise adviser to her in many things, she being so attached to him as her father-in-law and pastor. He was much interested in her and her two children and he used to say to her, "I will never turn my back upon thee, nor upon thy two children, Betty, as long as I live"; which promise he faithfully kept to his dying day.

In 1842 there was much rioting in the town of Rochdale, caused by the introduction of power looms, when many provision and bakers' shops were broken open and plundered; and Mr. Kershaw, knowing that a large crowd was to pass through the street she lived in, came down from his house, and he and she went into her front room to hand out loaves of bread to the rioters, which entirely pacified them, so that no attempt was made to break into her shop by the unruly mob.

Before we continue with Mr. Schofield's account, we include a most interesting extract from John Kershaw's biography concerning Mrs. Howarth (Mrs. Chadwick as she was then). Mr. Kershaw is writing about raising money for enlarging the chapel (1848).

The first person I waited upon privately was our senior magistrate, from an impression I had upon my mind that he had a respect for me as a neighbour, believing if I could get his name, and a sovereign or two, it would have its effect with others. He received me very kindly, saying he understood that our chapel had for some time been too small.

He carefully examined my book, the names and sums put down, and said, "Although I am a Churchman, I am no enemy to dissenters," and, putting a £5 note upon the book, said, "It is with the greatest pleasure I give you this towards the enlargement of your chapel, for I have had my eyes upon you for more than thirty years. You have been a man of peace, plodding about the town, visiting and relieving the sick and afflicted, doing all the good you could, and such men as you we must and will stand by and support."

As he spoke these words, the language of Paul came powerfully to my mind (Romans 13. 3): "For rulers are not a terror to good works, but to the evil...Do that which is good, and thou shalt have praise of the same."

His liberality had the desired effect, as four of the other magistrates followed his example, also many other gentlemen in the town and neighbourhood.

In looking over my list of subscribers, the magistrate first named noticed the name of Elizabeth Chadwick, who had put down fifty pounds, and inquired who she was.

I told him she was a widow woman, who kept a baker's and provision shop, that her first husband was my son William, who died of cholera, and that her second husband was also dead, leaving her with two small children.

He answered that he thought fifty pounds was too much for her to give.

I said that I had thought the same; but when she gave me her reasons for doing so I was obliged to take it.

He inquired what the circumstances were.

I asked him for a Bible, as in giving him the account I should have to read a portion of it, which led to it. I then told him, as she was a widow woman and a member of our church, I felt it my duty to call upon her every week, and on a recent visit I asked her what she was thinking of giving to the enlargement of the chapel.

She replied. "If you will come to your tea next Monday, I will tell you."

I went accordingly, and renewed the inquiry, when she got her Bible and said, "I need not tell you that when my late husband died, he left me in insolvent circumstances, and had it not been for you and my uncle standing by me and helping me, my creditors would have come upon me and sold me up, and my poor children and I would not have had a bed to lie down upon nor a seat to sit on. Also I was in a poor state of health, encompassed with these difficulties, which often bowed me down, both in body and mind. I often went into my room to tell the Lord my troubles, and to plead His promise to be the Husband of the widow, and the Father of the fatherless. On one of these occasions, when faint and ready to give all up, I opened the Bible to seek a little comfort there. As the Lord would have it, I opened to the twenty-eighth chapter of Genesis, and began to read it, and I felt encouraged, especially when I read the fifteenth verse, where the Lord promised Jacob that He would never leave him nor forsake him. The Holy Spirit bore witness with my spirit that Jacob's God was my God, and that He would never leave nor forsake me. He enabled me to cast my burden and care upon Him who cared for me, and would sustain and make a way for me. My mind was so supported and comforted in reading this chapter that I went into my chamber and, like Daniel, kneeled before the Lord to thank and bless His dear name; and, like Jacob, I vowed unto the Lord, saying, 'If God will be with me, and shall keep me in this way that I go, and will give me bread to eat and raiment to put on, and prosper me in my business so that I can pay my creditors, whatever He might give me more, I would give a tenth to His house'; for at that time I had an impression on my mind that the chapel would have to be enlarged. The reason I asked you to my home today is that I might have time to reckon what I am worth, and what a tenth would be, and I find it will be fifty pounds." (This at the proper time she gave me in sovereigns.)

When the worthy magistrate heard this relation, he said, "God bless Betty Chadwick. It is the best tale I ever heard. Under these circumstances you could not but take it."

We now continue with William Schofield's account:

Mrs. Chadwick married again to a member of the church at Rochdale, of the name Michael Howarth, in the year 1851, who lived until the year 1868; so that it will be seen she survived three husbands. Meanwhile, she took a very great interest in the services of God's house, and assisted Mrs. Kershaw in the Sabbath school; and even at this date she was looked upon as being a mother in Israel.

On October 20th, 1863, our dear mother wrote in a memorandum book as follows:

"I heard Mr. Kershaw preach this morning from these words: 'Therefore be ye also ready; for in such an hour as ye think not the Son of man cometh. This sermon was occasioned by the sudden death of one of our members; I felt, as he was describing those characters who were ready, what a solemn and necessary thing it is to be *made ready* by the Lord's Spirit and grace.

'Prepare me, gracious God,
To stand before Thy face;

> Thy Spirit must the work perform,
> For it is all of grace.'

And as the desires and cravings of those who were being made ready were set forth, I felt that I possessed them, for I could honestly say that I desired to know more of Jesus Christ, and grow more into His image of holiness and humility; but O how unholy I feel myself to be at times, so that instead of going forward in this respect, I often fear I am going backward, and that I shall never reach the heavenly Canaan in safety: but I do so wish to be right with God.

"In the afternoon, Mr. Kershaw preached from these words: 'But I give myself unto prayer.' A portion I have often thought about, and wished that in every particular I could act upon it; for I can say before God that I do desire to 'give myself more and more unto prayer', and commit all my concerns into the Lord's hands, and leave them there. But how backward I am in the exercise of prayer, and how often it is with me 'that I know not what to pray for as I ought'. and therefore have to come before the Lord as a little child, saying, 'Lord, teach me how to pray, and what to pray for as I ought. Do come and control my affections, and let it not be what I would desire after the flesh, but let my petitions come before Thee in the all-prevailing name of Jesus Christ, as prompted from within by Thy Holy Spirit. Do help me to serve Thee as I ought, and to live more to Thy honour and glory.'

"In looking over the day's proceedings, and before retiring to rest at night, how I have felt a strong desire before the Lord for some token of His love to be made known to my soul. Once these words came to my mind with weight and power: ' The Lord thy God in the midst of thee is mighty; He will save, He will rejoice over thee with joy; He will rest in His love, He will joy over thee with singing.' I felt what an unspeakable favour and blessing it was to be one of the Lord's favourites; and how very condescending it was of the Lord to rejoice over such a poor sinner as I often feel myself to be.

"September 3rd, 1866. Early this morning when I awoke, I felt a strong desire to have my mind stayed upon the Lord through the day, when this verse came to my mind:

> ' Blest is the man, O God,
> Whose mind is stayed on Thee;
> Who waits for Thy salvation, Lord,
> Shall Thy salvation see.'

And I was led to meditate on these words: 'I had fainted, unless I had believed to see the goodness of the Lord in the land of the living. Wait on the Lord; be of good courage, and He shall strengthen thine heart: wait, I say, on the Lord.' And the words of the prophet Isaiah came very forcibly to my mind also: 'For they shall not be ashamed that wait for Me.' I felt much encouraged quietly to wait for God, and upon God, and to hope for His great salvation.

"September 21st, 1868. Feeling a great desire to get near to the Lord in prayer, the words dropped upon my spirit: 'A people near unto Him'; and I felt that I was one of those very people, having been adopted from everlasting into His family and redeemed by the precious blood of Jesus Christ, and called with a holy calling, by the power of His blessed Spirit, out of darkness into His marvellous light; and have now for nearly forty years had a name and a place among His dear people, which is better than all things else beside. The same day I was further encouraged with these words: 'The Lord taketh pleasure in them that fear Him, in those that hope in His mercy.' I hope I do in reality fear God, and I trust I have done so for forty-six years or more; and I desire to grow in this precious grace of godly fear which produces that blessed filial affection towards Him, which is peculiar to those who are loved of God, and who earnestly desire to love Him in return.

> 'O that my soul could love and praise Him more,
>   His beauties trace, His majesty adore;
> Live near His heart, upon His bosom lean;
> Obey his voice, and all His will esteem.'

"October 4th, 1868. Sabbath morning. As I was getting ready for chapel, my mind was occupied with these words: 'I have loved the habitation of Thy house, the place where Thine honour dwelleth.' O the love I felt to the solemn truths we are accustomed to hear: a free grace gospel, which secures spiritual benefits to poor sinners like me, and gives all the glory to a Three-One God. And I love the people of God, and the dear man of God, our minister; but above all, I love 'the God of my salvation'. In the evening, when meditating upon what I had heard in the morning, I was greatly helped by these lines:

> 'Shine, Lord, and my terror shall cease;
>   The blood of atonement apply;
> And lead me to Jesus for peace,
>   The Rock that is higher than I.
> Speak, Saviour, for sweet is Thy voice;
>   Thy presence is fair to behold:
> I thirst for Thy Spirit, with cries
>   And groanings that cannot be told.'

October 7th, 1868. About four o'clock this morning I was praying earnestly that the Lord would speak peace and pardon into my distressed and comfortless soul, when these words were brought with power to my heart: 'Comfort ye, comfort ye My people, saith your God. Speak ye comfortably to Jerusalem, and cry unto her, that her warfare is accomplished, that her iniquity is pardoned: for she hath received of the Lord's hand double for all her sins.' Is it possible, I said, that such a worthless sinner as I should come to a knowledge of so much sin pardoned, and to receive double for it? Wonderful mercy! and wonderful grace indeed!

'Grace reigns to pardon crimson sins,
To melt the hardest hearts;
And from the work it once begins
It never once departs.'

"February 6th, 1869. When I awoke this morning I was in great distress of mind, arising from many causes but chiefly on account of the absence of my heavenly Friend, which produced a darkness of mind which could be felt; but I was enabled to plead earnestly with the Lord that He would appear for my help once more, as He had done in days that are past – when He spoke with power to my heart these words: 'When thou passest through the waters, I will be with thee; and through the rivers, they shall not overflow thee: when thou walkest through the fire, thou shalt not be burned; neither shall the flame kindle upon thee.' It was so suitable and seasonable to the condition of my mind, and was in the hands of the Spirit such a comfort to my soul, and these lines of the hymn followed upon the heels of it so sweetly that I was greatly helped:

' When through the deep waters I call thee to go,
The rivers of woe shall not thee overflow;
For I will be with thee, thy troubles to bless,
And sanctify to thee thy deepest distress.'

I felt for the time being that I could leave all with the Lord, both for body and soul and circumstances, and truly it was blessed work to fall into the hands of the Lord, whose mercies are so great."

In order to relieve Mrs. Kershaw during the last illness of her husband, our dear mother became almost his sole attendant and nurse during the day; and they felt as much attached to each other as though they were father and daughter; the latter, with many other friends, lamenting their sad loss when the Lord should see fit to call him unto Himself.

"August 13th, 1881. The following portion of God's holy Word was very sweet to my soul today: 'Come, My people, enter thou into thy chambers, and shut thy doors about thee: hide thyself as it were for a little moment, until the indignation be overpast.' I felt quite a drawing aside from the world to hide my guilty soul beneath the wounded side of the dear Redeemer: even that Man who is to guilty sinners, 'a hiding place from the wind, and a covert from the tempest'.

'Other refuge have I none,
    Hangs my helpless soul on Thee;
Leave, ah! leave me not alone;
    Still support and comfort me.'

"December 15th, 1886. The Lord blessed me in answer to prayer with this sweet promise: 'I will never leave thee nor forsake thee'; then followed immediately these words: 'For the mountains shall depart, and the hills be removed; but My kindness shall not depart from thee, neither shall the covenant of My peace be removed, saith the Lord that hath mercy on thee.' I felt that God's almighty power was round about me to defend and protect me from all dangers, and His covenant mercy and love were within me, which gave me a sweet hope that I was His child, and that He would watch over me for good, and protect and support me down to my journey's end."

The jubilee of her membership with the church of Christ came on March 1st, 1879, but she commemorated it in the month of June 1888, by having a jubilee tea meeting, when several ministers and friends from other churches, along with her fellow members, were invited and accepted the invitation; when our dear mother submitted the following in writing to the meeting:

"My dear friends – I have written down a few things which I should like to read to you, as I cannot attempt to make a speech before you. I thought I should like *us* to have a members' tea meeting, as it brings us together in a friendly way and manner; and while it is not the time of my jubilee, it is the jubilee of two other members present, and I hope it may be a jubilee indeed to them; the Lord Jesus has been very precious to their souls, which I know from a personal knowledge of them, and their heart-felt experience. They can say, 'Hitherto hath the Lord helped us.' And they can speak of seasons when the Lord appeared for their help. How good it is when we can record His former visits to our souls!...I cannot give so distinct and clear an account of a work of grace upon my soul as some can, nor as our friend Mrs. Ramsbottom did at our members' last tea meeting: and this has caused me great trouble, and much heart searching before the Lord, to know whether I was right or not; for I solemnly know that while we may deceive our fellow creatures, we cannot deceive God.

'To Him I always stand revealed
Exactly as I am!'

"I well remember, when I was a schoolgirl about eight years old, we were reading about the sufferings of Christ, which affected me very much; and from that time I began to feel myself to be a great sinner, and one that needed a great Saviour. The subject matter of the 592nd hymn ('Mighty to save') was constantly upon my mind, together with the fact that my sins were such as to need this very Saviour to cleanse my soul from them. I mentioned this hymn when I came before the church, the last Lord's day in February 1829, when I was fifteen years and seven months old; so that on the first Lord's day in March last, I had been a member of this church at Rochdale, fifty-nine years. I have had much soul travail, and have gone through many a heavy trial since then. Sometimes I have felt myself to be such a sinner and so full of unbelief that I have thought I never could be saved; but I sincerely hope the Lord has many times spoken words of comfort to my heart, so that I have 'rejoiced in God my Saviour', and have felt with the prophet when he said, 'Behold, God is my salvation; I will trust, and not be afraid: for the Lord Jehovah is my strength and my song; He also is become my salvation. Therefore with joy shall ye draw water out of the wells of salvation.' I have often 'sat under His shadow with great delight', in hearing His ministers set Him forth in the ministry of the Word, and have found 'His fruit to be sweet to my taste'; but I want fresh helps for present troubles, for I feel my spiritual poverty more than ever I did. My winters are long, my hope is often chilled, and my harp is frequently hung upon the willows, so that the psalmist's prayer suits me well, where he says, 'Leave me not, neither forsake me, O God of my salvation.'

"A few days ago, I was reading the *Memoir of Sukey Harley,* and on page 119 she mentions many portions of Scripture, and some verses of hymns, which I have written down at different periods of time; but sometimes when I read them over again, there was no heavenly dew, nor any spiritual moisture to be found in them, so that they were not food for my soul to feed upon. For, as dear Sukey said, 'I want fresh manna every day, and I faint, unless by faith I feed upon the Lord Jesus Christ.' You will perhaps think that I am simple, but many years ago, I was very much tried about the word *grace,* and was so afraid that I was destitute of it, and I did not quite understand it; at least, I wanted to understand it more and more. Besides, I felt myself to be such a great sinner that, with the Apostle Paul, I often exclaimed, 'O wretched man that I am! who shall deliver me from the body of this death?'

'O wretched, wretched man!
What horrid scenes I view!
I find, alas! do all I can,
That I can nothing do.'

"I had an old Bible which Mr. Kershaw gave me, and I opened it at the second chapter of Ephesians, and when I came to the words: 'For by grace are ye saved through faith; and that not of yourselves: it is the gift of God,' I think I never saw anything so grand there before; there was such light shone into my soul, and such power attended these words: 'And that not of yourselves: it is the gift of God.' I felt that they suited just such a poor creature as I felt myself to be. And shortly after I turned to a hymn by Dr. Watts, and when I came to the verse which reads:

'Jesus, Thy love far, far from sight,
'Midst stars and seraphs pure and bright,
Stands high enthroned in worlds of light,'

how the name of Jesus stood out most prominent, and I think I saw more beauty in the Person and work of Christ than I had ever seen before: and there was such a sweetness and savour in that very name (Christ) that I can never forget. It was a deliverance indeed to my soul, so that I praised the Lord and took courage.

"After this I was very much exercised about the word *faith*. I seemed to be so unbelieving that I appeared to be destitute of faith, and yet the Lord says in His Word that 'without faith it is impossible to please God', and also 'that which is not of faith is sin'. What very great words did these appear to be to me, and how very far short did I feel to come with respect to what is set forth by those great words. O how I desired to be found in the use of all lawful means, and to be diligent in the use of them! Still, when I hear ministers speaking of principles of faith, and the working of faith in the hearts of God's people, I feel I have faith; for my heart's desires are continually going out to God that He would give me a clearer understanding in all these vital matters, that I might live more in the sweet enjoyment of them, and in the enjoyment of His gracious presence, and have continually in my heart a greater sense of His love and mercy, so that I might live more to His honour, praise and glory."

"I have often felt much encouraged in attending the prayer meetings, and I think it very desirable that we should show more earnestness and perseverance in attending them, for here it is that *real* Christians are expected to assemble together to breathe out their heart-felt supplications unto God,

'While one is pleading with our God,
May each one wrestle too.'

"It does seem so desirable that our prayer meetings should be better attended by those who profess to be the Lord's people, so that unitedly they might be led by the Holy Spirit to ask the Lord to support and bless each other, and by which means they would be holding up the hands of our ministers, as Aaron and Hur held up the hands of Moses, the servant of the Lord, while the children of Israel prevailed over the Amalekites. The Apostle Paul said, 'Brethren, pray for us'; and, of course, he meant all the Lord's servants down to the end of time, that they might be experimentally led into all truth and be enabled to declare it with savour and unction and power into the hearts of the Lord's people.

"There are three out of the many special seasons I have had at prayer meetings which I hope never to forget. One was a prayer meeting in our late minister Mr. Kershaw's house, and because of pressing matters at home I could not possibly get to it in time, and I stayed outside listening to the singing of the hymns and to the dear people pouring out their supplications to God, and I felt my heart to unite with them in the solemn worshipping of His holy name, and it was a blessed time indeed to my soul.

"Another time was when I was visiting at Mr. Horbury's House at Clayton West. I went to their prayer meeting, and when Mr. Horbury was engaged in prayer, I felt my heart go out with him in the prayer he offered up to God; and as Christians I felt that we were united to the Lord Jesus Christ in the bonds of the gospel, so that it was a time of rejoicing to my soul. There was such solemnity and reverence, coupled with his weighty petitions and confessions, that I could not help writing to Mr. Horbury afterwards, that he might rejoice with me at having obtained such a great blessing from the Lord, and which continued for some time.

"The third special time was on New Year's Day, 1887, when a few of us met together to recount the Lord's mercies and goodness, vouchsafed to us through the past year, and to ask His continued help and blessing in and upon our souls through the year we now had entered upon, should it be His sovereign will to spare us so long, and although there were but few of the friends present, yet I felt that the Lord had fulfilled His gracious promise, which says that, 'Where two or three are gathered together in My name, there am I in the midst of them.' Such were the hallowed feelings of my mind that I most blessedly realised the Lord was with us indeed, and in truth. The words of Holy Writ are most applicable here, which command us to 'provoke one another to love and to good works', and when we meet for prayer and praise, may our conversation and the services of God's house we are engaged in be such as are calculated to lead to our spiritual edification.

"We had some few years ago an aged, godly woman as a member of our church, and when I have been in a low state of mind, I have sometimes gone to visit her, and sometimes I have found her low herself, although she was generally a very cheerful Christian person. I remember one day finding her ill in bed, and when entering the room where she lay she said, 'I have been thinking of that sweet hymn which says:

> 'I'll praise my Maker while I've breath,
> And when my voice is lost in death,
> Praise shall employ my nobler powers;
> My days of praise shall ne'er be past,
> While life, and thought, and being last,
> Or immortality endures.'

What a lift that was to me, as well as a seasonable reproof for my unbelief, and how I was convinced of the fact that in the providence of God I was much more favourably situated than this poor woman, so that when our conversation is seasoned with grace it is very encouraging to visit each other.

"I thought I would mention among other things in these papers that most blessed ordinance, the Lord's Supper. For I have seen persons more frequently absent than members of the church of Christ ought to be. I can truly say for myself that only twice during my long connection with this church have I been absent, and even then by a determined effort I might have been present. It is more than fifty years ago since those two absent times occurred, and they have been a source of great grief to my soul unto this day. How much better it is for the Lord's people to avail themselves of every privilege afforded them to attend all the services of God's house, and as we are hoping to sit down with our Lord and Saviour Jesus Christ in His heavenly kingdom, it should be the chief concern of all His dear people here on earth to seek to have His company in the means of grace as much as possible, that they may through the Holy Spirit's teaching become more like Him."

Here the account given on her 59th anniversary ends.

"July 5th, 1888. I was crying unto the Lord in my many trials, and my mind was much exercised under the weight of them, when the Lord spoke to my soul the following words: 'They shall cry unto the Lord because of the oppressors, and He shall send them a Saviour, and a great one, and He shall deliver them.' I had such a sweet view of Jesus Christ as my Saviour who saves from wrath, sin and hell. The clouds dispersed, and the following verse was sealed with power upon my heart:

> 'Sorrow for joy I shall exchange,
> For ever freed from pain;
> And o'er the plains of Canaan range;
> For me to die is gain.'

What a blessed prospect!

"May 13th, 1890. 'For the vision is yet for an appointed time, but at the end it shall speak, and not lie: though it tarry, wait for it; because it will surely come, it will not tarry.' Although a clear revelation and manifestation of God's Word was made to my soul at times, yet at times it was withheld from me, so that I was often left to walk in much darkness, yet every testimony which God by His Spirit had favoured me with I felt would certainly come true.

> ' His word shall stand, His truth prevail;
> And not one jot or tittle fail.'

On November 14th,1890 our dear mother had a paralytic seizure which entirely took away her speech for six or eight weeks, and rendered her quite helpless, so that we had to attend to her like a child until the day of her death, which was within a month of being nine years. During which time she manifested much Christian patience and resignation to the will of God. But there were times with her when she longed to be gone and sometimes she would say to her daughter, "Hannah, I have a strong desire to depart, to be with Christ which is far better."

About a month after this attack, she made a great effort to tell us of a portion of God's Word that was upon her mind, but she could not utter a word distinctly, but we thought she wanted to say *blessed* and also the word *hope,* and she indicated that she wanted the Bible, which was given her. She began to turn from Timothy to Titus, and we soon found that it was these words she wished to repeat to us: "Looking for that blessed hope, and the glorious appearing of the great God and our Saviour Jesus Christ." She was delighted when she found that we understood her, and knew what portion she had upon her mind, which fully showed the blessed position she was in. I said to her, "But you are not satisfied, mother, that you have been looking for nearly seventy years, and are still looking?" And very imperfectly she said, with great emphasis to the former part of the question, *"No, no,"* and indicated that she was still looking to the Lord for help and salvation.

Mr. Eddison, the pastor, and the friends from the chapel began to hold prayer meetings occasionally in our house on a Lord's day evening. which she appreciated very much. At one of these meetings she had a very special time of communion with God, which arose from the following hymn being given out by one of the deacons:

"To know my Jesus crucified,
By far excels all things beside;
All earthly good I count but loss,
And triumph in my Saviour's cross."

She spoke of this season again and again to the friends and to the deacon who was the instrument in the Lord's hand of conveying it to her. About this time she so far recovered her speech as to be able to converse with those who called to see her, and unless the conversation turned upon spiritual matters she was far from being satisfied. She was often found quoting the lines of the hymn.

"Jesus, my soul's athirst for Thee;
Absent from Thee I cannot rest;
Come now, reveal Thyself to me;
I cannot leave Thy throne unblest."

So that she longed for closer communion with and more conformity to the image of Christ Jesus her Lord.

On one occasion the writer was very tried about giving up family worship, as he felt hard in the exercise of it and seemed to get no answer to his poor petitions. The enemy was raging and saying it was no use to pray, "for the Lord did not hear nor answer them, and those that had to listen to them were weary of the same confessions of sin, unworthiness and unprofitableness, etc., and the same petitions for mercy, mercy, mercy, and you know yourself that you are weary of hearing your own voice morning and night; give it up at once." And I was so much pressed that I sat with my Bible on my knees for some time, and the family were waiting and I have no doubt wondering what it all meant, but by and by I was led to open the Bible at the one hundred and twenty-first Psalm, and as I read it my heart was somewhat softened, and I thought if I were the special object of God's care and keeping I must have the root of the matter within me, and although much tried all would come right at last. We knelt down together at the footstool of mercy, and the Lord the Spirit helped me to breathe out my soul's supplications to God in a special way and manner, and upon rising from prayer the dear old saint said, "William, your prayers of late have been a wonderful help to me, and they have been the very breathings of my soul before God, both day and night!" I replied. "Well, mother, I have been of late much tried about continuing family worship, for the enemy told me you were weary of hearing me, and you saw how I kept you waiting this morning before I opened the Bible." She said, "So far from that, I can say that I value them as my greatest comforts and privileges, and also for the fact that I live in a house with those who fear God and where His Word is regularly read, and prayer and supplication is made unto God." I record this to show how much our aged mother appreciated the company of God's saints and their supplications before the Lord on the one hand, and to encourage on the other hand those that are similarly tempted, for I am sure the Lord tries the righteous.

On June 1st, 1895, she was greatly blessed with the following words coming into her heart with power: "Yea, I have loved thee with an everlasting love: therefore with lovingkindness have I drawn thee." She felt how sovereignly the love of God had been displayed in herself, and how softening and drawing its power was in her heart, that the response was,

> " O that my soul could love and praise Him more,
> His beauties trace, His majesty adore;
> Live near His heart, upon His bosom lean;
> Obey His voice, and all His will esteem."

On September 7th following she was reading Hawker's morning portion for that date, the heading of which was, "For the Lord God of Israel saith that He hateth putting away," and she felt so much comforted in that the Lord did not put her away, guilty and filthy as she felt herself to be in His sight. No, He would not disregard her earnest plea, nor spurn her from Him, for she was engraven on the palms of His hands, and her needs were continually before Him. The following lines were sweetly applied:

> " 'Graved on His hands divinely fair,
> Who did their ransom pay,
> The golden letters still appear;
> He hates to put away."

Then followed, "I will trust, and not be afraid: for the Lord JEHOVAH is my strength and my song; He also is become my salvation." and she felt much sweetness and savour from the following verse:

> "Then will He own my worthless name
> Before His Father's face,
> And in the new Jerusalem
> Appoint my soul a place."

She had been a constant reader of the *Gospel Standard* since its commencement in 1835, and has many times been encouraged by the writings and sermons which have been published therein. The sermon of Mr. A.B. Taylor of Manchester, which appeared in the G.S. some time ago, which treated on "The Inheritance of the Saints", she wanted to be read to her again and again, as she was longing to be put into the possession of the same. It was a favourite subject of hers. I remember four or five years ago, when very ill, she said most earnestly, "The Lord is the portion of my inheritance, therefore will I hope in Him." She was a woman who kept close to her Bible and hymn book, which together with the *Gospel Standard* and *Hawker's Morning and Evening Portions,* formed nearly her whole library. The friends from the chapel, with Mr. Eddison, and other ministers, visited her from time to time during the whole of the nine years she was afflicted and laid aside, and their visits she much appreciated. Therefore this record of her might be lengthened out from many sources.

On July 28th, 1899, she had a second seizure which entirely took her speech again, after which, and up to the day of her death, she was only once able to take any solid food, but lived almost entirely on milk. For a few days she was unconscious, but about the first week in August consciousness was restored to her, so that she could even utter some short words, and it was very clear to all who saw her that her end was drawing very near, and it was equally clear that her mind was steadfastly fixed upon divine realities, for she was from day to day directing us to some portion of the Word of God, or to some of her favourite hymns, of which she had many. And I have noticed when she has been in an unsettled state from some physical cause, and which we could not fully understand, that the best way to compose her was to read to her a chapter, or a Psalm, or some of her favourite hymns.

She lingered on in this way until the end of September. and about a week before her death she became unconscious again, and we never could be certain that she understood anything we said to her. In this state she quietly and peaceably breathed her last on October 7th, 1899. She was interred in the Rochdale cemetery on October 12th, when the following ministers took part in the burial service: Mr. John Smith, Mr. McKee, Mr. H.E. Greenwood, Mr. Chandler and Mr. Eddison, the latter officiating at the graveside. Thus ended a life morally unblemished, chequered, but upright and consistent as a Christian. So that we may say she was "well laid in the grave", leaving two children to mourn their loss.

Gospel Standard 1995, first published in the 1900 *Gospel Standard.*

THROUGH MUCH TRIBULATION

Anne Coates

By James Dennett (1828-1900), minister at Salem Chapel, Birmingham.

The subject of this account was born at Beckley, Oxfordshire. Her parents being Church people, she was brought up in the dead forms of that Establishment, and continued in them until God opened her blind eyes to see the emptiness of such mere outward worship. Nothing particular took place in her life until after her marriage to Mr. John Coates in the year 1837, when they settled at Chalgrove, a village about three miles from Stadhampton, where Mr. Philpot used to preach, and in which Mr. Doe afterwards laboured and experimentally preached the great and grand doctrines of free and sovereign grace. Both of these dear servants of God were held in high esteem by Mrs. C., and by many others who heard them.

Mrs. C. not having left any written account of the Lord's dealings with her soul, I am (with a little help from friends, for which I tender them sincere thanks) almost entirely dependent on my own personal knowledge and memory of what I knew of her, and what she has related to me of the Spirit's work of grace on her heart. Truly God is a sovereign in giving grace to whom He will give it, and also in ordaining the paths in which His own dear children shall walk after they are called to the knowledge of His great and sacred name, which are so various and in many cases so opposite as to baffle our reason, so that no one can mark out a uniform pathway to the kingdom of God except, as Christ hath promised, that all who know and fear His name shall in the world have tribulation.

About the year 1840, at which time Mrs. C. was with her husband attending the Church of England, the Lord began to open her blind eyes to see the emptiness of such a system of forms, and brought upon her such feelings of soul-trouble as she had never known before. She could then no longer go on with a mere formal religion, and her husband, being a rigid Churchman, began to oppose her; and now began a conflict for the one who was called and quickened by grace, both from without and from within; for Satan raged furiously through her husband, who became her bitterest persecutor, and as furiously against the life of God in her soul.

The clergyman who preached in the church where they attended was brother-in-law to Mr. Coates, having married his sister, and this made the separation the more trying to Mrs. C., and as she would no longer attend church with her husband, to go through what she felt to be a mere formal service, this made him rage the more. When her husband came to know that her mind was favourable to dissenters, to whom he was much opposed, and that she had embraced the doctrines of free and sovereign grace, his anger and rage were intensified, and such ill-usage and cruelty were added to it as were almost unbearable, and her life was often in imminent danger. But the Lord, who knoweth how to help and succour His people in trials, raised up one and another to comfort and help her.

Opposite to Mrs. Coates's home lived Mr. and Mrs. Crake, who kept a school, and who afterwards removed to Clifton, near Abingdon, and finally to Eastbourne. During Mrs. C.'s great soul-trouble. Mr. and Mrs. Crake were true helpers and comforters to her, and they, being intimately acquainted with Mr. Tiptaft, named her case to him. Mrs. C. now attended the little chapel at Stadhampton, where God often blessed her soul through that dear, simple, honest servant of Christ, Mr. William Doe. She frequently went to chapel with her soul full of trouble and overwhelmed in outward trials and sorrows, when Mr. Doe was so led to trace out her inward experience and describe her outward pathway that she often thought someone must have told him all about her, and she has returned home full of joy and peace and love to God and His dear servant.

On one occasion when her husband found out that she had been to chapel, he was so enraged that he tore her hymnbook into pieces, but there was a leaf left on which she saw the name of Jesus, when she was so comforted that her tears of sorrow were all wiped away. Frequently Mr. C. would hold her Bible over the fire, but always seemed afraid to destroy it. Miss Hatt, now Mrs. Godwin [Thomas Godwin of Godmanchester's wife], was a true friend to Mrs. C. They often walked to the house of God in company, and spoke of the exercises that their souls had passed through during the previous week, and were surprised to find how Mr. Doe told them all their heart exercises and desires. During this time of intimacy with Miss H., the Lord was pleased to set Mrs. C.'s soul at liberty, taking away her burden of sin and guilt, and giving her peace and pardon, when she spoke with much confidence to Miss H., and endeavoured to assure her that the same blessing was in store for her; and in this she prophesied truly, for in the month of June of the same year (1844) the Lord came down and took away the mountain of sin and guilt under which Miss H. had been labouring, and the Holy Spirit revealed Christ in her the hope of glory.

Mr. C. eventually left Chalgrove and took a farm at Great Milton in which undertaking he at first prospered, and being a good business man, he might have continued to do well. A neighbouring farmer once said to him, "If you would only be steady you might soon ride in your carriage"; but drink became his besetting sin, and when under its influence, his conduct and cruelty to his wife was such that she felt her life was in constant danger and that she must leave him, which course, with the advice of some kind friends, she determined to take; but when all had been arranged, and she was just on the eve of departing to live alone, God by His Word intervened, applying the following scripture to her heart: "And the woman which hath an husband that believeth not, and if he be pleased to dwell with her, let her not leave him" (1 Cor. 7. 13). She was thus stopped from following her own plans and the advice of friends, and was enabled with prayer and supplication to commit her way and herself for safety into the hands of a good and gracious God, that she might experience more of His supporting grace and power in her soul, and realise most clearly how He preserved her life and restrained her violent husband from executing the will of the devil towards her.

At this critical time persecution raged high, and her husband became most desperate, and used at night to place under his pillow a razor and, supposing his wife to be asleep (when, dear woman, she was awake and secretly calling upon God for preservation), he would take the razor and audibly say, "Now I will do it," meaning that he would cut her throat; but God restrained him, and would not suffer him to carry out his purpose. Mr. C. was determined to make his wife go to church, but this she could not and would not do; therefore he resolved to prevent her going to chapel, and used to beat her so unmercifully that at times she was tempted to accede to his wishes, and give up her religion.

In the year 1849, Mr. Tiptaft being intimate with Mr. and Mrs. Crake, was through them well acquainted with the trials of Mrs. Coates, but under the circumstances knew not how to advise her; therefore he wrote to Mr. Philpot respecting the matter, and asked for his advice. Mr. P.'s reply is in Letter 107 of his Book of Letters, and runs as follows:

"I consider poor Mrs. C.'s case is a very trying one, and one very difficult to pronounce any decided opinion upon. Say, for instance, that we gave it as our decided advice that she should stay away from the chapel; that would seem shunning the cross. Say that we advised her still to go, and she should lose her life in consequence, painful reflections might be cast upon us. Such dreadful brutality we rarely hear of – indeed, I might say, such murderous proceedings. I think, however, there is a decided difference between doing evil and forbearing to do well. Thus, I think, she might resolutely refuse to go to church, whatever the consequence. *There,* I think, my mind is pretty clear. But whether she might not abstain for a season, during his present dreadful madness, I might call it, from going to chapel, is another matter.

"Christians, when persecuted in one place, might flee to another. Here was an allowed declining persecution by flight; but on the other hand, God, we know, can make a way of escape even by persons persevering to go. Look at D.C. of A–, how her husband stood with a knife at the door, the morning she was to be baptized, to stab her, and how she crept out at the window, was baptized, and how all was overruled, as we hope, for his eventual good. A leaf which fell into my hands this morning gives an account of a poor woman much in Mrs. C.'s situation.

"I think much must depend on the state of her mind – what she feels led to do, what promises the Lord has applied to her soul, what faith and strength she has in exercise, how her own conscience is exercised in the matter. It is so hard to lay down rules of action in these matters, for what one can do another cannot. Peter, who once denied his Master, could afterwards be crucified with his head downwards. Nicodemus comes first by night, and afterwards goes boldly into Pilate's presence. Elijah flees before Jezebel, and then meets Ahab in Naboth's vineyard. David kills Goliath, and then flees before Absalom. Thus, good men act differently as faith is weak or strong; and we would not counsel any man to walk on the waves unless we knew he had Peter's Master near, and Peter's faith in exercise.

"Thus I feel slow to offer advice, or give counsel in this painful and difficult matter. We feel, however, encouraged to hope the Lord will appear for her from the promise He has given her."

She often spoke with much esteem of Mr. and Mrs. Crake and Miss Hatt, who afterwards became the wife of Mr. Godwin, as in her sorrows and trials they showed her great kindness. Some time after this the parish church at Great Milton was about to be renovated, when Mr. Whiting, a very godly man, who lived at Weston-on-the-Green, and who was a member of the little Strict Baptist church, which at that time met in an upper room at the back of Mr. Higgins's business premises, Jericho, Oxford, obtained the contract to do the required repairs at the church at Great Milton. Mr. W. had heard of Mrs. Coates and her troubles, but knew not how to gain an interview with her. One day he resolved that he would go and ask if he could borrow a ladder, when Mrs. C. came to the door, and said he could have their ladder. Mr. W. then said to Mrs. C., "Do you know anything about Jacob's ladder?" This led on to a conversation and soul-union which ever after remained unbroken, and Mr. W. proved a lasting friend to her both temporally and spiritually.

One morning Mr. Coates met Mr. W., and knowing that he was executing the work at the church, and feeling a special esteem for him, though he could not tell why, said, "Mr. W., would it not be better for you to get apartments at Milton, and not go such a long journey home every night?" Mr. W. replied that he would be very glad to do so, but stated that he could not get apartments at Milton. Mr. Coates's house being large, he at once offered Mr. W. the use of three or four rooms for himself, wife and two sons, which was gladly accepted, and specially regarded as the hand of God; and there they came to live, and remained for twelve months. This arrangement was made a great blessing to Mrs. C., for she now had the privilege of conversing with a godly man in her own house, a constant interest in his prayers, and less to endure from her persecutor. Thus God stayed His rough wind in the day of His east wind.

One evening Mr. W. went to Stadhampton to hear someone preach, but Mrs. C. was afraid to go, as her husband had threatened what he would do if she went. After Mr. W. was gone she fell on her knees and implored help and mercy from God under her troubles, when the Lord drew near and blessed her soul, and filled her with His love and grace.

Mr. C. still continued his drinking habits and neglected his business, until in 1850 they were obliged to leave M., which was a great trial to Mrs. C., but she used to say, " The Lord is good in giving me strength equal to my day." Her husband's father, who was a large farmer at Brightwell, again helped him, and started him in business as a cattle dealer, but his whole course was a constant cross to his wife, and he was soon in difficulties again, and so grieved his father that he said, "I will see to his wife and family, but my son I will not have in my house."

At last Mr. Coates committed himself, and was imprisoned for four years. This set Mrs. C. at liberty, and she was privileged to attend the house of God and meet with the saints of Christ; and a great blessing it was to her. Thus the scripture was fulfilled, "The wicked shall be a ransom for the righteous, and the transgressor for the upright" (Prov. 21. 18).

Mrs. C. had for some time past been desirous of honouring and following the Lord Jesus Christ in the ordinance of believers' baptism, and as her persecutor was for a time taken away from her, the way was made plain, and she was baptized at Abingdon by Mr. Tiptaft in the summer of 1852 when, coming up out of the water, she was so happy that she said she could have sung aloud for joy, and was much favoured with the presence of God when she sat down to the ordinance of the Lord's Supper and partook of the bread and wine, the emblems of the broken body and precious atoning blood of Jesus Christ. After thus honouring the Lord by openly professing His name, she was much indulged with His gracious presence and enabled without fear to meet with His saints in His earthly courts to worship His holy name. She was also favoured in the year 1853 to realise the Spirit of adoption, which enabled her to cry, "Abba, Father." Of this precious visit she wrote to a dear friend as follows:

I have received your kind note with pleasure, as I do like to know how you are getting on in the best things; for by knowing the dark side, we are better judges of the bright side, when light is given. I like to hear of people's troubles, for it often helps me on my way. You know I have been in a poor place for a long time. I tried to pray with all my might and could not; then I thought I was cut off, and could not pray at all; so shut up that I could not see how God could be just in saving one like me, for my religion was all natural. And you know how Satan and the heart can make up religion. At times how short do we feel, fearing our religion being natural! And do we not feel all sin and iniquity before God? We have received light from God, and yet dishonour Him in word, thought and deed; and how exceeding sinful we are, and yet how He comes over our mountains of sin!

"There was one word in the hymn last Sunday week that expressed my desire, and that was, 'O Lord, remember me!' It made me feel my sadness. On Monday I took that book of Huntingdon's, seeing my sad state, and all in a moment my hope sprang up and anchored in Christ. I never felt such a sensible springing up of hope as I did just then. It made all right in a moment. It made my heart leap for joy. I called Him my God and Father in truth; I praised Him, honoured Him, and crowned Him Lord of all. The more I praised Him, the higher He got in my estimation, and the lower I sank in myself to think He had not forgotten me. It made me low, it made me weep at that dear Jesus' feet, to see all my mountain of sin removed. I thought I should not sink quite so low again; but you know how simple I am, and I do act the fool's part so much if only left to myself for one moment, that it even makes God's grace a snare. I think unbelief is rooted in me, for I told Mr. Y. that I had had a sip. He asked me what words attended it? I answered, 'None.' It then struck me all at once, 'It is not all right now.' I thought if I had a word or two, that would have made it more sure that it came from God; but I sank in a moment. I had only strength to say that there would be no heaven for them that knew not God and His Spirit. But it seemed as though I could not keep it or let it go. The hope did not quite leave me; the spring rose a little when Mr. C. visited me; for I do love to see them that love God.

"I went to S— on Sunday, and while going, pondering on the mysteries of godliness, these words struck my mind with power: 'But ye have received the Spirit of adoption, whereby ye cry, Abba, Father.' And I did cry 'Abba, Father,' in truth; and the Spirit of adoption seemed to clothe my soul, and then led me into all the train of the Spirit's work and the Trinity, such as I knew not before; and all the names of the work of the Spirit came as correctly one after another as though I knew them all by heart; as the Spirit of adoption, of intercession, of supplication, of humility, of meekness, and many more such as the Spirit works. In short, it seemed open daylight to my soul's feelings. In the afternoon I searched the Bible to find the words, and I found them in Rom. 8. 15; and indeed all the Bible seemed full of the Spirit's work. Yes, the Spirit of the living God, honours crown His precious name, bore witness to His own work. Do not dishonour Him like me, for he is the best of friends."

Mrs. Coates had a sister living in Birmingham, and in the year 1861 she came to spend a few days with her. There was at this time a hay and corn business to be disposed of in this neighbourhood, which they thought would suit Mr. C., and which was purchased for him, and in a short time he and his wife and family came to live here. When Mrs. C. told her Oxfordshire friends that she was going to live in Birmingham, they strongly opposed her, and thought she was almost beside herself; but she said, "I am firmly persuaded that Birmingham is to be my future home, and to Birmingham I must go"; and often did she bless God for thus ordering her footsteps and giving her a name and a place in His church at Frederick Street.

Hope was entertained that as her husband was now removed from his old companions, and had obtained another fair start in business, he would be more steady and kind; but this hope was soon blighted and withered away, for he returned to his former habits of drunkenness, and recommenced his cruel acts towards his wife, so that she was again overwhelmed in outward sorrow and troubles. The treatment to which she at this time was subjected became unbearable, and she was in constant danger of losing her life.

She now began to attend Frederick Street Chapel, where for the first time I saw her, and on December 29th, 1861, she related her experience before the church, and was unanimously received a member. She was present when I preached my first sermon in Frederick Street Chapel, on

Sunday, October 27th, 1861. From that day she became one of my warmest supporters, and according to her own statements she was often filled with joy and peace in the Holy Ghost. She had been told, as many others have been told, that the people at Frederick Street were a cold, hard-hearted people, who thought none were right but themselves, but she said she proved them to be just the opposite.

About this time her husband, upon several occasions, came to chapel with her, and after hearing the Word preached, said, "That man, whoever he is, has preached the truth." For a short time he appeared an altered man, and even came to our prayer meetings or week-night services, which were held in the vestry. But alas! man may be restrained and awed by hearing the solemn Word of God and have many changes, and yet be destitute of a real, vital change of heart, which was the case with Mr. C., for in a short time he became worse than ever. Night after night he placed the razor under his pillow, and when he thought his wife was asleep he would take it and flourish it over her, and in a sort of angry whisper, loud enough for her to hear, he would say, over and over again, "Now I will do it. Now I will finish her." But instead of being asleep, Mrs. C. was mentally calling upon God, though she did not show any signs of terror or distress.

One day she felt her trouble intolerable, and in ascending the stairs to go to her bedroom she fell on her knees on the stairs in deep distress of soul, and begged of God to deliver her from her wicked, persecuting husband, who often said she was a good wife, and he had no fault to find with her except her religion and the *set*, as he called them, to which she belonged. Whilst on her knees on the stairs begging for help, the Lord very graciously and very powerfully applied the following scripture to her soul: "David said moreover, The Lord that delivered me out of the paw of the lion, and out of the paw of the bear, He will deliver me out of the hand of this Philistine." This was a great comfort to her.

Before the next Sunday arrived she had been tried in her mind about this promise, and secretly wished and prayed that if it came from the Lord, she might have it confirmed when she came to chapel on the following Sabbath. Having just commenced my ministerial labours at Frederick Street, and meeting with a storm of opposition and persecution from professors of truth, God poured out upon me continually a spirit of grace and supplication to prepare me for the day of battle; so that at that time I spent days and nights together in prayer to His sacred Majesty, mixed with praise and thanksgiving and love to His holy name; and this enabled me to take hold of His strength, and by the sweet and precious promises which

He gave me, and the power that attended them, I was assured that neither men nor devils could overthrow me, for God was with me. At this time I was much comforted, encouraged, and strengthened in reading the account of David, and how he slew the giant Goliath. When Mrs. C. came to the chapel on the Lord's day after being so comforted, I read, with much feeling, part of 1 Sam. 17, and afterwards in my sermon spoke of what David said to Saul in the 37th verse: "The Lord that delivered me out of the paw of the lion, and out of the paw of the bear, He will deliver me out of the hand of this Philistine." After service Mrs. C. came into the vestry with tears rolling down her cheeks, and her soul, as she said, full of God's love, assured that He would deliver her. She said, "Where have you had these things from? However were you led to speak as you have done? The Lord has answered my prayer. He is my Lord and my God."

But her cross was still heavy, *so heavy* that at last her relatives, considering her life to be in constant danger, and she herself feeling that she could no longer endure such treatment, she left her home and her husband, and saw him no more. He was at this time in good health, and possessed a strong and healthy constitution, but he was now entirely given up into the hands of Satan, and attempted to take away his own life, and although through this mad act he died not immediately, yet in the end it proved to be fatal; for after lingering a few days he died, at the early age of 48 years, and his wife was delivered to live quietly with her children. Thus the Word of God was fulfilled to the oppressor and the oppressed: "The upright shall dwell in the land, and the perfect shall remain in it. But the wicked shall be cut off from the earth, and the transgressors shall be rooted out of it."

Left without any means of support, Mrs. C. was entirely dependent on the Lord, who had thus far led her, fed her, stood by her, and enabled her to honour Him by trusting in Him; and He still supported her and supplied her, both temporally and spiritually. She was so continually favoured and blessed under the preached Word that she often said she had never seen the things of God so clearly nor felt them so precious to her soul as she now did. God, who is a husband to the widow, raised up for her friends who greatly helped her in temporal matters, and often in answer to her prayers did He send her relief. Being at this time brought into a closer intimacy with her, she often related to me some of the things which she had to endure from her husband on account of her religion. On one occasion he said that unless she would give up her religion, and promise him that she would not go to Stadhampton chapel, he would certainly kill her. She said to herself, "Shall I, *shall I*, give it up?" Then the Lord gave her strength and courage to say she could not do so. He then took hold of her, pulled her out of bed, and dragged her down the stairs by the hair of her head, and her head bumping from stair to stair until she was insensible, and then left her to recover as best she could. Sometimes he would strike her most severely about the face, and once or twice broke her nose and face. He would then say, "Now, will you give up your religion?" At other times he would go to the stable and fetch the halter, tie it in knots, and, when she had nothing on but her nightdress, would beat her with it until, as she stated, her flesh was black and blue. More than once, after using her most cruelly, he turned her out of doors at night almost naked, when, had she not found a friend in Miss Hatt, in whose house she found an asylum, she felt that she must have perished. This was taking up and enduring the cross for Christ's sake; this was the trial of faith; this was religion tried in the furnace; and all because she could not and would not go to church, nor give up what God by His sovereign grace had done for her soul.

Being such a tall and stately looking person – for such she was in outward appearance, and which she retained to the last – some friends may have thought that she might have retaliated and defended herself against this unjust and uncalled-for treatment; but she with great patience endured the cross, and realised the preciousness of the Saviour's words, "Blessed are they which are persecuted for righteousness' sake; for theirs is the kingdom of heaven." In the midst of this undeserved treatment, and when asked if she would give up her religion, she would sometimes, when she could get her husband to listen to her, say, "John, how can I give it up? I did not make the change which I have experienced in my soul; it came upon me from above. I sought it not. It is the Lord's work, and I had no control over it, nor power to resist; therefore what could I do? You know, John, we lived happily together, and I was obedient to you as my husband, and grace has not changed me from being a good wife to become a bad one. I will obey you in all things that are right according to the Word of God; but I cannot give up my religion, nor deny what God has done for my soul." By thus speaking to him he was sometimes quite overcome, and appeared sorry for the way he had treated her, and promised that in future he would do better.

Mrs. C. was the first who joined the church at Frederick Street after I commenced preaching there, and after her husband's death her whole heart and soul were engaged in the welfare of the church and the prosperity of the preached Word, and she with others helped me much in prayer and supplication, feeling assured that God would stand by me. The chaff fled before the wind of God's holy Word, and a grain or two of wheat went with it but afterwards returned to the heap on the barnfloor, which the whirlwind did not scatter. She, with a few others who are still living and are still members with us, whose souls were at that time led out in a remarkable way in prayer for Zion's increase at Frederick Street, have lived to see their prayers answered and God's promises to us fulfilled; for the Lord has raised up under the ministry of His Word a new church and a new congregation, and united us in the unity of the Spirit and the bond of peace. Honours crown the adorable brow of our majestic Prince of peace and power; for *all* the glory and every whit of praise are His due!

The last few years of her life Mrs. C. was afflicted with bronchitis and weakness of her heart, and this prevented her attending the house of God as much as she wished; but when able she was always there. In her latter days she was subject to many changes, but never lost her hope in God. Though she was a woman of strong faith, she was often tried with unbelief. She often said, "What should I do now if God were to leave me? O, I cannot live without my God!" These changes and exercises, and longings for the presence of God and Christ, made her a good hearer of the Word, which the Spirit made life and power to her soul. She was present on the evening of October 22nd, 1893, when I spoke from the words, "Behold, I will do a new thing; now it shall spring forth; shall ye not know it? I will even make a way in the wilderness, and rivers in the desert," when the Lord so blessed her soul that she said the savour and sweetness of that discourse abode on her spirit for quite a fortnight afterwards. On this occasion, a man who was visiting the various places of worship in our town, and publishing his opinion on the congregations and ministers in a weekly newspaper, was present, and in the next issue of his periodical spoke contemptuously of the sermon which had been so signally blessed to her soul. When she heard of it she said, "Awful, awful! Next to blasphemy. I would not be in his place for ten thousand worlds." How this shows that "the preaching of the cross is to them that perish foolishness, but unto us which are saved it is the power of God".

After this she was not often able to attend the house of God. She now became heavily afflicted and confined to the house, and often to her bed, and had much to try her faith and patience, which she bore with remarkable resignation to the will of God. During her illness my wife once read to her Ephesians 3, which was made a blessing to her soul. She said, "I never saw such beauty in the chapter before." She was frequently longing to die and be with Christ, and enabled to believe that He was her Lord and her God.

Verses of various hymns in Gadsby's selection were very precious to her soul, which for want of space I cannot insert. She was at times in much distress, and often prayed to God for grace and patience, and begged that He would not leave her in the hour of death. On one occasion she was heard to utter the words, "Glory, glory!" On March 8th the last verse of hymn 591 was much blessed to her soul. She said, with a smile, "How long, dear Lord, how long? Crown Him! Crown Him! My God, my God! Amen, amen!" On March 9th, 1895, she quietly passed away in her sleep to join the ransomed host above, and to behold, without a veil between, the face of Jesus, the King of kings and Lord of lords.

Mrs. C. had been much blessed and comforted many times from Psalm 107 and Romans 8, and was able to claim them as her own. By grace and the Lord's strength she held fast to the end what the Lord had done for her soul, and what He had taught her.

Gospel Standard 1998, first published in the 1896 *Gospel Standard*.

"I AM ON THE ROCK"

Ann Pickup

By William Whittaker (d.1902), a Lancashire supply minister.

"Tell your father that I am on the Rock," said a dear, dying saint on Monday night, December 11th, 1899; and before the next night she had gone to see Him upon whom her hope was built. She was born nearly 68 years ago, on the side of a bleak moor, opposite where these lines are being written; and with the exception of a brief period her entire life was spent in that neighbourhood.

It was in the summer of 1881 that the friendship commenced which only concluded in death; and even to this day we feel the fulness of the words that, "The memory of the just is blessed." For years scarcely a week passed but we were together; she being the only member of one of our churches who lived near here. On these occasions of our meeting, she often told me how the Lord had graciously appeared for her and what heart-cheering words He had been pleased to speak; but the union became deeper and stronger when her eldest daughter, Betsy, was called by grace, whose experience appeared in the *Friendly Companion* for January 1892, and her obituary in the *Gospel Standard* for October 1896. [Her name was Betsy Robinson.] As some of the readers of these pages may not have those magazines, permit me just to say how this deeper and stronger union was brought about.

On the first Saturday in October 1890, a note was sent me from my dear friend, expressing a desire that I would go and see her daughter who, to all human appearance, lay at the point of death. One of my old scholars at Goodshawfold had to be buried that day and, for a short time, I did not know what step to take. However, the words, "Let the dead bury their dead," settled my mind, so I went to see the sick friend.

After being seated a time, her mother (Mrs. Pickup, of Acrefield Head Farm) said to me, "Will you come up and see Betsy?" When the name was mentioned, how upset my mind became, for I thought it was one of the others, who attended their mother's chapel at Haslingden, that was sick; but when it proved to be Betsy, one who seldom, if ever, went there, "Whatever must I say to her?" was my first thought.

The stone steps which led to the bed-chamber were not harder or colder than my heart and feelings; but when once in the room, she held out her thin arms, saying. "O, Mr. W., and have you come to see a poor, lost sinner like me? O, I am lost!. There does not seem to be the least hope for such a wretch as me!" My heart felt broken to pieces, no longer cold and hard as marble, but melted by her words of feeling and power. Despair was indeed deeply written on her face, but what a well-grounded hope I had of the safety of her immortal soul! After reading a part of the 102nd Psalm, and naming portions suitable to the state in which she was, we parted, commending her to Him who soon after wrought deliverance for His child.

At midnight on the Sunday, as the mother was praying in the porch for the Lord to appear for her dear child and deliver her from the despair and anguish in which she was, those two lines in hymn 92 came with power and assurance to her mind:

"And her request, and her complaint,
Is but the voice of every saint."

"And she is a saint then," the mother, now in glory, said to herself. O, how she blessed and praised the Lord at that midnight hour! She had not thought to find dear Betsy alive; when, however, she went back to her bedside, instead of misery there was happiness and joy. Yes, joy almost or quite unutterable. When her daughter could speak, she said, "I can die now! All my sins are pardoned. The Lord is good! Help me to praise Him!"

From that hour the dear mother had a spiritual child and sister in dear Betsy, who from that time began slowly to improve; but it was just a year before she had sufficient strength to go and hear me speak at Goodshaw-fold. In November 1891, I had the joy and pleasure of baptizing her at Haslingden.

In the autumn of 1895 the family were afflicted with typhoid fever and Betsy took it, which, in December of that year, ended in her resting from her labours and entering into the joy of the Lord. After her death, her dear mother and myself were often together, at which times she told me what the Lord had done for her, in grace and providence.

About two months before her departure, she expressed a wish for me to go up some time and she would try to tell me her case right from the beginning. Accordingly last October, just nine years after her daughter's deliverance, I went and sat by her side and wrote down the words as she spoke them.

She began: "It is about forty years since the Lord, I hope, began His work with me. From a child I had a desire to be a Christian; and if watching my words and trying to be good would make me one, then I would be one; but when I was about 28 years of age, the Lord showed me that it was His work and not mine to make a Christian. It was brought about in this way. By degrees my eyes were opened to see what a great sinner I was and my guilt became as a heavy weight upon me. O, how distressed I felt, and would have given anything to have been a dog, or cat, or anything that had no soul."

As she uttered these words she was sitting by her fireside, in the house that has often been called by me "The Modern Dairyman's Cottage" [referring to Legh Richmond's *The Dairyman's Daughter*]. I sat by her with my pencil and paper and as she spoke my eyes were fixed on her beautifully expressive face, although she was so nearly 70. The place was the picture of cleanliness; no palace could be more so. Behind, only a few yards off, is the quarry that the stones came from for the Manchester Assize Courts; and here was a "polished stone" being prepared by the eternal Spirit for the King's house. From where I sat, a lofty monument on the opposite hill could be seen [Holcombe Tower]; it was erected to the memory of that great statesman, Sir Robert Peel, who was born in Bury; but at my side sat one who was a monument of rich mercy and free grace, erected by God Himself on the Hill of Zion. On the monument men put up is the one word "Peel". On this that God had raised was the one word "Christ!" who was her "All and in all". She spoke in a very solemn manner, for she knew her time on earth would not be long; and she desired to make all preparations and to "set her house in order" before she died.

Let me continue her own story in her own words. She said, "Satan at this time tempted me so much that I durst not go to bed, never name to sleep. O, how wretched and miserable I felt! The words, 'O thou afflicted, tossed with tempest, and not comforted,' were my experience. My uncle, Henry Platt, came to see us about this time and he could see there was something the matter; he knew, too, what it was and that it would end all right. He told me to go to Sarah Howarth,* at Kay Barn, and she would be able to tell me something. So I went over to see her, and O, how pleased she was to know what a sinner I felt to be! Many a time did I run over the fields from Fearnley Barn Farm to tell her my troubles. My uncle came again and advised me to go to Haslingden, to Cave Adullam Chapel; for there, he said 'would be preaching that would suit me'."

---

* Sarah Howarth was a most gracious member of John Kershaw's church at Rochdale. See G.S. 1890.

How easy it was to go back with my dear friend, to the days of her youth. I knew the Mrs. Howarth she spoke of, and wrote her obituary for the *Gospel Standard* about ten years ago. Her farm and dear Mrs. Pickup's were not far apart, and often were the two seen together: indeed they were united as Naomi and Ruth. Her sister, Miss Stansfield, who is now a member at Haslingden, has told me about one of her early visits to that place. She said, "She called at our house, and before she had been in long she began to say what a sinner she was and that she felt as if there was no hope for her; but when she got to chapel she heard what it was that Jesus Christ came into the world for, even 'to save sinners', and so faith came by hearing and hope sprang up in her heart that, 'if for sinners, perhaps for me'!" Ever after, so long as health and strength were given, the five miles were not too far for her to go.

She proceeded: "The first real relief I got was from the words, 'I have prayed for thee, that thy faith fail not'; and when once listening to a sermon in Cheesden Pasture – I don't know who the minister was, but it was not Mr. Kershaw – the preacher spoke about the Lord being taken up from His disciples at Bethany. I had such a view of Jesus Christ, I seemed to watch Him go up; and O, how I did want to go up with Him! That night my burden was taken from me, my sins were felt to be forgiven, and I returned home 'a happy pardoned child'."

When she got thus far with her history, she said, "Perhaps I've said enough for this time; but you know, Mr. W., I don't want His mercies to lie

'Forgotten in unthankfulness
And without praises die.' "

"Thou shalt remember all the way which the Lord thy God led thee these forty years in the wilderness" (Deut. 8. 2) is a truth my dear friend and mother in Israel, Mrs. Pickup, lived long enough to prove. As I sat by her side, recording how the Lord had led her about and instructed her, new life, light and power was felt in that old and often-proved scripture, and our spiritual feet mutually fitted in each step, although she had been in the way many years before I knew what that way meant or was.

On my annual autumn visits she usually began to speak about what the Lord had either said or shown her since I was last there; then she would begin gathering together the "stones of help" with which, in bygone days, she had made "high heaps"; in which employment of "looking back", even from the banks of Jordan, she was favoured. Her face beamed with joy and gladness as she spoke of how the Lord had "made bare His holy arm" in her defence and deliverance. While thus pleasantly engaged, we seemed to see that same arm again; for it *is* the same that has helped and upheld the saints in all ages and under all circumstances.

On another visit she continued her life's story thus: "Well, about this time Mrs. Howarth, of Kay Barn, told me that A.B.Taylor was going to preach at Bury and advised me to go and hear him; and that was the day I ever shall remember. He preached as if he knew everything I had passed through. He told me everything. I did not know then that there was a vestry where strangers could have their tea, so I went out somewhere to get something to eat, and when I came back I stood at the door waiting for the chapel to open; as I stood there this line came so fresh and powerful:

'Are not Thy mercies sovereign still?'

and my heart at once replied -

'And Thou a faithful God!'

My soul felt so full of the Lord's blessing that I said, 'This is the gate of heaven.'

"Some time after, old James Kay, the deacon, came to see me and in the course of our conversation asked me about joining them at Bury, but I felt that Haslingden was the place where my lot should be cast. As two others were going before the church there my desire was made known that I would like to go with them; 'but what must I tell them?' This caused me some anxiety, but the words, 'Nor death nor danger fear,' and this text, 'Who shall lay anything to the charge of God's elect?' came with sweetness and power: so I felt, 'I will go and tell them that.' "

After thus much had been written and read to her for correction, there was a pause, while the dear one gathered fresh strength; then, instead of looking backward, she looked forward to her end; and it struck her that she might, like my own dear wife with whom she was so long acquainted, be taken with a stroke, and so be unable at the last to give instructions about her burial. She said, "I want John Buckley to make my coffin, and I should like all at The Room at Ramsbottom to be invited, you know there are not many, and also my old friends at Haslingden, and it is you that I want to bury me; and if you cannot get away from your work, try to get Mr. Sutcliffe, who buried Mrs. W., but if I die so that I can be buried on a Saturday, then you will perhaps be at liberty. I have been telling our people all this today, but they wanted me to speak on a more cheerful subject. I told them that I must speak now, for it may be that I cannot speak when you want me."

She was sitting in her chair downstairs, and spoke as composedly as if only going for a walk in the field. The house in which this solemn conversation took place may be clearly seen both from the highway at the bottom of the meadow, and from the railway running to Accrington and Bacup, but few passing either way knew what was taking place in that old farmhouse. After another pause she continued about her going before the church, and how the Lord enabled her to tell far more than she thought she could; she proved the Holy Ghost to be her Remembrancer.

After her funeral, as a few friends sat with the bereaved husband and family, the husband related what took place some time before she was baptized. He returned home much earlier than usual, and when he entered the house he found her weeping. He did not know what was the matter, and she felt she could not tell him; all that she could say was, "I shall have to go over yonder." He did not know where she meant, but feared she intended to drown herself, as there was a deep reservoir near the place. However, she at length told him it was to Kay Barn and not to drown herself. She found in her who lived at Kay Barn what Ruth found in Naomi, and as often as she could go with her hopes and fears, joys and sorrows, she would if possible be there. Not that she was a gospel gad-about, far from that: after God's house came her own. Indeed, although we lived for nearly sixteen years within two miles of each other, she was only in my house *once*. She was often invited, but she would answer, "When I have got back from chapel there is so much to do and I don't like to go much from home." But at the beginning of her spiritual career it seemed never too soon to rise nor too late to return to rest, so as that none of the household affairs were neglected. O that more followed her as she followed Christ, for she was enabled for over thirty years to adorn the doctrine of God her Saviour. But to return to her experience.

She told me that when the Lord laid it upon her mind that she should be baptized, she found much persecution and opposition. She said she told one woman that if there was nothing but devils between her home and Haslingden, she felt she must go. On the first Lord's day in August 1867 she was buried with her Lord in baptism.

Methinks I still see her in my mind's eye as she smilingly related the following:

"That was a good day to me. O how I felt the Lord's presence in that chapel, and the day following felt even better, for I had expected to have a deal of trouble through taking the step. On that day I was asked if I had 'been in the water' and I said 'Yes'; then, instead of a frown there was a laugh, for he went out and never said another word: but the Lord broke into my heart with these lines:

'Ye fearful saints, fresh courage take,
The clouds ye so much dread,

– and I had dreaded those clouds –

> Are big with mercy, and shall break
> In blessings on your head.'

It was in *that* way they broke, for my soul felt so blest that I sat on a chair in that corner and scripture after scripture flowed into my heart, so that I could scarcely contain myself. I kept saying, 'For me, Lord? All this for *me?*' O, how I sang and praised the Lord for His mercy!" We wept together, but they were joyful tears.

As I look back to when she related these things, sadness creeps over me to think they will never occur again. We were friends for nearly twenty years, during which length of time I never had from her one unkind word or look. She was indeed a mother in Israel to me.

In September 1882 she had a terrible trial. Her eldest son Samuel, aged 27, fell off his lorry and was instantly killed. Two years after, her youngest son's life was despaired of, but after many weeks of anxious watching, his life was spared. In 1895 her husband, daughter and two grandchildren were laid aside with typhoid fever. Although herself then somewhat advanced in years, she nursed them all. The doctor said, "Mrs. Pickup, I'm surprised at your keeping up so well week after week." Her reply was, "Doctor, my strength cometh from the Lord, who made heaven and earth!"

One winter evening, at dark, she lit the lamp but forgot to draw the blind. I went to visit her in her sorrow. The husband and grandchildren were in another room and she was alone. The light attracted my attention and, on looking, I beheld what I shall long remember. She was sitting at the table, with her Bible open before her and, with arms and eyes uplifted, she was engaged in prayer. I dared not for a while disturb her devotion. What sincerity was in her look! Indeed, I have not seen the like before nor since. It seemed a week-night service for us both.

About two years ago her health began to fail. She was laid aside for several weeks, and her affliction left marks which told plainly she would never be the same strong person again. About this time she had a very marked answer to prayer. Her spectacles fell on the floor and the frame got somewhat bent. As she was putting them on, the crooked part went into her eye. She told me, " 'O Lord,' I cried, 'whatever shall I do now, if my sight is lost and I cannot read Thy Word?' The pain was terrible to bear, and unbelief and fears filled my heart for I felt sure I was blind. They went to get something for me, and while they were away, the Lord blessed me with such a spirit of prayer that I felt I could not let Him go. I pleaded whatever should I do, now that I could not go to His Word, nor even read it? Bless His precious name; before they came back the Lord had heard and answered my prayer!" This was one of many instances of the Lord's interposing for her.

All her spare time she spent with her library. First and foremost was her well-read Bible; then came her hymnbook, the *Gospel Standard,* the memoirs and works of Kershaw, Warburton, Huntington, etc. Whatever or whoever had a word to say against any of the above could not be affectionately received into her heart. Her Bible was always in sight.

One person asked her why The Room at Ramsbottom [not too far from where she lived] was commenced. She said, 'For such as myself, who are too infirm and afflicted to go as far as we have done these many years." "Well, are there not chapels near here?" was asked. "None," said she, "where the truth is preached as set forth in the Scriptures." She then began to relate what was truth and how she was brought to know it. Then she asked her questioner what he knew about it, but the poor man could not reply.

Some will be ready to ask, "How did this fair vessel reach her desired haven? Did she come through the seas of sorrow and distress without making shipwreck of faith?" Let us see. On September 7th, 1899, early in the morning, these words came to her with power. "I will never leave thee nor forsake thee"; and later in the day, the two lines.

> " More happy, but not more secure,
> The glorified spirits in heaven."

Then followed, "Heaven and earth shall pass away, but My Word shall not pass away." She was so lifted up in the feelings of her soul that she said,

> " Death is no more a frightful foe,
> Since I with Christ shall reign;
> With joy I leave this world of woe;
> For me to die is gain."

On October 10th, much comfort was brought to her by, "The eternal God is thy Refuge"; also, "The memory of the just is blessed."

On October 21st, this was sweet: "Mary hath chosen that good part, which shall not be taken away from her." The next day, "I am thy Rock and thy Fortress."

One evening in November, she told me how good the Lord had been to her since my previous visit. "O," she said, "I have had such fellowship with Jesus in his sufferings! I could see Him, by precious faith, bearing my sin. O, to think that He should suffer for such a wretch as I and these two lines came so sweetly:

'Sinners have bound th' Almighty's hands,
And spit in their Creator's face.' "

On the last Lord's day in November, just eight years after I baptized her daughter, Betsy, I, accompanied by Mr. Croft [Jesse Croft of Sale] and a member at Haslingden, spent a very profitable time with her. She told us what a happy day it had been and how sweet were the lines,

"And yet how oft did Israel prove
Thy constancy and grace."

And she blessedly spoke of having proved the same. I read, at her request. the 103rd Psalm. That was her last night downstairs.

On December 5th, while musing on the dear Redeemer's sufferings, the lines came with power.

"He wept, He bled, He died for you;
What more, ye saints, could Jesus do?"

On December 8th, "The mountains shall depart, and the hills be removed: but My kindness shall not depart from thee." Next day, "Though I walk through the valley of the shadow of death, I will fear no evil; for Thou art with me." O, happy saint, is not this the way and manner thou enteredst thine eternal rest and longed-for home? As I stood by her bedside on that 9th of December, I spoke to her about its being the anniversary of dear Philpot's death, and repeated to her his dying sayings, which she much enjoyed. Mr. T. Walsh, son of the late minister was with me. She said, "Mr. W., I can now say to you as our dear Betsy said, 'Don't pray to the Lord for me to recover; but ask Him to take me home, if it be His blessed will!'"

The Monday following was our last meeting and last parting. Yes; the last of many. Mr. Croft's son, Walter [many years later pastor at West Street, Croydon], was with me, and it was to him that she said, *Tell your father that I am on the Rock!* " O, that night! Before I left her, I said, "Mrs. Pickup, you are now in the place for proving what real religion is, and what truth is; will the doctrines you have heard preached for nearly forty years do for you now?" I can almost hear her now silent voice answering me, "O, yes; they will do now; they will do here!" "And what about free-will and duty faith?" "I don't want to have anything to do with them; nor have I ever wanted to since the Lord showed me these things." How affectionately she took hold of the hand that now holds the pen and gave a dying grip, as she said, "The Lord bless you, Mr W., and help you still to preach His truth as I have heard you; and if we never meet here again, we shall meet, I hope, in heaven, where there will be no parting." How true!

The day following she exchanged death for life. The last word she tried to speak was, "Hallelujah!" A sweet smile came over her face, and just past four on Tuesday afternoon, December 12th, 1899, the Lord granted her sweet liberty. On the following Saturday, on the same side of the valley where she had experienced natural and spiritual life, in the graveyard adjoining Park Chapel, it fell to my lot to commit her mortal remains to the silent grave, there to lie until that period when "the dead in Christ shall rise first". She was 68 years of age.

The husband has lost a most devoted wife, the children and grandchildren a parent of the best kind, and myself and others a kind, sincere friend. My earnest desire is that Zion may be blessed with more such-like mothers in Israel.

Gospel Standard 1999, first published in the 1900 *Friendly Companion.*

THE SHINING OF THE LIGHT OF LIFE

Susan Sarll

For many years I have had it upon my mind to write down some of the Lord's dealings with me in providence and grace. I wish to do it with a single eye to the glory of God. We are told, "Whether therefore ye eat, or drink, or whatsoever ye do, do all to the glory of God." How much more then should I wish to do this for His glory! And I believe that the blessed Spirit will bring to my remembrance what the Lord has done for me, for He is the Remembrancer of His people. My earnest desire is to keep self in the background.

I was born in August 1835. My parents were professors, and members of the Congregationalists. My father was very strict in attending all the services at the chapel, and was a Sunday school teacher. He took me to the same school when I was four years of age. He was very particular about our behaviour on the Lord's day; my sisters and I were never allowed to laugh and be trifling on that day. I think it is quite right to teach a child to reverence the Sabbath; however, I am thankful I was taught to do so.

I remember being very much troubled in my mind when very young about my state as a sinner. This verse of Watts's troubled me:

> "There is a dreadful hell,
> And everlasting pains,
> Where sinners must with devils dwell
> In darkness, fire, and chains."

My teachers in the Sunday school used to tell me I must have faith, I must repent, I must pray. And I thought by so doing I should obtain the favour of God. As I was very fond of reading, and had not many books, I read the Bible a great deal, and found I must be born again before I could enter heaven. But my teachers said very little about the new birth. One thing I remember, our teacher asked us all round the class if we could say to the first commandment that we *did* love the Lord with all our heart, and with all our soul, and with all our might. The other girls would answer, "Yes, Teacher"; but I dared not say, "Yes." And she would tell us we ought to be able to say as Peter did, "Lord, Thou knowest all things; Thou knowest that I love Thee." But I could not say it, for I knew in my heart I did not love God, but thought of Him as a dreaded Being who was angry with me every day. And although I tried to pray, I never felt I had any answer to my prayers. How hard I tried to find out what faith was, as I read in my Bible that without faith it was impossible to please God. My teachers told me I ought to have faith; and when I told them I wanted a new heart, and wanted to know if I was converted, they told me they believed I *was* converted, and that now my aim must be to try and convert others. But they could not make me believe it.

So that all through my childhood I can say I was troubled to know how I could please God, and what I must do to be saved; but I kept these things to myself, could not mention them to my parents. My father was very much against election. I used to listen eagerly to controversies he had with different persons upon that subject. He used to call it "that high doctrine" and a "dangerous doctrine". He had some relations who took in the *Gospel Standard;* and when I was going there on a visit, he told me not to read "that red book",* for it was a "dangerous book". But when I was there, I ventured to peep into one of the numbers when no one saw me. I began reading the experience of one who, like myself, had been striving to keep the law, and was in bondage. O, how astonished I was to find someone else was tried just as I was! "But," I thought, "I must not read this book, my father told me not"; and now I was disobeying him. How I wished it was a book I might read! I think I was about eight or nine years of age then.

But I think I must go back to an earlier time of my life, even to when I was but five years old. I remember telling a falsehood to my little sister who was two years younger, and I thought it was fun. My father overheard me, and spoke to me very solemnly about the sinfulness of lying, and about Ananias and Sapphira and Gehazi. I believe I did not know before that it was a sin, but what my father said to me then made such an impression upon my mind that I remember it as well now as though it were only yesterday. It shows plainly that we go astray from the womb speaking lies, for it seemed natural to me to tell falsehoods for fun and mischief. But after this occurred I was very careful to try to speak the truth; in fact, I date from that time the beginning of a fear of offending God, who could see me at all times. My dear mother taught me Watts's hymns for children, and they made a lasting impression upon my mind. The superintendent of the Sunday school used to tell us that Jesus stood

* In the early days the *Gospel Standard* had a pale red cover.

with outstretched arms calling us children to Him, and we would not go to Him. How this puzzled me! for I wished He would call me. I asked my teacher once how it was that as God was all-powerful, He could not make sinners come to Him. I do not know what answer she made me.

Now I must return to the time when I was eight or nine years of age and first saw the *Gospel Standard*. At the same time I went to stay with an old lady, my father's aunt, who I believe was a good woman. She showed me an old Bible, which had some very quaint prints in it. One was of the call of Abraham, and another, of the call of Samuel. I asked what that meant; and she explained it to me as well as she could, saying the Lord would call me in His own time, if I was a vessel of mercy. I remember I burst into tears, and said, "O that the Lord would call me as He did Samuel!" and what she said comforted me more than I had ever been comforted before.

About this time I had a dream. I thought I was falling down a well, and was going down, down. I felt a heavy weight fastened to my feet, which was dragging me downwards. I thought to myself, "O, I am sinking into the *bottomless pit!*" and I heard a voice say, "It is your sins that are the weight bound to your feet. If the Lord Jesus takes your sins away, you will be delivered." Then I cried out, "O deliver me from going into the pit!" Immediately I felt the weight taken off, and I went up to the top in a moment. O what a deliverance it was! I understood by that dream it was sin that dragged mortals down to perdition. After this, how I used to pray to the Lord to take away my sins! I very often was kept awake nearly all night striving hard to make my peace with God, as some told me to do. But the Lord seemed not to hear nor regard me, and I felt I was like the prophets of Baal, who cried all in vain.

I went on like this until my parents removed to London, and then my father took me with him to hear the different preachers. We went from chapel to chapel, but I could get no comfort. It was the same thing over and over again; the bed was too short and the covering too narrow to wrap oneself in it. I was in Egyptian bondage, and these ministers seemed like the taskmasters, who took away the straw and yet demanded the same tale of bricks. I went to Mr. Henry Allen's, Islington, for some time, and attended the Bible class. One Sunday evening he took for his text: "Behold, I stand at the door, and knock," etc., and he said the Lord knocked at everyone's heart, and people would not open to Him; but there would be a *last* time, and then if we rejected Him, He would not come again. The next time I went he took for his text: "If the righteous scarcely be saved, where shall the ungodly and the sinner appear?" This time salvation seemed a very difficult matter; we should have to do something very wonderful to be saved in any way. I was so overcome with terror and distress that I was obliged to leave the chapel; I felt almost beside myself. The pew-opener asked me what was the matter with me. I told her I would never enter that chapel again; and I kept my word. At this time I was staying with some members of Mr. Allen's church, and they were very much put out to see me in such distress. They told me I must have committed the unpardonable sin.

My trouble increased to such an extent that my health gave way. I began to think I was like the man who was shut up in the iron cage we read of in the *Pilgrim's Progress*. I could not pray; I had no hope. How I wished I had never been born! I concluded I was a reprobate, hated by God as Esau was. I cannot describe the distress of mind I was in for nine months. At the end of that time I was sent to a doctor, as my health was bad; and he said I had better go into the country to my native air. Some ladies in the country who knew my family well, both on my father's and mother's side, hearing of my distemper (for I was not quite ill), sent for me to stay at their house, to see what the change would do for me. And I went.

These ladies were very religious; they had no cooking done on Sundays, and the servants all went to chapel on Sunday mornings as well as evenings. Now these ladies and their minister did all they could to pacify me, and make me believe I was converted. They told me I must not expect to have such a wonderful change and conversion as Paul had; but that if I did my best, read the Scriptures, gave myself to prayer, and did my duty, I should soon find peace of mind. I took their advice, and after a time fell in with them. And I began to think, "Well, after all I am not so bad. Why, when I look back, and think how hard I have tried to do right, and be right, and of that nine months of trouble – why, that was repentance, of course." And I began to be quite lifted up with pride, and to make plans that I would be like Daniel, and make it a rule to kneel down three times a day; and if I stayed there, that I would join their church and become a teacher in the Sunday school, and should soon be a bright Christian. O what a mercy I was not permitted to stay there!

After some months I was sent for, to go to live with my father's relations, whom I have spoken of before, who took in the *Gospel Standard*. They attended where the truth was preached, and expected me to go with them; and I went just to please them. But how I hated the preaching there, and the doctrine of election was detestable to me. As I was fond of singing, I bought a Gadsby's hymnbook to use at chapel, but I hated the book because it was full of high doctrine. And, to my shame, I remember when alone I stamped upon the book on the floor, and thought to myself, "Ah! when I have been here awhile, I will tell them that I will not go to their chapel, but will go to the other one in the village." But as I had a very happy home with my aunt and cousins, I did not say anything. When I went to chapel, I did not try to listen, but despised the ministers in my heart. After going on a long time in this manner, one Sunday a Mr. Martin had been preaching, and he used the words several times in his sermon or in his reading, "Thus saith the Lord"; and they sounded in my ears with some power. As we were leaving the chapel I turned and looked at the dear man, and the words seemed to sound inwardly, "This man speaks with authority, and not as the scribes – not as the men you heard in London, and the minister who preached smooth things to you at R____." This produced a strange feeling. I felt different from what I had ever done before.

To add to my trouble, I had to leave this happy home quite unexpectedly, which was a great trial to me, as I should now have to seek a situation. I had another aunt in the village, and she kindly let me make my home with her until I could see my way clear; and as my father's mother was with her, and was bedridden, she was glad to have me for a time.

While I was staying with this aunt at Ashwell, I had two remarkable dreams, which I must relate, as they were the means the Lord used to show me where I was. The first was this. I dreamt I was in a small boat on some very dark and muddy water. This boat was full of cracks, so that the water came in, and I had to be constantly sticking paper over them to keep it out. I felt in a sad plight, as I feared I should sink; and I heard a voice telling me I must be very diligent, and keep the boat well pasted up, or I should sink to rise no more. I heard another voice saying, "Arise, and depart, for this is not your rest." With that I cried, "O that I could arise! but where, O where can I go? I see no way of escape." Then I looked up and saw a rock some distance off, very high, and I saw some persons walking on its summit. I cried out, "O that I was on that rock! for then I should feel safe; but now I am in constant fear." Then I felt the water was coming in, and I was sinking. I was obliged to cry, "Lord, save, or I perish." And in a moment I was lifted up by an unseen hand and placed on the rock. O, I cannot describe what a deliverance I felt! But I said, "Thou hast lifted me up out of the horrible pit, and the miry clay, and set my feet upon a rock, and put a new song in my mouth."

With that I awoke, and was astonished at the dream. I did not tell anyone of it then, but pondered over it, hoping it would be fulfilled, as I felt such joy in it. When I opened my Bible, I came to the 40th Psalm, and the second verse being the very words I had in the dream, I was quite amazed; for they seemed so fresh to me, as though I had never seen them before. After this a little hope sprang up.

About this time an uncle called to see us, and he began to talk to me about election. He said he hoped I should not be drawn away, by the preaching I was hearing there, to believe the dangerous doctrine of election, as my father would be in trouble if I were. I felt very much tried about it, and desired very earnestly to be taught aright. Then I had the second dream. It was this. I thought I was on a large common, and it was very foggy or misty, so that we could scarcely see each other. A great many people were rushing about, some coming and some going, and they were all talking about religion. Some said one thing was right, and others said something else; but I thought I was very anxious to find Mount Zion, and I was asking the way thither. Some told me there was no such place to be found; that the world was all over alike, and we should never see anything else but this thick fog; there was no other way to heaven. But I had the words continually sounding in my ears, "The ransomed of the Lord shall return, and come to Zion with songs and everlasting joy," etc., and also, "In this mountain shall the Lord of hosts make unto all people a feast of fat things full of marrow, of wines on the lees well refined: and He will destroy in this mountain the face of the covering cast over all people, and the veil that is spread over all nations."

I seemed to wander about a long time among this crowd of people. One man in particular tried to persuade me there was no such place as Mount Zion, and he told me I should never find it. But I told him I must go on seeking for it, when, lo, all at once I came to it. The fog and mist seemed to open and I saw with great delight a beautiful mountain. It was all clear. A few persons were going up, and at the top was a beautiful light. I turned round to the man, who had followed me, and said, "O, now do you not see what I have been searching for? Here is Mount Zion." "What?" he said. "You are deceived, for I do not see it." With that I looked under his broad-brimmed hat, and I saw he was *blind*. I answered him, "I see you are blind; that is why you cannot see. But I am thankful to say that whereas I was once blind, I now see." With that he went stumbling and grumbling away, and I began to ascend this glorious mountain with such joy as I had never felt before. And lo, I awoke, and found to my sorrow it was but a dream.

I pondered over these two dreams, and as I felt such joy in each of them, I hoped they would be fulfilled. Soon after, I opened the Bible in the Book of Job, at the 33rd chapter, and was astonished to read the 14th and following verses: "For God speaketh once, yea twice, yet man perceiveth it not. In a dream, in a vision of the night, when deep sleep falleth upon men, in slumberings upon the bed; then He openeth the ears of men, and sealeth their instruction." I had never seen so much in the words before; they seemed new to me. I could say the Lord had taught me more by those two dreams than I had learnt in any other way; although I cannot remember all, as it is now forty-five years ago. (Now it is 1901.) But if the dear Remembrancer is pleased to bring it to my mind and memory, I do want to record how I hope these dreams were fulfilled.

At this time I was staying at Ashwell, and before I went back to London I had a great wish to go to see my maternal grandparents, who lived at Saffron Walden in Essex. As it was cross country, I did not know how I should get there; but I had an uncle living at Guilden Morden, who kept a general shop, and once a month a van came from Saffron Walden to supply him with goods. So it was arranged that I should go in this way.

Now this was the most remarkable journey I ever took in my life, and I shall remember it through all eternity. I always compare it to Jacob's journey to Padan-aram. O that I could describe it! My dear uncle got up and got me some breakfast, and we started away from Guilden Morden before it was light, as it was at the end of January 1855. It was a covered van, and the man had to deliver goods at different villages all round the country. My uncle gave me a piece of cake to eat on the way, and I bid him and my aunt and cousins adieu, and went off. I had put my little Gadsby's hymnbook in my pocket – the same little book I had stamped my foot upon, as I have said.

When we had reached the open country, I got down and walked to keep warm, the van going on before; and thus I was left *alone with God*. That was how I felt. O how I cried to the Lord to have mercy upon me! and I had the words come with much power: "When the poor and needy seek water, and there is none, and their tongue *faileth* for thirst, then I the Lord will hear them." I said, "O Lord, I am indeed poor and needy, and my tongue faileth for thirst, even for righteousness; and Thou hast said, 'Blessed are they which do hunger and thirst after righteousness: for they shall be filled.' " And as I was going along, I well remember, I was very anxious to know what was meant by the term "free grace". I did not understand the meaning, and I remembered hearing that a boy in the Sunday school at Ashwell had written in his Bible, "This Bible was given to me by Mr. Flitton, minister of *a free grace* gospel." "Well," I thought, "this little boy understands the meaning, and I do not." I opened my little

Gadsby's upon the eleventh hymn,

> " Thy mercy, my God, is the theme of my song";

and when I came to,

> " Thy *free grace* alone, from the first to the last,
> Has won my affections and bound my soul fast."

I saw the doctrine in a new light, and was astonished. "Free grace" seemed to sound in my ears, and yet I did not fully understand it. I had not heard it preached by the free-will preachers. Then I opened my little book again, and saw other hymns that gave me some encouragement, so that a hope sprang up. I was like one in a dark prison, and seeing a light coming through the dark crevices. I walked on, crying to the Lord to appear for me, and then was obliged to get up and ride for a rest; then got down and walked again. So I went on all day; and such was my distress of mind that I did not touch the cake my uncle gave me, nor had anything to eat all day. Once the man who was with the van insisted upon my having a cup of hot tea, and that was all I had, until we reached Saffron Walden; and we did not arrive there until nine at night. It began to snow towards evening, and by the next morning the snow was deep; so that I reached my grandparents' home just in time, for the next day the roads were impassable.

My grandparents lived in the almshouses which face Abbey Lane, leading to the park, and were intended for such as had been tradespeople in the town. My grandfather had been a miller. As I look back to that time, what a lovely spot that is in my memory, as it was to be the place of my deliverance! Now I must just say that my grandmother was a member of the General Baptists, and did not like the Strict ones, who had a little chapel in the London Road. But I knew there was one there, for I had heard my father speak of it as one of "those high-doctrine places"; and when Sunday came I had fully made up my mind to try and find it.

By Sunday the snow was so deep that the path which led to the chapel was filled up level with the hedges; and when I told my grandmother where I had made up my mind to go, she lifted up her hands with astonishment, and was quite angry with me. But I had a solemn feeling that the dear Lord was going to meet me there, and go I must. So I walked on the top of the snow with the greatest ease to the chapel. And when I entered, I think I felt something like Moses when he turned aside to see the burning bush, and the Lord said, "Put off thy shoes from off thy feet, for the place whereon thou standest is holy ground."

Now the minister and the few people that were there were perfect strangers to me. I had my hymnbook, and the 134th was given out, which I shall never forget:

> " Hail, sovereign love, that first began
> The scheme to rescue fallen man!
> Hail, matchless, *free,* eternal *grace,*
> That gave my soul a hiding place!"

I believe they sang all the hymn, and every verse seemed more and more wonderful to me. It was a summary of my feelings; and I was so melted down that I was glad I sat in a pew by myself, and no one saw me. Then I was all expectation for the word the Lord would send me by His servant. His text was from Acts 9.4: "Saul, Saul, why persecutest thou *Me?* " I thought to myself, "What a strange text!" and feared after all I should be disappointed – "surely that could not be a message for me" – and I almost felt angry. This I think must have been from the enemy of souls, trying to rob me of my comfort.

But when the dear man went into his subject, he spoke of the union that existed between Jesus and His people, showing how dear His saints were to Him whom Saul had been persecuting, and that in touching them he was touching the apple of His eye. He spoke also of God's choice of His people before the foundation of the world, and of His electing love; and the word came to me with power. I saw election in that little word *"Me"*. I saw that glorious doctrine in a way I never had before; it seemed to shine like a brilliant light. When I look back to that time, it seems but as yesterday. For it was as though the heavens opened, and the Lord Jesus spoke to me inwardly, saying, "I am Joseph, thy Brother." I had been for so many years thinking of Him as Joseph's brethren did of Joseph before he made himself known to them. I had thought of Him as a stern Judge, as an angry God; and that I must do something to appease His anger. And now how wonderful! He seemed to me as a Brother. I cannot describe what I felt. But I well remember that when I stepped out of that chapel, I felt I could say, old things had passed away and all things appeared new. Although it was everywhere covered with snow, it was springtime with my soul; and I went over the high bank of snow with the greatest ease. The old people in the almshouses were amazed to find I had gone that way; but I could not mention anything to them of the matter.

In the afternoon, as I was musing over the wonderful change I felt, all at once a voice seemed to ring in my ears: "Yes, it is all very well for you to believe in election, and in all you have heard this morning, but how do you know that you are elected? How dare you, such an insignificant creature, think that God would choose you and leave others to perish? What are you more than they?" With that I sank down as it were fathoms. It was like getting near the gates of heaven, and then sinking down to the confines of hell. I retired into a room by myself, and fell down before the Lord; for I felt like Peter when he was sinking, and as I felt in my dream when the waters were come over me - "Lord, save, or I perish."

With that I saw by the eye of faith the dear Redeemer hanging upon the cross; and He seemed to look at me and say, "*I died for thee.*" I said, "What, Lord, can I not do anything for my salvation?" He answered, "*By grace* are ye saved through faith; and that not of yourselves: it is the gift of God." I said, "Cannot I do anything to be saved?" Then the words came with such power, "*My grace is* SUFFICIENT *for thee*"; and with them I was brought into the glorious liberty of the children of God. I then understood what free grace meant. O the happiness I felt! What love I felt to Him whom I had seen by the eye of faith hanging upon the cross. I felt like Bunyan's Pilgrim when he came to the cross, and his burden fell from him into the sepulchre. I could say,

> "Blest cross! blest sepulchre! blest rather be
> The Man that there was put to shame for me!"

Such joy, such peace flowed into my soul that I could not describe, and the words came; "The ransomed of the Lord shall return, and come to Zion with songs and everlasting joy upon their heads"; and I felt that peace which passeth all understanding. I could say the Lord Jesus was "the chiefest among ten thousand and the altogether lovely". But O! I cannot express one half of what I felt. I can say,

> "E'er since by faith I saw the stream
> Thy flowing wounds supply,
> Redeeming love has been my theme,
> And shall be till I die."

I well remember soon after this sweet manifestation, I was sitting in the room pondering over it all, when it was just as though Satan came (not bodily, of course, but as Apollyon came to Christian), and I seemed to have a battle with him, for he said, "What about all this rejoicing and all this assurance that you seem to have? It is only enthusiasm, it will all pass away like the morning cloud. How dare you claim to be a favourite of heaven? You know how shocked your father and uncle will be to know you have turned a Calvinist." And withal he brought to my mind many of my sins and follies, so that for a time I was as it were cast down to the ground, and I knew not what to do, when I had these words given me with such power: "Now the God of hope fill you with all joy and peace *in believing,* that ye may abound in hope, through the power of the Holy Ghost" (Rom. 15. 13).

These words were as a sword to thrust at him, and I could say, "Begone, thou enemy of souls, for if God has given me a good hope through grace, and a joy unspeakable, and peace which passeth all understanding, neither you nor any earthly power can take it away from me"; and with that he fled, and I was permitted to enjoy such happiness as the worldling knoweth not. When night came I was afraid to go to sleep for fear that in the morning I should have lost all the happiness I felt. But when I awoke it was a lovely morning, the sun shining into the window, the white snow sparkling in the sun; and some time in that day, I cannot remember if it was morning or afternoon, I felt a desire to go into the park, which was close by. I could not tell why, as everywhere was still snow-bound; even the trains were stopped, so that the hotels had many passengers staying at them weather-bound. It was the time of the Crimean War *(1854-6).* But into the park I must go, to the astonishment of the almshouse people.

When I had gone some distance, and not a creature to be seen, I had a wonderful solemn feeling – I felt "alone with God". I had been led into the grace of the Lord Jesus Christ, and now I wanted to experience the love of God the Father; and the words came: "I will allure her, and bring her into the wilderness, and speak comfortably unto her." O, how shall I express what I then enjoyed? Although it is so many years ago, for that was in the year 1855 and this is January 1902, and my memory is so bad now that I forget events which took place last year, yet how fresh it is on my memory sometimes. It was as though the Lord said to me: "I have loved thee with an everlasting love; therefore with lovingkindness have I drawn thee." I answered, "What me, Lord, unworthy me?" and I was favoured with such communion with the Lord that I could say, " Lord, Thou knowest all things, Thou knowest that I love Thee"; for I felt the love of God shed abroad in my heart in such a manner that I cannot find words to express. I was obliged to say, "Stay Thy hand, for I am sick of love." I was brought into the banqueting house, and His banner over me was love. I felt I wanted to sing myself away to everlasting bliss – I could say,

"O for such love, let rocks and hills
Their lasting silence break,
And all harmonious human tongues
The Saviour's praises speak!"

But O, what at poor account I have written of that wonderful visit of the Lord to my soul at that time! I want a seraph's tongue to tell one half of it. I often wish I had written it at the time – I did send a letter to my father giving him some account of it.

But the time came that I had to leave Saffron Walden and return to London. I was with my grandparents about a fortnight. What a wonderful fortnight it had been to me! I told them I was not able to pay them for their kindness to me, but as soon as I was able I would make them some recompence. My grandma said, "My dear girl, we have been so richly supplied with everything since you have been here, even from strangers to us, it has been quite surprising" – so that I saw the Lord had been mindful of me in providence as well as grace.

When I took my journey to London, how earnestly I begged of the Lord to preserve me from the snares and temptations of the great city, where I was going to seek for a situation. When I reached my parents' home, they were living at Whitechapel, and I longed to tell my father what a great change I had experienced, but to my great surprise he received me very coldly, and my mother told me, in his absence, he was very much put out at the letter I sent him. He was very grieved that I had turned a High Calvinist. I had been so simple as to think I should soon convince him, but I found to my grief he was quite turned against me. He used to argue with me for hours, so that I was obliged to cry earnestly to the Lord to search me and try me, and lead me in the way everlasting. My prayer was, "Open Thou mine eyes, that I may see wondrous things out of Thy law." It was the means of bringing me to the throne of grace with great earnestness.

The first Sunday I was at home my father said. "Well, where are you going today?" I said, "I have heard of Zoar Chapel, Great Alie Street, and I have made up my mind to go there." "What," he said "that dirty chapel?" "Yes," I said, "I *must* go there." As I walked along the street on my way to Zoar, I had to go along Lemon Street, and I believe at that time a great many shops were open, and there was such a noise of the buyers and sellers that I felt like the pilgrims in Vanity Fair. And what with the free-will arguments my father had brought forward, I felt very sorrowful.

When I reached the chapel, I went up to the gallery and took a seat there. The minister in the pulpit was a rather robust-looking man with a pleasant face; and although I cannot remember his text or anything he said, yet I had such a wonderful confirmation sermon that I felt like one refreshed with wine. Ah, I was strengthened and comforted, so that I could say, "Surely this is the house of God and the very gate of heaven." I asked the friends as I went out the name of the minister, and they told me it was Mr. Mortimer (William Mortimer, pastor at Chippenham). And I remember as I stepped out into the street I felt all fear taken away. I walked home unconscious of all the noise in the street, and felt that all my father could say would not shake my confidence again in the blessed truths I had heard. I went again in the evening. and received another blessing. And all the next week I lived upon what I had heard, although I had the same trial to go through with my father, as he would begin arguing every time he came home.

While I was at Saffron Walden my grandmother had a book, Mason's *Spiritual Treasury, Meditations for Morning and Evening throughout the Year*, and it was very much blessed to me while there. I missed it very much. My father had a lot of books, but none I could read then: but he had one book which was sent him once in mistake. It was the *Gospel Ambassador*. I remembered when quite a child his being so vexed about this book, as it was a high-doctrine one. I went to his book-case and there was the book; it had been there for about ten years, and hardly ever been opened before. I found it very suitable to me; it was like a kind friend. When my father found me poring over it he said, "What! reading that book?" I said, "Yes, father; and I believe it was predestinated and foreordained that the publisher should make a mistake and send you this book, to be a comfort to me now." (I have it in my possession now.)

Well, all that week I was looking forward to Sunday, to go again to Zoar, thinking I should hear that dear man again, for I did not know the people there had supplies. When the Sunday came I took the same seat in the gallery, full of joyful expectation, when to my great disappointment a very different looking man came into the pulpit. He was a little man with rather a bald head, and, I thought, looked weakly. "Ah," I thought to myself, "I shall not be able to hear you, I should think." I felt quite to despise him. I do not remember much about his prayer. But O, when he gave out his text it was in the third of Ephesians, eighth verse: "Unto me, who am less than the least of all saints, is this grace given, that I should preach among the Gentiles the *unsearchable* riches of Christ" – in the first place it came to me as a reproof, as I was despising him in my heart because he looked a little, weakly man. But O, when he was led into the subject, such power attended the Word that he seemed to me like an apostle. It was indeed wonderful to me. I felt as though my heart was melted when he spoke of "the *unsearchable* riches of Christ", and our lost condition by nature. I had never heard anything like it before; his face seemed to shine, and he spoke with such energy that I felt it must be the power of the Spirit of God. It was indeed a feast of fat things to my soul.

So that once more I went on my way rejoicing. He was Mr. Roff, of Stow-on-the-Wold, they told me when I asked his name. (I call Mr. Mortimer and Mr. Roff the two bishops by whom I was confirmed.)

The next Sunday I went again, and felt prepared to hear whoever might be in the pulpit, believing I should have another confirmation of the blessed truths I was longing for. That day it was Mr. Gorton (pastor at Milton-under-Wychwood) who preached; and his text was Hebrews 6. 17, 18. I found it a sweet and precious subject – the heirs of promise.

As I had been looking out for a situation in these weeks, now I wished I could live where I could always attend Zoar Chapel; but I earnestly prayed that the Lord would place me where I could hear the same sweet truths preached. And O, at that time what access I had to the throne of grace, what communion I had with the Lord! I could go to Him and tell Him all my trouble. and pour out my heart before His blessed Majesty. And I could say, "This is my Beloved", and, "The Lord is my Friend." I had no one to tell my happiness to, I felt all alone with the Lord.

> "What peaceful hours I then enjoyed,
> How sweet their memory still!"

My father had a cousin named Mrs. Stevens. whose husband was a deacon and they were members of Mr. John Hazelton's* church, Mount Zion, Chadwell Street. During the time I was at home I went to see them and they asked me to go with them to see a baptizing that was going to take place at their chapel some time in the end of February. Now I had a great aversion to baptism, as I had been some years before to a General Baptist chapel, somewhere in London, to see a young woman baptized whom I had known for some time, and knew her to be a very worldly, vain and frivolous girl. She went quite back into the world (however, she never came out of it). And I was so disgusted and shocked at what I saw at her baptizing that I felt I should never want to see another. So when my cousin Stevens asked me to go with them to their baptizing I did not feel any wish to go, but went just to please them; for I did not say a word to them of what I had passed through.

I believe it was on a Thursday evening I went with them. Mr. Stevens put me in a seat near the pool, so that the candidates passed close by me. I believe Mr Hazelton took for his text, "My son, give Me thine heart, *and let thine eyes observe My ways.*"
He then spoke of the ordinance in a very powerful convincing, manner,

---

* Father of the John Hazelton, minister at Streatley Hall, London.

and how the Lord Jesus went through it Himself, expounding the Scriptures referring to it. I saw the candidates come forward and Mr Hazelton spoke to each one solemnly as they went down into the water. And O, how I felt I cannot describe. I felt, "Surely this is the house of God, and the very gate of heaven." I was so overcome, my heart was as it were melted within me, and I felt a vehement desire to go through the ordinance myself. O how earnestly I begged of the Lord that He would make a way for me to fulfil and follow Him in His sweet command! I have thought sometimes I was like the queen of Sheba, for I could say half had not been told me. And the Lord gave me such sweet promises that evening that He would grant my request that as I went home I hardly felt the ground I walked on, although I had to go to Whitechapel, where my parents lived then. I did not say a word to my cousins of what I felt, only that I was very glad I came. (And, what is so remarkable, I was baptized in the same place exactly a year afterwards.)

How I wish I could have written then of the many promises that were given me. But although this is the 2nd of February, 1903, yet I remember so well how happy I felt. It was a foretaste of heaven. O what a blessed month that February of 1855 was to me! How I think of it every year! It was the time of my espousals. I could say,

> " O for such love, let rocks and hills
> Their lasting silence break,
> And all harmonious human tongues
> The Saviour's praises speak!"

Soon after this I obtained a situation at Barnsbury, and I found I could attend Mr. Hazelton's ministry, although there was some distance to walk. The situation I entered just suited me then, as I was much alone. The family were very strict Church people, but I was very particular to have an agreement that I could go to chapel. The first Sunday evening I went to hear Mr. Hazelton I had such a good time that going home I seemed scarcely to feel the ground under my feet. I found there was a prayer meeting in the afternoon and the next Sunday I went to it. I very much enjoyed it and afterwards went every Sunday, and then again in the evening. I took a sitting, but I did not say a word to Mr. and Mrs. Stevens or anyone of what I had passed through, but what I want to record is that for nine months in this place I had such sweet communion with the Father, the Son and the Spirit that I cannot find words to express. It had been just nine months of misery, darkness and bondage, shut up in an iron cage, as it were. And now I had the same number of months of such happiness it was a taste of heaven below.

In the first part of the time I was tried about the Holy Spirit. It was in this way. I had sweetly entered into the enjoyment of the grace of the Lord Jesus Christ, and into the love of God the Father; but I now wanted to understand the communion of the Holy Ghost. I did not fully understand His office to my satisfaction. All one week it troubled me, and I begged the Lord to teach me aright on the solemn subject. On the Sunday evening (and how I used to long for the time to come!) it was pouring with rain. It was said, "Surely you won't go all that way in this rain." But I said, "I must"; and I remember the water ran off my clothing in the pew. Mr. Hazelton took for his text John 16. 13, 14; "Howbeit when He, the Spirit of truth is come, He will guide you into all truth," etc. O how astonished I was that he should have the very subject that evening that I had been so tried about all the week! If I had told anyone, I should have been ready to think Mr. H. had been told; but I knew it was not the case, but felt it was a direct answer to prayer. My mind was so enlightened by what I heard that I felt there was love shed abroad in my heart to God the Holy Ghost as the great Teacher. And after that I had such communion with Him, He did indeed take of the things of Jesus, and show them to me. And for nine months I had a wonderful time of love. Not a dog was allowed to move his tongue. I lived upon the manna of the gospel, and it was a foretaste of heaven. I used to say, "O Lord, Thou makest my feet like hinds' feet."

Now at the end of the nine months I thought, as I was out a little earlier one Sunday evening, I would call and see Mrs. Stevens, as I never hardly spoke to her, although I had a sitting in their pew, having to leave when the sermon was finished. I was afraid to tell anyone of my joy for fear it would be intermeddled with. When I reached my cousin's house, I found she had cut her hand, and was going to stay at home. She said to me, "I should be glad if you would stay with me." I felt reluctant at first, as I had been looking forward to the feast of fat things I had every Sunday evening. But, however, she prevailed upon me to stay. And when we were quietly settled down she said to me, "I should like to know if you profit under the Word, as you appear to pay great attention." And after a little while I felt my mind drawn to tell her a little of what I had passed through. And as I was telling her, I felt my heart burn with love towards her, for she wept for joy, and she rejoiced with me for the great things the Lord had done for me, and was exceeding glad. And after we had had a nice long talk together, I remembered I said to her, "Dear cousin, I hope I have experienced and entered into the grace of the Lord Jesus Christ, and the love of God the Father, and the communion of the Holy Ghost. And now

I know what the communion of saints means." (*Written May 22ⁿᵈ, 1904.*)

May 1909. After all these years I want to write a little more of the Lord's dealings with me. I am now seventy-three, and feel the infirmities of old age; and I think my time will not be long.

If I continue where I left off in 1904, I must tell of my going before the church at Mount Zion, Chadwell Street, after I had been visited by two of the deacons, the late Mr. Burrell being one of them. The night before I went I was full of fear at the thought of it, when I had the words, "My soul shall make her boast in the Lord; the humble shall hear thereof and be glad." I was helped to tell a little; but in the midst of my speaking, it was just as though Satan said to me, "How dare you be so presumptuous?" The insinuation was so powerful that I made a sudden stop, and was silent for a few moments, when inwardly I said, "The Lord rebuke thee, Satan; am I not a brand plucked out of the fire?" With that he seemed to vanish, and I felt a confidence given me to proceed. I was received by the church unanimously. Some of the friends asked me what made me stop so suddenly.

I was baptized by Mr. Hazelton on February 27ᵗʰ, 1856, just a year after I had such an earnest desire to follow the Lord through the ordinance. And He granted me my request in the same chapel. The young lady where I lived at the time turned a bitter enemy when she found I was a Baptist. The evening I was to be baptized I was suffering from a sore throat and bad cold; and it being a very cold evening, this lady told me I had better "order my coffin on the way, as it would be certain death" to me. Instead of that, I completely lost my cold, cough, hoarseness, and sore throat. It was the custom of the family to read the Scriptures every evening, each one, verse by verse; and my voice was quite clear, so that the young lady was astonished. Mr. Hazelton told me afterwards he had lost a cold in the same way after he had been baptizing.

[*From a letter dated 26th August, 1907.*] I do feel indeed that I am nearing my journey's end, but I think I can say that lately I have felt a great pleasure in thinking of my departure from this vale of tears... I trust that you and I not only know the Lord, but that *He knows us.* Have we not many proofs that He knows us? and is it not our supreme desire to know Him whom to know is life eternal? Do we not prize the visits of His grace more than anything this world can afford?...I was just nine months under the law, almost in despair, no hope; the heavens were as iron and brass. O how I wished I had been a bird or a beast, so that I had had no soul to be saved! But when the Lord brought my soul out of prison, and brought me into the glorious liberty of the children of God, when I had looked for hell and He brought me heaven, it was then I enjoyed for nine months such happiness that I have never been able to express. I seemed to live at the very gate of heaven. I enjoyed such sweet communion with the Three Persons in the Trinity, and the ministry of the Word was so blessed to me. My dear minister, Mr. Hazelton, used very often to take the very subject that I had upon my mind in the week, and open it up to my understanding; which was very wonderful to me. O how thankful I am that I had my *hearing* then! And although that is fifty years ago and more, yet how sweet the memory still!

> " How high a privilege 'tis to know
> Our sins are all forgiven;
> To bear about this pledge below,
> This special grant of heaven!

> " *To look on this* when sunk in fears,
> While each repeated sight
> Like some reviving cordial cheers,
> And makes temptations light."

Yes, and with me I can say it has made trials, afflictions and persecutions light. Dear R——, I verily thought then I had done with the world; but I had to come down from the mount, and like the disciples had to enter a cloud. I then met with persecutions and trials. But in after years I got into a backsliding state and a cold and lifeless frame, which caused the Lord to hide His face from me. And I can say, that has been the *greatest trial* of all. But of late I have felt such longings for the dear Lord's presence; my soul follows hard after Him. I have been led to feel my own helpless state when left to myself; so that my prayer is, "Hold Thou me up, and I shall be safe." S.Sarll.

[*From a letter, 5th October, 1908.*] I think perhaps the Lord is going to take me away suddenly, as so many old people are taken off. Lately I have felt perhaps that I shall not be here long, and I want to live every day as though it were my last. Not that I can prepare myself, or go on to perfection, as some talk of; for I feel my sinfulness more and more as I get older. But I can say that the things of time and sense seem all vanity and vexation of spirit, and I long for another token, another glimpse of the "sweet Lord Jesus", as Rutherford says, and that He would lift up the light of His countenance upon me, as in times past. I have enjoyed reading the piece in the *G.S.* for October by Mr. P., "Risen with Christ." That is my desire – to seek those things which are above. If we be risen with Christ, we are new creatures; "old things are passed away; behold, all things are become new." What a mercy to be able to say this!...I love to think of death and to look for the summons, "Come up higher"; where I shall see and hear and know all I desire and wish below. S.Sarll.

[*From a letter, 15th December, 1909.*] I was very ill in the night and I felt it very solemn for I thought perhaps my summons had come to depart. For I feel there is but a step betwixt me and death. I enjoyed Mr. P.'s sermon you sent me; and on Sunday evening I read the *Pilgrim's Progress,* where the pilgrims had such a glowing reception into glory; and I longed to follow them. S.Sarll.

Her last days.

My dear wife suffered much at times from heart failure and other afflictions for the last four or five years. She was very cheerful and patient to wait the Lord's time to take her to Himself. She said to me a day or two before she died, "O if it were possible, but I know it cannot be possible; after I am gone I would like to send down to earth such a shout of sovereign grace that the earth might hear! But it cannot be." She always said, "When I die, if I cannot speak, I will throw up my hands." As she was sinking very fast I said to her, "Do you feel the Lord Jesus precious?" The moment I spoke she threw up both hands and arms. While her voice was audible she tried to say, "Hark!" many times. The last time I spoke to her she was conscious, and answered a faint "Yes." That was about 4 a.m. She quietly lay free from pain, and gently breathed her last at 6.40 the same morning, 5th February, 1910. She always thought she should die in that month, for that was a month of months to her. She has now departed "to be with Christ, which is far better".

William Sarll
Stotfold.

Gospel Standard 1999, first published in the 1910 *Gospel Standard,* and recently published as a pamphlet.

J.C.PHILPOT'S DAUGHTER

Deborah Maria Philpot

Miss Philpot was the person who selected the daily portions for Ears from Harvested Sheaves *and* Through Baca's Vale. *She died in 1917.*

I was born into this world on April 21st, 1847, of godly parents, a heritage of far more value than of gold that perisheth or any amount of worldly possessions. I need not speak of my father – his life and career are wellknown amongst the inhabitants of Zion, and his praise is in all the churches. My mother was a very quiet, amiable woman, an exemplary wife, and devoted to her children, entering into all their little joys and sorrows. My father, good man, was strict and rather stern, so that we were considerably afraid of him. It was the custom in those days to make the difference between old and young, parent and child, far more distinct than it is now, and in later years we have been glad we were not spoiled by over-indulgence. As a child, I remember being somewhat impressed by a remark made by my uncle, Mr. Tiptaft [William Tiptaft of Abingdon], while preaching, to the effect that when as many years had passed as there were leaves on the trees in the park, eternity would have only just begun. And when my father, referring to the passage: "If God be for us, who can be against us?" solemnly asked, "But O! if God be *against* us, who can be *for* us?" I was awed by the tremendous thought.

But such impressions soon wore off, and I went on thoughtless and unconcerned till I approached my sixteenth year. At that time I was at the school of a godly woman who conceived a deep affection for me, and who talked to me about my soul. On one occasion she sent me a very affectionate letter, in which she said that though I was young and had known little of sorrow, yet times of trouble would come. I might be far from all who loved me, and then what should I do? Where should I turn? Would it be to the only Source whence help could come? "And then," she added, "then my faith grows strong in the promise, 'And whatsoever ye shall ask,' etc., and I long for you to know, and believe you will know the happiness of having an almighty, all-sufficient friend in every time of trouble."

A month or two passed on, and then the signal time arrived. It was one morning when we were out for a walk, and this good friend had been telling me that she never looked at me without the prayer that God would bless me. I was much touched by her kindness and affection, and that day while sitting at dinner, I remember staring at the wallpaper opposite and saying to myself, "What is it to be blessed of God? What is it?" Now for the first time I saw something desirable in it; and then I began to see that God had a people whom He would save and bless; and I felt I should like to be among them. Still at that time I had little or no sense of sin and its grievous nature, but a month or two after I was sent to school at Brighton, and there, under the ministry of Mr. Grace [John Grace, pastor at West Street, Brighton], which I attended, gradually there fell upon me a conviction that I was a sinner, and that before a holy God. It was not very deep but sufficient to make me feel uneasy and unhappy and to cause me to cry, "Lord, have mercy upon my poor soul."

One time I specially remember. I had been feeling depressed and unhappy, and was spending the week-end with Mrs. Grace and her daughters, and one of them was taking me back to school on Monday morning. We spoke to each other very little, as far as I recollect, when as I was walking along the word dropped gently and softly into my soul, "I will lead the blind by a way that they know not," which gracious promise has been and is being fulfilled in my experience.

After being at Brighton for about a year I left school altogether, and came back to my home at Stamford, but did not remain there long, as owing to my father's health he was obliged to give up his pastorates at Oakham and Stamford, and we went to live at Croydon. There we attended the ministry of dear Mr. Covell [Francis Covell, pastor at West Street, Croydon], but I grieve to say I did not greatly appreciate the privilege at first, for having worldly brothers, and my sister not yet being called by grace, I was drawn aside to do many things I did not see so much wrong in as I did afterwards. For instance, I was intensely fond of music, and there was the Crystal Palace close at hand with its attractive concerts. Also a School of Art was set up in Croydon which I attended, and pursued the arts of drawing and painting with great ardour, the prizes I gained from time to time being so many incentives to continue my studies. My father's death, 1869, which was rather sudden and unexpected, brought me to solemn considerations of eternal realities, and I remember bursting into tears, I think before he was buried, and imploring the Lord to be my God and Saviour too.

Later, during the next year, it seemed to be laid on my mind that I was making an idol of my painting, and that I ought to give it up; but my natural mind loved one of "the refined amusements" (which Mr. Hart speaks of) so dearly that I could not bear the thought of relinquishing it. And it was not till after repeated blows in my conscience, and my eyes showing signs of failing owing to the fine work in which I had been engaged, that I was compelled, as it were, to allow my idol to be taken from me. When I was engaged in my beloved pursuit, some thoughts of more important and weighty matters would intrude, and the words run in my mind:

> "The heart that wants this fear is poor,
> Whatever it possess beside."

O the kindness of God and His Holy Spirit in following up, and not suffering me to rest in anything short of Himself!

Well, the years rolled on until it pleased the Lord to put His hand a second time to the work, which was in the spring of 1876. I may mention that during the previous summer, typhoid fever being prevalent in the town, I had an attack which, owing to one or two relapses, lasted about eleven weeks. During this illness, I grieve to say, I amused myself with reading stupid, worldly tales, or novels as they really were, which came out in some numbers of a magazine which had been lent me; and to my sorrow, I must confess I was almost wholly oblivious of my wretched state – though my illness might have ended fatally – except for one gracious touch of mercy and compassion. I was lying awake alone in great pain, the rest of the household, not realising I was so ill, having gone to bed, when in my distress like Hezekiah I turned to the Lord and entreated His pity, crying that He had never failed to help me in trouble, and if He did now, it would be the first time. And, blessed be His name, He did not fail, for after a little while I got easier and fell asleep, and awoke in the morning with a little gratitude, I hope, and feeling I had not had such a bad night after all.

After my recovery, my sister and I went on the Continent for some weeks. Our younger brother took us by way of Brussels and the Rhine to Switzerland, and left us in the care of some friends at Lausanne, where we stayed for about three weeks, taking a few days for a trip to Chamounix and then to Paris, where we spent a week, a night at Rouen, and then by the Dieppe and Newhaven route back to my dear mother and home. But all this time of worldly pleasure, I grieve to say, I had but few transient thoughts of God and His salvation. So far had I strayed in my backsliding from the right way, as far, as the hymn says, "from God as sheep can run".

But in his great mercy He would not leave me to compass my own destruction. For the next spring, in the year 1876, I went to chapel and heard Mr. Covell as usual. I do not remember the text – it might have been in the exposition of the chapter he read – but he insisted very strongly on this passage: "If any man have not the Spirit of Christ, he is none of His;" and then went on to describe it as being the hatred of sin and the love of holiness. As I listened, I thought: "I don't hate sin like that; I wish I did, but I feel I don't. And I don't love holiness in that way. I am afraid, to be perfectly honest, I don't want to be quite so holy." Yet after I came away, the word followed me up closely, and made me feel uneasy, and caused me to cry, "What must I do? what must I do?" So I thought, "I suppose I must pray to be made to hate sin, as that seems the first thing." So I went about crying, "Lord, make me hate sin; Lord, make me hate sin." And I hope He did lay sin upon my conscience, and give me a sense of my lost, ruined condition.

One time during the next autumn I specially recollect. I think my trouble began one Monday evening, when a conviction of guilt and misery fell upon me; and it went on more or less the two following days. On the Wednesday evening I went to chapel, and dear Mr. Covell took for his text the last verse of Psalm 1: "For the Lord knoweth the way of the righteous," etc. When he gave it out, I said to myself, "That won't suit *me*"; for I felt anything but righteous, and at first he went too high. But presently he came lower and lower until he exactly reached my case. If he had been inside my heart, and known all that was passing there, he could not have spoken more to the point. "They shall mourn apart. They shall be as doves of the valleys, each one mourning for her iniquities. They grope for the wall like the blind, and they grope as if they had no eyes." O, it was just me! I sat in the chapel feeling ready to choke in the effort to keep back the tears, but O! it came dropping into my heart with such power and sweetness that I could not help feeling persuaded, for the time, that I was one of the righteous, and while memory lasts I can never forget that blessed time.

In the next spring Mr. Covell called one day, and finding me alone, took the opportunity of speaking to me about my soul's salvation. I replied, "I cannot say much; but I'd give all the world to have it." "I'm very glad to hear you say so," he rejoined, and talked so kindly to me and said, "May the Lord strengthen, stablish and settle you." From that time I think he kept a watch over me, and I cannot say what his ministry became to my soul. One or two gracious helps I specially remember. Once when he was speaking from the words: "That the Gentiles should be fellow-heirs" (Eph. 3. 6), and speaking to some who could not get very far, he said: "You say,

> 'The soul that with sincere desires
> Seeks after Jesus' love,
> That soul the Holy Ghost inspires
> With breathings from above'

That suits me. And

> ' Those feeble desires, those wishes so weak,
> 'Tis Jesus inspires, and bids you still seek;
> His Spirit will cherish the life He first gave;
> You never shall perish if Jesus can save.'

That suits me. And: 'He will not break the bruised reed' – that suits me.' "
Then He said, "Fellow-heirs! Fellow-heirs!" and I, feeling I could come in
there, said to myself, "Why, I do believe I am right after all! I shall get to
heaven." It was gone almost before I got out of the chapel, but it left a
sweet savour upon my spirit which I can never forget.

During the summer of 1878, I was on one or two occasions greatly
favoured. One lovely morning in July I was out walking, and as I was
going up a hill, I felt my heart strangely drawn out after the Lord, and I
said, "There be many who say, Who will show us any good? Lord, lift up
the light of Thy countenance upon me, and it will put more joy in my heart
than the wicked ever know when their corn and wine increase." And then
such love, joy and peace flowed into my heart as I walked up that hill as I
could never describe. I sat down on a seat at the top, and looked around
on all the objects in the glorious sunshine. "How beautiful it all is," I
thought, "and it is all God's handiwork!" I saw His glory shining through
creation, and I cried, "How good He has been to me all these years in
leading, watching over and guiding me." My heart was full of love and
gratitude. I was afraid to get up from the seat and go away lest I should
lose the sweet feeling, but I had it all the way home.

Later, in the autumn of that same year I had to pass through a season
of darkness and distress which lasted about a week. One morning I was
sitting in the drawing room, musing over my sad condition, when I
suddenly thought of a happy little time (I can't remember exactly how long
before) I had had while travelling by train to London. The previous
Sunday Mr. Covell had said: " This blew o'er my soul this morning, ' The
Lord taketh pleasure in them that fear Him: in those that hope in His
mercy.' " " Why, that's poetry," I thought; but it was something more than
poetry to me. For, remembering it in the train, I said to myself, " Well, I
am not sure I fear the Lord, though I wish to do so; but I'm sure I hope in
His mercy. Can it be possible that He takes pleasure in me? It doesn't

seem so, yet He says it." And for a few minutes I realised He did, and had such a happy little time.

Well, this said morning I was speaking of, this all came back to me, and I said "Why, I *did* believe. I did believe the Lord would have mercy on me"; when suddenly the words seemed spoken to me, "Then according to your faith be it unto you"; and at the same time such a ray of light shone into my soul that I can only compare it to a person throwing back the shutters in a perfectly dark room, and letting in a flood of glorious sunshine. Well, all my fears and distress were gone in an instant and I went about so happy all day, feeling:

> "Yes, I to the end shall endure,
> As sure as the earnest is given."

That was on a Wednesday, and in the evening I went to chapel, though as I had a cold my mother suggested I should stay away. Stay away! Why, I would not have missed it for anything. So we went, and having a few minutes before the service began, opened a hymn book and read that sweet hymn of Cowper's:

> "When darkness long hath veiled my mind."

It suited me well. Mr. Covell took for his text Isa. 35. 1: "The wilderness and the solitary place shall be glad for them; and the desert shall rejoice, and blossom as the rose." The whole sermon was very good to me. I felt the desert had rejoiced and blossomed as the rose that very day.

So I went on with ups and downs, my soul being kept more or less in an earnest, seeking state till I came to what proved to be the last few months of Mr. Covell's life (1879).

How low I sank in my feelings I cannot describe, and deeper and deeper in doubt and despondency I seemed to get day by day, till I had scarcely any hope of being saved at all. All the enmity of my heart was stirred up in a way I had not till then experienced. I felt I hated God and His ways, and yet underneath all this bitter enmity there was grief that it should be so.

One day I came across that hymn of Mr. William Gadsby's:

> "The path that Christians tread
> To reason's eye is strange";

and it seemed to describe my case, especially the verse:

> "Sin, armed with all the spleen
> Of enmity to God,
> Oft rises up within,
> And scorns a Saviour's blood."

O that was it! What a vile creature I must be to scorn that precious blood by which alone I could be saved, but there it was, and I could do nothing. I found indeed that the law worked wrath. I felt its iron grip, and groaned under the bondage, but was utterly unable to deliver myself from it. At times I clung to this passage: "Bring hither the blind, the halt, and the lame, and *compel* them to come in." How I longed to feel that soul-compelling power, to be "sweetly forced in", as the hymn says, and Toplady's lines suited me,

> "If e'er Thou art Lord of my heart,
> Thy Spirit must take it by force."

From this season of soul distress the Lord gradually raised me. Once I was comforted by the application of that word: "Blessed is the man whom Thou chastenest, and teachest him out of Thy law"; and then again with: "If ye then, being evil, know how to give good gifts unto your children, how much more shall your heavenly Father give the Holy Spirit to them that ask Him?" I caught hold of the last words, crying "O! I *can* ask!" and so I did, with some hope that God would grant my request.

Then to crown all, I heard dear Mr. Covell most sweetly a few days before his death. His text was 2 Thess. 2. 16-17, and he dwelt chiefly on the words: "God, even our Father"; preaching from the same text twice on Sunday, and on the following Wednesday evening. Strangely enough – and yet not strangely, for I believe it was the Spirit's doing – he was led to speak of one who might have been enabled to call God "Father" once in their life, and then had been tempted to believe it was all a delusion. This was just my case, for more than a year before, under a deep sense of God's goodness and mercy, I felt such love to Him that I cried:

> "Do I not love Thee, dearest Lord?
> O search my heart and see!"

and then something prompted me to look up and say, "Father." I felt no reproof, but the sweetest joy and peace, only I had put it away again and again, especially in my recent trouble, fearing it had been nothing but the most dreadful presumption, till under these three sermons, my hope growing brighter under each, I could at length go home on the Wednesday evening, and say, in the full assurance of faith, "O, my Father, my Father!" Then I entreated Him to let me call the Lord Jesus my Saviour also, and He did not deny me. Though, through the power of temptation, this blessing was quickly wrested from me, it was renewed after dear Mr. Covell's death; and under that trial, I was so blessed, and helped, and comforted, that I begged the Lord that all who mourned him might be comforted in like manner.

A few weeks after, at the beginning of the new year (1880), one morning I was musing over these blessings, and the thought came, "I have been enabled to call God, 'My Father,' and the Lord Jesus Christ, 'My Saviour,' but are my sins forgiven and put away?" I did not feel sure about that, for though my judgment would tell me that this must have been comprised in the former blessing, I was so anxious for satisfaction on this point that I could rest on nothing short of it. But while I was musing, as the psalmist says, "the fire burned," and down came the most blessed assurance of God's pardoning mercy, and such light, love, joy and peace flowed into my soul as I have no words to describe. No scripture or word accompanied the blessing, but it was so powerful that I felt for a moment as if my soul would fly out of my body, and I praised God – Father, Son and Spirit – with my whole heart. I thought dear Mr. Covell was praising God in heaven and I upon earth. There was no difference, and nothing between us but this body of sin and death. Indeed, I remember standing in my bedroom, and saying, "I feel as sure of going to heaven as that I live, and breathe, and move." How happy I was! The blessing lasted two or three days, and then the Lord gradually withdrew, and my joy declined.

"But grace, though the smallest, must surely be tried," as dear Kent says, and I shall never forget the time when, more than a year and a half later, I heard Mr. Popham for the first time. He had been to West Street [Croydon] before on a week-evening, but I was away from home, and so had not heard him. On the Sunday he preached most powerfully and made me question all my religion, but on the Wednesday evening his text was from Psalm 119, and all his remarks were so cutting that I came away saying to myself, "O, he's like a drawn sword!" I felt stripped of everything, and my recollection of the blessing I have just described only increased my misery, for I feared it was all a delusion, and I, nothing but a consummate hypocrite, had dared to call God, "My Father." If only I had not been guilty of such presumption it would not have been so bad, but I had done it, and there it was. I cannot describe my distress, but I know where I got that night. Dear Mr. Covell, in the very last sermon he preached, told us that he used sometimes to fear he was all wrong, and he would go to God and cry, "Begin now, Lord; begin now!" and then he felt, "Why it *is* begun." And so I, in the midst of my trouble, could not help crying, "If I am all wrong, do let me begin again. Begin now, Lord; begin now. I do not want to wait a minute."

And so the conflict went on till the next morning, when the word came, "There is hope of a tree, if it be cut down"; and with that a little hope sprang up in my heart, for I had feared it was not merely a cutting down, but a thorough uprooting; that I was nothing but the most wretched hypocrite, and that Mr. Popham had come to discover it to me. I did not think for some time of the conclusion of his text, though I do not recollect that he went into that: "Let Thy judgments help me"; but I could not help hoping and believing they did. Then when Mr. Popham came again some months later, he made a few remarks I was exceedingly glad to hear. He said it had been observed that some professors were like dram-drinkers, they must always have their drop of comfort; but it was good to be searched and tried, and good to have depths in one's experience pointed out. "There are reproofs of life, reproofs of life," he said; and I was so glad, for I believed I knew it.

> "As sons of thunder first they come,
>   And I their threatenings fear.
> But then they bring me to my home,
>   And sons of comfort are."

Also, when Mr. Popham had been speaking of a path of which I felt I knew little or nothing, which was that of fellowship with the Lord Jesus Christ in His sufferings, he said, "Do you want to know Him? Then you *will* know Him. Do you want to love Him? Then you *will* love Him." These words rang in my ears again and again, and drove me to the Lord, crying, "Lord, I *do* want to know Thee; I *do* want to love Thee." A few times the feeling rose in intensity to the cry, "I must have Him! I must have Him!" at others I seemed less in earnest. But I felt that was everything: "Whom to know is life eternal"; and though I had a wretched heart that was continually going after idols and forbidden things, I felt that had become my chief aim – to know the Lord Jesus Christ and to love Him.

I must now speak of a great deliverance I had in the year 1883, in connection with the illness and death of an aunt, one of my mother's sisters. I am sorry to say I had always disliked this poor aunt but, especially on one occasion, was brought to feel how wrong I had been, and to lament and confess my sin before God. Soon after, she wrote to tell me she was very ill, and coming up to St. Thomas's Hospital as a paying patient. There I went to see her, and arranged for her to stay with us when she came out of the hospital, which she did, and I was allowed to take care of her and nurse her, and quite won her over. She was most grateful for all that was done for her, and how completely I forgave her, there is no need to say.

About six months after, I was staying at Stamford with some relatives, about twenty miles from the place where she lay dying. My cousin, who was her niece also, and I went over to see her the day before she passed away. She did not know us, being in the state of coma which sometimes precedes death, and her dreadful appearance, for she was worn almost to a skeleton, and the fear that there was no hope of her body or soul – for she had been a bitter opponent of the truth – impressed me so painfully that I can never forget the horror and distress I experienced that night and the next. It so happened that two days previously, the daughter of a clergyman at Stamford had, in a fit of insanity, thrown herself into the river, and was drowned; and these two most painful cases so wrought upon me that I cannot describe how vividly the awful state of those who die in their sins, and are swept into the Red Sea of God's wrath for ever, was set before me. And then I was in a low place myself, and had many fears and questionings as to how it would be with me in the solemn hour of death. Two verses out of Psalm 91 were a little support; they just kept me from sinking entirely: "A thousand shall fall at thy side, and ten thousand at thy right hand; but it shall not come nigh thee. Only with thine eyes shalt thou behold, and see the reward of the wicked"; but O the storm that swept over my soul in those two nights. How I longed for a refuge in that dread hour when, as Kent has it, "terrors o'er the conscience roll." It seemed as though I did in a measure "see the reward of the wicked"; for it was like watching while someone stood for a moment on the edge of a steep precipice, and then fell headlong down it. I could not see the crash below, but I could imagine it, and my soul recoiled with horror and dismay.

The morning after the second night, a telegram came to say our poor aunt had died at midnight. I then decided to return home the next day, and what with packing my belongings, and going to bid "Goodbye" to one or two friends, I got through the day pretty well; but I so dreaded being alone again at night, for I thought: "Now I know she's gone, it will be ten times worse." But O the goodness and mercy of the Lord! I had not been in my room long before He came, and broke in upon my soul with the last three verses of Psalm 91: "Because he hath set his love upon Me, therefore will I deliver him. I will set him on high, because he hath known My name. He shall call upon Me, and I will answer him; I will be with him in trouble; I will deliver him, and honour him. With long life will I satisfy him, and show him My salvation." Well, all my fears were put to flight in an instant; joy and peace flowed into my heart instead, and I went to bed, fell into a sweet sleep, and felt that Jesus was with me. "O!" I cried, "it will take a whole eternity to praise Him!"

The next day I returned home. A verse of Berridge's kept coming to my mind, and how I felt the truth of it:

"All other refuge fails,
And leaves my heart distressed.
But this eternally prevails
To give a sinner rest!"

When I had been at home a short time, one day an old copy of Watts's Hymns fell into my hands. In it I came across this verse, and believed I could say it feelingly:

"Jesus, to Thy dear faithful hand
My naked soul I trust,
And my flesh waits for Thy command
To drop into the dust."

I have heard dear Mr. Popham speak of "a solemn surrender". I believe I knew something of it that day, and committed myself into the Lord's hands, body and soul, both then and for ever. And those verses which the Lord so graciously gave me I sometimes think are the sweetest in the whole Bible, though I have others, I trust, which are precious; but these seem to contain all I want. "*Because* he hath set his love upon Me; *because* he hath known My name." There it all is. And whereas I have feared exceedingly at times that there was some subtle secret in true religion I was shut out of, which the people of God could not reveal to me, and I was afraid He would not, this word: "I will show him My salvation," seemed to pick me up, and set my feet upon a rock, the blessed Rock of Ages, which can never be moved. And indeed if these promises are truly fulfilled in and for us, what can we more desire?

For a number of years after I began to seek the Lord, the subject of baptism appeared to me of little consequence. If I heard or read anything concerning it, my conscience was quickly quieted with the consideration that it was not essential to salvation, and that therefore I need not trouble about it. And when a dear friend told me of her exercises about being baptized, I was at a loss to understand her. I could well understand her being concerned about the salvation of her soul, but why she should be so troubled anything so unimportant as baptism, I could not conceive. Ah! I understood well enough when I came into the same conflict. But as dear Mr. Covell seldom brought the subject forward, and never urged anyone to join his church, I went on while he lived with scarcely any thought of it.

In the summer of 1880, some months after he died, I was staying with an uncle, a clergyman, who one evening earnestly entreated me to be baptized, as I had not undergone the rite in infancy, and he considered it essential to salvation; and so, though I placed no confidence in what he said, having every reason to fear he was a blind guide, yet I felt so annoyed at his persistency that I thought I would at least see what the Bible said on the point, and searched it for that purpose. I was struck with the reply of the Lord Jesus when John the Baptist demurred at His request that he should baptize Him: "Suffer it to be so now, for thus it becometh us to fulfil all righteousness," wondering what the "us" meant, whether it applied to the Lord Jesus and His followers or not. Then turning to the Book of Proverbs, part of the second chapter caught my eye and attention: "If thou criest after knowledge and liftest up thy voice for understanding" etc., so on I read to the ninth verse: "Then shalt thou understand righteousness, and judgment, and equity, yea, every good path," which verse seemed to speak to me and assure me that if I continued to seek the Lord and follow after Him according to His Word, "If thou criest after knowledge," etc. – He would in His own time lead me in every *good* path and teach me all that it was necessary for me to know. Then I closed the Book, satisfied for a time, and thought little more of baptism until the Lord's time came to make me hear His instruction

Not quite three years after this, our dear friend, Mr. Popham, was dining at our house. It was the first day he spent with us, and in the afternoon my sister asked him to tell us a little about himself and his call to the ministry. He kindly complied, and in his narrative told us how on one occasion an old lady spoke to him, and asked him what he thought of baptism. He replied that he had not considered the subject particularly; he supposed it was right, but he had not thought much about it: when she rejoined: "Did you ever ask the Lord to teach you baptism?" The subject thus brought before him was laid upon his mind, and increased in weight, until he was at length constrained to follow the Lord in His ordinance.

That same night I could not help thinking of it as I went to bed, but early the next morning, about six o'clock, I awoke, and the events of the preceding day coming to my mind, and dear Mr. Popham's conversation, the question was put to me as by an inward voice: "Did you ever ask the Lord to teach *you* baptism?" "No," I answered, "and I don't want to learn"; and the bitterest anger and enmity arose in my mind against the ordinance. Still it made me very unhappy, for I found I could no longer go to the Lord and say as I had often done, "Lord, do teach me: I am so willing to learn"; for here was something I did not want to learn: and I remember saying to myself with some complacency a little time before: "Well, at all events I cannot say I do not desire the knowledge of God's ways" but here I was, not desiring the knowledge of *all* His ways; and that day I had no peace.

In the evening I went to chapel, and Mr. Popham took his text from

Luke 12. 31: "But rather seek ye the kingdom of God: and all these things shall be added unto you." It was a nice sermon, still it did not impress me particularly; but after I got home, I was left in the room alone, and my mind went back to the previous Sunday evening, when Mr. Popham had preached from Psalm 107. 14: "He brought them out of darkness and the shadow of death, and break their bands in sunder" – having the same text morning and evening; and in the evening, after he had spoken about the different bands which hold the children of God, I returned home with a band on my spirit, which was caused by the fear I had never sought after the forgiveness of my sins as a special favour. But while I was musing about it alone, I could not help remembering how earnestly I had been led to seek God's blessing from time to time, and Hart's words came sweetly to my mind:

> " What is it to be blessed of God,
> But to have all our sins forgiven?"

and I saw that all His favours were wrapped up in this blessing, and under the sweet influence of that assurance I begged the Lord to make His glory dear to me, for I had been grieved I cared so little for His honour, and also that He would make Himself very dear and precious to my soul.

I had no thought of baptism then, but on the Wednesday evening, my mind going back to these exercises, something seemed to say, "Did not you ask the Lord to make His glory dear to you?" "Yes," I answered. "And did not you ask Him to make Himself very dear and precious to your soul?" "Yes," I said. "And here you are unwilling to do the least thing He requires." This I was obliged to own, but the consideration softened me sufficiently to cause me to cry, "Lord, make me willing to learn," and the next morning I found I could say, "Lord, do teach me, *even baptism,* if Thou wilt."

There for a time I rested, being made willing to learn, and waiting to be taught. And then all the trouble wore off for nearly a year, with the exception of a little touch in the autumn. Mr. Mockford [George Mockford of Heathfield] had been preaching from the words: "What will ye that I shall do unto you?" And the poor blind men said, "Lord, that we may receive our sight." In his sermon he made some allusion to baptism, and when I got home I said impatiently, "I don't see it; I don't see it"; when the question seemed to be asked, "Are you willing your eyes should be opened?" Well, I hoped I was; but with that exception the subject did not trouble me particularly again till the following May, when a sermon of dear Mr. Popham's came out in *The Gospel Banner.* A short time before, I had been trying one evening to feel after the Lord, when this scripture was brought to me: "He that cometh to God must believe that He is, and that He is a rewarder of them that diligently seek Him." Very soon, I think only a few days after, this sermon appeared in *The Gospel Banner* on the same text. I read it, and one paragraph took fast hold of me: "What a solemn ordinance is the Lord's Supper. But some may say, 'We cannot go to that, because we have not attended to the other ordinance.' Well, we cannot break down the wall that God has built up. There is a door in it, baptism. Do you believe the Lord is in it? There is the hinge, for if a man does not believe that He is, he will not seek Him in it. Do you believe there is a heaven where bliss reigns, and a hell where God's wrath is ever burning? If you do, you will seek to escape the one and enter the other." These words, as I said, took possession of me, and brought me into trouble again.

A little later in the month, Mr. Popham was spending the day with us while supplying here. He let fall some expression concerning the Lord's Supper, and I said, "I should think everyone must see that." He answered me quickly, "I am not talking about seeing it"; and this served to increase my trouble. One day it was so heavy I could only groan, "O Lord, I am oppressed; undertake for me"; but even this grief abated and then wore off, but it returned at intervals.

In the summer I left home for a time, and being cut off from the means of grace, I sadly departed in spirit from the Lord. But almost immediately after my return home, this wretched backsliding was laid upon my conscience, and such misery did I feel one night in bed, combined with a nervous state of body, that I had fears I should go out of my mind, and thought I discovered symptoms of it. Under this trouble (which I believe was an assault of Satan), I turned to the Lord, but He had gone, and I thought He would never return. With what bitterness I cried out. "My God hath forsaken me! my God hath forgotten me!"

The next day was Sunday, and I went to chapel feeling so glad to meet among God's dear people again. Mr. Wakeley [Thomas Wakeley of Rainham] was preaching, and said some things that suited me. "Thou takest away their breath; they die, and return to their dust," etc. All that day my heart was going after the Lord with, "I must have Him! I must have Him!"

The next morning a grievous temporal trouble broke upon me, and when the two met – trouble of circumstances and trouble of soul – I felt almost distracted. But the promise was graciously brought to mind, "Call upon Me in the day of trouble," etc., and I was enabled to cry to the Lord for succour and deliverance, which I did most vehemently; and about noon, in tenderest mercy, He came and visited my soul, put all my fears to flight, and gave me the sweetest assurance of my interest in Him, so that my sorrow was turned to joy; and though the temporal trouble continued a day or two longer (God was very gracious to me in that also), I was calm and happy in the midst of it.

But while I was in that blessed state, the thought of baptism returned. I had said over and over again in my spirit that I could never go before the church, that nothing should induce me, that I would rather walk over burning coals, but now in the midst of my happiness the subject again rose up in my mind. Until I read that sermon in *The Banner,* though I hope I had known the breathings of a longing soul, I had never thought of seeking the Lord in His ordinance; but while I was rejoicing in the mercy my previous misery had made so sweet, something seemed to say, "Now how do you feel? You said you would rather walk over burning coals." "O!" I cried, "I should not mind walking over burning coals to get at Him, if that was the way – through the ordinances," and so for a short time I felt a blessed willingness to walk in the path appointed for me. How happy I was all that day and the next! A hymn of Toplady's suited me:

" This proof we would give that we Thee receive,
Thou art *precious* alone to the souls that *believe;*
Be precious to us; all beside is as dross,
Compared with Thy love and the blood of Thy cross."

I felt I believed, and He was precious to my soul, and the next day I sat peacefully sewing, and felt I was a Naphtali "*satisfied* with favour."

After this never-to-be-forgotten time, I went on for more than a year, sometimes troubled about baptism, and sometimes not, little thinking that the Lord was laying my case in this matter upon the minds of two or three other godly friends. At last, to my surprise, a member here spoke to me, quoting the words: "The Spirit and the bride say, Come"; telling of her own experience in being led to go through the ordinance as an encouragement to me. Deeply impressed, I returned home, and I found the Spirit had been saying, "Come," for a long time in my heart, though I had been trying my hardest to quench His sacred influences. After this Mr. Mockford spoke of baptism in the pulpit, but advised any of those who were troubled about it not to speak to man about it, but to God alone. The next day, or day after, he addressed me on the matter, when I quickly rejoined, "Don't you know what you said?" "O!" he replied, "I've tied my own mouth"; so I was saved from speaking on a subject, which from what I was passing through, added to my natural reserve, would have been very painful to me.

Then in December that same year (1885) one of the deacons spoke to me about joining the church here, and now my trouble went on with scarcely any intermission until my heart being brought down with labour, I was constrained to follow the Lord in the way He had appointed. But O! how wretched I was throughout that winter. I used to go to the Lord sometimes and say, "O Lord, I am so unhappy: I am so unhappy!" but could add no more. And yet I thought He pitied me; for once, and I think twice, this scripture came, "His soul was grieved for the misery of Israel."

But I was so stubborn, it was long before my hard heart would give way. "I will make thee sick in smiting thee," He said, and sick indeed I was made to feel; and then again it seemed the Lord would turn in compassion, and plead with me, "Have I been a wilderness unto Israel?" "He that loveth Me not keepeth not My sayings"; until I felt I could not bear His reproaches. A letter from dear Mr. Popham served to increase my exercises, he having had my case upon his mind without my having mentioned baptism in any way, and I felt quite cross with him at times for speaking of it as a "dear ordinance", when I was so full of bitter enmity against it. And so the trial went on, until the same deacon asked me in March if I would consent to his proposing my name at the next meeting, and a little time was given me for consideration.

One day about this time, to my surprise and that of my sister, our mother expressed a willingness to leave Croydon and go and live at Tunbridge Wells. My sister and I had often wished to do so, but had looked upon it as a castle in the air, and thoroughly impracticable. But when our mother's mind was turned in that direction, we readily acquiesced in her decision, and I was glad to find what I thought would be a nice loophole out of my trouble and difficulty. But I was presently made to feel that the Lord would not allow any excuse for continued disobedience, and one unhappy afternoon, when I stood irresolute, something pulling me first one way and then another, the word was spoken with authority: "This is the way, walk ye in it"; and to anyone less stubborn and wilful it should have been conclusive. But my God was merciful to my unrighteousness. "Sin shall not have dominion over you," was spoken to me one day in the conflict. "O, but," I cried. "it *does* have dominion." "Grace shall reign." "O, but," I answered in bitterness of soul, "it *doesn't* reign." Thus I went through the waters of affliction, but all the while my gracious God was leading me, and eventually brought me out into a wealthy place.

On the Sunday following the day the word came to me, "This is the way," etc., Mr. Prince [George Prince of Forest Hill] preached at Croydon, and to my surprise took that verse, and the preceding one, for his text. I could not help being struck with the coincidence, and though he did not get so far as the words: "This is the way," the former verse forming the subject matter of his discourse, yet he so described my exercises and conflict of mind, that I could not help falling under the Word; and when I returned home in the morning, the Lord came and spoke to me, "Daughter, be of good cheer; thy sins are forgiven thee"; and how could the stoutest rebel withstand such goodness? I was made willing to follow such a glorious guide.

But, "Wilt Thou be with me?" I anxiously inquired. "Certainly I will be with thee," He kindly replied, and O! how true He was to His promise. In the afternoon He again drew near, and said, "I know thy poverty" (I had at times so bemoaned my poverty, and Hart's hymn, "Lord, when I hear Thy children talk," was one day a help to me); "I know thy poverty, but thou art rich"; and I answered, "Yes, Lord, I am rich if I have Thee."

> "I'm rich to all the intents of bliss,
> If Thou, O God, art mine."

In the evening I went to chapel again, and found the Word still encouraging and confirming; so much so, that when I had to give a final answer as to whether I would come forward or not, I was obliged to answer, "I dare not refuse."

So at the quarterly church meeting my case was mentioned, and the deacons were deputed to see me, which they did at my home the following Thursday, April 8th, and I was enabled to give them some account of the Lord's dealings with me, and of my exercises concerning baptism. And indeed I did realize that sweet promise: "Thou wilt keep him in perfect peace whose mind is stayed on Thee, because he trusteth in Thee." So I went before the people and was helped to give some account of what I hoped the Lord had done for my soul, beginning at the beginning, and going step by step to finish with my recent exercises about baptism. I do think the Lord gave me entrance into the hearts of His people, who kindly and unanimously received me.

Then I went home, and I can hardly tell of the peace and happiness that followed. For one whole week, I walked in the light of the Lord's countenance, in the enjoyment of His love and presence. My birthday came during this time: it was the happiest one I ever had. On that day my mother and sister left me on a visit to Tunbridge Wells, and usually I did not like them to go and leave me by myself, but on this occasion I did not regret it. I felt so glad to be alone with my dear Jesus. It was lovely weather, I remember, and the bright sunshine without corresponded with the brightness within. At the end of the week my joys gradually declined, but the sweet recollection remained.

About a month after, I was baptized by Mr. Popham, and was mercifully helped through the ordinance, though I did not feel the joy I had after going before the church.

Gospel Standard 1984, originally published in the 1932 *Gospel Standard*

GOD ALONE THE REFUGE

Catherine Alice (Katie) Pepler

Mrs. Pepler (often known as "Aunty Katie") is still affectionately remembered by many. She died on April 23rd, 1963, aged 79.

O that the Lord would do for each of our family what I humbly hope He has done for me, in calling me out from the giddy multitude. I believe He spoiled these pleasures for me while in tender years, perhaps about ten years old. I well remember how I used to wish my parents were more like my school companions', and would take me to concerts, and such like, as they did. I made up my mind when I grew up I would have my fill, but God's thoughts are not as ours, and in much mercy He stopped me.

A concert was being arranged at the school I attended, and the teachers insisted I must go. I dare not ask my father, and so the head teacher called on him, and the next day my father told me I could go just once but never to ask again. How I enjoyed the concert, and how unhappy I felt when another was arranged soon after! I watched my school friends going along to it. I went outdoors to conceal my feelings, and as I crossed the yard I reasoned thus: "If only I was more like my sister and had no love for these things, how much happier I should be." I thought, as God can do everything, He could take away this wish, if I asked Him; so I stole away behind a heap of rubbish in my father's barn and made my request. I went back to the yard, and examined myself. Was the wish still there, or had God answered my prayer? There was a feeling of relief, and I felt I could sincerely say I had no desire whatever to go to that concert. That first answered prayer left a deep impression on my mind, and a good many times after that, if the old rubbish heap could speak, it might have told a few tales.

It must have been soon after this I went with my parents to Grove, when dear old Mr. George Mockford was preaching. His text was "Elect according to the foreknowledge of God the Father, through sanctification of the Spirit," etc. Doubtless I understood but very little of what he said, but I felt my eyes glued to the dear man as a holy man of God, and I well remember how earnestly I desired that I might some day possess that blessed something which he possessed, and my feelings gave vent to tears when Mr. Alfred Belcher gave out hymn 215 to close. The last verse reads:

"May I be found a living stone,
In Salem's streets above;
And help to sing before the throne,
Free grace and dying love."

Mr. Mockford was staying with my parents, and it was my job next morning to clean his boots. What an honour I felt it, and how I made them shine; the dear old saint rewarded me with a kiss and a penny. This was when we lived at Hanney Mill, where I was born in 1883, and where, three times in infant days, the Lord preserved me from death by drowning. Twice I can scarcely remember. I was playing near the edge of the water at the mill tail and fell in. As it was foaming out of the great wheel, the noise doubtless drowned my cries. I am told I sank twice, and just at that moment one of the tallest men in the village passed over the bridge and lying flat held my head above water till someone came to his assistance. When I came round I was lying on the sofa, and my dear mother was bending over me. I do not remember much of my mother, as she died at the age of 37, when I was six, and was buried at Grove Chapel, with the little coffin of the babe of five weeks resting on the top of hers. How little I then realized what I had lost – a mother's love – but I do remember that my attention was mostly taken up with my new clothes. How the seeds of pride thrive even in early childhood!

After two years a widower, my father married again, and my mother was very rarely mentioned. Many years after my mother's death, I felt a great wish to know if she was a gracious woman. I had, by this time, married and become a mother, and I longed to know if I had ever been to my mother the subject of the many prayers and exercises I have felt for my offspring. I was laid aside for a month with flu, and this matter lay heavily upon my mind. I found on the death card were the words: "Blessed are they which do hunger and thirst after righteousness, for they shall be filled." It gave encouragement, as I felt led to ask the Lord for a confirmation by causing the minister to bring these words into his discourse when able to get to chapel. We were then attending South Moreton, and the minister got up and gave out this very portion for a text. I felt full, to think the great God of heaven and earth should have paid heed to my poor breathings, and the matter was truly settled respecting my dear mother, and O how it made me long for a blessed assurance that my unworthy soul might be found in that covenant of grace.

Shortly after my mother's death, I was sent to an aunt of hers, where I was allowed to have my own way and was thoroughly spoilt by her four grown-up sons. She was of a very tender spirit, and I think it hurt her more than it did me to correct me. However, one day, after I had been very disobedient in climbing on top of a very high wall, she told me that she really would have to give me a whipping. She left me in the room and fetched a stick, which she laid on the table, and then knelt down at her old armchair and buried her face in her hands. Naughty child that I was, I thought it a good opportunity to run out of the room, and there the matter ended (as I thought).

Forty years passed away. My dear old aunt had long since been laid in the grave, and I was lying on a bed of affliction in St. Thomas's Hospital awaiting a major operation, from which there appeared little hope of recovery. It was a solemn time to me. Sins of the past, as well as the present, rose up before me till I felt like one hemmed in with no way of escape, and the way I treated my dear old aunt seemed to stand out so prominently amongst the mass of iniquity. I learnt the meaning of the wormwood and the gall; my soul hath them still in remembrance. What would I not have given to have been able to throw my arms around her and seek forgiveness. Mercy was my one and *only* plea in that solemn hour, and, blessings on His dear name, Mercy's angel form appeared and led me on to Jesus, a precious, sacred Hiding Place. This was in October 1931, a very memorable year to me.

But my mind seems to dwell on youthful days. We left Hanney Mill in 1897, and went to live at Garlands Farm. My father had had great difficulty in getting milkers, and used to get very worried over it, so I promised to learn to milk and to stick to it for as long as he needed me, which was sixteen or seventeen years. What ups and downs I met with throughout those years, and though I could not claim to be among the seekers in Zion, how many an errand took me to the throne of grace, for my path was not altogether a smooth one in my youthful days! If that precious work of grace had ever been begun, how slow its growth! There was an aching void, it ebbed and flowed, no satisfying rest in anything here below. My dear father was a godly man, but his natural disposition was often a trial to those about him. His word was law to his children, and woe betide us if we dared to thwart him.

Soon after we moved to Garlands, my eldest brother formed an attachment to a gracious young person he met during his apprenticeship in Sussex. He was rather young, and the young lady a bit older. Father set up opposition from the first, without much enquiry, and O what a bitter trial it was for our poor brother, who felt he had the Lord's approbation and could not give it up, and how bitter it was for us at home, only ourselves knew! How many cries went up in those days to the Lord that He would ever preserve me from inheriting my poor father's hard spirit, but grant that his God might be my God.

Not very long after this, my second brother ran away from home, and for several days kept us in suspense as to his whereabouts. Eventually he let us know he was on the Atlantic, bound for Canada. I loved my brother dearly, and felt very troubled about him, and one day, when trying to take the matter to the Lord in the old bedroom next to the cheeseroom at Garlands, these words came to me with such a comforting, yet solemn, feeling: "Thy shoes shall be iron and brass, and as thy days, so shall thy strength be." As I look back on the years, what support and comfort in other trials has that blessed promise been to me! How sweet the verse:

> "Only when the way is rough,
> And the coward flesh would start,
> Let Thy promise and Thy love
> Cheer and animate my heart."

What the dear Lord begins, He'll surely finish, and as "thy days" include, I believe, the great day of death, it gives me hope in my end. The greatest foe and robber of my peace I've ever had is the wretched unbelief and infidelity which dwell within my wicked and deceitful heart.

A few years after my brother went abroad, my future husband approached me by letter. I handed it to my father and, after thinking it over, he told me he very much liked the spirit of the letter and also the young man, and he dared not oppose it because he felt it was of the Lord. My father's words were a great comfort to me, as the matter caused me much exercise of mind for some time. I earnestly desired the Lord would be our Guide, for there was a strong affection between us. Six years passed before we could marry, and my spiritual exercises seemed to wear off and I settled down to a happy courtship and became swallowed up in my new happiness. Only now and then did the thought of my soul's salvation disturb my peace.

We married on September 2nd, 1915, and the following Christmas an uncle of mine (my mother's brother) invited us to spend an evening. Song singing and card playing, etc. was the order of the evening, and I felt very ill at ease, and on the way home how I begged of the Lord to decide this inward conflict, "Am I His, or am I not?" If I am not one of His, why O why cannot I enjoy myself as others? If I am, then help me to come boldly out and be separate, and let it be a clear cut, for the Word says, "Ye cannot serve God and mammon."

The following July our first baby was born, and there was trouble; my life and the dear babe's life hung in the balance. The Lord extended mercy to us both, so we called her Mercy, and from that time I believe He deepened my desire after a precious Christ. Till then I had felt, "Give me Christ" but now my need became so acute and I had to add, "or else I die." I told the Lord I was willing to bear anything He was pleased to send if only He would make it manifest I was His. How little we realize sometimes what we are asking for!

Our Mercy had grown a lovely child, just seventeen months old, the apple of our eye, and I am afraid the idol of our hearts. I believe it was in one of Samuel Rutherford's letters I read a remark I never forgot. It was to this effect: "Let your children be beside your heart, but don't let them get into the yolk; that is the place for Jesus only." One of our hymns says, "We may let idols in, But cannot turn them out." How solemn when God comes and does it, for none can stay His hand!

One day in December, I went into the next room to remove a saucepan from the fire. The dear child toddled along behind me, and tripped over the hearthrug. Her little hand touched the handle and it fell over, splashing some of the contents over her. For three never-to-be-forgotten nights we watched beside her, and on the third day she passed for ever from us. The scalded places had healed nicely, but the shock had been too much. I was distracted, the more so because I felt it was due to my carelessness. Carnal reason set to work, and I thought if only I had done this, or not done that, it would never have happened. I could not seem to alter myself, and however I could face the inquest on the following Monday I did not know, nor did I feel any freedom in taking it to the Lord, for I felt verily guilty before God and man.

There was a ray of comfort respecting our dear child. The doctor had drawn the sheet over her face when she died, and after he left I turned it back. How beautiful she looked, and just at that moment the words seemed to sing in my very soul:

"Safe in the arms of Jesus,
Safe on His gentle breast;
There by His love enfolded,
Sweetly her soul shall rest."

and faith seemed given me to believe it was even so. Another glimmer of comfort was in the hope that the Lord might use this bitter sorrow for my soul's good.

The next day was Sunday, and on his way from the morning service at Uffington, Uncle Jacob [her brother, Mr. Jacob Pocock] called to sympathise, following the exhortation "to weep with those that weep". We said but little; grief seemed to close our mouths; but just as he was about to leave, he leaned against the mantelpiece and quoted the second verse of hymn 261:

"It is the Lord; should I distrust
Or contradict His will,
Who cannot do but what is just.
And must be righteous still?"

I do not remember that anything struck me as he repeated it, but after he had gone, it seemed to open up to me as a break in the dark cloud, and what I saw in the first four words, "It is the Lord", I cannot fully express. But if "it was the Lord," then all the responsibility was lifted off me, for who could stay His hand, or say unto Him, "What doest Thou?" My natural sorrow remained, but the heaviest end of my burden was lifted, and I well remember there was some little sweetness in the thought that the Almighty God in marvellous condescension had visited us (even though it was with a chastening rod), and gathered one to Himself who was a part of us. How utterly unworthy I was of His choice, and after some meditation I felt not a little comforted.

I rose up and bestirred myself, for there was much to be done. My mind was calm where all had been turmoil. I was enabled to prepare the room ready for the inquest, and to attend it and say all that was required of me. Only once did the tears come, and that was when our doctor stood up and spoke so kindly of me as a mother, etc., and I was told there was scarcely a dry eye among the roomful of men. This was on Christmas Eve 1917, and on the Boxing Day we laid our greatest treasure on earth in the cold grave, but with the comfort of a good hope that the ransomed spirit was with Jesus around the throne. In our grief I think we both felt the light had gone out of our lives, never to return.

One afternoon soon after, when taking a rest on the bed in the long bedroom at Garlands, I took the little hymnbook we used to use at Grove Sunday school, and O how sweet was the hymn, especially the last verse:

"She's safely sheltered where she'll miss
The turmoil of a world like this,
Obtain the victory ere she fight,
And walk with Jesus Christ in white"!

For some time the Lord gave a measure of submission, and then Satan seemed to get me into his clutches, and for weeks I was tormented with terrible unbelief and infidelity. I felt unfit for anyone's company, and was afraid others could see my dreadful state. I felt so ashamed I dared not say a word to anyone. It took all the comfort out of our trouble, for Satan (though I did not then realise it was he) suggested her little body lay in the cold earth, and mine would one day follow, and that was the end, so why worry about God and religion? plunge headlong into the world and its pleasures, and forget. But I could not do that for conscience worked, and the evils of my heart were so stirred up. If only I could have realised (as I hope I do now) that the Lord was dealing with me after the manner of hymn 295: "I asked the Lord that I might grow in faith, and love, and every grace."

The following May, after we lost our little girl, another baby was expected, and how I feared as the time drew near! I imagined all sorts of things as a result of what we had passed through, and the prayer of necessity drove me to the Lord. "To whom or whither should I go, if I should turn from Thee?" On May 17th John was born, and I proved the truth of those lines:

"Creatures of fear, we drag along
And fear where no fear is."

When he was about 18 months old, I was brought into affliction, and had to go to hospital. While on my bed at home, the words seemed to abide with me: "Whom the Lord loveth, He chasteneth." They gave me both comfort and hope. It was the first time I had ever been in hospital, and my surroundings seemed to take all my attention and, try as I would, I could not get my thoughts higher than the ceiling, and I went into the operating theatre as hard as a stone. When I began to regain my senses, O what a difference! How precious was my heavenly Friend! I believe for a few moments I learnt what the poet meant when he penned hymn 637:

"Jesus, Thou art my only rest
From sin, and guilt, and fears";

and I had to speak aloud to His praise, and I also had to bear reproach for it afterwards.

After three weeks I returned home, and here I pause to look back and see the links in the chain of God's providence. For some time before this affliction, I had felt to long for living bread, and had many times asked the Lord to make a way for me to this end, for though I loved our dear old pastor at Uffington, he gradually became mentally afflicted. Sad though it was, his poor wife was in the same way, and eventually both had to be put in a mental home. But the years while the affliction was developing were very trying both for pastor and people. He was a very tender-spirited and gracious man, and although he was never known to divert from the truth, he was very trying to listen to. I was very weak when I left hospital, and our doctor forbade my driving in a pony trap (which we used in those days) on any shaky roads such as to Uffington, but I might go to Grove if we kept to the main road. How unexpected was this answer to my prayer! We went to Grove until after our third child was born, where I heard some good ministers, and I hope picked up a few crumbs and felt encouraged at times. As I got stronger, we went to Grove in the mornings and Uffington in the evenings, till in the providence of God we moved our tent South Moreton way.

January 22, 1948. I heard cousin Caleb (Sawyer) preach at Uffington from the first two verses of Isaiah 43. I went seeking for a dead lift, and came away feeling very encouraged, for I felt to have a good hope that I knew in some humble measure the path traced out, and that when the furnace has done its work, my poor unworthy soul will come forth from the fire with no smell of singeing, but O, that it may be with the sweet savour of sanctified affliction, well pleasing to the Lord, its Author and Finisher. He spoke of being reminded of trials and exercises of younger days, when passing through Goring station the previous day, and that led my mind back to the 15th November, 1923, in the darkness of the early morning.

I left our old home at Garlands, where I had lived since 1897, to go to a new abode, among complete strangers, where we had taken a farm. For some months before, the words had seemed much on my mind: "No evil shall befall thee, nor any plague come nigh thy dwelling." But that particular morning, as I took my seat in the train, my heart seemed drawn up to the Lord in such earnest desire, in the language of Jabez's prayer; those few words expressed everything I desired for time and eternity. When I reached Cholsey station, I had to change for a side line to Wallingford, and how glad I was to find an empty carriage and be alone, yet not alone, for I felt the Lord had me in His keeping, and would eventually fulfil that blessed prayer of Jabez in my experience.

But alas! we had been there only a few months before it seemed that nothing but evil was befalling us, and within eighteen months we were compelled to leave that place with our family of four small children, and the Lord provided a halting place close to the little cause of truth at South Moreton, where, as I look back, I believe my poor, hungry soul was provided with living bread, particularly under the ministry of dear Mr. Hope, and it became a sacred place to me, though our outward trials seemed to increase. Yet the Lord had so unmistakably provided that little home, and I felt I could not leave it till He had granted my oft repeated request, and given me an "indeed" blessing.

When this farm (Goosey) was offered to us, my husband felt disposed to take it, but I felt I must have a word from the Lord Himself. I shut myself in my bedroom, and in desperate need I fell on my knees, with my Bible, and told the Lord He must let me open it on His own word for me, and it opened on Joel 2. 25-27. I felt *full*, and so sure our move was of the Lord. On our last Sunday at South Moreton, dear old Mr. White, who was preaching, asked me where we thought of attending. I told him our future abode lay mid-way between Grove and Uffington and I felt a warm love to both places, but we could not make up our minds, or get a word of direction. He answered me like this: "I have always found, if no word of direction is given, you cannot go far wrong if you take the path of duty," and as my husband's mother was still living at Uffington, I knew that to be where our duty lay, but the final decision was made by the pony we drove – we let the reins loose at the turning, and he made for Uffington.

About three weeks after, I heard of one and another coming forward as candidates for baptism, and I felt such a constraining. I could not be left out after all His goodness to one so desperately unworthy. O how I loved this precious Jesus in those days. It seemed impossible that He could love me, yet how often my plea was expressed in these lines:

> " Dear Lord! and can Thy pardoning blood
> Embrace a wretch so vile?
> Wilt Thou my load of guilt remove,
> And bless me with Thy smile?"

I was warned it would be wiser to wait on account of my condition, but I felt so satisfied that He, who had managed all our things so far, would manage this likewise, and go forward I must. But when that memorable morning arrived, before I was scarcely awake, such a terror came over me so that I shook beneath the bedclothes, and the awful thought arose that if I persisted in that mad act of going through the water on such a cold day, I should be no less than the murderer of my unborn babe. I do not know how long this fearful temptation lasted, but at length the dear Lord came to my relief with: "Them that honour Me I will honour." O how it stilled that inward tempest, and I felt such freedom in committing my all into His gracious hands, and among other things I asked of Him that morning was that I might feel the movement of that child before I was received into the church, which was to be that same evening. Strange to say, I forgot this request until I was asked to move into another seat at the front just before the evening service, and as I rose to comply, my request of the morning was so unmistakably answered that it almost overwhelmed me with wonder, love and praise, and the effect was to enable me to sit down at the Lord's table with a feeling of humble boldness, "not like a stranger or a guest but like a child at home". How many times since then have I longed to feel the same childlike right to sit at His table! But we have had to go into the wilderness, and how many and how varied have been the trials we have met with, and as we look back over the way He has brought us, dare we say He has ever left us in trouble to sink? Indeed, we would say, we hope for His honour and glory, that out of our bitterest trials have come forth the sweetest comforts, so that, just now and then, we have felt from the bottom of our hearts we would not have one thing altered.

About three years after my baptism, I had a dream, which left a deep impression. I thought I was walking very airily across the meadows at my old home, everything looking so beautiful, and in my dream I felt so happy and carefree, till I was suddenly confronted with a most awkward looking stile, and as I stood wondering how I could climb over it, I was arrested by a voice on the other side. It was a man lying on the grass, reading what looked like a Bible. Somehow I got over and stood to listen, and in a clear, solemn tone he read these words: "These are they which came out of great tribulation, and have washed their robes, and made them white in the blood of the Lamb." I awoke and pondered over this dream.

Some few days after, our youngest boy, about three years, was taken very ill with bronchial pneumonia and whooping cough. He would sit up in bed and fight and scream in delirium, then sink back exhausted, as if his little life was ebbing out. After one of these distressing scenes, I fell on my knees beside his bed almost distracted with anxiety. The heavens seemed as brass, and I had nowhere else to go. But the set time had come for the Lord's appearance. That still small voice whispered sweetly, and so comforting, "This is that path of tribulation which leads to the kingdom, *where Jesus is."* I cannot put my feelings into words, but I told this precious Friend, "The kingdom that I seek is Thine. Then let the way that leads to it be Thine," and I felt willing for just whatever was His way for me, even to the giving up of our dear child. From that time he began to get better; he had lost flesh so rapidly but now he put it on just as quickly.

I look back sometimes to these times of trouble, and I say, "Lord, what of the many inward tears shed over the never-dying souls of our offspring?" How helpless we are in these matters! April 2nd was his 21st birthday. Twenty-one years last December I went through the baptismal water at Uffington with this unborn babe. What exercises of mind, what cries went up, that he might prove to be a child of grace! How long, O

Lord, how long? "Shall I for ever be forgot, as one whom Thou regardest not?" We try and pray that we may not grow weary by the roughness of the way. The 76th hymn is still God's way with sinners.

> "O, give him Samuel's ear,
>   The open ear, O Lord,
>   Alive and quick to hear
>   Each whisper of Thy Word.
>   Like him to answer at Thy call,
>   And to obey Thee first of all."

One bitter ingredient in this cup of sorrow is that sometimes invitations to go to vanity fairs come from some who sit under the sound of the truth and have heard the call "to come out and be separate". These things cause mourning in Zion.

> "While Thy dear cause is thus oppressed,
>   My burdened soul can take no rest."

Dear Lord, we desire to pray that Thou wouldest look in pity, give godly repentance and bring us each into the blessed experience of the hymn writer:

> "Let others stretch their arms like seas,
>   And grasp in all the shore;
>   Grant me the visits of Thy face,
>   And I desire no more."

We moved to Goosey in 1925, and I had joined the church at Uffington, perhaps about two years, when I seemed to get into a very dark path, could see no evidence of life within: freshly contracted guilt seemed daily to add to my burden, and the feeling that I had presumptuously joined myself to the Lord's people caused me some bitter thoughts. While in this despondency, John was taken very ill with flu; the doctor said he needed great care. All the children took it and the little girl who helped with them, and I felt ill too, but worse than all, I felt alone. The question kept rising, "Where is now thy God?"

I sought Him but I found Him not. We were delivered out of these temporal troubles, but I got no relief from my burden of soul until one morning these words came and abode for several days: "I have set before thee an open door, which no man can shut." I pondered over them, but got no light upon them, till late one night I was taken very ill, and about midnight it became necessary to send for a doctor, and my poor John was so distressed because he had to leave me alone. But as soon as he was gone, it seemed as if those clouds of darkness, which had been around me so long, parted asunder and revealed an open door, the door of mercy, the way made clear to the throne of grace. It was *open,* and for *me,* unworthy me; a light streamed from it; as I lay on my bed, that light took me in, and O the peace and quiet joy I felt in the thought that Jesus *knew* and *cared.* All my troubles, temporary and spiritual, were gone, and for a while I felt I could say, "My Lord and my God." Tears flowed freely, tears of sorrow over my sins, and tears of joy that He should thus take notice of such as me, and O how bountifully He supplied our needs in raising up kind friends to help us in our trouble!

What can this lower world afford compared to Jesus' love, and O what a good God He has been to us, as we look back over past years, and what a needs-be for His chastening rod! We have been blessed with six boys; the youngest was born in 1930. On the morning of the day he was born, I was much impressed with the portion on the calendar: "Take this child, and nurse it for me." How it pressed the cry out of me that it might be a child of grace! When about my work one morning, that verse in hymn 708 came so powerfully to mind:

> "Thy whole dependence on Me fix;
> Nor entertain a thought
> Thy worthless schemes with Mine to mix,
> But venture to be nought."

They seemed to impress me with more troubles ahead, and so it proved, but they were a wonderful stay and comfort at times in the midst of it. Within two months of this dear lad's birth, the Lord put me into a furnace of affliction. My right arm and hand became almost useless with neuritis; then chronic appendicitis set up with various complications. I had had it for years in a mild form, but now it reached a drastic stage. O the agonising pain I suffered in those days! Our doctor injected me with morphia, and sent me a 15 mile journey to Oxford Infirmary by ambulance where I was immediately prepared for an operation, but when the principal surgeons saw me, they decided it would be a big responsibility, and as the pain had somewhat eased, they wished me to be kept under observation, and finally they sent me home incurable. But that first fortnight in hospital I shall never forget.

I had felt very comforted on my bed at home by the words: "Yea, though I walk through the valley of the shadow of death, I will fear no evil, for Thou art with me." On that dreadful journey, they seemed a sort of pillar as the ambulance bumped across the tram lines in Grove Street. I felt so ill and the driver stopped, they, as well as myself, feeling the end had come, and O how sweetly those words supported me! But as soon as I settled in hospital, a kind of confusion started in my mind. I tried to pray, but it was suggested I had no warrant, being a professor, but not a possessor. Why did I mock God, and thus add sin to sin? Where should I spend a never-ending eternity? Sleep was out of the question. No interest in Christ, and no covering, my guilty soul seemed laid bare before a holy God with no Mediator, no Refuge. I, who had longed and hoped for heaven, was doomed never to see the King in His beauty. The anguish of mind I can never fully describe, and all about me could see what a vile character I was. For three mornings I bought a newspaper to cover myself and be hidden from view.

In this state I lay for several days. Then one particular night Satan appeared in a most horrible form just outside the glass doors opposite my bed. I could not move my body for the pain of my complaint, but now my limbs became rigid, and I felt certain he was waiting to receive my spirit. A kind nurse tried to comfort me, but I told her I was lost for ever. Would she draw the sheet over my head that I might be hidden? And then – how can I describe the horror as Satan appeared at the side of my bed, and the evil smell and atmosphere I can never forget, and how these words seemed to mock me, which before had been such a comfort, especially, "For Thou art with me." It seemed like hours I remained in this state, when two nurses came and removed my bed right away from the glass doors. I then became a little quieter, but I dared not sleep, though I had not slept for a week. I felt to be under the wrath of God, and could no more go to Him than a child to a stern parent.

How I got through the next day I know not, but towards the evening I became aware of some extra excitement among the staff, and was told that at 7 o'clock the New Year's Ball would commence, and the patients would be able to hear the music. What a den of iniquity within and without I felt to be in, and I thought "this is the company I shall have to dwell with for ever in hell." Then in desperate need arose that cry, "I will venture in unto the King, and if I perish, I'll perish at His feet," and I begged for respite in sleep. I have been very glad since that the Lord preserved me from a rebellious spirit towards His holy majesty. No, I had no hard thoughts of God. I felt He was just, and had right as the potter over the clay, to do as He would.

My next recollection was that of hearing in the distance the sound of soft music. I asked where it was, and the nurse replied, "You've had a lovely sleep, my dear, six hours, and now you think you're awake in heaven and listening to the angels, but 'tis the last of the ball." The question at once arose, "Shall I ever reach that glorious place?" but from that time my mind gradually cleared, and how relieved I felt that I was out of hell, but I could not get beyond that. It had been a tremendous shock to me, and my little hope seemed, as it were, swallowed up in the whirl.

O how thankful and, I believe, solemnly humbled I felt, as I passed through those glass doors to get into the car which took me home, and O the joy of being once more amongst my loved ones! Our humble home seemed like a palace. But at the back of my mind, what a burden I carried. I could not go on acting the hypocrite by sitting down at the Lord's table among His people, and felt the only course open to me was to lay the whole case honestly before our deacons.

However, the dear Lord's appointed time for my deliverance was at hand, and the first morning I was home the post brought a magazine, which was laid on my bed. I picked it up with a "who can tell?" I saw the signature of "Harry Patterson" to a letter entitled, "Who can utter the mighty acts of the Lord?" I began to read. He had quoted the whole of hymn 917, "Cease, O believer, cease to mourn." I cannot describe my feelings better than this – it seemed as if His love (more precious far than any earthly love) wrapped itself about me as I read on till I came to: "Thy warfare shall in triumph end, With thee it shall go well." It sounds presumptuous for one like me, but I say it to His honour and glory, I believe I felt a little of what the poor prodigal did when his father fell on his neck and kissed him. The next verse was just as sweet. It assured me of what the Lord had been to me, "a wall of fire", for all my foes had not been permitted to touch my life, which I hoped and then believed to be hid with Christ in God. And the third verse, O what a blessed promise for the future! I cannot express (it is no use to try) what it meant to me, but I did not want any one in my room to interrupt my joy. The Lord had appointed for me long months of suffering after this, but He never permitted me to sink so low again in soul matters.

In less than six weeks I was back in hospital with a very acute attack and other complications. My life hung in the balance, and there were times when I felt too ill to concern myself about the solemn position I was in, and when revived a little, how this tried me. A dear faithful old friend came to see me, and asked the question, "How do you feel, my dear, in the prospect of leaving your dear husband and the little ones?" I said, "Don't ask me, I dare not think about it." But O what exercise of mind this remark gave me for four or five days, and I could only beg of the Lord to spare me that I might recover strength, strength of hope and love and every grace, before I go hence and be no more.

But instead, the furnace seemed to get hotter, and Sunday came – and what a Sunday! My fellow patients (six of us in a small ward) were obsessed with three things, "The Oxford and Cambridge boat race", "The Grand National", and "The great Irish Sweepstake", The newspapers rustled from morning till evening, and it seemed more than I could bear. The earphones of the wireless lay on my bed. I had been very prejudiced against the wireless as one of Satan's allurements, but I thought even this is better than all this rabble, so I put one earphone on, and immediately that beautiful hymn started: "When I survey the wondrous cross", every word so plain, and I believe faith was given me to believe it was "for crimes that I had done. He groaned upon the tree, Amazing pity, love unknown, And grace beyond degree." There is one verse they sang, not in our book, but it was the climax to my feelings, and ever since that memorable evening, I always feel that hymn stops short and leaves out the poor sinner's thanks for "love so amazing, so divine, demands my life, my *love,* my *all".* I felt like one carried above my surroundings into an atmosphere of peace and rest.

The next morning, I asked for my hymnbook, and the nurse reached one out of my locker, left by a visitor the day before. It was David Denham's, a stranger to me, but not for long. I opened it on a blessed hymn which was so in unison with my feelings that morning:

"And am I blest with Jesus' love?
And shall I dwell with Him above?
And will the joyful period come
When I shall call the heavens my home?"

How this confirmed my joys of the evening before, and how I have loved that book ever since. I hope it is not presumption for me to say out of my bitterest trials have come my choicest sweets.

I was brought home once more, and within two months again collapsed, and within a few hours I felt as if every heart beat would be my last. Doctor said had he been three minutes later, it would have been too late. O the lovingkindness and tender mercy of a gracious God! I was semi-conscious, but what a sweet feeling I had as my poor husband was hastily ushered out of the room, that I was shut in with the Lord, sheltered under His wing, as a hen gathereth in her chicks, hidden in that cleft of the Rock, the Rock Christ Jesus! I said aloud, as well as I could speak, "On Christ the solid Rock I stand." That same afternoon I was injected and sent to hospital, and a dreadful sickness set up. I fully realised the doctor could do no more, but after such a sweet time, I felt all my concerns were in His hands. "Other refuge have I none, hangs my helpless soul (and body) on Thee."

After some time I began to revive, and then our doctor told me my case distressed him, as Oxford surgeons had refused the responsibility of operating, and he would like me to see a Harley Street specialist, and try and get me into St. Thomas's Hospital, London. This caused me much exercise of mind. All the help of man had proved vain, and I wanted faith to trust the Lord alone, and as I look back I see how wondrously He worked for us in our trouble. I was sent home, and our doctor set the wheels in motion for me to go to London, and the Lord seemed to clear all obstacles out of the way. I had felt very anxious about finances, as times were pretty hard with us in those days, and who knows, perhaps this may be read by my dear boys in years to come, and I would say to them in passing through trying times, "Take it to the Lord in prayer," for nothing is too *great*, nothing too *small* for His notice.

Our doctor called one day and asked me to unbosom all my cares to him, and the dear Lord used him, as a means, to dispel all my fears respecting money matters. I was afraid an operation might mean a hundred pounds or more, instead of which seven or eight covered everything including the fee at Harley Street. When final arrangements were being made, a kind friend called and offered to take me to London in his car. I felt deeply touched by his kindness, and as I stood at the window watching his car drive down the road, trying to lift up my heart in thankfulness for yet another token of lovingkindness from the Lord, His word came with power: "I will go before you into Galilee." For a few moments I felt quite overcome. It seemed to take all my strength, and I sank into a chair, willing to be led just wherever the Lord should choose:

"Lord, take my hand as Thou hast said,
Not one, but both my hands instead;
Lest with the other I should cling
For help to any earthly thing."

On that journey, and particularly on the way from Harley Street to Westminster, the Lord seemed to make over again that precious promise. Before I went our doctor had advised me on various points, and one thing he impressed upon me was that if the X-ray revealed my trouble, I was throwing away my last hope of life to refuse an operation; but if it did not reveal it (which had happened before) and they would like to operate for investigation, then his advice was "to set my face as a flint against it", as I should not survive it, he felt sure. Well, after three days in hospital with two X-rays, and lots of doctors, they told me it did not reveal the trouble, and the only thing they could do for me was to operate and investigate. It came as a shock, for three times the specialist had told me there would be no operation. The news was brought to me about 8 o'clock one evening.

The operation was to be the next day, and my husband must be sent for. "I was dumb with silence. I opened not my mouth, because Thou didst it."

My bed was situated so that I looked out into the face of Big Ben (the clock on the Houses of Parliament); it was a quarter to nine. What a solemn question loomed up before me! Tomorrow evening at this time perhaps, O where should I spend a never-ending eternity? After (as I hoped) I had enjoyed so much of the dear Lord's lovingkindness and tender mercy of late (how little I knew of Him!), did I really or truly know anything at all? My sins seemed to rise and swell like an ever-growing sea. I felt hemmed in on every side. It was then that my unkind treatment of my poor old aunt in childhood days rose up, and all my comforts fled and left me nothing, though I could not give it all up. After a time, one thing after another came up to my remembrance, and I was enabled to stretch out, as it were, a little hand of faith and cling on, till I felt a little comfort begin to flow, and a little boldness to tell the Lord, "Thou didst say,"and then He broke down all the barriers with the second verse of hymn 259:

> "Why should I shrink at Thy command,
> Whose love forbids my fears?
> Or tremble at the gracious hand
> That wipes away my tears?"

In spite of our doctor's warning, I *knew* the Lord's way for me was to accept that operation. My poor husband was very distressed about it, but I believe I learned a little of the meaning of: "If He speaks peace, who then can make trouble?" His goodness indeed passed before us, even in small matters, one of which comes forcibly to mind. I had watched others taken to the operating theatre, and our fellow patients trying to cheer them up (as they called it) with all kinds of jokes and excitement, and I felt I could not bear it, and I asked the Lord to manage this for me. And He did, in a very unexpected way. When all preparations were completed, the Sister said to me, "Now, my dear, you are all ready. Would you like me to remove the screens? Or perhaps you would prefer to be quiet on your own?" That little circumstance touched me. It seemed to say, His eye was upon me, His ear open to me. How utterly unworthy I felt as I passed unnoticed by others out of that ward along spacious passages to the theatre. The language of my heart was:

> "A guilty, weak, and helpless worm,
> On Thy kind arms I fall;
> Be Thou my strength and righteousness,
> My Jesus, and my all."

When I came round, how precious He was to me! Before I could speak, I longed to burst forth with, "Bless the Lord, O my soul, and all that is within me, bless His holy name"; and when my senses fully returned, what disappointment! I loved Him. I longed to be with Him. I shrank from the trials in front of me, and begged for submission to wait His time. One evening soon after, I felt so weary and full of self-pity, when the lines of hymn 872, verse 6, came so sweetly:

"His chastening, therefore, prize,
The privilege of a saint;
Their hearts are hard who that despise,
And theirs too weak who faint."

How it broke me down, and how unworthy I felt to come under the blessings of the saints, one owned and loved of God! I hid my head under the bedclothes, and wept to the praise of the mercy I'd found.

Another bright spot comes to remembrance. In that hospital they had morning and evening prayer, and very nice it is to see any outward respect, but, O the difference between a formal worship and to *feel* Him precious. A poor woman lying in a bed opposite mine sent a message, asking if I would go and sit with her in the evening when allowed out of bed before my operation. I was pleased to go, expecting nothing beyond a chat about our complaints, the usual topic in hospital: but as soon as this was over, she looked me full in the face and said, "But what is all my pain compared to what the Lord Jesus suffered to put away my sin?" It took me so by surprise. In that blessed name was no formality; the very look on her face, the anxious enquiry, seemed to say, "Do you love Him?" and the response from me was, "Do you love the Lord? He's very dear to me." I don't think I shall ever quite forget that evening, or the joy it was to me (and I believe to her also) to have found a companion in one to whom the name of Jesus was sweet. We wept together, for she had been asking the Lord for three weeks to send her a companion in one of His people, and as I was wheeled up the ward, she felt the Lord was about to answer her request, and so she watched me before she sent for me. How I missed her when she was sent home, and in six months she was called, I fully believe, to be for ever with the Lord. Her husband wrote and gave me a few particulars of her last days. She begged him not to pray for her recovery, she so longed to go.

The kind friend who took me up to London came and fetched me, and in due time I regained strength, and was able to go up to His earthly courts among His dear people, and I felt there was no other hymn in the book which suited me quite as well as 699: "Lord, we adore Thee, and would fain express Thy matchless goodness and our worthlessness."

But we had not come to the end of our trials, and often I felt how true was the hymn,

> "Sees every day new straits attend,
> And wonders where the scene will end."

On the farm we had many losses among the cattle, and it looked as if all these things were against us. We could not keep up with the rent, and it seemed only right we should look out for a smaller farm. We went to view several with no success, and after being led, as I felt, so conspicuously to Goosey, I did want to see the Lord's hand in leading us away, if ever we were to move. What an exercise of mind it was, till one day a letter came from Mr. Frank Belcher. He began his letter with the verse of hymn 70:

> "Thrice comfortable hope
> That calms my stormy breast;
> My Father's hand prepares the cup,
> And what He wills is best."

He then went on to say he knew of a farm to let, and wondered if it might suit us, a very lonely place, sadly neglected, but cheap rented. We went to look at it, and on the way I wondered how often we would be able to get to chapel, it was so out of the way. When we got to the house, which was empty, I felt tired, and seated myself on an old wicker chair, while baby played on the floor and Dad went to look round the farm. I tried to lift up my heart to the Lord, but I could not say much. The prayer of necessity is often very short: "Lord, help me," and I believe the Lord heard it, for as I sat there a sweet and comfortable persuasion took possession of me that all I had to do in this matter was to sit still, and I felt there was no need for me to stir or even go upstairs. I felt the Lord had something different in store for us, and so it proved, for within a week our landlord came and made suggestions of help, which reduced our rent, and enabled us to get along more comfortably.

We had many an errand to the throne of grace, and we would not be unmindful of the many answers mercifully bestowed. His dear people, how kind they were to us! Many a parcel of clothing was sent for me to cut up into garments for the boys, and when I left home for that operation in London we had as many as twenty-five pairs of knickers in reserve for them. One morning, about this time, I came across a pair of boots which had been put too near the fire and spoiled. How annoyed I felt, and had the culprit come in at the moment, he would have had a scolding, but in the midst of my passion the word came: "Your heavenly Father knoweth what things ye have need of." O, how it broke me down! My "heavenly Father". What blessed relationship; my heart was full, I could do nothing but weep. The lad came in, but I could say nothing. Later in the day the post brought me a registered letter. It contained 50 shillings [£2.50], and a note saying the writer felt constrained to send it, and added, "I do not know your needs, but your heavenly Father knoweth." What a sweet confirmation it was to me that it was of the Lord, and in the springtime of the same year (1932), I felt the Lord gave me a blessed confirmation through His dear servant Mr. Tingley that He had put me into the furnace for my soul's good. He was preaching at Grove for the first time, and took for his text: "I will be glad and rejoice in Thy mercy; for Thou hast considered my troubles: Thou hast known my soul in adversities." I followed step by step as he traced out my experience and exercises in my recent afflictions. I was very overcome, for it left no doubt that I was in the footsteps of the flock. Then he looked up, and said, *so* emphatically, "If you know these things by experience, I have God's warrant to say to you, 'With thee it shall go well.' " The service closed with that hymn 917 ("Cease, O believer, cease to mourn; Return unto thy rest, return; Why should thy sorrows swell? Though deep distress thy steps attend, Thy warfare shall in triumph end; With thee it shall go well.")

About this time I heard Mr. H. Patterson for the first time, a wish gratified, since his writings were made such a blessing to me. His text was: "It is appointed unto men once to die, but after this the judgment." What a solemn service it was!

In 1937 my dear father passed away in his eightieth year. I was privileged to be with him. What a blessed end after severe conflict! I verily thought I should never again be so tempted with unbelief and infidelity after witnessing the reality of religion in my dear father on his death-bed, but alas! our besetting sins are only kept under as God keeps them.

For some time I had felt my health giving way, and in September 1939, just as the Second World War started, I found myself again in Oxford Infirmary for an operation, which kept me there a month. How different I felt from the previous time! I longed for some token from Him, but I had to prove that what He gives we gather, and I felt to come out of that trial as I entered into it, nothing bettered by the cross. I had to part with two of our boys for the Services, and they were soon sent overseas, one to Ceylon and India and the other to the Middle East. After four-and-a-half years the Lord permitted their safe return. In much mercy He had watched over them, amongst so many dangers, of which, at the time, we mercifully knew nothing. How many, many cries went up from the depths of my heart in those anxious days, that He would preserve them from the many snares laid for their young feet! Being unable to sleep one night on account of these far-away lads, I got out of bed, and was trying to spread it before the Lord, when the word came with some power: "In all labour there is profit," and I felt free to tell Him He knew the "labour" of my poor prayers, and for a time I felt I could be still and leave the matter in His all-wise hands".

A few months before our dear boys went overseas, we passed through one of the bitterest sorrows of our lives in the death, so suddenly, of our fourth boy Philip, seventeen-and-a-half years old, a fine lad, over 6 feet tall, taken ill and gone within 48 hours with cerebral meningitis. I watched by his side as he tossed to and fro; then for hours a death-like silence and he passed into the great beyond without speaking one word. What had become of his never-dying soul'? I knew that none could enter into the presence of God without that all-important new birth. "Ye must be born again" sounded over and over again in my ears. The dear boy had always gone regularly to chapel, and had never given cause for anxiety in his daily life, but as the tree falls it must for ever lie; yet I could not quite give up a glimmer of hope, and I believe it just kept my head above water.

It came about like this. About ten days before he died I was cooking at the kitchen table when the first verse of hymn 622 came very powerfully to my mind:

"Poor fearful saint, be not dismayed,
Nor dread the dangers of the night;
Thy God will ever be thy aid,
And put the hosts of hell to flight."

It so broke me down that I could not finish my job till I had got away by myself and somewhat recovered. Naturally my mind went to our absent boys, for I *felt* a fiery trial lay ahead and what a blessed promise the Lord had given me, and when that dear lad passed away, I did beg that I might be enabled firmly to lay hold of it, and I dare not say it had not been a comfort at times. But O how I have longed that the Lord would give me a sweet *assurance* that our dear boy is safely housed in heaven!

While walking round his bed as he lay dying, how sweet were these lines, "God shall alone the refuge be, and comfort of my mind," and that hymn was sung at his funeral. Some two years later, when secretly fretting for some unmistakable sign, these words came with a little softening comfort: "And grief indulge no more." Seven years have passed, and still I wait, and wait again and never can give it up. Some things I have been trying to pray for a good many years longer. I cannot give them up either. We read, "And David encouraged himself in the Lord his God." My soul, wait thou only upon God; the expectation of the poor shall not be cut off.

A few months after our dear boy died, another great sorrow entered our family circle in the death of a dear young niece, about 13 years, killed instantly by a car on the road. It was no small comfort to feel there was some hope in her end. What an unspeakable mercy when grace is put into the hearts of the young, sheltered in time and throughout a never-ending eternity!

Some time after this I began to feel a very sharp pain in a nerve of my face, which gradually developed and at times became very acute. It is called tic douloureux. During the bitter weather of 1947, I had the greatest difficulty to speak, or eat, or swallow even a cup of tea at times, and perhaps the greatest trial of all was that Satan took adva tage of the low state of my mind to infuse all sorts of fears. There were times when I greatly feared my mind would give way under it, and O if only I could *feel* to have a solid standing on the Rock Christ Jesus, instead of which I had many fears that this trouble would end in my making shipwreck of faith, and thus prove that all I felt I had ever known of the Lord went no deeper than my head. It was a trying path, my poor mind so confused when I tried to pray, all seemed turmoil, the mind wandered hither and thither. I could not concentrate, or scarcely put a sentence together in prayer before the Lord, but I did feel some little comfort many a time in the thought that "man looketh on the outward appearance, but God looketh on the heart", and sometimes I felt enabled from the deep-down desire of my soul to appeal to Him and say, "Dear Lord, Thou knowest."

After some time our doctor began to worry about further advice, which I did not wish for on account of the consequences. One evening in May 1947, my dear brother at Uffington held a little prayer meeting on my behalf after the week-evening preaching service. O what a priceless gift are praying friends and what a sweet union was felt among us! I had been obliged to be absent some weeks, but was privileged to be present that evening, though quite unaware of their intention. How unworthy I felt and how Satan tried me afterwards, suggesting I had deceived the very elect, and I had many fears lest it be true, and the parable of the ten virgins seemed much on my mind. How very alike they were, the difference not detected till the Bridegroom came! O that the precious oil of grace may not be found wanting when we come to die.

In June our doctor said he would give me no more medicine for a time, and his next move would be to a specialist. It became easier and early in July, I suddenly found myself quite free from pain, and up till now (March 1948) I have had no recurrence. What can we say to these things? I believe more things are wrought by prayer than this world dreams of.

Whatever it may please the Lord to send for my chastening and moulding in the future, I do desire that He would give me *real* gratitude for all His goodness and O what a lot that takes in. Freedom from pain is a great blessing. The lovingkindness of godly. praying friends is a priceless possession. O that one thing needful, a passport into the presence of the King of kings, and Lord of lords. "One thing have I desired of the Lord, that will I seek after." Others have found it, some whom I have known and loved, and, "Why, my soul, why not for thee?" O to be part of that heavenly building, and He has said, "Not a hoof of that blessed number shall be left behind." Part of the host have crossed the flood, and part are crossing now. Dear Maude, our childhood friend, has just safely landed. After all her doubts and fears, it was light at evening time. She died in simple child-like trust. The Word says, "Of such is the kingdom of heaven." "Except ye become as little children, ye shall not enter into the kingdom of heaven." What will become of this great *I,* dear Lord? Do put me in my right place, and bring me to Jesus' feet.

I sometimes think of a dear old saint, a father in Israel to me years ago. On his tombstone in Cholsey churchyard is the one word "Peace". I believe it is even so. He was only a humble shepherd, could neither read nor write, knew what it was to work for no more than 9 shillings (45p) a week and bring up a family of six or seven children. Yet what wonders he could tell of how the Lord supplied his needs, temporally and spiritually. He has many times told us of one occasion when his poor wife and himself were sorely troubled, having nothing to put on the table to eat, and he walked out into the meadow to be alone with his God when to his great surprise a hare came bounding out of the hedge and ran straight into his legs. He grabbed it and it was soon cooking on the fire. The children ate it ravenously but he could scarcely swallow for tears.

We were singularly brought into contact through a heavy shower of rain. We saw him from our window sheltering under a tree after a morning service at South Moreton and called him in and while having dinner he began to tell of the Lord's dealings with him. As we listened, the time sped away till we found we had only just time to get back to the afternoon service at chapel, but from that day a sweet union existed between us, and what a faithful friend dear old Charlie was to me!

My memory does not quite serve me to tell the details of his call by grace but he used to say with grief how he was wont to persecute his godly sister, and her patience under it used to aggravate him. But when he was brought into concern about his sins, it had to stop and then for some years his wife used to persecute him, often hiding his clothes or his boots to prevent his going to chapel. His sister noticed the change but for some time said nothing. Then she suggested: would he care to go with her to hear a certain minister? He made excuse that his clothes were not respectable, which difficulty she overcame. After all he had said, he felt so ashamed to be seen going. However, his case became more and more desperate and at length he had to go, and O what straits that poor man went through in conflict of mind and in outward circumstances! His poor wife did not understand him. She would not allow him to take any dinner on Sundays to chapel, and if he came home between services, he would have the same struggle to get back, so he would roam off and sit under a hedge or anywhere out of sight till service time so the friends should not know he had nothing to eat.

He told us of a time when he had a great wish to go to Reading special services but he had no money and his wife had only one shilling (5p), so after beating about the bush for some time, he told her if she would let him have the shilling, he would bring her back two in place of it, though he had not the slightest idea where he was going to get it. However, eventually she agreed and he set off by train which cost him 6d (2½p). The other 6d he put on the plate for collection. Tea was provided at the chapel but his money was gone and he went off looking for some job such as holding a horse (very customary in those days) to get the promised 2 shillings (10p) but nothing came his way. He had heard well in the afternoon and felt confident the Lord would grant his request, but his faith began to droop during the evening service. How could he face his wife with empty hands?

He started the long walk home, stopping at a bridge deep in thought (and I daresay prayer), when a waggonette load of chapel friends stopped and offered him a lift. He would most gladly have accepted but it seemed like throwing away his last hope of earning the money, but they pressed and prevailed and as they drove along, a lady sitting next to him slipped 2s 6d (12½p) into his hand, and once more he proved that "when the Lord's people have need, His goodness will find out a way".

The Lord led him into some very deep waters in spiritual exercises as well as in temporal matters, and at one time the enemy so tormented him, he made up his mind he could stand no more; he would end his life and know the worst. Accordingly he laid his plans and set out in the dusk of the evening to a pond sheltered with trees. He took off his coat and was just about to plunge into the water when the pond seemed to divide. The half nearest to him was clear water. In the other half a mist rose up and in the mist right across the pond was one great word ETERNITY. He picked up his coat and fled in terror from the spot, and as he ran the Lord met with him and spake those blessed words, "Yea, I have loved thee with an everlasting love," etc. How it changed the scene! His heart was full to overflowing with joy and I have often heard him say, how he got home that night he never knew; but it was his meat and drink for many days.

When we first met with him, he had retired from work and was living on the old age pension, and would often spend a week or two with us when we moved to Goosey. And how he loved to get out to any evening services or among the Lord's people, a privilege denied him among his own family. Eventually he was compelled to leave his old home and go to live with a son near Reading, where his health rapidly failed. One of his daughters kept us informed.

A particular desire to see our dear friend once more seemed to press on me one morning after hearing he was very ill, and my husband took me up to Reading with a motor bike and side car. When we got there, it proved to be his last day on earth. He had wished all his family goodbye that morning and told them he had but one earthly wish left, and that was to see his friends from Goosey, and as he had taken this wish to the Lord, he felt sure we should come. As he talked to us of the glorious prospect so near, what a blessed privilege we felt it to sit at his bedside! I have wished many times that an abler tongue than mine could have seen and described that death-bed scene. *All* fear was taken away and his tongue set at happy liberty and how precious the blood of atonement was to him! I can never forget the expression on that dear old face as he slowly repeated the verse, "Here's pardon full for sin that's past; It matters not how black their cast; And O my soul, with wonder view. For sins to come here's pardon too," or the kiss he gave me as he said farewell for the last time on earth. I am not ashamed of that kiss. Had it been possible to exchange it for all the lovely treasures of earth I saw in the shop windows on our way home, I would not have exchanged it for it seemed to savour of heaven. He was buried by dear Mr. Hope whose ministry he loved.

Several things connected with his blessed death come to mind. A certain person who had wronged him and shown no repentance came to his bedside and kissed him goodbye. He said it was a Judas kiss but with tears running down his cheeks, he told us of the bitter spirit which rose up in his breast and said, "It seems as strong as ever it was, this heart plague and sore, which dwells within and I shall carry it till I breathe out my last breath on earth, but it won't be long now. O, how I long to be free of it, to be with Him , and like Him, a vile wretch that I am!"

We heard Mr. Curtis from Tunbridge Wells in our little sanctuary last evening from 2 Samuel 14 and verse 14: "We must needs die, and are as water spilt." It was a very solemn discourse, yet I felt very encouraged, and how I wish I could retain more of these good things; how little all the things of earth matter if we are in possession of the one thing needful! How I loved the ministry of his dear father! That scripture is fulfilled in their case: "Instead of thy fathers shall be thy children." In my younger days how sweetly the father seemed led to encourage seekers.

One particular occasion I remember, when we were living at South Moreton. Mr. Curtis was expected to preach the autumn services at Uffington. A kind friend offered to look after the children and I went, but what a disappointment I got in the afternoon! Most of the time seemed to be taken up with admonitions to young ministers, needful no doubt, but it did not touch my case. In the evening he took for his text: "I will feed the flock of slaughter, even you. O poor of the flock." He began at the beginning and described the feelings of the weaklings in faith – that aching void – one scarcely knows what or where it springs from; and I followed on step by step till he came to the place I then felt to be in: "Give me Christ, or else I die." "I must have Christ as All in all, or sink in ruin, guilt and thrall." After so clearly describing my exercises, he looked up and said with such confidence, "These shall at last to glory go, as trophies of His grace," and for the time being I felt to have a good hope that I should be among them in that great day.

Very shortly after this the dear man was taken ill, and I felt a desire to write and tell him what a comfort that sermon had been to me, but it seemed presumptuous, and I kept putting it from me, till one day I heard that he was worse and we could never expect to see him again. I made a vow to the Lord that if it remained on my mind, I would try to write, and eventually I did so. A few weeks after, to the surprise of all, the dear man was so revived as to be able to come to Grove for their anniversary on July 22nd, 1926. Then Satan began sorely to plague me about that letter – more especially for my presumptuous pride – but I felt I must go and hear him, and as he had to rest between the services, I told myself I could easily keep out of his way. He took for his text Luke 24: "And they told what things were done in the way" (verse 35), and O what a refreshing time it was to me, and we sang that hymn where it says, "If endless life be their reward, I shall possess the same.

After the service he sent for me to tell me how the Lord had been pleased to bless the few lines I had sent to comfort him in a time of need and the Lord had given him his afternoon text through them. I could say nothing. I felt full, and the following Sunday he preached again at Grove from Psalm 27. 4: "One thing have I desired of the Lord, that will I seek after." He seemed to portray my inmost soul in describing these exercises. This was his last visit to these parts but he still lives in our hearts and memories.

> "What peaceful hours I then enjoyed,
> How sweet their memory still!
> But now I find an aching void
> The world can never fill."

I feel as one grows older, the conflict increases. In younger days we used to look upon our elders as well established in these vital matters, feeling the ground firm under their feet, and how we longed and looked forward to the same security and settled peace, but alas, how different it is with us! We have had to learn and unlearn, and sometimes it has been a great encouragement to us to find that similar fears are experienced by others of whom there can be no doubt. Even that great and gracious leader of our denomination, Mr. Philpot, speaks much of fears, lest after all he might prove a castaway. No wonder the enemy torments such as me, but how I wish I could be quite sure of the difference between Satan's darts and the inward monitor speaking!

Some weeks ago I was brought in contact with Mr. Broome of Southampton. From a few verses of Scripture he read and a few words in prayer, I felt led to ponder over the history of Joseph, particularly that part when his brothers went down into Egypt to buy corn. Joseph knew his brethren but they knew not him. What a beautiful type of the Lord Jesus Christ! How often He is hidden from us and when we seek Him, it brings out the cry at times, "O that I knew where I might find Him!" What clouds and crowds come between and hide Him from our sight!

> "Yet all the vain and noisy crowd
> Is but a thin and lowering cloud,
>   A mist before thy eyes;
> If thou press on, the crowds will fly,
> Or if thou faint, to Jesus cry,
>   And He will send supplies."

All the while His eye is upon His dear people, His ear is open to their every cry. Joseph spake roughly to his brethren and acted strangely to them, but what seemed so sweet to me – he turned aside to weep in the midst of his apparent hardness. As one wrote of the Lord Jesus, "His sympathising heart feels for them in distress," and when Joseph could bear up no longer, he sent everyone else out from his presence while he made himself known to his brethren. How sweetly typical of our spiritual Joseph, for does He not call every one apart? Even the partners of our lives, and our own flesh and blood have no place here. Moreover Joseph kissed all his brethren and wept upon them, and after that his brethren talked with him.

While musing on this matter, I went to stay a few days with some dear friends at Wootton Bassett, and looking casually through their bookcase and scarcely knowing which book to choose, I picked up an old *Gospel Standard* (April 1862) and opened on a sermon by Mr. Vinall, preached over a hundred years ago, on the very subject (Genesis 45. 15), and what a sweet portion that sermon was to me! Joseph caused grief to his brethren to make way for a further taste of his love and Christ does the very same thing to His people here below, and O what can compare with this blessed reconciliation when a poor, hell-deserving sinner and a precious Jesus meet?

> "How vain a toy is glittering wealth,
> If once compared with Thee!
> Or what's my safety or my health,
> Or all my friends to me?"

But even as I write, how far off I seem from these sacred realities my soul has, I do hope, known and felt in bygone days. My language so often now is expressed in hymn 997.

> "Lord, while I wander here below
> What ills my soul annoy!
> For 'tis of Thee I little know,
> And ah! still less enjoy."

Infirmities increase and many are my fears that my working days are well nigh spent. All unknown the future lies. Would that I could let it rest. God shuts it from our eyes – He knows best. Thirty-two years ago, when our first-born came into the world, the following lines arrested my attention, hanging on a card over my bed:

> " Strength for the day, 'tis all that I ask,
> Strength for each duty, trial or task.
> This He has promised, 'tis all I need,
> And I shall find it sufficient indeed."

How sweetly they harmonise with the first promise the Lord ever gave me, when my poor, wayward brother ran away from home: "Thy shoes shall be iron and brass!" Through this brother leaving home, I was obliged to take on some very heavy work, carrying pails of milk and loading churns. They held seventeen gallons in those days and I did it for eleven years, which in after years unfitted me for motherhood. Our doctor strongly advised that our first should be our last, but I believe the Lord enabled me to lean hard upon that promise, and I refused an operation which would prevent any future family. If it has made for me a rough pathway and a daily cross, I desire humbly to bow to His will. His way was much rougher, and shall I repine? Mr. G. Rose told us the other evening that real submission means a complete acquiescence in the will of God in all His dealings, a falling down flat, and for our wills to flow evenly with His. How very rarely do we get there!

> " Dear Lord, to Thee I breathe my prayer;
> Reveal, confirm my interest there;
> Whate'er my humble lot below,
> This, this my soul desires to know."

January 1949: Another year has passed away and as we look back over the fast fleeting days and the ever-changing scenes of the chequered pathway, can we not lift up our hearts and say:

> "Thus far our God has led us on.
> And made His truth and goodness known;
> Our hopes and fears alternate rise,
> And comforts mingle with our sighs"?

Mercies, countless as the sands, have followed us through the year, and yet O the self-pity and rebellion of my wretched heart; shame and confusion of face belongeth unto me.

In May my painful face trouble returned worse than ever before. I could get no word of direction for relief save "Be still," which seemed to meet me everywhere I looked. I dared not go to my doctor till my health began to fail. I felt literally starved for want of food – I scarcely dared to open my mouth to speak on account of the pain. My friends insisted, and an Oxford specialist advised injection into the nerve. Would the Lord make my way plain?

Mr. F. Bennett came to Uffington to preach. I told him the Lord had bid me "be still". He replied with much kindness, "Perhaps the Lord means 'Be still' to your rebellious spirit, my friend." He took the text, "Rejoice not against me, O mine enemy: when I fall, I shall arise," etc. How plainly I saw my awful sin of rebellion and self-pity! I felt like one who had fought against a good and gracious God, with hand uplifted high, and I grieved over my sin, and begged of the Lord for forgiveness and that He would remove it or make me willing to follow in *His* way, not mine. A quiet calm gradually came, and at the time appointed I felt the Lord went before me and enabled me to bear patiently the painful ordeal, and what a *wonderful* relief it has been! The 699th hymn expresses my feelings better than I can. If we can attain no higher than a desire for a little *real* gratitude to the great Giver of all our mercies, Lord, let that desire arise as incense at the throne of Thy heavenly grace. Grant that desire for Jesus' sake, and give us grace to leave the unknown future in Thy hands, to Him who never slumbers or sleeps, who is the same yesterday, today and for ever – the God of love who has never yet failed us in our time of need.

At the opening of this New Year, how many needs we would bring to Thee: we've tried to manage many of them ourselves, but alas, we have to prove, "without Thee we can do nothing." "Except the Lord build the house, they labour in vain that build it." My dear husband has been in hospital since November 5th with a broken thigh. O that the suffering and the sore trial may be richly sanctified is the desire of my heart! How we long to see the peaceable fruits of righteousness springing out of this seeming evil! Our trials seem to shift from one shoulder to the other, and Bunyan's words seem often on my mind: "The Christian's seldom long at ease. Before one trouble's gone, another doth him seize." Good Bunyan found it so, and all the Lord's people more or less tread the path. What wondrous compassion in the dear Saviour to bear a part in all our afflictions! O for faith to enable us to obey the divine and blessed invitation to "cast thy burden upon the Lord", and what a sacred promise He has put with it: "I will sustain thee!" Why is it that we try every other means to get out of our troubles, till finding them fruitless, necessity drives us to the only source of refuge?

> "Other refuge have I none,
> Hangs my helpless soul on Thee."

These lines are on a stone in Goosey churchyard. I recall the time when they were put there. What volumes they seemed to speak to me concerning the poor man over whose grave they are placed! He was much afflicted from his youth with asthma. We often met him on his way to church on Sunday evenings, his head always bowed, his manner very sober. I had never spoken to him beyond a nod on passing, yet I often wondered how he felt in the prospect of death. Perhaps it was a natural sympathy on account of his affliction, but when I heard of his death and that two of his favourite hymns were to be sung at his funeral, whether out of curiosity or not I cannot tell, but I felt I must go. It was in the year 1931, a year of much affliction to me, both in body and soul. Till that time the wretched unbelief of my heart used to cavil so much at the incomprehensible mystery of the resurrection of the body. I could believe the Lord rose from the dead, but to think of that which was sown in corruption rising in incorruption in a glorified body, how it seemed to feed the awful infidelity of my heart, and what exercise it caused me, seeing I had put on an open profession, and how many times I had begged the Lord to clear my misty sight respecting this great mystery! Little did I think of its being shown to me at that poor stranger's graveside.

When I took my seat in the church, I noticed the two hymns posted on the pulpit. The first was, "Thy way, not mine, O Lord,." O how sweet that was to me in regard to my afflicted body and the way the dear Lord was dealing with me! O to fall into His hands in the language of that blessed hymn. I felt I could say, " 'Tis all my soul desires." The second hymn was "Jesus, Lover of my soul," and these lines "Other refuge have I none, Hangs my helpless soul on Thee," seemed the very language of my soul, and I felt if this was the poor man's real desire, he's got safely home, and so shall I.

With these feelings uppermost, I walked to the grave, and as the coffin was lowered into it, a solemn, sacred persuasion took possession of me that the poor corrupt body would one day arise a glorified body, to be united to the spirit of a just man made perfect. I seemed to lose sight of everything else for a few moments, and felt somewhat embarrassed to look up and see men coming forward to fill in the grave, and all the people dispersed. Some years later, when our dear Philip passed away so suddenly and the question of burial arose, I desired the spot close to where the Lord delivered me and brought me to see the wondrous beauty of the resurrection of the body to life everlasting.

Swiftly the months and years fly by, and at most it cannot be long before our earthly journey is finished. O may the dear Lord, whom I hope I can say I love, make over to me the choice blessing contained in the 91st hymn:

"Poor, weak, and worthless though I am,
I have a rich, almighty Friend;
Jesus, the Saviour, is His name;
He freely loves, and without end."

> "Swift to its close ebbs out life's little day,
> Earth's joys grow dim, its glories pass away;
> Change and decay in all around I see.
> Help of the helpless, O abide with me."

How good the dear Lord has been to me all my life long and now as I reach the close of my 72 years and "earth's joys grow dim, its glories pass away", I want Him more than ever before to assure me that He is mine and I am His. Death casts its shadows, and we know it can't be long before our poor, vile, clay tabernacles will be laid in the clods of the valley. It matters little *where* they are laid for when the last great trumpet sounds on the resurrection day, that which is sown in corruption will rise in incorruption at His command, to dwell for ever in the glories of His presence. "May my blood-washed soul be found, among that favoured band."

One after another of my old friends I have known and loved for many years are passing into the great beyond. I feel fully persuaded some have now reached that blessed state of "peace, perfect peace" after all the ups and downs of the chequered pathway. How varied have been their trials – in providence, in the family, in the church, and deep and sore bodily afflictions – yet we believe if they could tell us, it would be to the praise of their God. "He hath done all things well." Having walked in sweet union with a few such, who are loved of God, dare I hope I may some day be reunited and help to "sing around the throne, free grace and dying love". How sweet, at times, I have found that 171st hymn: "Join all who love the Saviour's name"!

We had hoped to hear Mr. J.H. Gosden at Uffington last evening but he was too poorly to come so Mr. Styles kindly filled the vacancy – our prospective pastor. My mind can scarcely comprehend the greatness, the weight of this *big* step. We daily try to lift the dear man up at the throne of grace, but O what feeble arms are mine!

May the dear Lord overlook our poverty and give us each a humble, contrite spirit, a spirit that *trembles* before Him in sincerity and in truth. May He guide our every step as a little church and teach us to walk as little children, to fix our whole dependence upon Him, and not leave us to seek great things for ourselves. "Let Christ be first, and Christ be last, and Christ be all in all." We want to walk in love and union with each other as it becomes the professed followers of Jesus. How *good* that Lord – the eternal God is thy refuge, and underneath are the everlasting arms, with such super-abundant support. He holds the world and *all* things up, this Rock, this Refuge, this Hiding Place. O may I call Thee mine! In Him I every glory view. He is the one thing needful for time and eternity.

> "Bless Him, my soul, from day to day,
> Trust Him to bring thee on thy way;
> Give Him thy poor, weak, sinful heart;
> With Him, O never, never part."

A pamphlet printed privately by the family, published in the *Gospel Standard* 1994.

FROM DEATH TO LIFE

Dorothy King

Miss Dorothy Turk King was born in London on 20th February, 1880, but after her father's death, when she was about 18 years of age, she and her mother moved to Brighton. She was by profession a school teacher and lived with her widowed mother until Mrs. King died on 11th February, 1913. Miss King was baptized by Mr. Popham and joined the church at Galeed, Brighton, where she was an honourable and highly esteemed member for nearly 70 years.

She became a resident at the Brighton Bethesda Home on 8th January, 1960, and passed to her eternal rest on 16th January, 1977, aged nearly 97.

First Impressions, 1897

It was during the autumn of 1897 that I received my first clear convictions, and also some spiritual encouragements, though for more than a year previous to this I had felt real love to godly people and an earnest desire to be found among them, and numbered with them and not be left in the world. One morning while busy with my duties, and at the time not thinking about religion, I felt sweetly persuaded I was saved, and at the same time my soul was powerfully drawn after Christ, and O how precious and desirable I saw Him to be! This was on a Wednesday, and I remember when I went to chapel in the evening feeling such a union to the people, that I was no longer outside, but one with them, and going to heaven with them.

Another time the 293rd hymn was much blessed to me, especially the following two lines:

> "Speak, Saviour, for sweet is Thy voice,
> Thy presence is fair to behold."

I seemed almost to see the Saviour by faith. I did indeed by faith see all in Him that I needed for my soul's salvation, and in spirit loved and worshipped Him. This was the first time I had really worshipped and felt sacred liberty in praise and love.

All through the autumn I was much helped. At times I felt Christ to be so near to me, and real and precious, and I was enabled to pour out my heart to Him, and to want Him only, for at times He gave me such glimpses of His beauties that I was shut up to one petition and desire: to have Him fully revealed to my soul.

Conviction of Sin

Up to this time I had had no clear conviction of sin, but one Wednesday evening Mr. Popham said, "You can't be saved before you are lost." The words sank into my heart. I do not remember the text nor any other part of the sermon, but that one sentence abode with me, and made me feel uneasy. I tried to forget the words but could not. I knew I had never seen or felt myself lost, and a feeling of unrest and fear came into me, yet up to Christmas I had sweet and powerful drawings after Christ, and at times felt such love to Him that I wished I could die, and I envied old people because I thought they were so much nearer death than I.

But gradually darkness came over me and a deeper conviction of sin, but not total darkness, for during the year 1898 I had several good helps. One was in the early part of the year. I was reading the 183rd hymn; the third verse was applied with power and much sweetness, especially the lines:

> "To faith I'll My fulness display,
> And bid the poor sinner look there."

I saw so much in the words, "My fulness," and I found liberty and earnestness in pleading for a revelation of Christ.

Darkness and Encouragement

The following Good Friday while at chapel, I was feeling very exercised and distressed, the sermon was nearly over and I had not received anything, when a sense of the love of God filled my heart; I felt surrounded with it. The power and sweetness of it remained with me for several hours.

I do not remember anything else until the following December when I received a very clear answer to prayer. It was only a small providential matter, but I had felt a good deal troubled about it and cried to the Lord to help me, and He sent me such a clear answer, it melted my heart and encouraged me to hope that He was not against me.

It was early in the following January when I sensibly entered into darkness of mind, and felt distance from the Lord, and silence. At first I used to count how many days it was since He had spoken or manifested any favour to my soul, but they became too many to count. I had entered a long, dark time of sorrow, famine, darkness, conviction of sin and the dreadful silence of the Lord, a silence which I could feel, and which crushed me down, and which lasted quite two years almost unbroken. During this time I was hard, cold and dead, as if the Lord had visibly left me. Yet even in the midst of this dreadful desolation I remember a few

times of sweetness when my soul went out to Him in love and praise.
One time was in the summer of 1900 from these two lines:

"When thou art nothing in thyself,
Thou then art close to Me."

They brought to my remembrance with much power and sweetness the good time I had that first autumn when I felt I was one with the Lord's people, and for a short time I enjoyed a sweet melting of spirit, and love and praise to the Lord.

Exercises about Baptism

It was during the year 1900 that I first began to feel exercised about baptism. Once particularly I felt a great love to the ordinance and from time to time an earnest desire to be brought to walk in it and one day early in the following year, 1901, I was feeling very exercised about it, but realising such a bitter sense of complete emptiness and lack, total lack it seemed to me, of any mark or evidence of grace, that I felt hopeless that it ever would or could be. I tried to lay all before the Lord, and was enabled to beg very earnestly that He would work in me and for me. I was turning over the leaves of my Bible at the time, when I came to these words: "Who would set the briers and thorns against Me in battle? I would go through them."

O what a blessing I realised in these words! It was as if the Lord really spoke them to me, and by faith I saw Him going before me, and He seemed to say to me, "All you have to do is to follow Me." I saw Him going through the thorns and through the briers. I can hardly describe what I saw in these words. I saw Him so suffering, but so glorious, so powerful, and it was a feeling sense of His great might that overcame me. My emptiness, helplessness and all the numerous impassable difficulties that had arisen before me were gone. I saw them to be less than nothing before Him. I saw myself passing through them all, and not feeling them because I was behind Him, He passing through every obstacle, or rather walking over them, treading them under His feet.

O I did see Him as almighty, as having all power in heaven and in earth, and I was praising and thanking Him as if I were already received into the church and baptized, so sure did it seem it would be so, that it seemed as if it were already come to pass!

A Season of Sore Affliction

Shortly after this I passed through a season of sore affliction in the illness of my dear mother, but during the trial a spirit of prayer was granted me, and several times I had sweet access to the Lord. Once particularly I seemed in faith to touch the hem of His garment, and all through the illness I had such a distinct feeling that I could only get through or be upheld by keeping very close to Him, as I must keep my hand on the hem of His garment all the time. The 107th Psalm and the 11th chapter of John were very good to me. I can say of this trial, that it "brought me to His feet, laid me low and kept me there."

A Deep Sense of the Need of Mercy

In the following August I was walking in the country with a friend when suddenly a deep sense of my great need of mercy came over me. I could have sunk on the ground and begged for mercy, and had I been alone I should have gone behind the trees to beg for pardon.

The following October I came into a deep painful trial which threatened to crush me, yet great mercy was mingled with it, for many times the Lord helped me in it, and turned the bitterness to sweetness and sanctified it, so that as time went on I could say I would not have been without it. I was brought to see it was only the flesh that suffered, for there were times when faith did truly approve the way and choose it, and I believe *love* it, for sometimes Jesus was so precious, and several times I had solemn, sweet views of His sorrows, which melted my hard heart in love to Him, and I believe in a very humble measure enabled me to choose affliction, and as I realised His presence I felt He was with me.

Deepening of the Work

I believe at this time the Lord began to deepen His work in my soul, but so gradually it seemed imperceptible to me at the time. Indeed it was the effect of His teaching I realised more than His actual dealings. From time to time I felt His hand separating me more from the world, and taking it and its things from me. At times I was in much bitterness of spirit. I felt I had neither this world nor the Lord, nor any marks of real religion. The Lord was silent, and I believe He has convinced me of sin more by silence than by accusation, but now it seemed as if He began to show me myself, my sins, my failings and utter destitution, but it was little by little, day after day, and month after month, like a cloud hanging over me and my whole life, and under it I felt helpless and powerless, and without repentance, life or light. I had not a sharp law work, and I envied all who had. How very, very long I was learning I was lost; for several years the Lord seemed to show me self, guilt and corruption, and at times I felt I was under His convicting hand, "though not a word He spoke", but by His silence I received my bitterest condemnation and sense of guilt. This was a time of darkness in which I must have sunk, or wholly and finally departed from that dear Saviour whom I was seeking, if He had not kept me and now and again granted me tokens of His favour.

Sacred View of God's Faithfulness under Renewed Trial

One morning while teaching a pupil, He drew near and I felt persuaded that He loved me. In a moment my heart was melted and I sweetly realised He was with me, and that He had been with me in the darkness. I had such a sacred view of His faithfulness, that He still cared for me and that He had cared for me all through my unbelief – for that seemed to stand out – and hardness and deadness. This did not last long, but it was like a bright flash of light in the darkness, and a sure intimation that the Lord was with me.

And now the trial I had entered into the previous October began to press more heavily, and became more cutting and painful. One Sunday morning I felt so wounded and crushed in spirit, and I told the Lord I could not bear the trial any longer. I took my Bible and was reading about being conformed to the sufferings of Christ but I only read a few verses for such a light shone on my path, I had enough (O more than enough!). My heart was full. I shut the Bible and went upstairs and fell on my knees and poured out my heart before the Lord. I begged Him not to take away the trial, but feared my rebellion would provoke Him to. I believe I then knew a little of having fellowship with Him in His sufferings. It was a blessed time. I earnestly begged Him to sanctify the trial, though it no longer seemed a trial, but a great privilege of which I was unworthy, to carry a sanctified cross.

I had not been long in prayer when it was as if by faith I saw the Lord before me, and O the glory I saw in Him! I could not describe it in words. It was as if He said to me, "I am before you, in front of you. Whatever they say or do to you will come to Me first. I shall suffer it and bear the bitterness of it before it reaches you." How I loved Him, and worshipped Him, and grieved for Him! He looked so suffering and yet so mighty to save. He had all power. He was God. I could not say a word for as I saw Him, I felt my vileness and yet He was saving me. I have never felt so vile, nor worshipped Him so sweetly as at that time. I knew however the trial increased, it would fall on Him before it reached me, and His power and glory joined with His sufferings was so great.

When I grieved over Him I felt I could only worship. He was so great, and all the feelings came together, so that I cannot properly describe them. His love and suffering, His glory and power, my vileness and yet His mercy to me.

I can now look back and feel I would not have been without this trial, so mortifying to the flesh but O how much less than I deserved, and if sanctified, which I hope and believe it was, what a great mercy! Though it was not removed at this time, nor for several years altered, the bitterness was gone and strength and help graciously granted, and for the time I was truly raised above the trouble. How often I have heard Mr. Popham say the Lord can come in affliction and give such help and comfort that though the cross is not removed, nor the circumstance altered, we are enabled and encouraged to go forward in His strength, and this I proved at this time.

Further Exercises about Baptism

For about two years after this I went on seeking but in much darkness and confusion, yet not altogether without help. Again and again baptism came before me, but I had lost the sweet feeling of help I had enjoyed about it, and all hope that it would come to pass seemed to get less and less, only my love to the ordinance did not get less; it increased to an earnest longing. Very often and several times I felt such a pressure on my spirit about it that I had to leave what I was doing and go away alone to beg the Lord to appear for me in the matter, and open the way. At times I was enabled earnestly to beg of Him to open the way for me to be baptized. These words in the 119th Psalm were sometimes a comfort to me: "My soul breaketh for the longing that it hath unto Thy judgments at all times," and the 35th verse was indeed the language of my soul: "Make me to go in the path of Thy commandments, for therein do I delight." This latter verse I many times pleaded before the Lord; it seemed to comprise all my desires in this matter, and sometimes I felt relief in pleading His own Word.

Helps under the Ministry

In the spring of 1906 we went to Heathfield and on the Good Friday Mr. Eddison preached. I did not get any special profit from the sermon, but the first hymn was 156: "If dust and ashes might presume." It so expressed what I was longing for, and my heart was touched and softened by it, so that whenever I read that hymn, I think of the first time when it was so good to me.

A few weeks after our return my dear mother had a long, serious illness, which was a time of great trial to me. O the hardness and

bitterness that I felt, and the thick gloom that rested on my spirit for many
weeks! I think it was the beginning of August before I received any real
help. I was out alone and as I walked, I thought of my wretchedness.
Temporal trouble and sorrow seemed as if it would crush me, and
spiritually I felt utterly destitute, and then a wicked, angry feeling arose, as
if something said, "What do you gain by seeking the Lord?" and I mentally
answered "Nothing but misery."
Just then some lines came into my mind which a friend had sent me:

> "He has come down in mercy,
>   And spoiled my earth-built nest,
>   And given me grief and conflict,
>   For happiness and rest.
> 'Tis well! the joy was worthless,
>   It flowed not from His love,
>   The peace was all delusive,
>   It came not from above."

The words, " 'Tis well," brought a soft, gentle feeling, and then the
words came: "Is it well?" My hard heart was broken, the bitterness gone,
and I said, "Lord, it is well." Providence was right, everything was right. I
did not want a thing altered, nor one sorrow less. I loved the Lord, and
could leave all in His hands, and I felt a sweet hope it was well with my
soul. I felt I could praise Him for sending me trials, which were a means
in His hands of bringing me out of the world.

I think it was in the following October, when Mr. Prewett was
preaching at Galeed, he quoted the words:

> "But Zion cries to God on high,
>   Do Thou Thy face reveal."

They seemed to speak aloud the one desire of my soul. I do not remember
anything else coming with power, but those words abode with me, and I
was enabled to plead them in prayer to the Lord over and over again. To
see Him by faith was what I wanted, and what I still want. O, I can say the
chief desire of my soul is:

> "A bleeding Jesus seen by faith,
>   A sense of pardoning love,"

to see Him, hear His voice and know Him for myself.

On looking back I can see how very gracious the Lord was to me in
the ministry, in allowing me the great privilege of hearing such a gracious
minister, and then blessing his preaching to my soul. Dear Mr. Popham!
All through these years of darkness and bondage the Lord made him His
instrument to show me where I was, and what I was, although I did not

then think that the Lord was having anything to do with me by means of the preaching in a way of blessing, because I did not get any comfort. O I have sat and listened to Mr. Popham and longed for a blessing, and I used to see him shut the Bible and feel another sermon was over, and nothing for me. There seemed two things set before me in the ministry: death and life. How I saw and felt my death, hopeless death it seemed to me, and how Mr. Popham showed me life in Christ, but I felt there was a dividing line, and I was on the death side. Yet how the ministry drew me on, and attracted me to Jesus; it seemed to tell me and tell me of my death, and then point to Christ, and show me life and salvation in Him.

Death in Everything

Once these words fell with power on my spirit; "Though He slay me, yet will I trust in Him," and a few days later, "Be thou faithful unto death, and I will give thee a crown of life." At first I tried to put them from me, but they abode in a measure of power, and I felt sure I should be still more killed than I had been, and should be brought down to death in self, and death in the world and the things of it, and I only wished to fall at His dear feet, to be saved by Him out of all of it. And so I proved it to be. For some time I had bitterly to learn death and destruction in self, yet at times I felt a sweet and entire submission to His way with me, nor could I pray or wish to have one thing altered, and from time to time He softened my heart, when I could love and praise Him.

Spiritual Conflict and Blessing

One Wednesday evening I came out of chapel feeling very cast down. I had received no comfort, and felt so lonely, out of the world, and out of the church, and destitute it seemed to me of any marks of grace – when I saw the Lord again in front of me, bowed and stooping. He turned and looked at me, but with such tender reproach, and said, "Won't you follow Me?" I felt all this long, long time He had still been in front of me, carrying the burden of my hardness, unbelief and death, yet without one complaint, and that His silence atoned for me (see Isaiah 53. 7). Had He spoken I could not have been forgiven. He had felt the full burden of my misery all this time, but He had borne it in perfect patience, and it was His bearing it that saved me. I saw He had to live on earth a suffering life to save me from my death. It was as if He said, "I have borne it all, and all your hardness and complainings." I said, "Lord, I will follow even if I have trouble all my days," and immediately I had a sweet persuasion He was leading me, and the sermons which I had felt were only to condemn me were not sent in condemnation, but in love to my soul, and I loved the ministry which, I now believe, had been the Lord's leading and teaching in my heart. I felt love even to all the bitterness and convictions that had pressed me down. All seemed stamped with love instead of condemnation. I felt it was, and had been, a right way He was leading me.

This help greatly comforted and encouraged me, and kept me from sinking so low afterwards. But my exercise about baptism increased, and I think I can truthfully say that for a year previous to my baptism, the ordinance was seldom out of my thoughts. I felt such earnest concern about it, and longing towards it. I remember the deep pain I felt when witnessing the Lord's Supper administered, feeling I was no nearer being one with the dear people of God than I ever had been, and I could not describe how low I sank, and how broken in spirit I felt. Once particularly, while thus mourning, I felt so near to Jesus, and such a tender sympathy with Him in His sorrows, and a precious sense of His knowing the great sorrow I felt.

A Sweet Confirmation

The baptizing services tried me very much. The one previous to my own I dreaded more than any former service of a similar kind, and as I walked through the town that day, I begged the Lord to help and uphold me through the service that evening, for I felt too low and unbelieving to pray for a blessing. How little did I think my deliverance was near!

Mr. Popham took for his text the 10th and 11th verses of the 45th Psalm: "Hearken, O daughter, and consider, and incline thine ear; forget also thine own people, and thy father's house; so shall the King greatly desire thy beauty; for He is thy Lord; and worship thou Him." It was all for me. Mr. Popham traced my path, exercises and desires. It was as if he gathered up the way I had been in for years, showed me where I was and who was my King. It was wonderful to me, for several times through the sermon he used exactly the same words that I had used on different occasions in prayer to the Lord. I followed him with an inward witness that I had experienced what he was saying, that I had left the world, and was following the Lord Jesus. He traced the way through the doubts and fears, and showed me it had been the Lord's work. That sermon was like a sweet confirmation to me. I believe the Lord made His servant His mouth to me that evening; it was like an open answer. I received nothing fresh, but a removing of clouds of uncertainty, the Lord telling me it had been His leading and teaching time after time, and in so many exercises and ways. This was on Wednesday, 13th May, 1908, and the effect of this sermon was as if someone had opened a great iron door before which I had been standing helpless. This is the only way I can describe the open way I felt before me. Just as hitherto I had felt it impossible to move one step forward, so I felt I could not, dare not keep back.

At times there was not one barrier in the way, not one little thing to hinder me from being baptized. How faithfully, how surely, the Lord had fulfilled His promise spoken to me seven years before, that He would go before me through the briers and thorns! I felt then I had only to follow Him, and now blessedly realised I only had to follow Him in this precious way out of which He had moved every obstacle.

Application to Join the Church at Galeed

On the Saturday morning I went to see Mr. Popham to ask him if I might venture forward. I felt my experience to lack the depth and fulness so many are favoured with, and I feared my lack would be a death to him, and that he would feel he could not receive me. I asked him if I had better wait, but he said he did not think so. He then spoke very solemnly that we might each be enabled to seek the Lord in this matter, and see His hand.

During the Saturday afternoon I sank very low; all seemed a delusion, and I feared I was a deceiver, and being deceived. I felt I must write to Mr. Popham and tell him how wrong my visit to him had been. It was powerfully suggested to me that the Lord would fill Mr. Popham with darkness and confusion in the matter, instead of letting him see His hand, thus showing him the truth. After tea I was reading aloud to my dear mother. It was the 17th chapter of Luke; as I read the 14th verse, the words, "And it came to pass, that, as they went, they were cleansed," completely broke the snare. I felt once more free, and an open way before me.

On the following Tuesday morning I was reading the 69th Psalm, and as I read the 6th verse, I had a most blessed sense of Christ interceding for me. I felt an inward witness that I was waiting on the Lord and seeking Him, and the words, "For My sake", were so beautiful, so full of power, and must prevail. I knew Christ was praying for me, that His prayer must be answered. I felt there was nothing left for me to pray for, but that His prevailing intercession covered my whole life and everything in it until my last breath. My heart was broken, and I fell on my knees before Him in tears and praises. I have never felt more dissolved and broken under His goodness.

I saw the deacons a few weeks later, and the Lord inclined their hearts to receive what He enabled me to say, but still the church meeting was before me, and sometimes it seemed to fill the future. Once when feeling very tried and exercised about it, these words came to me with power and sweetness: "Where two or three are gathered together in My name, there am I in the midst of them." The thought of the Lord's presence removed the fear. I saw a sacred beauty in saints meeting together with Him in their midst, and I did not wholly lose this feeling.

On the 10th September, 1908, I went before the church and the Lord inclined His people to receive me as a member with them.

Baptism

I was baptized with three others on the 14th October, 1908. Mr. Popham took for his text the last two verses of the 6th chapter of Romans. I received nothing special in the sermon, and felt a measure of disappointment, but I was looking for a season of thanksgiving and joy in the ordinance; but when I went down into the water a great awe fell on my spirit. I did not feel joy, but a great solemnity truly expressed in the words: "How dreadful is this place!" I felt tried afterwards as to why I had experienced no joy, as so many do while going through the ordinance, and continued to feel exercised about it until the last day of the year. Early in the morning of that day I was reading the 53rd chapter of Isaiah. The first three verses came with sweetness and a measure of power, and as I read on through the chapter, and of the sufferings of Christ's soul for sin, my baptism came before me, and I saw in it a solemn emblem of His awful sufferings for sin. The question came, "Can I expect joy in a place of such solemn sorrow?" and I felt it had not been the Lord's will to grant me joy in the ordinance but that perhaps the solemn awe was especially sent to me as a check on my naturally light spirit.

The Saturday after my baptism, while reading Psalm 71, the last clause of the 23rd verse came with such power and sweetness: "My soul, which Thou hast redeemed." I felt in my spirit He had redeemed my soul, and the word "redeemed" was so great and full. The next day Mr. Prewett preached. The morning sermon was very good to me; the text was Galatians 3. 13-14. Mr. Prewett began by saying, "We will consider the Redeemer and the redeemed." O what a sweet hope sprang up in my heart that I was one of the redeemed, such a confirmation of the same hope I felt on the previous morning! Mr. Prewett also spoke of the Lord praying for His people, and how He prayed for Peter, and I felt I knew He had prayed for me.

Help at the Early Morning Prayer Meeting

Sunday, November 30th, 1913, I had a good help at the early morning prayer meeting while Mr. Banfield was reading the 6th chapter of John. The 44th verse shone into my soul. I felt I really knew what it was to come to Christ, but I had never before seen as I did that morning that to draw near to Christ was an act of God the Father wrought in me. I cannot express the beauty I saw in being brought to Christ by the Father Himself, not the outcome of any effort or desire of mine, but wholly and only the sovereign act of God. It seemed to bring me a little into this beautiful verse which for years I have longed to experience fully:

> "In Him my weary soul finds rest,
> Though I am weak and vile;
> I read my name upon His breast,
> And see the Father smile."

I felt He could only smile on me while in this blessed spot; there could not be any condemnation here. It showed me also why Christ cannot cast out a sinner who thus comes to Him (verse 37).

A Good Day

Sunday, December 21st, 1913, was a good day. Before going to chapel in the morning, while reading the 14th chapter of John, the third verse was very precious: "And if I go and prepare a place for you, I will come *again*, and receive you unto Myself; that where I am, there ye may be also." The word "again" was so powerful. I felt I could say it would be "again"; that when I enter heaven it will not be the first time I shall see Him, nor the first time I shall hear His voice, but it will be "this same Jesus", who has come to me here and spoken to me here in times of sorrow and affliction. It led me to pray very earnestly to be so prepared for death that when it comes it may have no terror in it to me, but only be the Lord coming to receive me to Himself.

Our pastor was away in the morning through illness, and we had a prayer meeting. During one of the prayers the words came: "They will see His face." My spirit melted, and I began to love and worship Him. Heaven has never been so real, or seemed so near. The words grew and increased in power; seeing Christ, looking on His face, heaven filled my heart and I felt sweetly to melt and dissolve.

In the afternoon I took up a book to read, and unexpectedly came to a most beautiful description of heaven: "Upon the streets there went and came a holy people, clad in white, with faces sealed to peace unspeakable. I did not see His face who sitteth King within the shining city, but I saw reflected in each face His wondrous look, and I could read that every eye within the city saw Him, though I saw Him not." I thought it was wonderful to come upon such a description of what was in my heart. I was unable to go out in the evening as I had a cold, and was at home alone. It was a sacred season; portions of Scripture and hymns flowed into my heart with almost overwhelming power and sweetness: "He shall present you faultless"; the second chapter of Ephesians; especially the 103rd hymn, and 125th hymn, and the line: "I stand upon His merit". I knelt down and poured out my heart to the Lord. I told Him it was only His blood, His righteousness, His merit that would enable me to look on His face. I realized what purity, what almost awful purity, is necessary to enable us to look upon Him without a veil between.

The Blessing Renewed

Sunday, December 28th. The savour of the last Sunday abode with me during the week, and while reading early this morning through the Revelation, I felt the blessing was renewed. I was so much struck with the continual mention of the "white robes", which had never before occurred to me as being the righteousness of Christ, and I felt a gracious liberty in prayer to be clothed in this glorious dress, that the Lord might look on me as faultless. The last chapter was particularly good to me. The first hymn at chapel in the morning was 920. It seemed so suitable.

Wednesday, January 7th, 1914. Text this evening: "Behold the Lamb of God." I had a good hearing, a renewing of December 21st, as if our pastor had known all about it. I was glad he did not, as then the sermon would not have been so sweetly applicable.

September 1914. I feel I cannot let this summer pass away without mentioning the Lord's goodness to me during the past months. The ministry has been so blessed to me; sometimes I have felt I was the only one to whom Mr. Popham was preaching. For many weeks I was favoured with a spirit of prayer and felt access. Prayer was sweet and I felt encouraged to hope it was indited by the Lord, for strong opposition worked in me. " There is no help for you," "It is useless to pray," and many other discouragements fell like ice at times on my spirit, but instead of having the effect to check prayer, I felt faith rise in me, and was enabled to pray more earnestly than ever. Often I said audibly, "Lord, it is good to pray, it is of use to pray," and when thus enabled to cleave to the Lord, I felt such a sacred sense of faith triumphing over unbelief.

At the Friday evening prayer meeting on July 10th, our pastor read the 3rd chapter of Zephaniah, commencing at the 8th verse: "Therefore wait ye upon Me." The word "Me" was so great. It was the Lord. Mr. Popham read straight through without commenting and as he read I worshipped Him as God, and mentally repeated over and over: "The Lord, He is God, the Lord, He is God." When Mr. Popham expounded, he took up my case in a wonderful way though he did not know anything about it. I received a double blessing.

Sweetness in Pleading before the Lord

One Wednesday evening, I think the following, I was greatly favoured. Our pastor began his sermon with reasons why we should pray, and quoted passages through the Bible that exhort to it. They were the same that for some days I had felt much sweetness in pleading before the Lord in continual prayer, and which had encouraged and emboldened me to urge my case. He then spoke of how the Lord reveals Himself to us, sometimes in his Word, sometimes a view by faith, and I felt a sacred persuasion I had seen Him in these ways. Lastly he spoke of the sealing of the Spirit, and here I was left behind; I have not had it. O that I may not feel unconcerned about it but more and more concerned and exercised until it is bestowed.

One Sunday morning Mr. Popham was speaking of the atonement fitting us to enter heaven. It sweetly brought to my remembrance December 21st, 1913, and I said to myself, "I know it, I know it."

Sunday, July 19th, 1914. Our pastor preached from Matthew 28, verse 18. My path was described, my exercises clearly traced. A blessed hearing! Surely I may say: " This God is my God for ever and ever; He will be my guide even unto death," and then receive me to Himself. Our pastor's words, "Pray, pray," described my life. O the sweetness to pray in trouble and not tell a creature. He also said, "Sometimes we have to fall bound into the furnace." There was so much in this to me.

Wednesday, July 22nd. Text: Psalm 102, verse 18: prayer and its answers. Our pastor exhorted to watch any sense of liberty the Lord grants in prayer, and said that if we are enabled to lay all before Him, being compelled to pray, it is the sure token of an answer. He said: "A sight of Him by faith, a sense of His presence, surely this calls for praise." Blessed sermon! I had the inward witness.

Sunday morning, July 18ᵗʰ 1915. Text: Luke 18, verse 1. Our pastor showed the new and living way whereby we may approach in prayer; then the invitation to come; the power of the Spirit and nature of grace to pray. Just as it is in our nature to walk, so it is in the nature of grace to pray. He said, "To whom do you go in trouble? To whom do your thoughts turn?" Also he spoke of how the Lord's silence tries us when we have gone to Him for a long time about one thing and we get no answer, but instead everything gets worse and Satan says, " The Lord has shown you by His silence He does not intend to answer you. Now if you presume to go on asking, you will only make Him angry." "But," said our pastor, "what does the Lord say to you? *Pray on.* He will send you an answer." In his closing prayer he asked that we might make a fresh start in prayer.

"He is thy God, and Worship thou Him"

May 30ᵗʰ, 1916. While reading *Daily Light,* the last clause was applied with power and sweetness: "Thy God thy glory." My heart dissolved and the tears flowed down my face. I kneeled down and said, "Lord, it is too much. Is it really for me?" And it came with even more power: "He is thy God, and worship thou Him." I could only worship and weep. I felt I could have died without fear, for there was nothing against me.

A few mornings later as I read the words, "I will go before thee," they produced such a spirit of faith and worship and such quietness and assurance that enabled me really to trust in the Lord, and constrained me to believe they came from Him.

May 1917. One Sunday morning, hymn 469 was sang at chapel. As they sang the 5ᵗʰ verse, I was lost to all around,

> "Burdened and groaning then no more,
> My rescued soul shall sing,
> As up the shining path I soar,
> ' Death, thou hast lost thy sting.' "

O what I saw and felt in the word "rescued", – after all saved! For a few seconds I felt free, free from sin and every burden, redeemed; but it was like a flash, for the power was passed away by the time they finished the hymn.

Sanctified Affliction

For many years I was greatly tried and harassed by the fear that although I had been brought on thus far, something would yet come completely to overwhelm me, and particularly I feared that if I were taken suddenly ill, I should either die from fright or be speechless with alarm and terror. At times I greatly sank under a feeling of dread, and wondered whatever I should do if my fears came true.

On Friday evening March 28th, 1919, I was suddenly and alarmingly taken ill in chapel and while returning home with a friend it was suggested, "Now your terror will begin," but it did not; my mind was kept wonderfully quiet. I lay down in bed quite willing to be alone through the night. The next day when wondering how the illness would terminate, I felt a comfortable hope that my religion would do to die with, even if I did not receive any further blessing. On the Sunday morning as I was reading the 25th chapter of Isaiah, the first clause of the 8th verse was applied with considerable sweetness to my soul – "He will swallow up death in victory." The snare which had held me so long was broken in an instant. It was all in the word "He". I saw the Lord Jesus would do it all: defeat and conquer Satan, and swallow up all his lies, and that I should be a conqueror through Him. For a short time I was enabled to rejoice in His mercy, and wept under a sense of it.

January 7th, 1920. During the sermon this evening our pastor quoted the words – "Behold Me, behold Me," and instantly my heart replied, "My Lord and my God," but O the sweet brokenness of heart and melting! I was glad the lights were turned down for the tears ran down my face and I could not keep them back.

May 1920. One morning this month I was much comforted. I was feeling unwell and I considered how it would be with me if I were to die suddenly, and I had a sweet and solemn sense that God the Father was well pleased with me, that there was no frown on His face towards me but that I was under His smile, and that if I died He would receive me, and the words came with solemn satisfaction and peace, "I will receive you," and I knew it was God the Father. For some days I was in quiet, solemn peace; no great joy but a sober satisfaction as if my soul were enjoying a Sabbath, but I could not have explained how I was feeling.

Application

On Sunday the 20th May, Mr. Gosden preached both times. I had a good hearing in the morning, but in the evening I felt a distinct application of what he said. The text was Isaiah 25, verse 9, "And it shall be said in that day, Lo, this is our God; we have waited for Him, and He will save us: this is the Lord; we have waited for Him, we will be glad and rejoice in His salvation." During his sermon Mr. Gosden said, "Think for a moment that Jehovah is the only free Being in existence, and that His will is the only free will." As he uttered these words I felt the sweetest hope that God had willed my salvation. It threw such a clear light on what I had been enjoying for some days, but I could only express it in the words of the hymn—

> "'Tis even so, Father, we ever must say,
> Because it seemed good in Thy sight."

Eternal Security

March 28th, 1924. While reading the *Daily Light* I had a blessed in-shining as I read the words, "Where the priests' feet stood firm." The covenant was there, the Trinity was there, I was there, but the view I had of eternal security and firmness I am unable to describe; only I had a faint sense of my interest in it.

The Saviour's Intercession

September 9th, 1924. While reading this afternoon, these words were applied with much sweetness and power, "I have prayed for thee." I had such a blessed sense of my interest in the Saviour's intercession and assurance of my security. I felt,

> "More happy, but not more secure,
> The glorified spirits in heaven."

and as I mentally repeated the words, a spirit of love and worship sprang up in my heart and I kneeled down and said, "Lord, I cannot be more secure." I wept tears of love and praise before Him under a melting sense of His goodness to me.

October 19th, 1924. Our dear pastor preached this morning from John 17, verse 9. "I pray for them." I could follow him with the sweet inward witness that I had experienced this blessed truth for myself. As he spoke of all our state and case being covered with this prevailing prayer, I had a sweet remembrance of how I realised many years ago that my whole life was covered with the intercession of Christ, down to my last breath.

> "Should death be at hand, I'll fear not undressing,
> But cheerfully cast off these garments of clay;
> To die in the Lord is a covenant blessing,
> Since Jesus through death for His church made a way."

A Sealing Time

Towards the end of 1926 my health began to fail, but my spiritual hope was clear, and at times strong. In January 1927, the words "They shall not be ashamed that wait for Me," were applied with some power. As the year advanced, my health decreased but my inward peace and comfort increased, and I experienced daily comfort in waiting on the Lord and my intercourse with Him swallowed up the bodily affliction and all fear as to its issue.

In August I saw a specialist. A few hours before the consultation, the words were again sweetly applied, "They shall not be ashamed that wait for Me," but I would say here that they had no reference to any deliverance from the affliction, but they came to me as an earnest and pledge of the Lord's faithfulness to me, and pointing me to eternal victory in Him. I was told that a serious operation was necessary. As I heard this I felt almost joyful, and I seemed to see only Jesus and His faithfulness.

During the next few weeks my faith was greatly strengthened in the Lord and my mind was quite peaceful. The Sunday before the operation, during the morning sermon, our dear pastor said or rather quoted, "For the Lord God will help me," adding, "Perhaps you can even go farther and say with that suffering, but glorious One, I shall not be confounded." As he said this, I so realised my union with Christ that I had difficulty not to say aloud, "I know I shall never be confounded."

When the morning of the operation came, my spirit was peaceful and at rest. "Yea, though I walk through the valley of the shadow of death, I will fear no evil; for Thou art with me," was my inward feeling and as I lay down on the table I was full of peace.

I had one fear lest by word or act I should bring dishonour on His dear name, for I felt I should be in the midst of the world and they would be watching me, and it had been suggested that if my comfort left me and I sank in fear and dismay they would say religion was of no real use.

For several days I was too weak even to think, but the fourth morning I was clearer and I began to consider, and my heart went up to the Lord that I might not lie as a lifeless log. Then the thought came, "How have I been brought through!" and a sense of the Lord's goodness filled me and I felt my heart ascending to Him in praise and gratitude. I felt melted and broken in spirit, when the following words came slowly, but clearly, "But I wrought for My Name's sake, that it should not be polluted before the heathen, among whom ye were." These words filled me with a solemn awe, and a sense of how dear the Lord's glory is to Him. I felt crumbled into less than nothing before Him. He showed me it was not for my sake He had done this, but to preserve the honour of His glory while working in me and for me.

He drew very near to me; I was too weak to pray in any order, but again and again He gently whispered, "Fear not, it is I," and, as it were, showed me His impress on everything to do with me.

As my bodily strength increased so did my spiritual comfort. I seemed to walk out the Scripture, "Thou shalt remember all the way which the Lord thy God hath led thee." Former blessings were confirmed and each Scripture which had been applied through the past years was fulfilled in me and I could truly say all came to pass; not one word failed.

I had a particular view one day of how the Lord had gone before me and made all ready for me, before I entered into the illness. I saw the impress of His handiwork in everything, from the most important circumstance to the smallest matter and that all had been wrought for me by Himself. I lay in wonder and praise as one thing after another passed before me, and how good His working appeared.

At a prayer meeting previous to my illness our pastor had alluded to Christ as a crowned Priest, and it arrested me. During my convalescence I had a glimpse of the beauty of it in the two scriptures – "Let not them that wait on Thee, O Lord God of Hosts, be ashamed for my sake; let not those that seek Thee be confounded for my sake, O God of Israel;" and the word our pastor quoted in Zechariah – "Even He shall build the temple of the Lord; and He shall bear the glory, and shall sit and rule upon His throne; and He shall be a Priest upon His throne; and the counsel of peace shall be between them both."

This application was a sealing time. The Lord graciously and clearly confirmed His work in me, and His word to me. I saw all in a different light from what I had ever experienced before. It was as if He had allowed His word to be put to the test, and then gave it back to me, proved and sealed as having borne the test.

Deliverance under Temptation

July 25th, 1929. This, and the following day (Friday), I had conflict more severe than I can remember heretofore. It was not so much my safety that was assailed, but a flood of temptation hurled at me on all sides without cessation. I was too agitated to kneel and too confused to pray in order, but as I walked about, short cries were wrung out of my heart to the Lord. My mind was more like a cloud of dust whizzing about, and I had not time to consider whether it came from sin in me or temptation. I only believed it to be the hand of God on me to bring me to nothing. As I was going to the prayer meeting on Friday evening, the following verse came with some distinctness–

"Lord, to Thee I trembling run,
Void of refuge and undone,
And if Thou reject my prayer......"

But I could go no further. I said almost aloud, Lord, I cannot have the "if": I must have Thee," and I felt a little strength to try and hold Him. As I sat in chapel, the verse, and blessing already alluded to, came to my mind,

"Burdened and groaning then no more,
My rescued soul shall sing,
As up the shining path I soar,
' Death, thou hast lost thy sting.' "

The word "rescued" was even greater than before, and I felt the power of the temptation was broken, and my spirit also. Our pastor read the 57th Psalm, and to me each verse was wonderful, but when he began to expound he was truly made God's mouth to me. He said "Until these calamities be overpast." The psalmist had faith to believe that all the trials he was then surrounded with would have an end and in the meantime he would trust in the Lord. "He shall send from heaven, and save me from the reproach of him that would swallow me up." This reproach our dear pastor said was the tempting and assaulting of Satan, and here he mentioned the very temptations which Satan had unceasingly been hurling at me, endeavouring to swallow me up; but I had the deliverance he spoke of, in the Lord sending from heaven to save me from this reproach. He went on to say, "Some of you have a past," and then discoursed most blessedly on how the Lord renews past visits, and I was sweetly experiencing one little bit of my past "made o'er again". And then the last clause, "Let Thy glory be above all the earth" – the Lord's work in us, and for us, glorifying God in our deliverances and praises to Him.

Pleading for Justifying Faith

Sunday, June 18th, 1939. I awoke very early this morning before it was light, and I thought, This is the Lord's day, the day of resurrection, and I earnestly pleaded that Jesus would put forth His resurrection power in me. Very solemnly the words came, "He was raised again for our justification," and I saw my sins as one huge black mass, as expressed in the hymn,

"How huge the heavy load of all,
When only mine's so great."

I besought the Lord to give me justifying faith, and to make me a real believer.

Here Miss King's writings end.

From an original manuscript, first published in the *Gospel Standard* 1978.

HITHERTO

Ruth Beesley

Early Days

I was born at Polebrook, near Oundle, Northants, in 1889 and was favoured with godly parents, both being members of Oundle Strict Baptist church. We moved to Peterborough when I was four years old and attended Salem Strict and Particular Baptist Chapel there. As a child I had many solemn thoughts of the day of judgment. My dear mother taught me that little prayer:

> "Lord, teach a little child to pray,
> Thy grace betimes impart;
> And grant Thy Holy Spirit may
> Renew my youthful heart."

But these desires passed off and I began to want to go into the world. Going to chapel one week-evening to see a dear friend baptized, these words came solemnly to me, "Where will you spend eternity?" yet my desire was to go into the world. After this I was in great sorrow, feeling I had resisted the Holy Spirit. My beloved mother had always taught us to read God's Word and good books. One evening when fourteen years old and reading John 15, the Holy Spirit convinced me that there was something in real religion that I was a stranger to. Instantly the desire to go into the world left me and my desire was to seek the Lord with all my heart. This led me to the week-night services at Salem. My cry was:

> "Convince me of my sin,
> Then lead to Jesus' blood;
> And to my wondering view reveal
> The secret love of God."

One dear aged friend used to pray at the prayer meeting for those who desired to desire. This suited me well; I did so long for true conviction of sin. The first two verses in hymn 1092 ("Till God the sinner's mind illume") were suitable to me. I felt so dead and lifeless and longed for eternal life and true conviction of sin. A sermon preached by Mr. Stonelake of Nottingham: "And did all eat the same spiritual meat," made a deep impression on me. It made me long to eat the same spiritual meat that His dear people eat. How I loved His dear people and loved to be in their company! Then a sermon preached by Mr. Fred Kirby of Staplehurst made a deep impression on me from the text, "But my God shall supply all your need according to His riches in glory by Christ Jesus." My desire was to be deeply convinced of sin as Mr. Kirby was and to have the same revelation of the Lord Jesus Christ as he had to my soul, but I used to feel like "a limping beggar, clothed in rags".

Deep Distress and Liberty

Sorry to say I went on like this until I was eighteen and then had to go to Leicester to nurse my eldest sister over her last confinement. She had heart trouble and the dear baby boy was afflicted with hare lip and split palate, which was very serious. The doctor told me it depended on me whether the child lived or died. I must feed him every half-hour with one spot of food at a time. He had great difficulty in taking this; also he was to be prepared for an operation when he was six weeks old. This caused me constantly to pray that I might be enabled to feed him and not choke him and that God would let him live. He graciously answered my poor prayer. Having to feed the dear baby, and my sister ill, I had to remain in Leicester.

When nineteen, the Holy Spirit convinced me deeply what a great sinner I was in His holy sight. I felt lost and that perish I must and drop into hell. I felt entirely ignorant of the way of salvation, although having always attended chapel. That verse helped me: "Who can have compassion on the ignorant, and on them that are out of the way." This experience lasted for some weeks but the burden of sin became heavier and I felt completely lost and that I must sink into hell. Eventually the dear Lord came with almighty power and spoke these words to my soul: "Your life is hid with Christ in God," and I was given such a faith's view of the Lord Jesus suffering on the cross for my sin, together with the words, "He shall see of the travail of his soul and shall be satisfied." "There is joy in the presence of the angels of God over one sinner that repenteth." The mercy and love of God to my soul was amazing. "Amazing grace! (how sweet the sound!) That saved a wretch like me." I was taught a much deeper knowledge of myself as a sinner in God's holy sight, and sank in great distress of soul, when these words were applied with divine power: "His sweat was as it were great drops of blood falling down to the ground," and I had a sweet assurance that they were shed for me.

Trials and Deliverances

The dear Lord hid His face again and being in great trouble and distress I went to Zion Sabbath school. Our beloved teacher, Miss Josephine Orton, took for our lesson Solomon's prayer at the dedication of the temple, and I received such great help from the verse, "Moreover concerning a stranger, that is not of Thy people Israel" (1 Ki. 8. 41); if these strangers pray towards this house, the Lord Jesus Christ, He would save them. Miss Orton said if the Lord could save her, he could save any one of us, and a little hope was given that He could save me. That evening Satan dared me to go to Zion Chapel because I was such a sinner, and that if I went, I should drop down dead and be in hell; but I was compelled to go. Mr. Hazlerigg was not well enough to preach that evening so Mr. Lenton, our deacon, read Isaiah 55 commencing with the words, "Ho, every one that thirsteth, come ye to the waters, and he that hath no money; come ye, buy and eat; yea, come, buy wine and milk without money and without price." It just seemed as if there were only the Lord and myself in the chapel as the Lord sweetly spoke those words to my soul. I was a bankrupt soul, nothing to pay with, and my soul did thirst for the living water which only God could give.

But the Lord soon withdrew His blessed presence. We had a read sermon that evening from the text, "The Lord thy God in the midst of thee is mighty; He will save, He will rejoice over thee with joy; He will rest in His love, He will joy over thee with singing," and the service closed with hymn 912, "Salvation by grace, how charming the sound." I went straight home and to my bedroom, and had to fall on my knees begging for mercy. Suddenly the Lord came with divine power into my soul with the above text; also, "The Lord that made both heaven and earth, And was Himself made man," etc., showing me that He had chosen me in Christ before the world began. I realised the eternal love of God and that Jesus was the eternal Son of God and that I could never finally fall; that "His delights were with the sons of men"; and that He was rejoicing over such a wretched sinner as me with singing; that He had saved me with His everlasting salvation. I sang for joy at His great mercy.

I went to my home at Peterborough for Christmas and there, in the very room where for years I had begged to be truly convinced of sin, I could now thank Him for answering my poor cries and rejoice in Him as my Saviour and Redeemer. I was completely overcome with the love of God to me and wanted to be alone to praise Him for His covenant love and faithfulness. This rich blessing lasted many days.

I was very troubled one evening by the following words coming to me:

"But when, like a sheep that strays from the fold,
To Jesus thy Lord thy love shall grow cold,
Think not He'll reject thee, howe'er He reprove;
For though He correct thee, He'll rest in His love."

In my first love I felt it impossible to stray from my beloved Lord, He was so precious to me, and little thought at that time what a heart like mine would do, how the devil would aim at my overthrow. Returning to Leicester feeling sad at leaving home again, the words came with power and gave me submission to His will: "What though I can't His goings see," etc. Then shortly afterwards the dear Lord gave me the following words with divine power: "The Saviour lives no more to die," etc. Thus the dear Lord brought me to realise that I was justified, that He rose for my justification, and that now He lives to intercede for me. O the joy and peace this truth gave me! I felt filled with the love and mercy of God. Shortly afterwards He gave me these sweet words: "To present you holy and unblameable and unreproveable in His sight." Thus the dear Lord gave me sweet assurance. I was lost in wonder, love and praise and longed to be taken to heaven to praise Him.

I did not know how to work I was so filled with the love of God and had to ask Him to stay His hand. My body was overcome with His love and mercy. I felt I must "tell to sinners round, What a dear Saviour I had found", and that if I did not, the very stones would cry out. Jesus said to me, "If ye love Me keep My commandments," and I longed to keep His commandments. To take this step seemed impossible as I had only been attending Zion for such a short time, and felt the church could not receive me on that account. I had never spoken to anyone on these things and feared to approach Mr Hazlerigg on the matter. Not daring to take this step, I just felt cast from heaven to hell.

[Miss Beesley then gives an account of several profitable hearing times during the next few years.]

Eventually Mr. S. Champion became pastor at Leicester. The first text that I was specially helped under was Psa. 103. 3: "Who forgiveth all thine iniquities, who healeth all thy diseases." Then Psa. 31. 15: "My times are in Thy hands." This was a very special help as, at that time, I was ill and was forced to resign my post. When able I applied for another post and should have liked it, but it would have meant my selling novels, which I could not possibly do. I went home and as soon as I got in, I was told that a lady had sent for me. I went to see her and she engaged me straightway. I have so many times proved that all my times are in His blessed hands.

A Mysterious Experience

Then came a special blessing, when I felt constrained to come forward as a candidate for baptism. A dear aged deacon said to me, "Tonight's sermon was all for you, and if you do not come forward, you will be in trouble." I replied, "I feel the same." I went to see Mr. Champion and he arranged for me to see the deacons. As soon as I had spoken to Mr. Champion, I was the subject of the most fierce temptations, Satan telling me I was not a real child of God, and the Lord hid His blessed face. I was in dreadful trouble, but was helped to see the deacons and they very kindly received me. I went before the church and was received unanimously. But the severe temptations and the Lord hiding His face made me very ill and I felt there was no hope for me. I was in prison and felt condemned, and felt I should never come out of that prison. I had to go home with a complete breakdown and was not able to go back to Zion to be baptized. I was in severe pain spiritually and bodily; I felt under such condemnation.

One dear servant of God, Mr. J. T. Wiles of St. Ives, was preaching at Peterborough and, knowing how great was my distress, felt he must see me, so I went to see him. We had a close conversation, and he encouraged me to hope in God, and quoted the text: "Wherefore He is able to save them to the uttermost that come unto God by Him, seeing He ever liveth to make intercession for them." Mr. Wiles said, "It is absolutely impossible for you to get beyond God's *uttermost*. The Lord is faithful and He will bring you through." It helped me, and each time he came to preach at Peterborough, he tried to encourage me to hope in God, and he had the joy of seeing my deliverance, although it was years afterwards. Then how we rejoiced and praised God together for His mercy and love to such a sinner as me.

I was at home for eighteen months, and then went as temporary help to Mr. and Mrs. C. H. Gascoigne of Wellingborough, and there I had some profitable conversations with Mr. Gascoigne which helped me spiritually.

[Miss Beesley then records how a situation in London was provided for her.]

Sometimes I felt encouraged to hope the Lord would appear for me, but the full deliverance for which I longed did not come. During a visit to my sister in September, we attended the prayer meeting at Grove Road Chapel, Eastbourne, and very much enjoyed it. I had to return to London that evening which meant that I was very late reaching home, and never having previously slept in a house alone, I felt rather afraid. I knelt down and asked the Lord to take care of me, and instantly felt surrounded by the

Lord's presence. The words followed, "Take off thy shoes from off thy feet, for the place whereon thou standest is holy ground." This meant so much to me – to realise His gracious presence. All fear of being in the house alone was taken away, and I had a good night's rest. I received various helps by the way and longed to be baptized through the text being applied, "But it is good for me to draw near to God." "I have put my trust in the Lord God, that I may declare all Thy works." But I needed more divine assurance in my soul to take that solemn step.

A Dreadful "Accident"

On 15th August, 1932 I left London to spend a fortnight's holiday at Llandudno, North Wales, with a dear friend from Leicester, and we had many spiritual talks on the way. On Lord's day evening, we went to chapel, and the text that evening was: "And whosoever shall compel thee to go a mile, go with him twain." This had a weighty effect on me.

On Tuesday, August 23rd, my dear friend, Mrs. Anderson, and I went for a walk along the Marine Drive on the Great Orme, having a close spiritual conversation. It being near lunch time, we got on the tram at the halfway engine house to go down to the bottom of the Great Orme, and had only been on the tram two minutes when the draw bar, which controls the tram, snapped. The tram gathered speed and ran into a stone wall killing the driver of the tram. My friend and I sat behind the driver; she was not injured but received shock. The coping stone of the wall came through the tram window on to my head, and I received a lacerated brain and fractured base of the skull. I was quite unconscious and was laid on a lady's lawn by the tramway.

My friend was able to attend to my head until the doctor and ambulance arrived. The doctor plugged my head wound, and I was taken to Llandudno Cottage Hospital. Just at that time, the finest surgeon in Wales, Mr. Coleman, was at the hospital, and took charge of me; he said if he operated I should die, and if he did not I must die. However, he operated and sewed the brain together. The surgeon thought I was passing away on the table and administered life injections to keep me alive, but no hope was given of my recovery. I was taken to a private ward and all relations sent for, but the Lord's time to take me had not yet come.

I was unconscious for a month and on regaining consciousness for a short time, I felt this was the second mile which I must go. Being blind for a time, I had to be told that I was in hospital. Then, suddenly, the dear Lord came and I simply felt to lie at His dear feet. O the mercy and love I felt lying there – the sweetest spot on earth! I begged of the Lord to let me remain there but, to my great sorrow, I felt the dear Lord withdrawing His sacred presence and "I missed the presence of my Friend, Like one whose comfort's gone." But, blessed be His holy name, He gave me that sweet promise, "As thy days, so shall thy strength be," which was graciously fulfilled, for I was very ill and no hope of recovery given. The more pain I had, the more strength and help the dear Lord gave me to bear it. Then Satan came with sore temptations and told me that I was not a child of God, so I asked my sister not to let any minister bury me in sure and certain hope of a glorious resurrection; but the dear Lord broke through the clouds and gave me a little hope in His mercy. I was having life injections in one arm and sleeping injections in the other, to keep me alive, but I again proved that "as thy days, so shall thy strength be".

The kind surgeon said if they wished to take me home, it must be done before the eighteenth week, but he could not say that I should reach home alive, and if they took the risk to move me, he must contact a Leicester surgeon to meet me. On October 13th, 1932, I was taken by ambulance from Llandudno Hospital to my married sister's at Leicester. The ambulance men were afraid they could not get me home alive, but were assured by my friend that special prayer was being made for my safe arrival. I felt very ill, but the dear Lord gave me that sweet promise, "The eternal God is thy refuge, and underneath are the everlasting. arms." O what a support and strength the words were to me! Eventually I went unconscious (which was a great mercy) and remained so until I reached home. The doctor was there to meet and attend to me, and so we had great cause to thank God for a safe journey.

Gradual Improvement

God very graciously gave me a very good and kind surgeon who took a real interest in my case. I was completely paralysed down my left side. The surgeon at Llandudno had written to the Leicester surgeon and told him everything possible had been done for me, and he could only stand by and make me comfortable until I died. Many times did my surgeon say, while watching my brain knit together, "We are fearfully and wonderfully made: I have never known such a miracle."

Some months after, he took the risk of my life in moving my finger on my left hand, and also slowly moved my left side and got some use in it. I was brought very low spiritually, and could often only say, "Lord, help me."

"Pity my simplicity,
Suffer me to come to Thee.

"Fain I would to Thee be brought;
Gracious God, forbid it not;
In the kingdom of Thy grace,
Give a wretch like me a place."

I felt such a wretch, and undone, and begged of the Lord for a word from Himself. One evening, Mr. H. Haddow, a deacon at Zion, Leicester, came to see me and read a portion of God's Word, and prayed that God would give me a word for myself, which the dear Lord graciously did. He sweetly said, "Fear not, I will help thee," and I said, "Lord, a wretch like me?" He kindly said, "Thee." It was such a help and blessing to my soul.

Though I had believed that Christ was the glorious Head of the church, and we were dependent upon Him and the Holy Spirit for every desire and movement Godward yet, lying quite helpless, the doctor having told me that I could not move my little finger unless the brain gave permission, here I was taught more than ever my whole dependence upon God, our glorious Head of the church, for every spiritual desire and for every movement bodily. How I longed to know more of Him whom my soul loved, and how I have proved the truth of that verse many times since!

"No! we bless the Lord on high,
Not a single joint can die.
Every member lives in him;
He's the life of every limb."

Mr. S. Champion's visits were made a great help to me.

A year after the day of my accident, 23rd August, 1933, I received a notice that the Great Orme Tramway Company, Llandudno, had gone bankrupt. I wondered what I should do, as the old Health Service did not then provide for accidents, only for illness. I was paying privately for doctor and medicine, but the Lord gave me that sweet promise, "God all-sufficient," and so I have found Him to be. My doctor was most considerate and kind, and also my late employer and his wife, Mr. and Mrs. Hicks of blessed memory, who kindly helped me as long as they lived, and since then, their two daughters have done the same. O blessed be God for answering prayer spiritually and in providence!

More Trials and Mercies

I felt full of earthly concerns and had to pray, "Unite my heart to fear Thy Name." Then came the word with divine power into my soul: "Bless the Lord, O my soul, and forget not all His benefits." Then I was enabled to thank the Lord for the home that He would provide. That evening my dear sister was at Zion and a friend, Miss L. Robinson, whom I did not know at that time, enquired how I was, and she told Miss Robinson I was needing another home. Miss R. went home and told her sister and they decided to come and see me, Miss R. having had the word applied to her, "Take this child and nurse it for Me." They kindly offered to take me, but I should have to be upstairs for some time. I went to Miss Robinson and her sister in November 1934, and was with them a good number of years.

At that time my doctor was teaching me to pull myself up from a chair by the bed rail and then stand alone for a minute with his arms each side of me. This took me four months to do, and then I was taken ill with appendicitis and there was also an abscess. I was taken to hospital for an operation; I was also on the verge of peritonitis and very ill. The surgeons dare not operate because of the serious brain operation, but did their utmost and dispersed the abscess and sent me home, as they could not do any more, but the dear Lord graciously helped me through.

On one occasion I needed ten shillings more to pay my board which was due that morning and I was just reading that precious promise, "My God shall supply all your need according to His riches in glory by Christ Jesus," and had my finger on that very text, when the postman brought me a letter containing a ten shilling note.

" For the wonders He has wrought,
Let us now our praises give;
And, by sweet experience taught,
Call upon Him while we live."

On account of the Tramway Company going bankrupt, it was three years before my compensation case was settled, and then the compensation was so small, I wondered what I should do if I lived. I broke down thinking of the struggle ahead when, instantly, I felt surrounded with the Lord's presence and He spoke the words to me, "The Lord is my Shepherd; I shall not want." I felt to be on holy ground and said, "Dear Lord, I never shall," and, bless His holy Name, I never have.

The fifth anniversary of the accident I had a special time. The Lord gave me those words: "Set thee up waymarks, make thee high heaps," and I was led back to the blessed waymarks the dear Lord had given me. The seventh anniversary, I woke up very early with the words: "O magnify the Lord with me, and let us exalt His Name together." I longed for someone to come so that we could exalt His Name together. I was put down for my usual afternoon's rest but I could not rest; I wanted to praise the Lord for His mercy and care. At that moment dear Mr. S. Champion came and so we tried to exalt His blessed Name together.

Chapel after Nine Years

I was not able to go to chapel for over nine years; my heart did thirst for the courts of the Lord. At length, through mercy, I was enabled to be taken by car to Zion Chapel. The friend I lived with wished me to ask my kind doctor's permission which, to satisfy her, I did. The doctor said, "You will go prepared to be very ill, won't you?" I replied, "No, doctor, I hope to enjoy the service." I said, "You took the risk of my life in moving my fingers and the Lord helped us." The doctor said, "Yes, He did; He always helps you. Your faith will bring you through. I'll give my consent." So I was carried to the car by my dear nephew and laid on a bed in the chapel and we had a real thanksgiving service. Early that Sabbath morning I felt very ill, yet I felt sure the Lord would take me to His house, and the Lord gave me that sweet promise, "My grace is sufficient for thee, for My strength is made perfect in weakness," and the Lord gave me a refreshing sleep. I did not even feel ill during that service and when I got back to bed, the words came with divine power. "Blessed are all they that put their trust in Him."

My arms being very weak I hardly knew how to use them and I asked the Lord to help me and He gave me that portion, "The arms of his hands were made strong by the hands of the mighty God of Jacob." Thus the dear Lord strengthened my arms. The worst head attack I ever had was one midnight. I could not move or speak and was alone, yet not alone, for the Lord came with the words, "His left hand is under my head." It was as though Jesus stood by me supporting my head. Then He spoke these sweet words to me, "The eternal God is thy refuge, and underneath are the everlasting arms." Words fail to tell the inward peace He gave me. We must go into affliction and trial to know His worth and love.

I had many sore temptations and trials; faith was keenly tested at times, yet the Lord very graciously brought me through. I was very ill on one occasion and the doctor thought I must pass away. So did I, but the dear Lord came and sweetly assured me that my hope was founded on Christ, the eternal Rock of Ages, that, "My hope was built on nothing less than Jesus' blood and righteousness". Then at chapel a long time afterwards, Mr. Champion took for his text, "The King is held in the galleries." The Lord came and overwhelmed me with His love and mercy to my soul. I did not know how to get home; I was lost in wonder, love and praise. I wanted to be alone with Him whom my soul loveth. He was my Beloved and I was His. I wanted to prostrate myself before Him; He was the altogether lovely One to my soul. Another time I had a sweet blessing from the text, "For surely there is an end; and thine expectation shall not be cut off." How many times I have feared my expectation would be cut off! I seemed to be passing through a series of destructions; I longed for the Word with power.

I had longed to go to the prayer meeting at Zion and my dear sister took me, and Mr. Champion read that portion and spoke from the text. "And being in an agony He prayed more earnestly: and His sweat was as it were great drops of blood falling down to the ground." I did enjoy the prayer meeting and felt helped; I little knew what it was to prepare me for.

Another Sore Affliction

The next day I had a fall and fractured my thigh and the shaft of the femur was displaced. At this time I was learning to walk by the furniture. I was in the most severe pain, it being the leg which had been paralysed, and I had to pray more earnestly for strength to endure the pain. I was taken to hospital for an operation but the orthopaedic specialist refused to operate and said to give an anaesthetic would be immediate death after such a serious brain operation; but, far worse, I felt the Lord had forsaken me. I could only cry, "My God, why hast Thou forsaken me?" and being in severe pain in soul and body, I knew not what to do. However, reading that portion one morning where the Lord Jesus cried, "My God, My God, why hast Thou forsaken Me?" the Holy Spirit revealed to me that I was having a tiny little fellowship with my blessed Lord in His sufferings. I felt how huge the weight of all His saints' sins since mine were so very great. But I had such a view of the dear Lord Jesus in His sufferings. I did weep at His dear feet and He did bless and help me.

I was in hospital over eight weeks and then was sent to a nursing home for six weeks, not to be moved off the bed until I went back to hospital for an X-ray. I was in such severe pain that my wicked, sinful heart felt rebellious at the pain and suffering. I felt helped by the prayer of one of our deacons and also by the first part of a sermon in the *Gospel Standard* by Mr. J. Delves where he related his like experience in a serious illness he had. I had a little hope that my sins might be forgiven. I was taken back to hospital for an X-ray and had to be re-admitted into hospital and go back on the fracture extension for a month. I had a lot of X-rays and my leg stretched, but they could do nothing more for me. The first Lord's day of that month, the *Gospel Standard* was brought to me and I read the second part of dear Mr. J. Delves's sermon where the Lord had visited him with His love, mercy and compassion; and the dear Lord visited me in like manner. I was completely overcome with the love and mercy of Jesus my beloved Lord. The hospital ward became the gate of heaven.

At length I was discharged from hospital to lie in bed for life. I went home feeling sure my good Doctor Greer would be enabled to do something for me, which he did. It meant a painful process of exercises; there was a leg shortage of four inches so the doctor ordered me a surgical boot. One evening being in such severe pain I hardly knew how to endure – it was midnight and I was alone – the dear Lord came at once with these words:

"I feel at My heart all thy sighs and thy groans,
For thou art most near Me, My flesh and My bones;
In all thy distresses thy Head feels the pain;
Yet all are most needful; not one is in vain."

The dear Lord gave me a sweet assurance that I was a member of His body, the church. I could but say, "Bless the Lord, O my soul, and all that is within me, bless His holy Name." The first four verses of Psalm 103, Psalm 107 and hymn 420, "O bless the Lord, my soul," have often been my sweet experience. "They that go down to the sea in ships, that do business in great waters; these see the works of the Lord, and His wonders in the deep." And so I proved it.

After being in hospital and at home for fourteen months, I had such a desire to go to Zion Anniversary, and was taken there by ambulance. Mr. Champion took for his text in the morning "Thy God hath commanded thy strength: strengthen, O God, that which Thou hast wrought for us" (Psa. 68. 28). It proved such a word of help and blessing to me then, and has been many times since. Then my doctor was anxious for me to be out as much as possible. The dear friend that was with me at the accident in 1932 was then very ill and had gone to be looked after by another friend and she kindly offered my sister and me the use of her house. I shrank from it but the Lord gave me the word, "He pleased not Himself," and that made me willing to go. From there I was able to be taken in an invalid chair to chapel and was carried up the steps by very kind friends, not being able to walk alone. Many were the ups and downs in those days but, blessed be His holy Name, He brought me through. My beloved friend, Mrs. Anderson, passed away on August 9th so that meant another change for us, but dear Mrs. Bree of blessed memory offered us a home with herself, which we gladly accepted. How often would she say in the midst of trials and afflictions:

"In heaven, and earth, and air, and seas,
He executes His firm decrees;
And by His saints it stands confessed,
That what He does is ever best."

Baptized on a Stretcher

At this time I was very exercised about being baptized, the words being given: "He that hath My commandments, and keepeth them, he it is that loveth Me." I felt the first Person we should meet in heaven would be a baptized Lord Jesus Christ. I longed to follow Him. I knew there were many difficulties in the way bodily, it being very difficult to get down *one* step, but the dear Lord swept the difficulties away and gave me such sweet portions of His blessed Word, and assured me that "with Him I should be in safeguard"; also, "My grace is sufficient for thee, for my strength is made perfect in weakness"; "I can do all things through Christ which strengtheneth me," so I was enabled to speak to Mr. Champion, and he came to see me. He asked if I had considered how it could be done. I said, "Yes." Mr. C. then said, "Will you leave it to the deacons and myself?" and I replied, "Yes." Mr. Champion arranged for me to see the deacons and I felt helped to tell them what I humbly believed the Lord had done for me, and they decided it would be best for me to be baptized on a stretcher. I went before the church, was helped to speak, and was unanimously received.

The baptism was arranged for the Thursday evening. A friend wished me to ask my kind doctor's consent but this I felt I could not do, feeling the dear Lord had given me His divine consent. I said, "I will *tell* the doctor, if you wish," which I did. I told him I wished to be baptized by immersion, and he replied, "Whatever next, Ruth? You realise it may be the death of you?" I replied, "I don't feel it will; the Lord has promised to help me; and should it prove my death, it would be nice to die following the dear Lord who was baptized." The doctor replied, "I'll give my consent; I know the Lord will look after you. He always does. I believe you will be brought safely through. The Lord bless you."

I went to the service ready dressed for my baptism and lay on the stretcher, which had a piece of rope at each corner. Just before hymn 427 was sung ("Jesus, and shall it ever be"), that verse came with power:

"When I survey the wondrous cross
On which the Prince of Glory died,
My richest gain I count but loss,
And pour contempt on all my pride."

Then as the deacons and one male member carried me on the stretcher to the water, that verse came so sweetly:

"We to this place are come to show
What we to boundless mercy owe;
The Saviour's footsteps to explore,
And tread the path He trod before."

Then they gently let me down into the water and Mr. Champion baptized me. I saw Jesus only and, to His honour and glory I would say it, I never even felt ill. To God be all the praise.

I felt very tried about coming to the Lord's table. Satan kept telling me that I was not a real character but I begged of the Lord to enable me to go to His table and He gave me that sweet verse:

"Jesus is my great High Priest;
Bears my name upon His breast;
And that we may never part,
I am sealed upon His heart."

It was sweet indeed and such a help. On receiving me into the church, Mr. Champion gave me the text, "I have chosen thee in the furnace of affliction." I was helped through the service and afterwards being put into my chair to go home, the dear Lord gave me that blessed portion "And as we have borne the image of the earthy, we shall also bear the image of the heavenly." The dear Lord has favoured me much at His table.

Another Sore Trial

[Miss Beesley recounts a few changes, and then speaks of staying at Croydon for a time.]

I was so looking forward to the Centenary Services to be held at West Street Chapel, Croydon, but alas! I had another accident (so called) on the Wednesday previous to the day of the Services. My very kind friend, Mr. Hicks, had bought me a chair, driven by electric power, to enable me to get out more. I had made this chair a very special matter of prayer that I might be able to use it, and felt that prayer would be answered. But I was mistaken. The Lord said, No. The first time Mr. Hicks took me out in it at Croydon, it developed a fault, mounted a grass verge, and overturned. Mr. Hicks received shock and a cut face. I had fractured a collar bone, fractured ribs, a fractured knee, and hurt my arm and chest. No operation was performed in West Croydon Hospital because of my serious brain operation. I felt distressed while in hospital and felt that all these things were against me. Dear Mr. Foster came to see me and I told him how I felt. The portion he was led to read, his remarks on God's everlasting love and His care, and his prayer were all made a blessing to me. But again I sank so low. Then the dear Lord came with a word, "For He maketh sore and bindeth up: He woundeth, and His hands make whole." Then I could rejoice in Christ as my Saviour.

After being in Croydon about three months, I was taken to Raunds in

Northamptonshire. There I had a fall while trying the leg, which made it worse.

After being at Raunds several months, I was taken back to Leicester to my dear sister's, and was then under the skill and care of my good Dr. Greer. He was shocked at my condition, but his great patience and skill were wonderful. By tiny exercises three times a day, and being in bed eight months, the use began to come back into my leg. Then at the Anniversary at Zion, I was able to be taken to chapel by ambulance for the services. In the morning, dear Mr. Champion's text was: "Happy art thou, O Israel: who is like unto thee, O people saved by the Lord?" It was a time of rejoicing to my soul.

Another time in great distress, going to the prayer meeting and feeling too ill to continue the journey, I had to cry out to Him for strength to continue the journey, which He mercifully gave. That evening the reading was John 14. The first verse came with divine power: "Let not your heart be troubled" (or "violently agitated"). Mine was; but the dear Lord came and lifted my burden right off my heart and bore it for me.

> "I would for ever speak His Name,
> In sounds to mortal ears unknown;
> With angels join to praise the Lamb,
> And worship at His Father's throne."

[After writing of good hearing times and many changes, through which she passed, Miss Beesley continues.]

Concern about a Home

On May 17th, 1962, I came to dear Mrs. Pinnell again. On May 27th I was favoured to be taken to Edmonton Chapel for evening service, when dear Mr. Pack preached from Genesis 22. 13, 14. I was specially helped in this service by Mr. Pack's reference to verse 8: "My son, God will provide Himself a lamb," and by the way he spoke of the thickets and trials some of God's people have to pass through. I was very tried about getting another home, but through that service I was enabled to believe that God had provided His dear Son, the Lamb of God, and that my sins were laid upon Him, and that He would provide me with another home in His own time. "Jehovah-Jireh; the Lord will provide."

On June 14th I was taken to Edmonton Anniversary Services, when dear Mr. J. W. Tyler took for his text: "Then Samuel took a stone, and set it between Mizpeh and Shen, and called the name of it Ebenezer, saying, Hitherto hath the Lord helped us." The afternoon service was a most solemn one, Mr. Tyler asking the question: Were we real children of God, or only like Ichabod? What proof had we of the Holy Spirit's work in our hearts? I felt I was not a real child of God and yet had made an open profession of His Name. The trial of faith was very severe for an hour and I had to cry for mercy, and that I might know I was a real child of God. Then the dear Lord most blessedly came and brought again to my soul His former promises: "Your life is hid with Christ in God"; and, "He will save, He will rejoice over thee with joy; He will rest in His love." This brought peace and joy. Then as dear Mr. Tyler spoke (at the evening service) of raising another Ebenezer stone to His praise for help given, and saying, "Hitherto hath the Lord helped us," my soul was sweetly blessed. I felt such a desire to sit under Mr. Tyler's ministry, although at that time it seemed impossible.

However, I went home and was alone in the house for another six months with only daily help. I cried to God to open a way for me, and used lawful means (as I was getting worse), or begged that He would send me a resident help; but nothing came. I felt all these things were against me, and the enemy said, "Where is now thy God?" At last I felt the iron gates must open of their own accord because the God of the iron gates still lives. To my sorrow, rebellion at the Lord's dealings at times arose. Yet I could only beg of the Lord to help me.

A Way Made

November 3rd, 1962, I felt to give up all hope of the Lord moving me, and felt it must be His will for me to remain where I was. On November 4th, being the Lord's day, I had a comfortable day reading His Word and a sermon. November 5th I woke with the words: "I will be with thee in all places whithersoever thou goest." I thought, "That means that I have to go into hospital again." But when the post came that morning, there was a letter from a friend that I had not heard from for some years saying that she had heard that I was living alone and needed help. If I would like to go and live with her, she and her sister would look after me. Also, when I was able to go, she would take me to The Dicker Chapel – the very spot where I wished to go! As I read Miss G. Verrall's letter, the words came with power: "This is the way; walk ye in it." "I will be with thee in all places whithersoever thou goest." And my reading that evening was: "Ye have dwelt long enough in this mount." So feeling it was the Lord's provision for me, and His will that I should go, I wrote and accepted my dear friend's very kind offer to go and live with her and her dear sister at Horsebridge, Sussex. There were many things to be attended to. The house would have to be sold. There was the clearing of the house and some things would have to be stored. I felt enabled to place everything in the dear Lord's hands. The solicitor and house agent were most kind to me, and my kind niece did all the packing. I could only say, "O magnify the Lord with me, and let us exalt His Name together." My very good doctor, who had looked after me for thirty years, was kindness itself. He had hoped to look after me to the end; the Lord had sent him to me, and his dear wife and family were so kind to me.

The Move to Sussex

During December 1962, we had much snow; the roads were frozen. Yet on December 13th the day arranged for me to come to Horsebridge all the way by car, it was a lovely sunny day. We had sunshine all the way. I could but praise the Lord for His great kindness to me. He did indeed make His goodness pass before me in the way, and I had no ill effects of the journey. On the Sabbath morning, December 16th, 1962, Miss Verrall took me to The Dicker Chapel, and dear Mr. Tyler took for his text: "Thy kingdom come." How I longed for it to come more into my heart! It was good to my soul and I wept at God's goodness to a wretch like me.

I felt rather nervous at the busy Dicker roundabout, having to cross it on the road in my chair, but the dear Lord gave me the sweet promise: "With Me thou shalt be in safeguard," which took all fear away. Owing to the severe weather and much snow, I was not able to go to chapel for nine weeks. This was a severe trial to me as I so longed to be in the courts of the Lord's house.

Early morning of February 24th, 1963, I felt very ill and wondered what might happen. It was a lovely day and, through God's great goodness and His healing power, I was able to be taken to The Dicker Chapel that afternoon. Our beloved pastor's text was: "I will not leave you comfortless: I will come to you." Mr. Tyler referred to the man who fell among thieves, leaving him half dead. That is how I felt spiritually. But at that service, Jesus, like the good Samaritan, came just where I was, pouring in the blessed oil and wine of His gospel, binding up my wounds. I felt Jesus had paid my debts on Calvary and had brought me to His gospel inn at The Dicker. Mr. Tyler asked the question: Have you been very ill in hospital and had a little fellowship with the Lord Jesus Christ? My mind went back to the sweet fellowship I had with Him in His sufferings in hospital and when at home in such severe pain, and He blessedly came again with the words:

> " I feel at my heart all thy sighs and thy groans,
> For thou art most near Me, My flesh and My bones;

In all thy distresses thy Head feels the pain,
Yet all are most needful; not one is in vain."

I received such a blessing that afternoon that I was lost in wonder, love and praise at God's mercy to me. He did comfort me indeed. Mr. Tyler was led into my soul's experience, and yet did not know how I felt at that time. The dear Lord continued to bless me so much, especially under the preached Word.

United with the Church at The Dicker

November 10th, 1963, was another day of blessing to my soul. My cup ran over with the love of God in Christ Jesus our Lord. Our beloved pastor's text: "Therefore they shall come and sing in the height of Zion, and shall flow together to the goodness of the Lord," etc. (Jer. 31. 12). It was so good to me as Mr. Tyler spoke of Christ Jesus the Foundation, Redeemer and faithful Friend. How I longed to praise and bless His holy Name! He gave me such sweet meditation in His Word, and often a song in the night. That verse was sweet to me:

"Goodness, immortal and divine,
The bliss of endless day,
The Lord my God has made to pass
Before me in the way."

I felt like Ruth of old: "This people shall be my people, and their God my God"; and, "There will I be buried." I felt such a love and union to the dear pastor and people at The Dicker that I felt constrained to join them, and begged for divine guidance and help. It came under the ministry of the Word when Mr. Tyler preached from: "My times are in Thy hands," and other sermons; also by texts and verses being applied with divine power to my soul. "They shall abundantly utter the memory of Thy great goodness." "Tell all who love the Lord below, The debt of love to Him you owe." "And I will give thee the opening of the mouth in the midst of them" (Ezek. 29. 21).

"And canst Thou, wilt Thou, yet forgive,
And bid my crimes remove?
And shall a pardoned rebel live,
To speak Thy wondrous love?"

Feeling constrained to join the church at Zoar, The Dicker, 1963,* I spoke

---

* We commend the step our friend took. Having been led to move in providence, and feeling a real union to the pastor and church, she gladly came before them (though in old age and affliction) to tell them what the Lord had done for her soul, and to unite with them as a member.

to our beloved pastor, and was very kindly received by pastor, deacons and church. It was a time of deep exercise and trial of faith as well as rejoicing. Soon afterwards, feeling very tried, Satan telling me that I was not a real Christian, our dear pastor preached from the text: "For he endured, as seeing Him who is invisible". Mr. Tyler was led by the Holy Spirit into the deep recesses of my soul, and the Holy Spirit brought to my remembrance some of the blessings He had given me in the past, and I was enabled to plead that the Lord would bless and help me for His great Name's sake. I was favoured with sweet meditation the next day and with a hope that, through His mercy, I should endure to the end "as seeing Him who is invisible."

[Miss Beesley having given an account of her life up to the time of joining the church at The Dicker, her manuscript, covering the last six years of her life, assumes diary form (though usually without dates). It consists almost entirely of profitable hearing times she enjoyed. The following are extracts.]

Jeremiah 29. 11

When our dear pastor preached from the text: "For I know the thoughts that I think toward you, saith the Lord, thoughts of peace, and not of evil, to give you an expected end," as he was led to speak of God's eternal thoughts of mercy, love and peace to His people in His well–beloved Son, to give them an expected end, the Holy Spirit applied the word with divine power. It was such a sealing time to my soul. I wept for joy and longed to be taken to heaven. Jesus brought me, a poor, vile sinner, into His house of wine.

I woke one morning with the verse:

> "I shall sleep sound in Jesus,
> Shall in His likeness rise,
> To love and to adore Him,
> To see Him with these eyes;
> My kingly King in heaven,
> My presence doth command,
> Where glory, glory dwelleth,
> In Immanuel's land."

I really felt the Lord was about to take me to Himself, and I longed to be with Him. Though spared a little longer, He has given me to feel – "to lean upon His arm; His breast has been my sweet repose."

Isaiah 65. 8. 17

When our dear pastor took for his text: "Thus saith the Lord, As the new wine is found in the cluster, and one saith, Destroy it not, for a blessing is in it," I felt very tried, and felt I was fruitless and should be cut off. The trial was very keen and Satan tempted me not to go to the Lord's table the following Sabbath, telling me that if I went, I should eat and drink damnation to myself, and should soon be in hell. However, I ventured to go. Our dear pastor was most solemn and searching, his text being: "For behold, I create new heavens and a new earth." He referred to the new wine in the cluster. Also, he referred to the man who came seeking fruit for three years and found none. He said to the dresser of the vineyard, Cut it down. Mr. Tyler spoke of a tree being cut down to see if there was any sap. I felt cut down, and had no sap. But immediately the blessed Holy Spirit led me to the pierced side, hands and feet of our Redeemer, and gave me His witness that they were pierced for me. O the blessed exchange of joy for mourning! A new heaven and earth! My heart did rejoice in Christ my Saviour.

When it came to sitting at the Lord's table, I felt His dear, sacred presence there. How I longed to glorify His Name! Hymns 158 and 667 were so sweet. The dew lay all night upon the branch, and I wished to be drawn closer and closer to Jesus as the living Vine.

Job 42. 10

I received another token when our beloved pastor took for his text: "And the Lord turned the captivity of Job, when he prayed for his friends: also the Lord gave Job twice as much as he had before." Job lost family, health, substance, friends. I have lost most of my dear ones. I lost my health, substance and a lot of dear friends. I often wondered where the scene would end; I was in the furnace of affliction. Yet how God graciously brought me through and enabled me to praise Him for all through which I had passed! Yes, as it was with Job, in many ways and spiritually, God gave me twice as much as I had before. I felt I could say with Job, "For I know that my Redeemer liveth, and that He shall stand at the latter day upon the earth...Yet in my flesh shall I see God, whom I shall see for myself, and not another." In heaven my choicest treasure lies.

Haggai 2. 9

I felt I had been given a little of His beauty for my sin and shame, and beheld His glory. I felt His blessed presence with me as I sat at His table. The verse came so sweetly:

> "How sweet and awful is the place,
> With Christ within the doors."

How sweet, after severe afflictions and testings of faith, to realise that nothing can separate us from the love of God in Christ Jesus! Afflictions and keen trials working together for good brought me to The Dicker, the house of God where He has helped, tried, reproved and sweetly blessed me.

Proverbs 23. 18

At the prayer meeting, our beloved pastor spoke from: "For surely there is an end; and thine expectation shall not be cut off." It was a special word to me as I went to the meeting begging of God to give me another token for good. Our dear pastor could not have been led to a more suitable text—an end of sin, trial and affliction; then heaven at last.

Ezekiel 37

At times I should have almost despaired of having eternal life had it not been for Ezekiel 37. The very dry bones have often said, "Can my dry bones live again?" But, blessed be His holy Name, He has caused breath to enter into them and they have lived – only through His sovereign mercy. At times I have felt to be in the grave, buried in doubts and fears, Satan's temptation, feeling I should be buried in hell. Yet the Lord's word came, "Thus saith the Lord God, Behold, O My people, I will open your graves, and cause you to come up out of your graves, and bring you into the land of Israel." O what a mercy it is when He does this; we feel to live again! When I am directed to "the bleeding wounds of my incarnate God", when I can "weep o'er His pierced hands and feet, and view His wounded side", this is a little bit of heaven begun below.

Jeremiah 31. 20

On Lord's day evening, September 20th, I was taken to Edmonton Chapel and heard dear Mr. R. J. Morris. I was feeling sad and far off. Mr. Morris read Hosea 13 and 14 and commented on the words, "So will we render the calves of our lips," and said, "Whoso offereth praise glorifieth Me." He spoke of the many mercies we had received. We cannot praise Him enough for all His mercies to us so we must ask His dear people to come and help us to praise Him. Text was: "Is Ephraim My dear son? is he a pleasant child? for since I spake against him, I do earnestly remember him still. Therefore My bowels are troubled for him; I will surely have mercy on him, saith the Lord." Ephraim – "fruitful in the land of my affliction". My hard heart began to soften. I hoped the Lord had given me a little fruit in my affliction. I felt I had often gone astray like Ephraim; the dear Lord had chastised me. I could only pray, "Turn Thou me, and I shall be turned." I knew only the Lord could turn me. I longed for true repentance and godly sorrow for my sins, and to experience His everlasting covenant love again; for the Lord saith, "I will surely remember him still and have mercy on him." I felt helped; but when Mr. Morris quoted the verse:

> "I've bound thee up secure,
> 'Midst all the rage of hell;
> The curse thou never shalt endure,
> For I'm unchangeable,"

the dear Lord came right into my heart, and I felt that He was mine. "He brought me into His banqueting house, and His banner over me was love." The Lord gave me sweet meditation on these things for some time.

1 Samuel 7. 12

Our beloved pastor was led to take for his text: "Then Samuel took a stone, and set it *between* Mizpeh and Shen, and called the name of it Ebenezer, saying, Hitherto hath the Lord helped us." After a very searching time as to whether we were the true children of God (had Jesus borne our sins in His own body?), I felt very tried; but Mr. Tyler so begged of God to give him the real meaning of why the stone had to be set *between* Mizpeh and Shen, and like a flash the answer came. *Mizpeh* meant "God's care and watchfulness over His people"; *Shen* meant "a dangerous piece of rock, a precipice". Put *between* the two – Jesus, our blessed Mediator, who stood between God and hell for His people. My hard heart was completely broken. I felt Jesus stood in my place, and died for my sins, and rose again for my justification. It was sweet to go to the Lord's table to remember Him in His dying love for such a wretch as me. I felt enabled to raise my Ebenezer stone, saying, "Hitherto hath the Lord helped me."

Genesis 43. 11

Such a help received under a sermon from my beloved pastor from the text given him: "If it must be so now." – Jacob's great sorrow at the loss of Joseph, who he thought was dead, and now he was called to part with Benjamin. He felt like we do – that all these things were against him. Yet God was making all things work together for his good. We have just the same thoughts in our wicked hearts. But God was preparing Jacob for this trial by the words, "If it must be so now." As God prepares us for trials, He never takes away our all, Himself He gives us still. He always gives us more than He takes away. I have proved this in my long, painful affliction. In affliction we learn more of His worth, His preciousness and suitability. Jacob could say, "It is enough." So can we when we see Jesus, our Elder Brother, living and interceding on our behalf.

Exodus 33. 19

January 7th that verse was given me:

" Thou shalt see My glory soon,
When the work of grace is done;
Partner of My throne shalt be;
Say, poor sinner, lovest thou *Me*?"

Then going to God's house that evening, I received such a sweet confirmation when my beloved pastor was led to take for his text: "And He said, I will make all My goodness pass before thee." Moses prayed that he might see God's glory, and this text was God's answer. As our dear pastor was led a little into beholding His glory, I felt the Holy Spirit had shown me a little of His glory – once in particular when I felt I could hold no more while in the body. How great is His goodness which He has made to pass before me in the way, especially so in these years of affliction, both spiritually, in providence, and bodily! I felt completely overcome with God's great goodness to such a wretch as me. He would have been just in cutting me off, yet He had compassion on me. I so often have to ask God to help me in movements of my body, and spiritually, that Jesus will intercede for me, pardon my sins, and enable me to go to His house where He feeds me by the way.

Psalm 55. 22

Thursday evening text was: "Cast thy burden upon the Lord, and He shall sustain thee." The burden has not been removed, but He has given me sustaining grace. I have been enabled to think of the great burden our precious Redeemer bore – His people's sins (and, I have a sweet hope, mine). I have had some sweet relief in having a little fellowship with Him in His sufferings in the Garden of Gethsemane. It's the safest place to dwell there. Keep me, Lord, at Thy dear feet. That sweet verse was given me early morning:

"Yes, dearest Lord, 'tis my desire
Thy wise appointments to admire;
And trace the footsteps of my God,
Through every path in Zion's road."

Isaiah 52. 14

I have often felt I could willingly bear all my infirmities if only the power of Christ could rest on me more. One morning on waking, the dear Lord gave me the words: "Look on His wounded hands and read your name in crimson lines." It was a solemn, searching day when our beloved pastor took for his text: "His visage was so marred more than any man." He described the intense sufferings of Christ – no sorrow like His! The Holy Spirit led me a little into the sufferings of our dear Saviour. I felt to "see in His dear, sacred face, Ten thousand sins forgiven".

Exodus 14. 13

I went to God's house feeling very tried. Our beloved pastor was led to take for his text: "Fear ye not, stand still, and see the salvation of the Lord." He spoke so well of how the Israelites were hemmed in on every side, and how God's people are often in a similar position in spiritual matters, tempted by the devil who tells them that God has forsaken them. I had the same temptation for some years. O the midnight darkness I passed through! But the dear Lord delivered me again when brought into deep affliction and helplessness in body. I was brought to "stand still, and see the salvation of the Lord". The Lord mercifully paid my debt by His sufferings, death, blood, righteousness, and His glorious resurrection and intercession. I did not want to sleep that night for joy. His precious promises overwhelmed my soul.

Concluding entry

We must be led to suffer with Him in a little measure for Him to make His divine goodness pass before us in redemption, in sanctification, in affliction and in providence. I felt He had made His divine goodness to pass before me many times when sorely afflicted and tried. How I long to crown Him Lord of all!

> "We too amid the sacred throng,
> Low at His feet would fall,
> Join in the everlasting song,
> And crown Him Lord of all."

Amen

[At the end, Miss Verrall was unable to look after her dear friend. Miss Beesley was grateful to be found a place in the Bethesda Home at Tunbridge Wells where she passed away peacefully on December 25th,. 1969. As had been her desire, she was buried by her beloved pastor at Zoar Chapel, The Dicker.]

From an original manuscript, first published in the *Gospel Standard* 1972.